DARK PASTS

Changing the State's Story
in Turkey and Japan

Jennifer M. Dixon

CORNELL UNIVERSITY PRESS   ITHACA AND LONDON

Cornell University Press gratefully acknowledges receipt of a grant from the Subvention of Publication Program of the Office of the Provost, Villanova University, which aided in the publication of this book.

First published 2018 by Cornell University Press

Printed in the United States of America

Library of Congress Cataloging-in-Publication Data

Names: Dixon, Jennifer M. (Jennifer Margaret), author.
Title: Dark pasts : changing the state's story in Turkey and Japan / Jennifer M. Dixon.
Description: Ithaca : Cornell University Press, 2018. | Includes bibliographical references and index.
Identifiers: LCCN 2018007699 (print) | LCCN 2018008081 (ebook) | ISBN 9781501730252 (pdf) | ISBN 9781501730269 (epub/mobi) | ISBN 9781501730245 | ISBN 9781501730245 (cloth ; alk. paper)
Subjects: LCSH: Armenian massacres, 1915–1923—Historiography. | Nanking Massacre, Nanjing, Jiangsu Sheng, China, 1937—Historiography. | Historiography—Political aspects—Turkey—History—20th century. | Historiography—Political aspects—Japan—History—20th century.
Classification: LCC DS195.5 (ebook) | LCC DS195.5 .D58 2018 (print) | DDC 956.6/20154—dc23
LC record available at https://lccn.loc.gov/2018007699

Contents

Acronyms

AKP	Adalet ve Kalkınma Partisi (Justice and Development Party)
ASALA	Armenian Secret Army for the Liberation of Armenia
ASAM	Avrasya Stratejik Araştırmalar Merkezi (Eurasian Strategic Studies Institute)
ASEAN	Association of Southeast Asian Nations
ASİMKK	Asılsız Soykırım İddiaları ile Mücadele Koordinasyon Kurulu (Committee to Coordinate the Struggle with the Baseless Genocide Claims)
ATAA	Assembly of Turkish American Associations
CHP	Cumhuriyet Halk Partisi (Republican People's Party)
CUP	Committee of Union and Progress (İttihat ve Terakki Cemiyeti)
DTP	Demokratik Toplum Partisi (Democratic Society Party)
ERAREN	Ermeni Araştırmaları Enstitüsü (Institute for Armenian Research)
EU	European Union
FBIS	Foreign Broadcast Information Service
GDP	gross domestic product
İAGM	İstihbarat ve Araştırma Genel Müdürlüğü (Directorate General of Intelligence and Research)
ICTJ	International Center for Transitional Justice
ICTR	International Criminal Tribunal for Rwanda
ICTY	International Criminal Tribunal for the Former Yugoslavia
İHD	İnsan Hakları Derneği (Human Rights Foundation of Turkey)
ISIS	Islamic State of Iraq and Syria
ITS	Institute of Turkish Studies
JCAG	Justice Commandos of the Armenian Genocide
JSDF	Japan Self-Defense Forces
JSP	Japan Socialist Party
LDP	Liberal Democratic Party
MFA	Ministry of Foreign Affairs, Republic of Turkey
MGK	Milli Güvenlik Kurulu (National Security Council)
MOE	Ministry of Education
MOFA	Ministry of Foreign Affairs of Japan
NATO	North Atlantic Treaty Organization

NGO	nongovernmental organization
NHK	Nihon Hōsō Kyōkai (Japan Broadcasting Corporation)
ODA	official development assistance
PKK	Partiya Karkerên Kurdistane (Workers' Party of Kurdistan)
PM	prime minister
POW	prisoner of war
PR	public relations
PRC	People's Republic of China
ROK	Republic of Korea
SCAP	Supreme Commander for the Allied Powers
TARC	Turkish-Armenian Reconciliation Commission
TBMM	Türkiye Büyük Millet Meclisi (Turkish Grand National Assembly)
TEİMK	Türk-Ermeni İlişkileri Milli Komitesi (Turkish-Armenian Relations National Committee)
TESEV	Türkiye Ekonomik ve Sosyal Etüdler Vakfı (Turkish Economic and Social Studies Foundation)
TTK	Türk Tarih Kurumu (Turkish Historical Society)
UN	United Nations
UNCG	United Nations Convention on the Prevention and Punishment of the Crime of Genocide
UNICEF	United Nations Children's Fund
UNSC	United Nations Security Council
USD	US dollars
USSR	Union of Soviet Socialist Republics
WATS	Workshop for Armenian/Turkish Scholarship
WWI	World War I
WWII	World War II
YÖK	Yükseköğretim Kurulu (Council of Higher Education)

Acknowledgments

Researching and writing this book has been a long journey that included advice, feedback, and support from colleagues, advisers, friends, family, and many people I met in the course of my research in Turkey and Japan. Without their help, this book would have been impossible to write.

I would first like to thank Margaret Lavinia Anderson, Ron Hassner, T. J. Pempel, and Gordon Silverstein for their advice, encouragement, and feedback on the early and later stages of this project. Gordon Silverstein helped me sound out my ideas and develop a vague interest into a clear research question. Ron Hassner encouraged me to pursue the nugget of an idea that became this project and later pushed me to focus and hone my argument. Peggy Anderson helped me improve my writing and clarify my argument, and offered generous and considered advice at many stages of the project. T. J. Pempel offered valuable guidance for my research in Japan and expert feedback on that portion of my project. I also received advice and feedback from Kelly Greenhill, Marcus Kreuzer, and Naomi Levy. In particular, I have appreciated Kelly's enthusiasm for my project and professional advice, Marcus's collegiality and intellectual engagement, and Naomi's encouragement and advice.

While writing this book often felt like a solitary endeavor, the final product reflects the thoughtful comments and suggestions of many colleagues and friends. In particular, I thank Michal Ben-Josef Hirsch and Sarah Bush for their friendship and feedback over the past several years. This book has been much improved by their insights and suggestions, and their encouragement and advice has helped me see the way through many challenges. In addition, Celeste Arrington, Bronwyn Anne Leebaw, and Tobias Schulze-Cleven generously read much or all of the manuscript, and their comments and suggestions markedly improved the final draft. Celeste offered numerous suggestions that helped me better contextualize my analysis, and asked probing questions that helped me clarify my argument and analysis. Bronwyn Leebaw's comments pushed me to develop my argument in important ways. Toby's close reading of multiple drafts and myriad conversations helped me develop my arguments and hone my writing. In addition, I am grateful to Roger Haydon for his interest in and feedback on the manuscript, and for shepherding it through the publication process. I thank Stephan Astourian, David Barrett, Lerna Ekmekçioğlu, Jennifer Erickson, Lily Gardner Feldman, Arman Grigoryan, Richard Hovannisian, David Mendeloff, Manjari

Chatterjee Miller, Khatchig Mouradian, Jeffrey Olick, Scott Straus, Uğur Ümit Üngör, and Jenny Wüstenberg for reading and commenting on parts of the manuscript. I am deeply appreciative of the time and insights each of these readers shared. Any flaws or mistakes in this final version are my own. Finally, the book has also been improved by comments and advice from Taner Akçam, David Art, Seyhan Bayraktar, Charli Carpenter, Fuat Dündar, Evgeny Finkel, Fatma Müge Göçek, Amy Gurowitz, Yinan He, Jennifer Lind, Benjamin Madley, Marc Mamigonian, Álvaro Morcillo Laiz, Greg Noble, Melissa Nobles, Shaul Shenhav, Cihan Tuğal, Zheng Wang, Keith David Watenpaugh, Jason Wittenberg, and Keiko Yamanaka.

The three years I spent as a fellow in the International Security Program at the Harvard Kennedy School's Belfer Center for Science and International Affairs were critical in helping me crystallize and hone my argument. I am grateful for the feedback I received from Sean Lynn-Jones, Steve Miller, Bob Rotberg, Monica Duffy Toft, and Steve Walt. In addition, I received valuable feedback and encouragement from the other fellows, particularly Sarah Daly, Ursula Jasper, Patrick Johnston, Jennifer Keister, Rose Kelanic, Peter Krause, Jonathan Renshon, Norrin Ripsman, Chiara Ruffa, Josh Shifrinson, and Melissa Willard-Foster.

I am also thankful for the good friends I made at Berkeley, including Şener Aktürk, Jen Brass, Jon Chow, Brent Durbin, Els de Graauw, Ken Haig, Sam Handlin, Jon Hassid, Kenji Kushida, Martha Johnson, Dann Naseemullah, Seung-Youn Oh, Regine Spector, Rachel Stern, Susanne Wengle, and Zach Zwald. These friends helped me navigate many aspects of graduate school and contributed to this book in myriad ways. At Villanova, I am grateful for many supportive colleagues, especially David Barrett, Janice Bially Mattern, Matt Kerbel, Christopher Kilby, Simanti Lahiri, Eric Lomazoff, Sara Newland, Kunle Owolabi, Mark Schrad, Shigehiro Suzuki, and Maria Toyoda. And in Philadelphia, I appreciate the friends and colleagues who have helped create an engaging intellectual community, particularly Phillip Ayoub, Zoltán Búzás, Maryam Deloffre, Orfeo Fioretos, Julia Gray, Alexandra Guisinger, Rosie Hsueh, Sara Jane McCaffrey, Mark Pollack, and Jane Vaynman.

Beyond these colleagues and friends, I owe many debts for funding, support, and opportunities to share my work. For funding that supported my research, I am grateful to the Department of Political Science, the European Union Center of Excellence, the Institute of East Asian Studies, the Center for Middle Eastern Studies, and the Graduate Division at UC Berkeley. My research was also supported by funding from the UC Institute on Global Conflict and Cooperation and the College of Liberal Arts and Sciences at Villanova University. In addition, I thank the Office of the Provost at Villanova University for a Subvention of Publication Program award. In addition to this financial support, I thank the Institute of

Social Science at the University of Tokyo for sponsoring me during my research in Tokyo, Temple University's Department of Political Science for offering me an office during my sabbatical, Michael Zürn for hosting me for a summer as a visiting researcher at the WZB Berlin Social Science Center, the Irmgard Coninx Foundation, and the Institute for Advanced Study at the University of Konstanz. For opportunities to present or publish my work, I thank Sebouh Aslanian, Anny Bakalian, Seyhan Bayraktar, Irit Dekel, Ayda Erbal, Maria Koinova, António Costa Pinto, Wolfgang Seibel, and Devrim Yavuz. I am grateful to Ayla Algar for teaching me Turkish, to Hiwatari Nobuhiro for hosting me as a visiting research fellow at the Institute of Social Science at the University of Tokyo, and to my research assistant in Tokyo, whose help was invaluable. For translation help, I am grateful to Şener Aktürk, Celeste Arrington, Shigehiro Suzuki, and Maria Toyoda. For copyediting help, I thank Linda Benson. For their excellent research assistance, I thank Laknath Gunathilake, Meredith LaSalle-Tarantin, and Joseph Lasky. For administrative support, I am grateful to Andrea Rex at Berkeley, Susan Lynch at Harvard, and Diane Mozzone and Katie Schneider at Villanova. Thanks also to Merrill Stein for help tracking down sources. In addition, a portion of the Introduction was originally published as "Turkey's Puzzling Response to the Armenian Genocide," *Political Violence @ a Glance*, 29 April 2015, available at: http://politicalviolenceataglance.org/2015/04/29/turkeys-puzzling-response-to-the-armenian-genocide/. I appreciate that the editors of *Political Violence @ a Glance* have permitted me to use this material in this book. Material in Chapters 2, 3, and 4 is drawn (in part) from "Rhetorical Adaptation and Resistance to International Norms," *Perspectives on Politics*, vol. 15, no. 1 (March 2017), pp. 83–99; "Norms, Narratives, and Scholarship on the Armenian Genocide," *International Journal of Middle East Studies*, vol. 47, no. 4 (October 2015), pp. 796–800; "Defending the Nation?: Maintaining Turkey's Narrative of the Armenian Genocide," *South European Society and Politics*, vol. 15, no. 3 (September 2010), pp. 467–85; and "Education and National Narratives: Changing Representations of the Armenian Genocide in History Textbooks in Turkey," *International Journal for Education Law and Policy* (2010), pp. 103–26. I appreciate that these journals have permitted me to reproduce sections of these articles in this book.

I am indebted to all of the people in Turkey and Japan who were willing to be interviewed as part of my research. Without their time and perspectives, I would not have been able to understand the dynamics and considerations that shape the politics of memory in each country. I am also grateful for the friends I made in the course of my research in Japan and Turkey, without whom my fieldwork would have been much lonelier.

Finally, I owe thanks to my family. My parents, Donna and Jim, and my sister Chrissy have supported and encouraged me throughout the long process of researching and writing this book. Completing this would have been much more difficult if not for their love and support. Thanks to my oldest friend, Diana, for laughing at my jokes and always being there for me. And most importantly, I am thankful for Toby, who has been with me through every step of this process and whose encouragement and love supported me throughout, and for Hanna, who has filled this past year with joy.

DARK PASTS

COMING TO TERMS WITH DARK PASTS?

April 24, 2015 marked the passage of one hundred years since the start of the Armenian Genocide. The centenary was a solemn date of commemoration for Armenians around the world. It was also a focal point for activism and protest against Turkey's continued denial of the genocide. As the anniversary approached, pressures on Turkey to recognize the genocide ratcheted up, while countries such as the United States and Germany faced pressures to officially recognize the genocide. At the same time, Turkish officials sought to minimize criticisms of the state's narrative of the "Armenian question" (*Ermeni sorunu*), taking a number of steps to try to tamp down international criticism.[1] A key example of such efforts came a year before the centenary, on the ninety-ninth anniversary of the genocide, when then prime minister (PM) Recep Tayyip Erdoğan issued a statement about the "events of 1915" that was praised as "unprecedented" and "conciliatory" for its expression of "condolences" (*taziyeler*) to the grandchildren of "the Armenians who lost their lives in the context of the early twentieth century."[2]

When the hundredth anniversary arrived a year later, however, the limits of Erdoğan's apparent conciliation were revealed. While PM Ahmet Davutoğlu echoed Erdoğan's wording from a year earlier and offered "deep condolences" to the descendants of "the innocent Ottoman Armenians who lost their lives," statements by now president Erdoğan and other officials conveyed a very different impression.[3] Erdoğan declared: "It is out of the question for there to be a stain or a shadow called genocide on Turkey."[4] Similarly, the Turkish Foreign Ministry condemned a European Parliament resolution acknowledging the genocide,

1

calling it a mistaken repetition of "the anti-Turkish clichés of the Armenian propaganda."[5] These statements signaled continuity—rather than meaningful change—in Turkey's official narrative, which has consistently rejected the label "genocide" and denied official responsibility for the destruction of the Ottoman Armenian community.

Turkey is far from the only country to wrestle with a dark past.[6] Twenty years earlier, Japan faced a similarly momentous anniversary and a similar constellation of pressures for greater contrition. As the fiftieth anniversary of the end of World War II (WWII) approached, calls escalated within and outside Japan for an official apology and compensation for its WWII-era crimes, including the Nanjing Massacre and the military's sex slave program (the "comfort women" program). In the wake of more than a decade of diplomatic tensions and crises over "history issues," and facing a growing transnational redress movement, Japanese leaders decided that the anniversary would be a good time to deepen official contrition by having the Diet issue an official apology for Japan's aggression and crimes in WWII.[7]

Intended as a groundbreaking apology, the resultant resolution turned out to be neither groundbreaking nor an apology. Conservative politicians and nationalist interest groups successfully mobilized against the planned apology, with the result that the resolution the Diet passed constituted no change—and in some sense a reversal—in the content of the state's narrative. The resolution expressed "deep remorse" but pointedly did not offer an apology. Moreover, the resolution relativized Japan's war crimes by situating them within the context of other countries' "colonial rule and acts."[8] Furthermore, as the journalist Wakamiya Yoshibumi notes, by using the phrase "acts of aggression," rather than the unqualified term "aggression" that had been used by PM Morihiro Hosokawa in 1993, the resolution "was clearly a step backward."[9] Consequently, instead of "settling" the issue, both the ambivalence of the resolution and the right-wing opposition that effected this outcome deepened international dissatisfaction with Japan's position.

Of course, many states have dark pasts, ranging from the violence and expropriation of slavery and colonialism to more contemporary abuses and atrocities. Although such wrongs might have been elided or rationalized in the past, expectations have changed in the past couple of decades. This shift is due to the ascendance of human rights and the strengthening of norms of legal accountability and truth-seeking in the post-WWII period.[10] With the advent of the "age of apology," states, political and social organizations, and corporations have been pressured by victims and others to apologize and pay reparations for past atrocities and wrongs ranging from the Holocaust to slavery and colonialism.[11] In addition, states emerging from conflict and transitioning to democracy are now expected to take steps to bring the truth to light and mete out justice.[12]

In response, some states with dark pasts have looked into and apologized for past crimes. For example, in 2008 the Australian PM Kevin Rudd offered an official apology to indigenous Australians for their "past mistreatment" and "for the laws and policies of successive Parliaments and governments that have inflicted profound grief, suffering and loss" on families, communities, and peoples.[13] However, many other states have continued to silence, deny, rationalize, and relativize dark pasts.

These trends underscore the complexities and difficulties of truth-seeking and truth-telling. In particular, they raise questions about the persistence of contention over and the difficulties of coming to terms with past wrongs: What is it about dark pasts that makes it so hard for states to come to terms with them? Given the apparent challenges of reckoning with the past, what are the sources of continuity in states' narratives of dark pasts, and when and why do states choose to change such narratives? Or put differently, what are the determinants of—and obstacles to—such change?[14]

Narratives of Dark Pasts in Turkey and Japan

To understand when and why states change official narratives of dark pasts, this book compares and analyzes the trajectories over the past sixty years of Turkey's narrative of the Armenian Genocide and Japan's narrative of the Nanjing Massacre and the Second Sino-Japanese War.[15]

The Armenian Genocide took place in the Ottoman Empire during World War I (WWI) and was organized by the leaders of the governing Committee of Union and Progress (İttihat ve Terakki Cemiyeti). In the genocide, an estimated 800,000 to 1.5 million Ottoman Armenians were killed, Armenians' property was systematically expropriated, and tens of thousands of Armenian women and children were abducted and forcibly incorporated into Muslim households.[16] In this process, the Armenian community that had lived for centuries in Anatolia was destroyed, declining from about 20 percent of the total population in the late nineteenth century to approximately 5 percent in 1923.[17] In addition, traces of Armenians' existence and culture were erased or destroyed.

The Nanjing Massacre, which occurred within the context of the Second Sino-Japanese War, began in December 1937, when the Japanese army invaded the Chinese city of Nanjing. During and after the capture of the city, Japanese soldiers massacred an estimated one hundred thousand to two hundred thousand Chinese civilians and prisoners of war (POWs).[18] The Second Sino-Japanese War was fought on the Chinese mainland between the armies of Imperial Japan and the Republic of China. The war unofficially began on 18 September 1931, became official in July 1937, and ended with Japan's unconditional surrender in August 1945. During this fifteen-year period, tens of millions of Chinese people died; many Chinese POWs were executed; tens of thousands of (and possibly as many as two hundred thousand) Chinese women were raped by Japanese soldiers; approximately forty thousand Chinese people were forced into slave labor, during which about seven thousand died; and Japanese biological and chemical warfare programs killed an estimated one hundred thousand Chinese civilians.[19]

Over the course of the past several decades, Japan's narrative has gradually come to acknowledge the Nanjing Massacre and to include statements of regret and apology. In contrast, the extent of change in Turkey's narrative has been much more limited. Over this period, its narrative has moved from silence and denial to relativizing, mythmaking, and a limited degree of acknowledgment. Meanwhile, Turkish officials have continued to reject official wrongdoing in and responsibility for the genocide, and have developed new rationalizations for and defenses of the Ottoman government's actions. What accounts for this divergence in the two narratives' trajectories, in spite of broad similarities in regime type, allies, and normative structures?

At the same time, there has been a significant degree of continuity in both narratives. Notwithstanding the greater degree of change in Japan's narrative, central themes in each narrative have remained unchanged. While both narratives have come to encompass a greater degree of acknowledgment, both continue to relativize key aspects of these dark pasts. Given these continuities, these narratives represent "hard" cases for analyzing the sources of change in states' narratives or memories of past wrongs.

Extrapolating from these two cases, I argue that international pressures increase the *likelihood* of change in official narratives of dark pasts, while domestic considerations determine the *content* of such change. International pressures—which include calls for a state to apologize, demands for a state to change its representation of an event, and actions that bring attention to alternative narratives of an event—can challenge the legitimacy of a narrative and alter the cost-benefit calculus underlying it. In so doing, they can prompt officials to consider changing the state's narrative.

International pressures are only part of the picture. Whether and when change occurs, and what it looks like, are also shaped by domestic political considerations. In particular, whether and how officials respond to international pressures are contingent on four factors: (1) material concerns, (2) legitimacy and identity concerns, (3) electoral-political concerns, and (4) domestic contestation. First, change in the direction of greater acknowledgment and contrition is less likely when the perceived extent and likelihood of material costs (e.g., reparations, restitution, territory) of greater acknowledgment and contrition are high. If officials fear that greater acknowledgment or deeper contrition might lead to the loss of territory or the payment of reparations, they will be reluctant to take such steps. The more important and extensive the territory at stake, and the higher the feared reparations, the more reluctant officials will be to express greater acknowledgment or contrition. Second, change in the direction of greater acknowledgment and contrition is less likely the greater the extent to which a narrative is connected with sources of legitimacy or identity for the state, its institutions, or its officials. If a narrative is central to a nation's founding narrative or forms the basis of state institutions' legitimacy, officials will be likely to resist change. Third, change in the direction of greater acknowledgment and contrition is less likely when political support for the state, regime, or political actors could be threatened or undermined by such action. If key electoral constituencies or political allies are strong supporters of the state's story, then officials are unlikely to be willing to change the narrative, because they will not want to threaten sources of political support. Finally, change in the direction of greater acknowledgment and contrition is less likely when domestic contestation is trending toward calls for less acknowledgment and contrition. If activists are pushing for the maintenance of the status quo, or for less acknowledgment and contrition, then officials are unlikely to deepen official acknowledgment and contrition. Together, these four factors shape whether and how government officials change a state's narrative at a given juncture.

At the core, therefore, patterns of change and continuity in states' narratives of dark pasts are the result of complex and contingent *interactions* between international and domestic political forces. While international pressures—especially sustained pressures from powerful states and allies—are likelier than other factors to prompt change in a state's narrative, they are insufficient for understanding the content and extent of change. In moments when change is considered, the domestic considerations outlined above shape officials' decision making about whether and how to change the state's narrative. For example, while the frequency and escalating costs of international pressures, especially diplomatic protests by China and Korea, have led Japanese officials to consider changing Japan's narrative at several junctures, electoral-political and material concerns, along with the push and pull of domestic contestation, have repeatedly shaped *whether* and *how* officials and politicians have changed the state's narrative. And although a series of terrorist attacks on Turkish diplomats and the beginnings of international recognition of the Armenian Genocide—both in the 1970s—led Turkish officials to break the state's silence on the "Armenian question," *when* and *how* they did were shaped by concerns about territorial claims, threats to domestic legitimacy, and domestic constraints on academic and popular discussion of the issue.

This argument also accounts for *continuities* in states' narratives. Continuity is more likely if international pressures for greater acknowledgment and contrition are scant, sporadic, or from weak sources. Moreover, when officials consider changing the state's narrative, domestic considerations can operate as important constraints on change. The stronger, more salient, and more numerous the domestic considerations enumerated above, the more likely officials are to resist pressures to change the state's narrative and the more likely the state's narrative is to exhibit continuity. For example, Turkish officials have long feared that genocide survivors, or the representatives or descendants of Armenian victims or survivors, could advance territorial and compensation claims against government agencies, businesses, and properties in Turkey. This concern has been a key constraint on Turkish officials' willingness to acknowledge the genocidal nature of and officials' responsibility for the historic violence against Ottoman Armenians.

Additional sources of change and continuity can arise over time as states' narratives are contested, defended, and updated. As a result of feedback effects—processes of "increasing returns" and "path dependence" that "can trigger a self-reinforcing dynamic"—the production of an official narrative, and especially change in a narrative, can set in motion actors and developments that influence the narrative and decisions related to it at later points in time.[20] For example, efforts by nationalists to limit contrition and acknowledgment can inspire others to take action to push for greater contrition and acknowledgment, which can generate new pressures for change. Alternatively, official efforts to defend the state's position can mobilize actors who become invested in the status quo. With time, such defenders of the official narrative can constrain officials who might be considering change.

In sum, accounting for when and why states change—or do not change—official narratives of dark pasts necessitates an understanding of the effects and limits of international pressures on states' narratives, and the ways in which such pressures are refracted through the prism of domestic politics.

The Stakes

Understanding when and why states change narratives of dark pasts is important because of the broader consequences for domestic politics and international relations.

At the domestic level, narratives of past events—particularly narratives of glorious victories and ignominious defeats—are often used to construct and reinforce national communities.[21] Such narratives help constitute citizenship and belonging, delineate the boundaries of public discourse, and influence the quality of democracy.[22] At the same time, narratives of past conflict and violence can establish or harden boundaries between groups, which can lead to persecution and repression, and can create grievances that contribute to the development of unrest or rebellion. Narratives of past conflicts and atrocities can also be used and manipulated for diverse ends, including stirring up nationalist sentiment and justifying aggression and war.[23] At the extreme, narratives of past violence can exacerbate tensions and prejudices that can contribute to future conflict and violence.[24] Internationally, narratives of past atrocities and conflicts can influence states' foreign policies, affect political and economic relations, and increase threat perceptions between states.[25]

In Turkey, the state's narrative of the "Armenian question" has facilitated the securitization of important aspects of domestic politics and has contributed to the exclusion and alienation of Turkey's dwindling Armenian community, justifying ongoing discrimination, expropriation, and violence.[26] The impunity at the core of the state's narrative has facilitated the power and lack of accountability of the "deep state," undermined the rule of law, and stymied the quality of democracy.[27] Turkey's narrative has also been a complicating factor in its European Union (EU) membership candidacy, and has adversely affected its relationships with key allies. For example, each time the US Congress has considered resolutions calling on Turkey to acknowledge the Armenian Genocide, Turkish officials' negative reactions have strained bilateral relations. In addition, Turkey's denial of the genocide has bedeviled relations with the neighboring Republic of Armenia since the latter's independence in 1991.

In Japan, contestation over the state's narrative has reinforced domestic political divides, fueled right-wing nationalism and violence, and complicated other political questions, such as debates over constitutional revision. Japan's narrative has also negatively affected relations with its neighbors. Between 2001 and 2006, PM Koizumi Junichirō's repeated visits to the Yasukuni Shrine, which were perceived as symbolically whitewashing Japan's war crimes, reinforced Asian countries' lack of support for Japan's bid for a permanent seat on the United Nations Security Council (UNSC). Signaling this, in April 2005 China announced that it would "not endorse Tokyo's UN ambitions efforts [sic] until it 'clarifies some historic issues.'"[28] Shortly thereafter, Chinese premier Wen Jiabao warned: "Only a country that respects history and wins over the trust of peoples in Asia and the world at large can take greater responsibilities in the world community."[29] In addition, Chinese officials refused to hold bilateral meetings for Koizumi's last few years in office. Japan's narrative has also had economic costs. For example, many Chinese consumers boycotted Japanese products in response to a 2005 Japanese Ministry of Education decision that was perceived to gloss over Japan's WWII crimes, including the Nanjing Massacre.

Looking beyond these two cases, many other countries have dark pasts that stain the present. In the United States, the destruction and dispossession of Native Americans and the violence, disenfranchisement, and expropriation of slavery constitute foundational violence on which current aspects of US identity rest.[30] As a result, narratives of slavery and its aftermath, and the genocide and ethnic cleansing of Native Americans, shape policies and outcomes in areas including education, civil rights, criminal justice, housing, and health care. In Rwanda, to mention another example, narratives and myths of past violence contributed to the occurrence of the 1994 genocide.[31] And in the post-genocide period, Rwanda's president Paul Kagame "justifies his stifling of debate, and the suppression of opponents, as a necessary evil in a country where the freedom to whip up ethnic hatred has taken so heavy a toll."[32] Moreover, the state's narrow and relatively simplified narrative of the genocide—which focuses on Tutsi victims and Hutu perpetrators—silences and alienates those whose experiences and suffering in the genocide do not fit squarely into these categories.[33] Finally, narratives of past violence have been central to the perpetuation of mistrust and the repetition of violence in the Israeli-Palestinian conflict and in the conflicts in the Great Lakes region of Africa.[34]

Given the importance of these issues for conflict and violence, citizenship and democracy, and domestic and international politics, there are compelling reasons to investigate states' narratives of dark pasts.

Structure, Agency, and Contingency in the Politics of Memory

In examining the sources of change and continuity in states' narratives of dark pasts, this book builds on and contributes to interdisciplinary scholarship on transitional justice, the politics of memory, and international norms. Broadly speaking, existing work in these fields has tended to focus on collective rather than official memory, on memories as instantiated in particular sites (such as museums or memorials) rather than in overarching narratives, and on the effects rather than the causes of memory. In contrast, this book focuses on official memories—or narratives—as a whole, and flips the analytical lens to explore the factors that shape and reinforce such narratives. Moreover, whereas existing work has emphasized the effects of structural factors on collective and official memories, and the role of agents who contest and challenge official memories, this book highlights *interactions between* structures and agents in shaping states' narratives.

Memory scholars have predominantly focused on the politics and content of societies' collective memories, and on sites and forms of memory such as memorials, textbooks, museums, and apologies.[35] Official memory as a whole has been less well studied. In the field of international relations, scholars have investigated the effects of memory on political outcomes, investigating, for example, the effects of memory on foreign policy, threat perception, reconciliation, and conflict.[36] While this work has demonstrated the importance of official memories and narratives for various outcomes, we do not have as good of a grasp of the politics that shape such memories in the first place. This book thus addresses the prior question of what accounts for patterns of change and continuity in official memories.[37]

Transitional justice scholarship has also tended to overlook this question, instead exploring normative and empirical questions related to the pursuit of truth and justice in transitions from authoritarianism and conflict.[38] In particular, transitional justice scholarship differs in three key ways from this book's approach. First, transitional justice typically refers to the period of a country's transition to democracy or emergence from civil conflict.[39] In contrast, this book employs a broader time frame, analyzing Turkey's and Japan's narratives far beyond their initial formulation in periods of transition. Second, transitional justice institutions and processes can contribute to the *initial* establishment of narratives of authoritarian and violent pasts.[40] In contrast, this analysis traces patterns of change and continuity in official narratives *following* their initial formulation, thereby capturing the politics that affect narratives' trajectories over time. Third, as Leebaw argues, transitional justice scholars and advocates have emphasized the "depoliticized" nature of transitional justice institutions and practices.[41] In contrast, I focus explicitly on the *politics* by which states' narratives are shaped and contested.

Notwithstanding these differences, these literatures offer insights into factors that influence states' narratives. In particular, existing arguments attend to important aspects of structure and agency in the politics of memory, but they do not pay sufficient attention to the contingent and interactive processes by which states' narratives are produced, contested, and defended.

Transitional justice and memory scholars emphasize structural determinants of collective and official remembrance, while norms scholars explore the structural effects of norms on states' practices. Importantly, structural factors can help maintain continuities in an official narrative by creating and reinforcing power asymmetries and by designating certain perspectives and issues as out of bounds or taboo. Conversely, structural changes—such as the emergence of new states, changes in the relative balance of power, regime change, or the coming to power of a new party or leader—can lead to shifts in a state's narrative. However, whether change occurs in a state's narrative and what form it takes cannot be predicted from structural factors alone.

Transitional justice scholars emphasize that understandings of past wrongs can shift via formal processes of truth- and justice-seeking that are adopted in the wake of regime change. However, regime change provides an indeterminate answer to the questions of when and why states change narratives of dark pasts. Trials, truth commissions, and other mechanisms of truth- and justice-seeking can have ambivalent effects, including "promoting denial and forgetting," as Loyle and Davenport argue.[42] Moreover, countries can adopt diverse policies in the name of truth and justice, for example, lustration or individual criminal trials, which typically have distinct effects. In addition, trials, truth commissions, and other steps are likely to constitute only the beginning of processes of reckoning with the past.[43]

Another structural argument is that generational change can lead to shifts in understandings of past wrongs.[44] However, even if the passage of time does lead to change in a state's narrative, it does not answer the questions of when change might occur, what prompts change, or how a narrative changes. Moreover, contrary to conventional wisdom, time does not "heal" all wounds or take the bitterness out of past wrongs. This is illustrated with the "irruption" of memories of civil war and dictatorship in Spain, more than three decades after the "Pact of Forgetting" (*Pacto del Olvido*).[45]

Scholarship on international norms also emphasizes the importance of structure. Defined as "collective expectations for the proper behavior of actors with a given identity," norms are a fundamental element of the structure of power, ideas, and interests that states face in the international system.[46] As "collective expectations" and "standards of appropriateness," international norms help constitute identities and influence the practices of state and nonstate actors.[47] Over the course of the post-WWII period, the growing attention to memory politics has heightened scrutiny of states' narratives of past atrocities and increased the perceived values of "recognition," "truth," and "reconciliation."[48] While this trend has impacted the practices of an increasing number of states, it has not had a consistent or direct impact on all states.

Turning from structure to agency, both memory scholars and norms scholars have investigated agency in relation to the politics of memory. Memory scholars have shown how domestic public debate, bottom-up social mobilization, and "memory activism" can lead to changes in public and official understandings of historical wrongs.[49] Somewhat in contrast, this book focuses on *official* agents of memory and on *interactions* between official and societal, and domestic and international actors.

Like memory scholars, norms scholars have long emphasized the agency of nonstate actors, such as norm entrepreneurs and activists, particularly in processes of norm emergence and diffusion.[50] By contrast, "norm takers"—typically, states—have been treated as relatively passive subjects who commit to and comply with norms or are punished for violating norms. However, work on norm localization, translation, and resistance has begun to catalog alternative forms of agency. For instance, "norm takers" can alter a norm's content to make it better fit a local context and can employ a variety of strategies to avoid or lessen the costs of noncompliance and violation.[51] This book joins this vein of scholarship, exploring the ways in which norms structure expectations and actions related to the politics of memory, as well as the varied ways in which official and societal actors draw on and respond to normative expectations.

More generally, I look beyond the limits of a structural or agential perspective to analyze interactions between structures and agents. Tracing changes and continuities in the content of each narrative over time, I identify the actors that produce and contest each narrative, the processes through which change occurs, and the mechanisms that reinforce continuities in each narrative.[52] In so doing, I highlight the agency of state actors in relation to international pressures and structures of meaning, the agency of societal actors in relation to official discourse, and the limits of both forms of agency.[53] I also unpack the range and complexities of responses to international norms, tracing the diverse ways actors have used and responded to collective expectations related to genocide, human rights, legal accountability, and truth-seeking.[54] Finally, by focusing on interactions between domestic and international politics, I reveal how domestic politics functions as a filter that shapes the ways in which states' narratives change—or do not change—over time.[55]

The analysis also yields several insights into the nature of change in states' narratives. First, states' narratives are prone toward continuity and inertia. When change does occur, it is typically incremental and often involves *layering*, whereby new themes are added onto existing ones. This stems from the fact that, as official and societal actors become committed to a narrative, and as actors and institutions become involved in its production, support for the narrative becomes more entrenched.[56] As a result, it becomes more difficult—and riskier—to make a change that fundamentally breaks with the existing narrative. Second, change is often multifaceted and sometimes ambivalent. For example, increasing international recognition of the Armenian Genocide was the main catalyst for changes in the content of Turkey's official narrative in 2001. Yet, while the narrative shifted to acknowledge some basic facts about the genocide, Turkish officials simultaneously took steps to more effectively defend core elements of the state's narrative. Consequently, movement in the direction of acknowledgment was accompanied by the continued—and arguably strengthened—rejection of the label "genocide."

Plan of the Book

The argument outlined above is developed and substantiated over the course of the following chapters. To construct the trajectories of Turkey's and Japan's narratives over the past sixty years, I analyzed a range of primary and secondary sources and conducted more than eight months of fieldwork, including over seventy-five semistructured elite interviews, in Turkey and Japan.[57] Triangulating evidence drawn from interviews, government documents, news accounts, and other primary and secondary sources, I trace the motivations and processes through which change occurs and continuities are reinforced.

Chapter 1 presents the conceptual framework developed to assess the content of and changes in each narrative, explains the logic of case selection, and lays out the argument in greater detail. The conceptual framework consists of eight elements, ranging from silencing to commemorating, each of which captures a possible facet of an official narrative. In the chapters that follow, this framework is used to identify periods of continuity and points of change in the two narratives' trajectories. The remainder of the chapter discusses the logic underlying the comparison of Turkey's and Japan's narratives, and explains the international pressures and domestic considerations that have shaped patterns of change and continuity in these narratives.

Chapters 2 through 7 analyze the trajectories of Turkey's and Japan's narratives. The first three chapters cover the Turkish case, and the latter three cover the Japanese case. Each set of chapters is similarly structured. The first of the three case chapters introduces the case, reviewing the history of the event and discussing the factors that shaped the initial formulation of the state's narrative. The chapter then outlines the trajectory of the official narrative over time, and discusses how the book's argument accounts for the pattern of change and continuity therein. The latter two chapters on each country analyze the trajectory of the state's narrative over the course of nearly sixty years. Changes in each narrative are analyzed in relation to the basic historical understanding outlined in the first empirical chapter, as well as in relation to the content of the narrative at earlier points in time. The chapters are organized chronologically to illuminate relationships between actors and developments over time.

Chapters 2, 3, and 4 focus on Turkey's narrative. Following Chapter 2's introduction of the case, Chapter 3 analyzes the content of, and changes and continuities in, Turkey's narrative over the period from 1950 to the early 1990s. In this period, the state's narrative shifted from silencing and denying the genocide to an actively defended position that relativized the violence and presented an alternative account of what had happened. This shift, which began in 1981, also involved substantial continuity, particularly in the denial of official responsibility for the deaths of Armenians. This chapter documents the international pressures that prompted these changes and the domestic considerations that shaped their timing and content. Chapter 4 analyzes Turkey's narrative over the period from 1994 to 2008. Beginning in the mid-1990s, subtle changes emerged in the tone and substance of the narrative. Overall, however, despite major structural changes at the international level—including the establishment of an Armenian state—and the beginnings of domestic challenges to the official narrative, the content of the narrative was remarkably stable, highlighting the persistence of significant domestic constraints. Beginning in 2001, the narrative shifted more substantially, coming to include a limited acknowledgment of Armenians' deaths and suffering, while rationalizing these facts and continuing to reject the label "genocide." These changes were made primarily in response to increased international recognition of the genocide, and also reflected the broadening of domestic challenges to and questioning of the official narrative.

Chapters 4, 5, and 6 focus on Japan's narrative. Chapter 5 introduces the case, and Chapter 6 analyzes Japan's narrative over the period from 1952 to 1989. In this period, the state's narrative shifted from a broad silence and lack of acknowledgment, to an acknowledgment of the event and the harm suffered, to a vague expression of regret and admissions of responsibility that were accompanied by undercurrents of relativizing and mythmaking. These changes arose from the normalization of relations between Japan and China, pressures from China and other former victim states, and progressive domestic activism. Continuities in the narrative were driven by domestic and international structural factors, attempts by Japanese leaders to move out of the shadow of the past, and conservative activism. Chapter 7 analyzes Japan's narrative between 1998 and 2008. In this period, the state's narrative shifted to include admissions of responsibility and apologies, and then backtracked to resume mythmaking and relativizing (while continuing to apologize). These shifts were made in response to pressures from China and South Korea, and amid major changes in the international and domestic structures that supported the state's narrative. At the same time, domestic political considerations frequently shaped both the content and extent of changes in the state's narrative.

The concluding chapter reviews the book's argument and discusses how it accounts for the different degrees of change over time in Turkey's and Japan's narratives. The latter half of the chapter highlights key findings regarding the effects of and responses to international norms, and closes with a discussion of the broader implications of this research.

CHANGING THE STATE'S STORY

States tell myriad stories about the past. The stories that they choose to tell, and the ways they tell them, forge the foundations on which national identity and claims to political legitimacy are based. They also shape and infuse meaning into actions and decisions in the present. Once formed, however, such stories can be difficult to change, particularly when they concern dark parts of a nation's past. What is it about dark pasts that makes it so hard for states to "come to terms" with them? When and why do states change the stories they tell about dark pasts? What are the determinants of—and obstacles to—such change?

Conceptualizing Official Narratives of Dark Pasts

Despite the breadth of research on historical memory, we lack a conceptual framework with which to analyze and compare the content of states' narratives over time and across cases. Existing conceptualizations fall short in two ways. First, a range of different, overlapping, and conflicting terms have been used to analyze how and what states and societies "remember." This conceptual proliferation includes mutual outcomes such as reconciliation and forgiveness; one-sided actions such as commemoration; the payment of reparations or restitution; and general processes or elements of remembrance, such as contrition, memory, regret, coming to terms with the past, historical consciousness, and narrative.[1] While this variety of concepts reflects the diversity of questions asked by scholars across a range of disciplines, it hinders comparison across cases and contributes to analytical confusion. Second, memory scholars in the humanities often characterize the evolution of a state's or a society's memory in rich descriptive terms, while social scientists studying memory tend to conceptualize levels of contrition or types of remembrance as dichotomous or trichotomous outcomes.[2] The former approach does not allow for generalization, and the latter approach—while useful for broad comparisons and for charting expansive shifts in discourse—cannot capture more nuanced forms and degrees of change.

To address these shortcomings, first the object of inquiry—official narratives of dark pasts—needs to be unpacked. A *dark past* is a large-scale or systematic human rights atrocity that occurred in the past and for which the state bears some responsibility, either directly or as a successor to the regime that perpetrated the crimes. Large-scale or systematic human rights atrocities that fall into this category include, but are not limited to, genocide, mass killing, ethnic cleansing, colonialism, and slavery.[3] An *official narrative* is a state's characterization of an event, including the nature and scope of the event, and the state's characterization of the role and responsibility of government officials and institutions in the event.[4] In contrast to the concepts of memory and remembrance, which have dominated the field of memory studies, the term "official narrative" avoids the suggestion that the state or its officials might "remember" or "forget" an event in a particular way. Instead, it focuses on whether and how an event is characterized, described, and marked by state officials and institutions.[5] Alternative terms include "acknowledgment," "reparations politics," "restitution," and the "politics of regret."[6] However, each of these terms implies a particular form or goal for the state's position, whereas "official narrative" is neutral with regard to the content of the state's story. *Official* characterizations are those made by government officials and institutions whose actions and statements are widely considered to represent the government's position. An official narrative comprises both statements and actions, since to exclude actions such as commemorations and reparations would omit important elements of the state's position. Moreover, to accurately capture a state's narrative, several types of sources—or indicators of the official narrative—are analyzed:

1. Statements and actions by state leaders and spokespersons
2. Accounts and coverage in school textbooks
3. Accounts in official publications
4. Legislative resolutions and bills
5. Government-sponsored commemorations, museums, and memorials
6. Reparations and other payments to victim states, groups, or individual victims[7]

Official narratives are rarely uniform across different indicators or in the actions and words of different official actors.[8] As a result, assessing the content of and changes in an official narrative necessitates attention to fissures and gaps among official actors and across different indicators, along with such narratives' multifaceted nature.[9]

The conceptual framework introduced here captures different facets of an official narrative as well as changes in a narrative's content, and allows for comparisons of changes and continuities over time and across cases. At any given point in time, an official narrative usually comprises one or more elements capturing possible content of an official narrative, ranging from silencing and denial to commemorating. The range of possible elements of an official narrative is shown in Figure 1.1, after which each element is defined in greater depth.

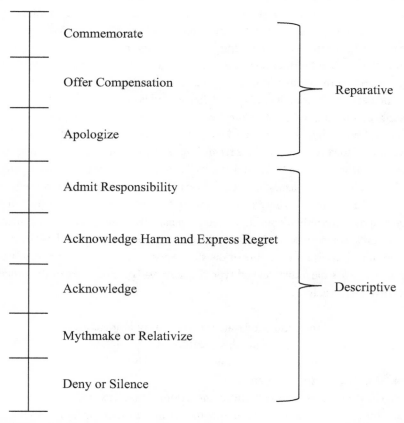

FIGURE 1.1. Framework for assessing the content of official narratives

The eight elements in this framework are arranged in an approximate sequence, based on the logical assumption that, for example, a state is unlikely to apologize if it has not acknowledged an event and admitted responsibility for it. This sequence is not intended to suggest that change in a state's narrative necessarily involves the sequential addition of one element after another. Moreover, change in one direction does not preclude change in the opposite direction at a later time, and there is no final place at which a "good" or "appropriate" official narrative has been achieved and an issue can be consigned to history. The elements from "deny or silence" to "admit responsibility" are *descriptive*, meaning that they capture a state's characterization(s) of an event, while the elements from "apologize" to "commemorate" are *reparative*, meaning that they capture actions taken by a state to make reparations for a dark past.[10]

The first element is to deny or silence an event.[11] *To deny an event* is to claim that something did not occur or to refuse to acknowledge that something happened.[12] Like other elements in this framework, denial is narrowly defined to capture more nuanced forms of change. This definition thus differs from broader conceptualizations of denial, which typically encompass outright rejections of the reality of an event, as well as disavowals of responsibility for or involvement in an event, and rationalizations and relativizations of an event. Illustrating a broader conceptualization, Smith writes that "denial involves not just refusal of facts, but the more active strategies of rationalization (giving a reason for the action, but not the real reason), projection (attributing one's own motives or acts to the victims), and justification (the victims deserved the suffering and death that was meted out to them)."[13] In contrast, the narrower definition offered here allows for the disaggregation of these and other possible characterizations of and responses to an event, which in turn makes it possible to identify more nuanced forms of change and continuity. *To silence an event* is to consciously elide or suppress a historical wrong. This can include saying nothing about an event, omitting an event from official histories, and suppressing discussion of an issue within the domestic sphere (through laws that limit or ban discussion and through the punishment of those who discuss an issue) or internationally (through persuasive and coercive diplomacy). Crucially, as Winter puts it, silence is "socially constructed."[14]

The second element is to mythmake about or relativize an event.[15] *To mythmake about an event* can involve claiming that an event was not what it looks like, but was instead of a different, more benign nature; acknowledging that something happened, but that its cause was natural, unintentional, or that someone else bears responsibility; or shifting attention to other events, either real or imagined. An example of mythmaking in Turkey's narrative is the claim that Armenians and Turks were engaged in a civil war that occurred within the Ottoman Empire against the backdrop of WWI. As with the definition of denial, this narrow conceptualization of mythmaking allows one to differentiate among distinct elements of an overall narrative and to identify more nuanced forms of change.[16] *To relativize an event* involves questioning or downplaying the severity of what happened, or arguing that an event should be viewed within a broader context that diminishes its severity. An example of relativizing in Japan's narrative can be seen in the aforementioned 1995 Diet resolution, in which Japan's aggression was situated within the context of "many instances of colonial rule and acts of aggression in the modern history of the world."[17]

The third element is *to acknowledge an event*, which is to admit that an event occurred and to recognize basic facts about the event. Acknowledging an event involves passing a relatively low bar of basic recognition of an event's occurrence, and often coexists with mythmaking and/or relativizing.[18] The fourth element is *to acknowledge harm and express regret for an event*, which involves recognizing the harm to and suffering of the victims, and expressing regret for that harm. This element thus involves recognizing that a wrong occurred.[19] The fifth element is *to admit responsibility for an event*, which is to acknowledge that an event was organized or perpetrated—at least in part—by agents or institutions of the state.

The sixth element is *to apologize for an event*. Following O'Neill's definition of a "full apology" for a wrong done by X to Y, to apologize requires "an acknowledgment of the harm done to Y, the moral wrong involved in the action, and X's responsibility for it."[20] A state is characterized as having apologized if it conveys all three of these elements and if it uses a variant of the words "sorry" or "apology."[21]

The seventh element is *to offer compensation for an event*. This involves offering compensation to victims or their families, to groups that represent individual victims or a victim group, or to one or more states in which victims or their relatives or descendants reside. The compensation needs to be explicitly identified as compensation or reparations for suffering in or harm from the event. Aid or payments that are offered in lieu of compensation but are not explicitly acknowledged as compensation or reparations do not count as offering compensation.

The final element is *to commemorate an event*, which involves actions or statements that recall, document, or honor an event or its victims in ways that acknowledge the event and the government's responsibility for the harm suffered. This can include holding ceremonies to remember an event or its victims; documenting an event in government-owned or government-funded museums, archives, or research centers; and constructing monuments to an event and its victims.[22] Note that commemoration could happen either before or after compensation, or in the presence or absence of compensation.

In addition to helping identify the content of a state's narrative, this framework allows one to delineate distinct phases, or periods of continuity, and points of change in the trajectory of a state's narrative. At any given point in time, an official narrative comprises one or more of these elements. *Change* is defined as the addition or subtraction of one or more elements from an official narrative. A change has occurred when one or more elements are added to or taken away from an official narrative. Of course, assessing whether a change has occurred is more than just a simple counting of elements. Rather, as the empirical analysis demonstrates, interpretation is central to assessing whether and how an official narrative has changed. In particular, determining whether a state's narrative includes a certain element requires drawing on and evaluating the content of various indicators, which then allows for the determination of whether change has occurred, and if so, the substance of that change. For example, the content of a narrative in one indicator (e.g., textbooks) might change, while the content in another indicator (e.g., official statements) might remain constant. In such cases, deciding whether change has occurred involves a subjective evaluation of whether the content of the overall narrative—which is a composite of various indicators—has been substantively altered. *Continuity* is defined as the lack of change over a period of time, and a *phase* is a period of time during which there is no change in the elements of an official narrative. Finally, the *direction* of change refers to whether an official narrative moves toward denying and silencing or toward commemoration.

In contrast to more descriptive analyses and to broader conceptualizations, the framework introduced here makes possible comparisons over time and across cases, and facilitates the analysis of changes and patterns that are missed in studies that classify states' narratives into two or three broad categories. Thus, beyond the study at hand, this framework should be valuable for scholars who want to analyze and compare the content of and changes in other states' historical narratives.

Why Turkey and Japan?

Employing this conceptual framework, I compare changes—and continuities—over time in Turkey's narrative of the Armenian Genocide and Japan's narrative of the Nanjing Massacre and the Second Sino-Japanese War.[23] These constitute good cases for understanding the sources of change and continuity in states' narratives for several reasons. For one, the stickiness of Turkey's and Japan's narratives is representative of other narratives of dark pasts, which as a rule are more prone to continuity than change. Moreover, the continuities in both narratives make them relatively "hard" cases for understanding change in states' narratives, while also facilitating the analysis of the sources and mechanisms of continuity.

In addition, because both states have experienced domestic and international pressures for change, they capture the full range of potential independent variables. Finally, because both narratives have been politicized for decades, they are good cases for probing the influence of international normative expectations regarding truth- and justice-seeking, which have strengthened and been institutionalized only since the 1990s.[24]

These two narratives are also promising subjects of study from a comparative perspective. As noted in the introduction, these cases are similar in a number of respects, and yet their narratives have diverged significantly over time.[25] The cases share five key similarities. First, each is a single narrative within a complex of related narratives about atrocities that took place under the broader umbrella of world wars.[26] Second, both are cases of mass killing, which Valentino defines as "the intentional killing of a massive number of noncombatants."[27] That said, the Armenian Genocide is a genocide, whereas the Nanjing Massacre is not. In spite of this categorical and legal difference, analyzing changes and continuities in each case separately over time holds constant a number of potentially relevant factors, including the nature of the event, and makes it possible to more clearly isolate and identify sources of change and continuity in each case. In addition, despite the opprobrium attached to the crime of genocide, Turkish officials have not always or solely rejected the label "genocide," and avoiding the stigma of genocide has not been the only factor motivating officials' defense of the state's narrative. Thus, while the content of Turkey's official narrative has reflected shifts over time in the content and strength of the norm against genocide, the broad patterns of change and continuity in the state's narrative are much better explained by the international pressures and domestic considerations discussed below.[28] Third, both Turkey's and Japan's narratives have been subjected to intense scrutiny and pressure from a range of actors, including victim states (e.g., China and Armenia), third-party states (e.g., the United States and EU member states), and domestic and transnational activists. Fourth, in both cases, members of the victim group primarily reside outside the perpetrator state. Consequently, both are cases in which the victims do not constitute a significant political or social force *within* the state.[29] This contrasts with a country like Rwanda, in which both the perpetrators and the victims of the 1994 genocide continue to live. Finally, both states are Western-oriented democracies, important regional powers, and strong US allies.[30] Thus, while US support has to some extent muted pressures on both narratives, this is a similarity across the cases, not a difference.

In spite of these similarities, the trajectories of the two narratives have diverged over the past several decades. Over the period since 1950, Turkey's narrative has shifted from denying and silencing the genocide to acknowledging some basic facts. From 1950 through the late 1970s, Turkey's official narrative denied and silenced what had happened to Ottoman Armenians. Beginning in 1981, the official narrative shifted to include references to the events, but that largely involved mythmaking and relativizing. After the end of the Cold War and the establishment of an independent Republic of Armenia, the tone of Turkey's narrative shifted, even as its content remained more or less unchanged. Since 2001, the official narrative has acknowledged basic facts about the deportation and deaths of Armenians, while more strongly relativizing those facts. Alongside these changes, the gist of the state's core position—the rejection of the fact that systematic and intentional violence organized by Ottoman officials led to the destruction of the Ottoman Armenian community—has remained constant.

In contrast, since 1952, Japan's narrative has moved from a position of silencing that was quite similar to Turkey's, to gradually acknowledging the Nanjing Massacre and Japan's aggression against China, acknowledging the harm suffered by Chinese victims, and admitting Japan's responsibility for this harm. Since the mid-1990s, Japan's narrative has also included general apologies for its past aggression and crimes, including the Nanjing Massacre. This deepening acknowledgment and contrition have, since the late 1990s, been accompanied by increased official mythmaking and relativizing. In spite of this backtracking and ambivalence, Japan's narrative has changed to a much greater extent than has Turkey's.

Given the broad similarities outlined above and the gradual divergence over time, the comparison of these two narratives sheds further light on the drivers of change and continuity in states' narratives of dark pasts.

Interactions between International Pressures and Domestic Considerations

On the basis of this research, I argue that international pressures increase the likelihood of change in official narratives of dark pasts, while domestic considerations determine the content of such change. International pressures—which include calls for a state to apologize for an event, demands for a state to change its representation of an event, and actions that bring attention to alternative narratives—make change in a state's narrative more likely, and are more likely to trigger such change than other factors, such as structural change or domestic activism. Such pressures can come from *victim states* such as China and Armenia; *third-party states*, such as the United States; *international organizations*, such as the United Nations (UN); *regional organizations*, such as the EU and the Association of Southeast Asian Nations (ASEAN); and *transnational nongovernmental actors*, such as the Armenian Secret Army for the Liberation of Armenia (ASALA), which was a transnational terrorist group.

International pressures are more likely to prompt change in a state's narrative when they are sustained and when they come from powerful victim states or allies. In particular, the relative material power of a victim state influences how likely a perpetrator state is to respond to a demand for change. If a perpetrator state's power is much greater than that of a victim state, then the former is less likely to respond to the latter's demands for change in its narrative, or is less likely to respond in the desired manner. If a victim state's power is increasing relative to that of a perpetrator state, or if the gap between their power is not great, then the perpetrator state is more likely to consider changing its narrative in the desired direction. Transnational activists' influence is greatest when they succeed in pushing a victim or third-party state to pressure a perpetrator state, or when they connect with domestic activists within a perpetrator state.

While international pressures are more likely than other factors to prompt official actors to consider changing the state's narrative, the *content* of change is shaped by domestic considerations. Thus, although state actors and institutions control the production of official narratives, their decisions about whether and how to respond to international pressures are contingent on four types of domestic considerations: (1) material concerns, (2) legitimacy and identity concerns, (3) electoral-political concerns, and (4) domestic contestation. These considerations are summarized in Table 1.1 and discussed below.

TABLE 1.1.   Domestic considerations influencing the content of change

DOMESTIC CONSIDERATION	CHANGE IN THE DIRECTION OF GREATER ACKNOWLEDGMENT AND CONTRITION IS LESS LIKELY . . .
Material concerns	When the perceived extent and likelihood of material costs (e.g., reparations, restitution, territory) is high
Legitimacy and identity concerns	When the narrative is highly connected with sources of legitimacy or identity for the state, its institutions, or its officials
Electoral-political concerns	When political support for the state, the regime, or particular political actors could be threatened or undermined
Domestic contestation	When domestic contestation is trending toward calls for less acknowledgment and contrition

Material concerns refer to worries about the perceived material costs of greater acknowledgment and contrition. The higher the perceived likelihood of having to pay reparations, offer restitution, or give up territory, and the higher the perceived costs, the more likely officials are to resist changing the state's narrative in the direction of greater acknowledgment and contrition. Both Japanese and Turkish officials have been concerned that greater degrees of acknowledgment or contrition could lead to material demands for compensation or territory, which helps account for continuities in both narratives.

Turkish officials have long worried—and continue to worry—that acknowledging the genocide could expose the state to demands for territory and compensation. Given the massive, state-organized appropriation of Armenian property that occurred in the genocide (and after), Turkish officials have worried in particular that descendants of Armenian victims and survivors could make claims against an untold number of properties and businesses in Turkey.[31] In addition, Turkish officials have feared that the state of Armenia (and earlier the Soviet Union) might try to claim territory in eastern Anatolia. These concerns were expressed, for example, in a 1990 speech by PM Yıldırım Akbulut, who explained that "leaders of Armenian communities . . . have declared . . . at every opportunity that these resolutions will constitute the basis for their future claims for compensation and territory. . . . In view of these facts, Turkey has come to the conclusion that efforts to make the international community accept and confirm the so-called Armenian genocide must be stopped. . . . Consequently, it is out of the question to make concessions from our fundamental position."[32] This concern has been an important motivating factor behind Turkish officials' robust defense of the state's narrative. While territorial claims are unlikely to gain traction in the post-WWII international system, Turkish officials' concerns were first activated during and in the wake of WWI, prior to the emergence of the "norm of border fixity" and at a time when national groups' claims to self-determination were being recognized.[33]

At key junctures, concerns about individual compensation claims have also limited the extent of change that Japanese officials have been willing to consider. That said, such concerns have been less acute for Japanese officials than they have been for Turkish officials. This is primarily because Japanese officials have argued that the issue of compensation was settled in the 1951 San Francisco Peace Treaty and in individual treaties that Japan signed with former victim states in the 1950s, 1960s, and 1970s. These treaties included state waivers of reparations claims (or reparations agreements in four cases), and the Japanese government has interpreted these agreements to mean that the compensation issue has been settled both with states and, crucially and not uncontroversially, with individuals.[34] While Chinese, Korean, and other war victims have sought compensation from Japan, the existence of postwar treaties absolving Japan of the need to pay reparations to various countries has helped contain Japanese officials' concerns about the *likelihood* of having to pay individual or collective compensation.[35] Even so, material concerns have influenced Japanese officials' considerations at various points, particularly given that Japan has faced compensation claims in domestic courts and internationally.

Although material concerns are unlikely to vary in the short term, they could change if territorial issues are settled in a treaty or bilateral agreement, if potential claims time out legally or are dismissed in other cases, if there is a shift in the consequences faced by other states that have committed similar crimes, or if there are changes in the content or strength of collective expectations regarding reparations and restitution.

Legitimacy and identity concerns refer to potential threats to sources of legitimacy or identity for the state, its institutions, or its officials. As scholars of nationalism have amply demonstrated, stories or narratives often serve as the glue used to bind together new nations and disparate peoples, and to legitimize state institutions as well as particular leaders and regimes.[36] Given this, Heisler notes that "a major reason . . . for the contentiousness of the past is that some revelations threaten the authority of those in power . . . and the positive self-concepts of societies and groups within them."[37] Consequently, officials are more likely to defend the state's narrative and resist changing it in the direction of greater acknowledgment and contrition if the state's narrative functions as a source of legitimacy or identity for the state, its institutions, or officials. The greater the extent to which the narrative functions as a source of legitimacy or identity, the more resistant officials will be to greater acknowledgment and contrition.[38] Note that this concern could change if the narrative connecting the state or its institutions to the event changes, or if the people and parties in power change.

In Turkey, concerns about national identity, along with the legitimacy of the founding narrative and key political institutions, have heightened the perceived costs of greater acknowledgment. The story of Turkey's founding is premised on the silencing of the violence that immediately preceded its birth, which is characterized as a historical juncture that broke with the Ottoman past and created a completely new nation and state.[39] The genocide, however, belies this purported break: the wealth of the new state was based on properties expropriated from Armenians, and the Muslim and Turkish identity of the new nation was made possible by the violent homogenization of the population.[40] Moreover, as Göçek documents, these linkages were buttressed by striking continuities in the people in power before and after the founding of the republic.[41] Consequently, acknowledging that what happened was a genocide that was organized and carried out by state officials could destabilize the founding national narrative and aspects of Turkish national identity. These stakes have left Turkish officials highly resistant to acknowledging the genocide (as such) and official responsibility for it.[42]

Japan's official narrative also connects with national identity. Many of the societal groups and individuals who contest "history issues" in Japan—and the politicians with whom they are allied and aligned—see the question of how the nation's past is remembered and commemorated as part of a larger struggle over what the nation is and should be. As Saaler observes, disputes over the extent to which textbooks should address Japan's war crimes are "linked to fundamental social and political issues such as the relationship of the individual to the state, the importance of national integration and national pride or patriotism, and the degree of control that the state can legitimately claim over the individual."[43] Those who criticize the state's narrative as too "masochistic" and who argue that the government should not (continue to) apologize for its actions in WWII often link these positions to the need to have pride in Japan's history and in being Japanese. Conversely, activists who push for greater acknowledgment and contrition from the government frequently link their advocacy to a desire to engender "a free and peaceful society."[44] Legitimacy and identity concerns vis-à-vis international audiences have also factored into officials' considerations. Notably, as Japan became one of the world's leading economies, Japanese officials sought an international political role commensurate with the country's economic status. In this context, Japanese officials concluded that to strengthen the country's international political reputation, it would be necessary to address external pressures for greater contrition.

Electoral-political concerns refer to considerations of threats to political support for the state, the regime, or political actors. This includes concerns about maintaining political support from important constituencies, preserving a political coalition, sustaining levels of public support, and preventing social unrest or violence. Officials are more likely to defend and resist changing the state's narrative in the direction of greater acknowledgment and contrition if doing so would threaten or undermine political support for the state, the regime, or particular political actors. Perceived threats can arise from dominant views among the electorate, the preferences of interest groups, or the views of political leaders.

For example, in late 2002 the Justice and Development Party (Adalet ve Kalkınma Partisi, AKP) came to power in Turkey. This was a watershed in Turkish politics, since the AKP is a socially conservative and Islamist party that did not espouse a strong commitment to the Kemalist ideology at the core of the avowedly secular Republican People's Party (Cumhuriyet Halk Partisi, CHP) and other mainstream and nationalist political parties in Turkey. Since then, the AKP has remained in power, leading to the gradual diminishment of the power and authority of the military, and the waning influence of the mainstream secular parties that have long defended the official narrative. This momentous shift in the domestic political landscape did not, however, lead to major changes in the state's narrative on the Armenian question. While the AKP has accommodated increasing domestic and international pressures on the official narrative in limited ways, with minor and largely symbolic adjustments (such as the one discussed in the introduction), the content of the narrative and the strategies used to defend it have exhibited remarkable continuities. One—but not the only—reason for the strong degree of continuity stems from AKP officials' electoral-political concerns that the Turkish public, which has been deeply socialized since the early 1980s to believe the state's narrative, would object to moves toward greater acknowledgment and contrition.

Japanese officials have often sought to strike a balance between external and domestic calls for greater contrition and sincerity, and opposing pressures from domestic right-wing groups, conservative interest groups like the Japan War-Bereaved Families Association (Nihon Izokukai, hereafter Izokukai), and conservative politicians. In a number of instances, Japanese officials have limited or resisted change in the state's narrative to maintain the support of conservative and nationalist interest groups that can mobilize and get out votes in an electoral system in which campaign and fund-raising activities are tightly controlled.[45]

Finally, *domestic contestation* refers to processes in which societal actors such as academics, activists, and journalists challenge or affirm aspects of the state's narrative. This can include uncovering new evidence that supports or undermines the official narrative, and advancing new interpretations of the underlying events. These actions can influence an official narrative in two ways: directly, by bringing new pressure on the official narrative or on the state actors who produce it; and indirectly, by changing understandings of the event among elites or the public, thereby shaping the context within which the official narrative is produced. These processes can reinforce officials' commitment to the status quo, or generate and reinforce pressures for change in the state's narrative. When officials consider changing the state's narrative, if domestic contestation is trending toward calls for greater acknowledgment, officials are more likely to shift the narrative in that direction. In contrast, if domestic contestation is trending toward calls for less acknowledgment, then officials are likely to be more resistant to changing the narrative in the direction of greater acknowledgment and contrition.[46] Frequently, activism by groups on one end of the political spectrum prompts a response from those on the opposite end of the political spectrum. Over time, the locus of contestation can shift back and forth between calls for greater and less acknowledgment and contrition.

Although domestic contestation about the country's dark past has been more long-standing and extensive in Japan than in Turkey, it has been a salient factor in both cases. In Japan, individuals and groups from across the political spectrum have contested and tried to shape how the past is remembered. Conservative and nationalist groups have had particular influence on the state's narrative, constraining the scope of change at key junctures as Japanese officials and politicians sought to meet the demands of right-wing activists and influential conservative organizations.[47]

In Turkey, legal and social constraints on speech, especially regarding sensitive issues like the Armenian Genocide, have long hindered the emergence of domestic activism on the issue. The most prominent of these constraints has been a series of broadly written laws that have made it dangerous to make public statements at odds with the state's narrative, since doing so risked being prosecuted and possibly jailed. In addition, until the early 2000s, a taboo on the discussion of this issue muted discussion in the Turkish media, while academics interested in studying the "Armenian question" were long made to understand that doing so would damage their career prospects in serious ways. In the past ten to fifteen years, some of these constraints have loosened, in part driven by and in turn contributing to the emergence of what Göçek has labeled the "postnationalist critical narrative" of the genocide.[48] The activism behind this critical narrative has influenced Turkish officials' considerations over the past decade or so.

Together, international pressures and these domestic considerations have shaped patterns of change and continuity in Turkey's and Japan's narratives. Moreover, the divergence between the extent of change over time in the two cases can be explained by the higher degree of international pressure on Japan, the higher material and ideational stakes for Turkey, and the more sustained nature of domestic contestation in Japan.

This argument should, moreover, account for changes and continuities in other narratives of dark pasts. A key requirement is that the state whose narrative is being studied should bear responsibility, at least in part, for the planning or execution of the underlying event. Three additional factors do *not* limit the applicability of the argument. First, where the surviving victims reside after the event is not relevant. To assess the influence of various international pressures on each state's narrative, I chose to analyze the Turkish and Japanese cases, in part because the victims largely resided outside the perpetrator states. That said, the argument should also apply to cases in which the victims largely reside *within* the perpetrator state. In such cases, however, I would expect change to be less likely because international pressures might be less likely to arise. Second, while both Turkey and Japan were on the losing sides in the wars within which the Armenian Genocide and Nanjing Massacre occurred, the book's argument is not limited to defeated states. Although the processes and actors that shape the initial formulation of a state's narrative are likely to be different for a defeated state than for a victorious state, the argument advanced in this book accounts for the causes of change and continuity *after* a narrative has been established. Finally, while a state's regime type is likely to have an impact on the production and contestation of official narratives, such effects are captured by electoral-political concerns and domestic contestation. Thus, while I would expect change to be more likely in a more democratic state, the argument's applicability is not limited to democracies.

The Nature of Change in Official Narratives

This analysis also sheds light on the *nature* of change in states' narratives. Change is typically incremental, frequently involves processes of layering, is often multifaceted and multivalent, and can give rise to feedback effects that affect the narrative at later points in time.

First, official narratives tend to change incrementally. This stems from the fact that, over time, it becomes more difficult to make a change that fundamentally breaks with the existing narrative.[49] One reason for this is that as official and societal actors become committed to a narrative, and as official actors and institutions become involved in the production of a narrative, support for the narrative becomes more entrenched.[50] In addition, reputational costs deepen over time for the actors and institutions involved in defending the state's narrative. Moreover, as competing narratives and facts are forgotten and silenced, citizens learn and come to believe the narrative, or simply do not learn about alternative narratives.

For example, as noted above, the coming to power of the AKP in late 2002 did not usher in major changes in Turkey's narrative of the Armenian question, as some might have expected. In addition to the aforementioned electoral-political concerns, another reason for the strong continuity in the state's narrative is that, over time, the production of the narrative has been embedded in a range of government institutions and powerful societal actors have become involved in and committed to its defense. These institutions have continued to produce the official narrative while societal actors who were enlisted to help defend the narrative in earlier phases have continued to militate against change by publicly speaking out against advocates of change and pushing their own views about the narrative and how it should be defended. Consequently, when the Armenian question came up, influential societal actors—most notably, retired diplomats—spoke out against change, right-wing ultranationalists agitated against change (sometimes violently), bureaucrats opposed change behind the scenes, and the broader public did not support greater acknowledgment or contrition.[51]

Closely related to the incremental nature of change is that changes in states' narratives typically involve layering. Layering is a process of gradual change whereby new themes are gradually added to an existing institution or policy while old elements remain.[52] Rather than being eliminated or rejected, old content is simply augmented with new themes. As a result, supporters of the old narrative are less likely to oppose the new elements.

The trajectory of Turkey's narrative reflects such processes of layering. In each phase, some new themes were added, some themes were slightly adjusted to accommodate new information or changes in the domestic or international context, while a majority of the themes continued unchanged. At the same time, the content of the narrative was adapted to new pressures and circumstances, thereby continuing to resist pressures to change the narrative in more fundamental ways. For example, in the mid-1980s Turkish officials began to argue that the Armenian question was an issue that should be addressed by historians, not politicians, and that more research and objective and unbiased analysis were needed to be able to judge the nature of the events. This has continued to be an element of the narrative since then. However, as more historians—especially *Turkish* historians—have studied and written about the genocide, this theme shifted to argue that all of the evidence has not yet been fully analyzed and that historians have not yet reached a consensus about the events. Thus, the underlying argument that this is an issue for historians, not politicians, has remained, but layered onto the older claim that more research was needed is a new claim that further *analysis* is needed in order for historians to be able to fully grasp the issue.

In the Japanese case, the wording of official statements about the past similarly illustrates the tendency for change to come in the form of layering. Over time, the key term in official statements gradually shifted from "regret," to "remorse," to "deep remorse," to "apology," and finally to "heartfelt apology." Similarly, the pool of victims acknowledged in official statements gradually expanded. Such shifts in the wording, framing, and context of official statements often involved layering to avoid provoking too strong of a negative response from powerful domestic groups. For example, in discussing the 1995 Diet resolution, Yamazaki notes that the terms "'colonial rule' and 'aggression,'" which had been controversially added to the official lexicon of remorse by PM Hosokawa in 1993, were, by 1995, accepted by conservatives and included in the 1995 Diet resolution.[53]

Changes in states' narratives are also often multifaceted and multivalent. Given the range of indicators of an official narrative and the range of voices that speak on behalf of the state, the state's narrative typically has multiple themes and includes more than one element in the conceptual framework introduced above. Moreover, when change occurs, it is rarely unambiguously univalent. Rather, movement in the direction of greater acknowledgment might be accompanied by increased rationalization or mythmaking. For example, Armenian terrorism combined with states' and international organizations' debates about the genocide prompted Turkish officials to end the official silence about the genocide in the early 1980s. While the changes that were made at the time included the beginnings of acknowledgment that something had happened to Ottoman Armenians during WWI, they also included the continued silencing of many aspects of the genocide and the renewal of rationalizations that had been developed in the post-WWI period. Moreover, state officials developed a set of strategies to more effectively defend and disseminate the official narrative. As a result, the net effect of these changes is best described as mixed.

Likewise in the Japanese case, deepening acknowledgment and contrition have, at crucial junctures, been accompanied by increased relativization and mythmaking. On the fiftieth anniversary of the end of the war in 1995, for example, PM Murayama issued an unprecedented personal apology for Japan's war crimes a little more than two months after the Diet had passed the resolution that relativized and failed to apologize for Japan's wartime actions. Less than a decade later, PM Koizumi attempted to balance his annual official visits to the controversial Yasukuni Shrine, which was interpreted as downplaying and eliding Japan's war crimes because of the inclusion there of the enshrined spirits of fourteen Class A war criminals, by repeatedly restating Murayama's apology.

Finally, states' narratives are both outcomes of political contestation and decisions, and institutions that influence and constrain the ideas and actors that are involved in later political decisions. The latter point highlights the fact that over time, states' narratives can have positive (i.e., self-reinforcing) and negative (i.e., challenging or undermining) feedback effects. In particular, the production of an official narrative, and especially change in a narrative, can set in motion actors and dynamics that impact the narrative at later points in time, either by reinforcing continuities or by pushing for change.[54]

In terms of continuity-reinforcing feedback effects, for instance, Turkish officials have created and supported societal organizations that have produced publications, research, and experts to help defend and disseminate the state's narrative. In particular, several think tanks have produced important publications on the Armenian question, including the Foreign Policy Institute in the early 1980s and the Institute for Armenian Research (Ermeni Araştırmaları Enstitüsü [ERAREN]) in the early 2000s. Their publications have reinforced continuities in the official narrative by bolstering the content of the official narrative with "new" research and by sharing it with Turkish politicians and academics, US politicians and policymakers, and the interested public. Moreover, two sets of actors that became involved in defending the official narrative in the early 1980s have continued to support the status quo. The first is Turkish diplomats, a number of whom continued to be prominent defenders of the official narrative after retiring from government. The second is organizations in the Turkish diaspora, which have been encouraged to advocate on this issue by Turkish officials and have functioned as strong defenders of the state's narrative.[55]

Feedback effects can also generate pressures for change in a state's narrative. Many of the international activist groups that have mobilized to pressure Turkey and Japan to change their narratives have done so in response to the ongoing production of these narratives or in response to shifts in one of the narrative's

indicators. Moreover, shifts in Japan's narrative have frequently led societal actors within Japan to mobilize, with some groups deciding to challenge the official
narrative and others taking action to oppose further changes in the state's narrative. Japan's narrative has thus generated and been affected by feedback effects
by groups across the political spectrum, from right-wing ultranationalists willing to use violence to preserve their vision of Japan's past actions to Commu-
nists, Socialists, and leftists who have pushed and fought—in courts, school
boards, classrooms, and elsewhere—for the state to acknowledge more of Japan's
wartime aggression and crimes and to take concrete steps to back up such acknowledgment with apologies, compensation, and commemoration.[56] Thus, while
some scholars warn of the potential risk of "nationalist backlash" in response to
pressures for greater acknowledgment or steps toward greater contrition, this is
only part of the story.[57] While the potential for a nationalist backlash is real, responses to changes in a state's narrative are typically multivalent, rather than univalent, with actors across the political spectrum responding to and pushing for
changes and continuities in the state's narrative.

THE ARMENIAN GENOCIDE AND ITS AFTERMATH

I read in various German newspapers official Turkish denials of the atrocities committed against the Christians and am surprised at the naivety of the Porte in believing they can obliterate facts about the crimes by Turkish officials by telling blatant lies.

—German vice consul Walter Holstein, 14 August 1915

It is a virtue of the Turkish nation that it quickly forgets the past.

—Turkish president Kenan Evren, 10 February 1989

The Armenian Genocide took place in the Ottoman Empire in the context of WWI. Between 1915 and 1917, the leaders of the governing Committee of Union and Progress (CUP) organized the forced deportation of the vast majority of Ottoman Armenians, during which an estimated 800,000 to 1.5 million Ottoman Armenians were killed, and thousands of women and children were abducted and incorporated into Muslim households and society. The genocide occurred within the context of a systematic effort to Islamize and homogenize the population and the economy, which included the ethnic cleansing and mass killing of Greeks, genocide of Assyrians, internal deportation of Kurds, and settlement of Muslim refugees from the Balkan Wars.[1] As a result, according to Ulgen, "at the end of the Great War, nine-tenths of the Christian population, which was around one-sixth of the total population in Anatolia, was cleansed through forced expulsion, massacre and population exchange," in addition to the forced Islamization of women and children.[2]

A variety of factors contributed to the genocide. A central factor was the impact of the Balkan Wars, particularly the empire's tremendous territorial losses, the massacres of Balkan Muslims in the war, and the resulting influx of Muslim refugees into the Ottoman Empire.[3] Göçek estimates that the territory of the Ottoman Empire decreased 60 percent in the several decades before 1912 and a further 35 percent during the Balkan Wars.[4] These losses fed CUP leaders' fear that Ottoman Armenians would be the next group to seek independence, threatening further territorial losses in the heart of the empire.[5] These existential anxieties influenced and were in turn deepened by the increasingly radical ethnonationalist views of the CUP's central governing committee and the per-ceived incompatibility of such views with the existence of large, non-Muslim populations concentrated in parts of the empire, particularly Eastern Anatolia. Finally, WWI significantly heightened CUP leaders' fears about Armenian inten-tions, and provided a catalyst and cover for the deportations and massacres.[6]

The genocide began in early 1915 and unfolded over a period of about two and a half years. Initial deportations of Armenians began in February 1915. The fol-lowing month Armenian soldiers were disarmed and placed in labor battalions.[7] Starting on 24 April 1915, Ottoman authorities arrested intellectuals, community leaders, and other prominent Armenians in Istanbul and other cities. Within a few days, between 1,000 and 2,000 Armenian elites had been arrested; most were subsequently killed. Following these arrests, the scope of the deportations and kill-ing began to expand. A month later, on 27 May 1915, the Ottoman government announced the "deportation decision" as a temporary law.[8] By late June 1915, the deportations had expanded to include all Armenians in the empire.[9] The deporta-tions and massacres continued until June 1917, although most of the deportations ended by late 1915.[10]

The genocide was planned and executed by a small group of radical national-ists in the Central Committee of the CUP, with the involvement of regional and local officials, elites, and others. Led by Interior Minister Mehmet Talât (later: Paşa), bureaucrats in the Ottoman Interior Ministry planned and orchestrated the details of the deportation, along with the confiscation and redistribution of Armenians' wealth and belongings. At the provincial level, local bureaucratic and CUP party officials, together with the quasi-official paramilitary known as the Special Organization (Teşkilât-ı Mahsusa), organized the deportations and mas-sacres. Police and gendarmes led the deportation marches, while many of the at-tacks on and massacres of deportees were carried out by the Special Organization with the help of Kurds and others recruited by local officials and CUP agents to join in the killing with promises of material gains.[11]

Multiple forms of violence characterized the genocide. Ottoman Armenian men were initially conscripted into the Ottoman army. They were disarmed and placed in labor battalions in March 1915; after some time, most of these men were massacred. When the deportations began, Armenian men who had not been conscripted, along with boys older than about age twelve, were typically killed before the remaining Armenian population of a town or village was deported. Consequently, most of the deportees were women and children. Along the de-portation routes, groups of deportees were massacred at specific points, while others died from violence, starvation, and disease. In addition, many girls and women were raped, and Armenian women and children were taken from the de-portation marches, forcibly Islamized, and incorporated into Muslim families as servants or wives.[12] Finally, although several hundred thousand Armenians managed to survive the deportation marches, many subsequently died from starvation, disease, exposure to the elements, and a second wave of organized massacres in 1915 and 1916.[13]

Alongside these processes of physical violence, the wealth, properties, businesses, and homes of Armenians were confiscated and declared "abandoned property" by the state. These "vacated" properties were then redistributed to hundreds of thousands of Muslim refugees from the Balkans who were resettled in formerly Armenian towns, homes, and businesses. This massive redistribution of wealth significantly enriched the state, advanced the nascent project of forging a more homogeneous population, and formed the physical infrastructural and economic basis for the creation of a new class of Muslim entrepreneurs.[14]

Unsettled Elements of This History

Scholars who would generally agree with this account still debate several issues. Significant discrepancies also exist between this account and the official Turkish narrative.

For a variety of reasons, it is difficult to precisely estimate how many Armenians were killed in the genocide. Estimates range from a low of 600,000 to 1.5 million, with most scholars agreeing on at least 800,000 deaths.[15] In contrast, estimates of the death toll in the official Turkish narrative are much lower, ranging from a low of about 55,000 to a high of 600,000.[16] The number of survivors is unknown, in part because census data from before the genocide are widely recognized as flawed, but the direction and extent of bias in the data are contested. The number of women and children who were abducted and Islamized is also unknown, although as Ekmekçioğlu notes, it "is conventionally estimated at about a hundred thousand."[17]

Beyond questions of numbers, some scholars argue that the campaign of elimination was planned in advance, whereas others contend that the state's actions were more "contingent" and gradually progressed toward genocide in a process of "cumulative radicalization."[18] Regardless of these differences, the deportations, massacres, and confiscations followed consistent patterns and evidence of the planning and intent behind these patterns can be found in foreign archives, Ottoman and Turkish archives, diplomatic correspondence, and the memoirs of survivors and Ottoman officials.[19]

In contrast, the official Turkish narrative maintains that this was not genocide. As the next two chapters document, the arguments advanced in support of this position have shifted over time. Since the mid-2000s, officials have argued that there is no evidence of the intent to destroy Armenians "in whole or in part," which is a criterion in the definition of genocide set forth in the 1948 United Nations Convention on the Prevention and Punishment of the Crime of Genocide (UNCG). The official narrative at times maintains that only those Armenians who were suspected of having allied with Russia or of organizing nationalist activities were deported. However, the deportations were not limited to these groups or to those near the front lines of the war. The official narrative has also argued that categories of Armenians were exempted from the deportations and that this demonstrates that the deportations were not aimed at the systematic annihilation of Ottoman Armenians. In reality, although some exceptions to the order to deport all Armenians existed, such exceptions were limited and inconsistently applied.[20]

The official Turkish narrative has also emphasized that massacres of Muslims by Armenians precipitated the Ottoman state's actions, that the deportation was a defensive response to rebellion, and that what transpired was "intercommunal warfare" in the context of a "civil war." Countering this claim, Akçam emphasizes that "not a single top secret document at the highest levels of the state makes the slightest allusion to a civil war or 'intercommunal warfare.' On the contrary, Ottoman documents show that Armenian areas were evacuated under tight government control."[21] Akçam also documents repeated references to fears of revolts and Armenian bandits in internal government communications during the war, but he argues that these were largely fabrications and misrepresentations.[22] He further reports that foreign diplomats stationed in the Ottoman Empire "were reporting back to their superiors that there was, for all practical purposes, no uprising whatsoever being prepared by the Armenians."[23] Rather, Armenian resistance was rare and largely constituted defensive reactions against repression and deportation.[24] Two Armenian nationalist organizations did aspire to independence and some Ottoman Armenians did join the Russian army at the beginning of WWI. That said, the nationalist groups were small in comparison with the Armenian population and did not represent the majority of Ottoman Armenians.[25] In addition, the numbers of Ottoman Armenians in the Ottoman army vastly outnumbered those who fought with the Russians.[26] Finally, some Armenians in the Russian-occupied areas of eastern Anatolia attacked Muslim villages and massacred "at most 40,000 to 60,000 Muslims."[27] However, these massacres occurred *after* the genocide (in 1918), so they cannot have been a cause of it.

Formulating an Official Narrative during and after the Genocide

Ottoman officials began to deny and rationalize the violence as it unfolded. Within the first two years after the end of the war, official discussions of the violence against Ottoman Armenians (and others) and prosecutions of some perpetrators took place. As the nationalists assumed power, however, discussions faded and by 1923, when the Republic of Turkey was established, the issue was silenced.

In late May 1915, a few days before the temporary deportation law was announced, the Allied powers issued a joint public statement to the Ottoman government, which stated: "In view of these new crimes of Turkey against humanity and civilization the Allied governments announce publicly to the Sublime Porte that they will hold personally responsible [for] these crimes all members of the Ottoman government and those of their agents who are implicated in such massacres."[28] In response to this criticism and to extensive coverage of the deportation and suffering of Ottoman Armenians in Western newspapers such as the *New York Times*, the Ottoman government produced several official defenses of the deportation during the war.[29] In these publications, Kaiser notes, "the Ottoman government maintained there had been no plan or attempt to destroy the Ottoman Armenians, and thus all the Entente accusations were lies."[30] In addition, the Ottoman government argued that the deportation was undertaken "to assure internal order and external security of the country."[31]

For a short period after the end of the war, the Ottoman government investigated the violence and prosecuted some of the perpetrators. In the immediate postwar period, the Ottoman government was under internal and external pressure, especially from Britain, to punish the perpetrators of the Armenian massacres. Near the end of the war, key organizers of the genocide had fled the country, making it impossible to punish those most responsible.[32] Nevertheless, the Ottoman government established a military tribunal to try individuals accused of organizing and executing the deportation and massacres of Ottoman Armenians. The tribunal, which lasted about two years and included more than sixty cases, sentenced seventeen individuals to death, of whom three were executed.[33]

Ottoman officials also openly discussed the violence, in some cases reiterating and reinforcing justifications first advanced during the war. The grand vizier acknowledged crimes, but deflected the question of responsibility. Instead, Hovannisian notes, he "shifted the blame to the Germans and Young Turk dictators and reminded the Allies of Armenian excesses."[34] Many non-Muslim members of the Ottoman Parliament went further, calling for the punishment of officials involved in the deportations and massacres, and arguing that the former CUP government should be held responsible for the massacres of Armenians and Greeks. Others—especially former CUP members—argued that Turks had also died during the war, some from attacks and massacres by Armenians, and that these Muslim deaths should also be punished and acknowledged.[35] According to Aktar, these former CUP members also "took the position that 'in the past, bad things happened; let's not stir up these issues.'"[36] In particular, one deputy argued that even though the Turkish side had massacred Armenians, "it was Armenians who started it all" with the development of an Armenian nationalist movement and later rebellion, which resulted in the "mutual massacre" for which all guilty parties should be punished.[37] As Aktar observes, "Many positions articulated by Turkish official circles today concerning the Armenian massacres were first developed at the Ottoman Parliament."[38]

These discussions, investigations, and prosecutions were short-lived. Between 1919 and 1922, a national resistance movement fought against and expelled the armies occupying Ottoman territory, leading to the preservation of significant portions of Ottoman territory, the renegotiation of the postwar peace settlement, and the establishment of the Republic of Turkey in 1923. As the War of Independence (Kurtuluş Savaşı) took shape and power shifted from the Ottoman government to the newly declared nationalist government in Ankara, official discussions and investigations of the massacres abated. By 1920, the leaders of the nationalist movement had turned away from the prosecution of perpetrators and disavowed official responsibility for the massacres of Ottoman Armenians.

There were three key reasons for this shift, connected with material concerns, electoral-political concerns, and legitimacy and identity concerns. First, the nationalists regarded the acknowledgment and rectification of these wrongs as threatening to their goal of securing Anatolia for the Turkish nation. A deep-seated fear, which had motivated the violence in the first place, was that Armenians' nationalist aspirations would lead to catastrophic territorial losses. In addition, nationalists believed that the monumental changes in the economy and demography of Anatolia that resulted from the genocide were essential for the Turkish nation's survival and future.[39] Illustrating this, in 1920 a parliamentarian declared: "This deportation business, as you know, has put the whole world in an uproar, and has branded us all as murderers. . . . But why should we call ourselves murderers? These things that were done were to secure the future of our homeland, which we hold more sacred and dear than our very lives."[40] In particular, officials feared that Armenians would return and reclaim their properties, and that an Armenian state might be created from parts of eastern Anatolia.[41] This latter concern was exacerbated by the demands of the Armenian delegation at the 1919 Paris Peace Conference and by the 1920 Peace Treaty of Sèvres, which stipulated that the (short-lived) state of Armenia might be entitled to part or all of the Ottoman provinces of Erzurum, Trabzon, Van, and Bitlis.[42] Second, the CUP had organized the national resistance movement prior to its dissolution, and when the British and the Ottoman government initiated arrests and trials of suspected perpetrators of the genocide, many CUP officials fled to Anatolia and became leaders of the national resistance movement. Nationalist leaders were highly unlikely to investigate themselves or their colleagues, particularly because doing so would have undercut the movement itself.[43] Finally, as Zarakol observes, "admitting guilt would have undermined the project of constructing a modern, proud, European Turkish nation, and it would have also perpetuated the hierarchical relationship with the West the new regime was trying to avoid."[44]

Reflecting these considerations, between 1918 and 1921 the movement's leader, Mustafa Kemal (later: Atatürk), shifted away from acknowledgment and criticism of the deportations and massacres, establishing many themes that later became central elements of the official narrative. In speeches and writings, he referred to "Armenian designs" on Turkish territory and characterized Armenians' massacres of Muslims near the Russian border, and Western claims of massacre as "nothing but lies."[45] According to Ulgen, while Kemal acknowledged "that some 'shameful act', some 'disaster' . . . had indeed taken place," he also argued that both Turks and Armenians had suffered, and that the deportation was "a decision that we had been forced to take."[46] Moreover, he asserted that "whatever has ever happened to non-muslim minorities living in our country, it has been the result of their own policies of partition."[47] Based on her analysis of Kemal's speeches and writings, Ulgen observes that, whereas "the 1915 deportations are usually restricted to being 'some unfortunate events', 'incidents' or 'mistreatment in which the people had taken no part', the violence Turks suffered at the hands of the Armenians is reified as a policy of extermination and savagery unique in history in the context of an ongoing narrative of the oppressed nation [*mazlum millet*]."[48]

As the nationalist movement's strength grew, international pressures to investigate and punish the perpetrators petered out. In the fall of 1921, Britain traded those who had been arrested for their suspected involvement in the genocide for British soldiers who had been captured by the nationalist movement, thus ending the official pursuit of justice.[49] Consequently, when Turkey and the Allied powers renegotiated the postwar peace settlement in 1923, the representatives of the soon-to-be-established Republic of Turkey refused to discuss the question of an Armenian homeland or allow any reference to the Armenian massacres or Armenians in the treaty. Bobelian writes that "Joseph Grew, the chief of the American delegation [at the negotiations], noted that 'there is no subject upon which the Turks are more fixed in obstinacy.'"[50] The resultant Treaty of Lausanne thus marked the silencing of this issue internationally and in official Turkish discourse.[51]

For decades after the October 1923 establishment of the Republic of Turkey, this official silence continued, enforced and perpetuated by constraints on the press and speech, and by the repression of Kurds and non-Muslim minorities.[52] This silencing of the dark past included the destruction of Armenian cemeteries, churches, and villages; the elimination of non-Turkish place-names; the surveillance of the Armenian-language press in Turkey; and the strict censorship of non-Turkish books and books about the histories and cultures of non-Turkic groups.[53] Highlighting the extent of the erasure of Armenians' historical presence in Turkey, Kouymjian estimated in 1985 that "roughly 90% of the names of historical Armenia have been changed."[54] In 2015, Cheterian reported that "out of the 2,538 Armenian churches originally in Anatolia, only 7 remain active, and only some 300 ruins remain."[55] In addition, in the decades after the establishment of the Republic, only a few books were published on the topic, and Turkish authorities actively worked to prevent foreign books on the genocide from circulating in Turkey.[56] And while Armenians appeared peripherally in history textbooks and the deportation was mentioned briefly in textbooks until the early 1940s, such references were brief and rare.[57]

Turkey also took steps to honor key CUP officials who had organized the deportations and massacres. Göçek reports that "in 1927, the Turkish National Assembly decided to allocate income to the families of prominent perpetrators. . . . They were pointedly assigned incomes accruing from properties unwillingly abandoned by deported and massacred Armenians."[58] And in 1943, Talât's remains were repatriated from Germany and interred in Istanbul in an official ceremony.[59]

Finally, on the rare occasion when the issue came up outside Turkey, the Turkish government fought to silence such references through diplomatic channels, international pressure, and a campaign to improve Turkey's image.[60] An oft-cited example is Turkey's success in preventing Metro-Goldwyn-Mayer Studios from producing a film in the mid-1930s based on Franz Werfel's best-selling historical novel *The Forty Days of Musa Dagh*, which tells the story of the collective resistance and survival of an Armenian village during the genocide.[61]

The Trajectory of the Official Narrative, 1950–2008

This active silencing of the issue within and outside the country extended for several decades. My formal analysis of Turkey's narrative begins in 1950, at which point an official silence had prevailed for nearly three decades. Over the subsequent sixty-plus years, Turkey's official narrative has steadfastly rejected claims that the events of 1915–1917 were genocide and has advanced an alternative and evolving account: from 1950 through the late 1970s, the "Armenian question" was denied and silenced. Beginning in the early 1980s, the official narrative emerged from silence and, alongside notable continuities, has changed at several junctures since then. In 1981, the official narrative shifted to include references to the deportation of Ottoman Armenians during WWI, but these references largely involved mythmaking and relativizing. In the mid to late 1990s, there were modest changes in the narrative, some of which presaged more extensive changes introduced in the early 2000s. Since 2001, the official narrative has acknowledged basic facts about the deportation and deaths of Ottoman Armenians, but has also more strongly relativized the events. The trajectory of Turkey's narrative from 1950 to 2008 is depicted in Figure 2.1 and briefly outlined below.

The first phase began in 1950 and extended to the end of 1980. In this period, the official narrative silenced and erased accounts of the deportation and massacres of Ottoman Armenians, both domestically and internationally. Since the 1920s, Turkish officials had willed the issue settled, and structural factors—including Cold War geopolitics and Turkey's highly constrained domestic politics—severely limited challenges to the official narrative. Latent concerns about material claims, along with legitimacy and identity concerns, shaped Turkish officials' efforts to silence and deny the reality of the issue. Starting in the mid-1970s, however, international pressures made it increasingly difficult for Turkish officials to maintain this silence.[62]

The second phase began in 1981 and continued through the early 1990s. In this period the official narrative emerged from silence to directly discuss some aspects of the issue, but not the deportations and deaths of Armenians. Thus, the official narrative continued silencing and denying the genocide, but it also relativized the deportations and deaths of Armenians and presented alternative characterizations of what had happened (i.e., engaged in mythmaking). These changes were accompanied by a set of strategies that targeted domestic and international audiences to spread the official narrative and discredit its challengers. The central drivers of these changes, which emerged within a few months of the September 1980 military

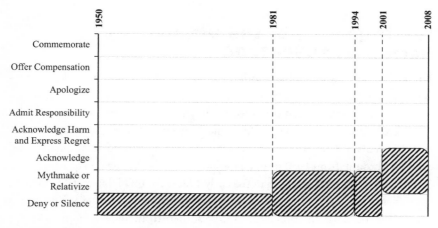

FIGURE 2.1.   Trajectory of Turkey's narrative, 1950–2008

coup, were sustained international pressures and negative attention focused on Turkey's official narrative. The content of the changes, meanwhile, was shaped by strong material concerns and deep legitimacy and identity concerns.

The third phase began in 1994 and extended through 2000. Subtle shifts occurred in the content of the narrative, some of which previewed themes that fully emerged in the fourth phase. Importantly, despite major structural change at the international level and the beginnings of domestic challenges to the official narrative, the content of the narrative was remarkably stable, highlighting the persistence of domestic concerns as constraints on change.

The fourth phase began in 2001 and extends through the end of my analysis in 2008. Within this period, the official narrative began to acknowledge and rationalize basic facts about the genocide while continuing to reject the label genocide. These changes were made in response to increased international recognition of the genocide, particularly around 1999 and 2000, as well as the emergence of domestic contestation that challenged the official narrative. In revising the narrative, Turkish officials drew on the set of strategies that had been developed to defend and disseminate the official narrative in the 1980s, replicating the earlier repertoire of action to defend the official narrative in the face of new pressures for acknowledgment. The strong continuities in the state's narrative were a reflection of officials' abiding concerns about potential territorial and compensation claims, along with feedback effects from influential actors who sought to preserve the status quo.

Explaining Changes in Turkey's Narrative

Over the past several decades, Turkey has experienced sustained international pressures to acknowledge the organized and intentional nature of the mass violence committed against Ottoman Armenians during WWI. Since the early 1990s, a small but growing number of academics, journalists, publishers, and activists within Turkish society have also challenged and contested the state's narrative. Despite these pressures and challenges, Turkish officials have resisted acknowledging the extent and genocidal nature of this violence. And yet, as outlined above, elements of Turkey's narrative have changed over the past six decades.

As the next two chapters document, interactions between international and domestic factors have shaped the trajectory of Turkey's narrative, resulting in four distinct phases between 1950 and 2008. Turkey's narrative changed at three points, but only after international pressures had significantly heightened international and domestic attention to and scrutiny of the state's position. In turn, when and how officials responded to these accumulated pressures were primarily shaped by domestic considerations, including concerns about threats to Turkey's territorial integrity and national identity, the emergence of domestic contestation, and feedback effects from institutionalized power bases within Turkish society and the Turkish state.

The continuities at the core of the state's narrative—the dual rejection of official responsibility and the label of "genocide"—have been driven by Turkish officials' persistent concerns about the material and ideational costs of greater acknowledgment. In terms of material concerns, officials have worried that acknowledgment of the validity of Armenian claims could open the door to territorial claims and demands for compensation or reparations from the state of Armenia or from descendants of Ottoman Armenians.[63] Turkish officials and citizens alike have feared that descendants of Ottoman Armenian victims and survivors could make claims for confiscated land, businesses, and homes. Illustrating the strength and persistence of this popular fear, Kaplan notes that in the Turkish village in which he conducted research in the late 1980s, "a visceral fear of Armenians returning . . . and reclaiming their lands still gripped local imagination. To prevent such a possibility, townspeople had leveled Armenian homes to their foundations and uprooted the orchards. . . . Fear of the Armenians' imminent return was equally present in the geography lesson I attended. At some point in the discussion about external enemies, some pupils wondered aloud whether I had come to spy on behalf of Armenian descendants or to unearth hidden treasures they may have left behind."[64] Officials' concerns are not completely baseless, as individuals and groups have brought individual and class action claims against the Turkish government, insurers, and others, both in Turkey and in the United States. That said, the post-WWII emergence of the "norm of border fixity" means that territorial claims are unlikely to lead to large-scale territorial losses.[65]

Turkish officials have also had strong legitimacy and identity concerns that have shaped their resistance to acknowledging the nature of and official responsibility for the violence against Ottoman Armenians. As discussed in chapter 1, acknowledgment of the genocide and of Ottoman officials' responsibility for it could undermine Turkish national identity and the state's founding narrative, and could call into question the legitimacy of state institutions and the securitization of many aspects of Turkish politics. Official rhetoric has long characterized Turkey as a nation beset by enemies, both internal and external, and Turks as a people who have no friends and can rely on no one but themselves.[66] According to this logic, Turkey's citizens and leaders must protect Turkey from threats to its unity, sovereignty, and security, just as the nationalists preserved the sovereignty and unity of Turkey's territories during the War of Independence.[67] The facts of the genocide, however, hint that the origins of Turkey's enmities might lie in the actions of Ottoman and, later, Turkish officials. Finally, greater acknowledgment could also undermine public trust in the state institutions that have been actively involved in denying and mythmaking about the genocide.

Consequently, at key junctures when officials have felt that international pressures were too great to ignore, and as domestic attention to the issue has increased, officials have updated the official narrative to maintain its plausibility and legitimacy, particularly for domestic audiences, but also for international audiences. And yet, as officials have updated the state's narrative, given the material and legitimacy and identity concerns outlined above, they have continued to avoid recognizing the genocidal nature of the violence as well as official responsibility for it.

FROM SILENCING TO MYTHMAKING (1950–EARLY 1990s)

> **Now, after we have kept an official silence for years and years, we are inundating (the world) with more or less propaganda material.**
>
> —Selçuk Bakkalbaşı, press counselor, Turkish embassy, Paris, 1982

> **We did nothing to make retribution for. We were on the land for 1,000 years. There was a civil war within a world war. . . . And even if we did have something to talk about, we would never talk under the threat of terrorism.**
>
> —Mithat Balkan, Turkish embassy official, 1983

While the genocide was silenced in the decades after the end of WWII, the silence came under increasing international pressure over the course of the 1970s. Armenian terrorism, combined with increased international recognition of the genocide, eventually prompted Turkish officials to end the official domestic silence about the genocide in the early 1980s. At that point, the official narrative shifted to denying the events and mythmaking about them, alongside the continued silencing of many aspects of the genocide and the renewal of rationalizations that had been developed in the post-WWI period. At the same time, officials initiated diplomatic, institutional, and rhetorical strategies to defend and disseminate the official narrative. The net effect of these changes involved the strengthening of official denial of the genocide, alongside a limited acknowledgment that *something* had happened to Ottoman Armenians.

Phase One (1950–1980): Silencing the Past

From 1950 to 1980, Turkey's narrative was characterized by an active silence that involved denials of the deportation and massacre of Ottoman Armenians and efforts to suppress references to the genocide domestically and internationally. Domestic constraints on democratic freedoms and on minorities, Cold War geopolitics, and the weakness of the Armenian diaspora limited attention to the issue and facilitated Turkey's silence. In addition, the weakness of the new international norm against genocide made it easier for Turkish officials to disregard its applicability to Turkey's own past. Together, these factors meant that until the mid-1970s, there were few pressures on Turkey to address or discuss the issue.

The starting point for understanding Turkey's narrative in this period is domestic politics: 1950 marked the beginning of Turkey's democracy, but the quality of that democracy was weak, restricting citizens' ability to question or challenge the government's silence about the genocide. Even though Atatürk's Republican People's Party was overwhelmingly voted out of power in May 1950, the Kemalist elites who had established the nation's founding narratives and successfully silenced domestic discussion about the massacres in the 1920s continued to dominate domestic politics. In particular, the military—the institution most active in defending the secular nature of Turkey's political system—increasingly dominated domestic politics, overthrowing elected governments in 1960, 1971, and 1980. As the military increased its power, change in the official narrative was unlikely, given the extent to which the institution and its leaders were committed to the state's founding narrative and to defending the country's territorial integrity from perceived threats.

Alongside these identity and material concerns, groups within Turkey that might have questioned the official silence were marginalized and disenfranchised. In response to discrimination, violence, and expropriation, Armenians and other non-Muslims emigrated from Turkey, reducing the numbers of citizens who had survived or experienced the genocide and whose memories contradicted the official narrative.[1] Among these discriminatory policies were the arbitrary and inequitable application of the Wealth Tax of 1942–1944 and the 6–7 September 1955 pogrom in Istanbul, in which Greeks and other minorities were killed.[2] In 1974, the Court of Cassation ruled that non-Muslim minority foundations were not entitled to own properties—such as churches and schools—that had not been officially reported to the state in 1936. Following this decision, the Turkish government began confiscating many such properties.[3] Alongside these policies, the "loyalty" of non-Muslim minorities was continually questioned. Exemplifying this was the Subcommission on the Minorities, which was created on 7 November 1962 and whose central "task was the 'monitoring of minorities within our country from the perspective of the security of the homeland.'"[4] These policies ensured the silence of those who remained in Turkey. Highlighting this silence, Göçek's analysis of the literary works of Turkish Armenian writers demonstrates an extreme degree of self-censorship and only "obscure and fleeting" references to the massacres.[5]

This self-censorship extended beyond the Turkish Armenian and other non-Muslim communities. As one academic explained, in this period, "strange things" happened to academics who tried to work on the "Armenian question."[6] Consequently, the only societal actors willing to address the issue were retired government officials, some of whom had participated in the genocide. Of the few books published in this period, the most notable is *Tarihte Ermeniler ve Ermeni Meselesi* (The Armenians in history and the Armenian question), written by the retired Turkish diplomat Esat Uras and published in 1950. A former CUP official, Uras had been involved in the genocide as a high-level bureaucrat in the Interior Ministry.[7] As Jørgensen notes, Uras argued that "it was in fact the Armenians who had murdered thousands of Turks, not the other way round. . . . [And] secondly, there were never any massacres of the Armenian population. The so-called 'relocations' took place in an orderly manner."[8] Uras's arguments served as the basis for many later works by the government and others. In addition, the few memoirs written in the 1950s by former CUP officials attempted to downplay the massacres and disavow their authors' involvement.[9]

Outside Turkey's borders, three aspects of the international context are important to understanding the overwhelming silence in this phase: the limited use of the nascent concept of genocide, Turkey's role in the Cold War, and the dearth of activism among diaspora Armenians.

In 1944, the legal scholar Raphael Lemkin coined the term "genocide."[10] Four years later, the UN passed the Convention on the Prevention and Punishment of the Crime of Genocide, which defines genocide as "any of the following acts committed with the intent to destroy, in whole or in part, a national, ethnical, racial or religious group, as such: (a) Killing members of the group; (b) Causing serious bodily or mental harm to members of the group; (c) Deliberately inflicting on the group conditions of life calculated to bring about its physical destruction in whole or in part; (d) Imposing measures intended to prevent births within the group; (e) Forcibly transferring children of the group to another group."[11] Aside from the passage and ratification of the UNCG, and from Holocaust-related trials and reparations, little international attention was paid to the issue of genocide in the first few decades of the Cold War. Thus, despite the fact that Lemkin had referred to "the massacre of the Armenians" as genocide, Turkish officials did not appear overtly concerned about the connection of this concept with the massacres of Ottoman Armenians.[12] That Turkey was one of the first twenty countries to ratify or accede to the Genocide Convention seems to reflect officials' belief that the country had moved beyond its dark past—or else a desire for that to be the case.[13] Lemkin argued to Turkish officials that being one of the first countries to ratify the convention would signal to the world that Turkey had broken "radically with the past" and would further signal Turkey's status as a "modernized nation" with "modern ideas."[14] While it is likely that these arguments helped convince Turkish officials to ratify the convention, their exact motivations are unclear. In any case, whatever concerns Turkish officials might have had were soon rendered moot, as the concept quickly faded from international discussions as the Cold War took shape.

Turkey's active role in the Western bloc also diminished the likelihood of external criticism. Suciyan argues that Turkey's strong turn toward the West at the beginning of the Cold War could in part have been a strategic reaction to territorial claims advanced by the Soviet Union (USSR) and transnational Armenian organizations between 1945 and 1947. These claims prompted a fierce response from Turkish officials and the Turkish press.[15] However, Suciyan reports, "both the US and the USSR distanced themselves from the territorial claims by August 1946. . . . For Truman, it was more important to have bases in Turkey."[16] Thus, from the beginning of the Cold War, the United States established military bases in Turkey, and the United States and the North Atlantic Treaty Organization (NATO) supported Turkey with high levels of military and economic aid. As one Turkish academic explained to me: after the Cold War started, no one would have listened to a few Armenians, as Turkey was the spearhead in the West's fight with communism.[17]

At the same time, Armenians outside Turkey did not mount any sustained political efforts related to the genocide, and scholarship on the topic was scant.[18] Although the genocide was commemorated within Armenian communities, activism related to the genocide was negligible prior to the 1970s. This was, in part, because Armenians were scattered in various countries—notably Lebanon, Syria, Iran, the United States, France, Canada, and the Soviet Union—and were divided among themselves, with some supporting and others fervently rejecting Soviet Armenia.[19] Moreover, as part of their suppression of political activities, Soviet authorities did not allow commemorations, research, or public discussion of the genocide within Soviet Armenia.[20]

Maintaining the State's Story

In the absence of both internal and external pressures, between 1950 and 1980 the official narrative continued to actively silence discussion of the Armenian Genocide. On the infrequent occasions when the issue did arise in international contexts, Turkish diplomats lobbied to quash it. As Roger Smith aptly puts it, this was a "policy of silence where possible and diplomacy when necessary."[21] Crucially, Turkish officials sought to avoid *any* reference to the deportation and massacres, not only those that included the term "genocide." For example, in the late 1960s, Turkish diplomats pressured US policymakers to stop the erection of a monument to the genocide in Montebello, California. According to Bobelian, the Turkish ambassador argued that the Turkish people "are very sensitive about reference to any partition of Turkey."[22] This statement illustrates that, in Turkish officials' minds, the Armenian question raised material concerns in the form of the threat of claims to Turkish territory. As a result of Turkish diplomats' lobbying, although the monument was built, it did not refer to "the Genocide or the Ottoman Empire." Despite this accommodation, Bobelian notes that the Turkish government was not pleased, complaining to US State Department officials that "because the plaque mentioned Armenians, 'it would be obvious' that it targeted Turkey."[23]

Aside from these diplomatic efforts, Turkish officials and agencies said and wrote little about the Armenian question. Domestically, Turkey published only a smattering of official books on the topic (see Figure 3.1), which reflected the overall policy of silence and denial. As Özdemir notes, until "1970, there was not a single publication in foreign languages [i.e., other than Turkish] that clearly elucidated the Turkish thesis."[24]

On the rare occasion when Turkish officials did publicly acknowledge the Armenian question, two themes predominated. First, they argued that the issue was best left in the past. In a letter to the editor of the *New York Times* in February 1957, Altemur Kılıç, the press attaché at the Turkish embassy in Washington, emphasized that bringing up the Armenian issue "could serve no purpose but harp on distant and bitter chords."[25] Instead, he suggested in May 1965, "the best thing to do now would be to forget them [i.e., "old and bitter memories"] and to strive together for a bright future for all citizens of Turkey in a better world."[26] Likewise, the Turkish representative to the UN successfully argued that a passing reference to the Armenian Genocide should be removed from a UN report because, among other things, it "would revive flames of hatred."[27] This argument resurrected claims made in the aftermath of WWI, when officials acknowledged the violence but warned that the nation should not "stir up" the past.[28] It also reflected the weakness of the emerging international norm against genocide and the prevailing belief among states and experts that investigating past human rights crimes was potentially dangerous and destabilizing.[29]

The second theme, which also renewed an argument made in the aftermath of the genocide, was that everyone had suffered, not only Armenians. An example of this is from Kılıç's 1965 letter, in which he wrote: "Those were indeed dark days, . . . full of misery and suffering for all our ancestors." Additional themes were that "there have to be at least two sides to every story" and that Turkey was a tolerant country. In support of the latter claim, Kılıç pointed out that Turkish Armenians "today live in our modern republic as equal and undiscriminated [*sic*] citizens."[30]

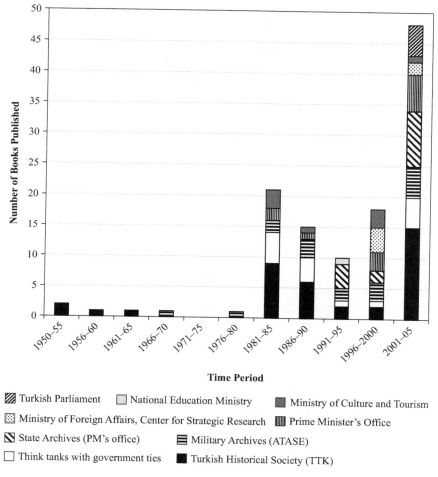

FIGURE 3.1. Official and quasi-official publications on the Armenian question, 1950–2005. See appendix 1 for a discussion of how this chart was created.

Note: Official publications are from government agencies or presses. Quasi-official publications are printed under the direction or at the instruction of government officials. Atatürk established the Turkish Historical Society (Türk Tarih Kurumu) in 1931. It is nominally independent from the government, but its publications frequently reproduce and advance official ideologies. Göçek 2007; Aktürk 2012, 283–84.

The most important aspect of the official narrative was what was *not* said. Notably absent were direct references to the deportation and deaths of Ottoman Armenians. Illustrating this, Turkish high school history textbooks were silent about Armenians, conveying an overall impression of their near nonexistence within the Ottoman Empire.[31]

The Emergence of International Pressures

Turkey's silence on the Armenian question began to be challenged in the mid to late 1970s. The fiftieth anniversary of the genocide in 1965 catalyzed political action in the Armenian diaspora. Commemorations of the genocide were held throughout the Armenian diaspora, the most significant of which was a massive demonstration in Soviet Armenia on 24 April 1965.[32] According to de Waal, Soviet authorities approved the planned commemorations "on the strict understanding that the territorial issue of the 1940s would not be revived."[33] Around the same time, Soviet authorities agreed to build a memorial to the genocide in Yerevan, which was completed in 1967.[34]

In the wake of the fiftieth anniversary, Armenians began working to raise awareness of and gain political support for recognition of the genocide.[35] Armenians started to use the term "genocide" more frequently.[36] In addition, Hovannisian writes, "Armenian memorials were erected, studies and memoirs related to the genocide appeared in various languages, and a rising generation took to the streets with placards and chants to remind the Turkish government and the world that the Armenian Question still existed."[37]

At the same time, two small groups chose violence as a means to gain the world's and Turkey's attention. In January 1973, Gourgen Yanikian, a seventy-eight-year-old Armenian American who had lost his entire family in the genocide, assassinated two Turkish diplomats in California.[38] Yanikian was not connected to a broader group, but his attack inspired others to use violence to bring attention to Turkey's denial of the genocide. Between 1975 and 1985, ASALA and the Justice Commandos of the Armenian Genocide (JCAG) attacked Turkish diplomats and others in a number of countries, demanding that Turkey acknowledge the Armenian Genocide, pay reparations, and return territory. Over the course of approximately 240 attacks, ASALA and JCAG killed 31 Turkish diplomats, diplomatic employees, and family members, and were responsible for dozens of other deaths and hundreds of injuries.[39]

Predictably, the attacks hardened Turkish diplomats' commitment to the state's position. As one foreign diplomat noted, many Turkish diplomats were directly affected by the attacks and felt besieged and physically threatened by them.[40] In 1982, the press counselor at the Turkish embassy in Paris observed: "Ten years ago we could have admitted there was some kind of massacre, but for some reason the Government decided not to. Now it's too late. Who can bend to the demands of terrorists?"[41]

The attacks brought the first awareness of the Armenian question for many in Turkey.[42] The violence also resonated with Turkish officials' claims of Armenians' violence and lack of humanity, which Turkish officials emphasized. For example, in a UN General Assembly speech in October 1982, the Turkish foreign minister İlter Türkmen stated:

> Armenian extremists began to resort to violence in the early 1890s in a manner very reminiscent of the activities of their successors today. . . . The outbreak of the First World War marks the most important crisis in relations between Turks and Armenians. The Tsarist Russian Government then instigated the rising of the Armenians against Ottoman rule in eastern Anatolia, by promising the establishment of an Armenian State. That was the signal which prompted the Armenian extremists to commit large-scale atrocities against the Turkish population in eastern Anatolia, as the Russian armies advanced. It was only after these massacres that the Ottoman Government decided to move the Armenian population out of range of the Russian invading forces in eastern Turkey to central Syria, which was at that time within the boundaries of the Ottoman State.[43]

As Göçek explains, "The Turkish populace therefore quickly believed and internalized the Turkish state's newly constructed justification that these recent Armenian actions were merely a continuation of the rebellious violence the Armenians had committed in the past against the Ottoman state."[44]

Thus, while the terrorist attacks put the issue on Turkey's political agenda, they made it impossible to challenge the state's narrative, since doing so would risk being accused of disloyalty and of sympathizing with terrorists.[45] Moreover, although Turkish officials sometimes acknowledged to domestic audiences that Armenians *outside* Turkey were responsible for the terror attacks, such claims were undermined by officials' and others' constant questioning of Turkish Armenians' loyalty. For instance, a 1981 article in the mainstream newspaper *Hürriyet* called on Turkish Armenian citizens to learn from "our Jewish compatriots in Turkey" and to show their "patriotic loyalty" by taking action to defend the Turkish nation and oppose the "villainy of their kinsmen in other countries."[46]

The 1970s also marked the beginning of international recognition of the genocide. The first sign came early in the decade with a report on genocide prepared by the UN Commission on Human Rights' Sub-commission on Prevention of Discrimination and Protection of Minorities. When a first draft of this report was completed in 1973, it included this passage: "Passing to the modern era, one may note the existence of relatively full documentation dealing with the massacres of Armenians, which have been described as 'the first case of genocide in the twentieth century.'"[47] This reference appeared in a short section that provided historical context for the report's discussion of genocide. According to the report, the Armenian Genocide was included because it was one of "the examples most referred to in the majority of the works on genocide that were available."[48] Turkey's ambassador to the UN quickly expressed his opposition to this passage, and over the next few years, Turkey successfully lobbied individual states and the subcommission to remove the passage. Consequently, the 1978 final report did not refer to the Armenian Genocide.[49] In response, Armenians and others protested and mobilized to oppose the paragraph's deletion, with the result that in 1983, the subcommission tasked one of its members to "revise . . . and update the study."[50] In spite of further efforts by Turkish diplomats, the revised and updated report, which was released in 1985, referred to "the Ottoman massacre of Armenians in 1915–1916" in its historical survey of genocide.[51]

The protests and lobbying surrounding these UN reports mirrored broader developments. For example, in 1975 the issue was brought up in a proposed resolution in the US Congress.[52] Turkey lobbied against the resolution, and both the White House and the State Department opposed its passage. As a result, although it passed in the House of Representatives, the Senate did not vote on it. Nevertheless, together with the UN report and the terrorist attacks, this signaled the advent of a serious problem for Turkey's diplomats.[53]

"Passive Effort[s] to Defend the Turkish Position"

In the face of these international pressures, one might have expected a change in Turkey's narrative.[54] In fact, Bali reports that in 1975, Turkish president Fahri Korutürk expressed the desire to "no longer remain silent" and to "explain . . . the righteousness of Turkey's position."[55] Despite this stated desire, Turkey's narrative did not change for several more years.

Instead, Turkish politicians were preoccupied with the country's political and economic turmoil and with problems stemming from the 1974 invasion and occupation of Cyprus.[56] These problems left little capacity for major changes in the official narrative or in the strategies to defend it. The Turkish government thus continued to oppose and suppress references to the genocide when it came up internationally. The National Intelligence Organization (Milli İstihbarat Teşkilâtı), the military, and the diplomatic corps focused on condemning the terrorist attacks, heightening security measures for Turkish diplomats and agents working abroad, and denying the veracity of genocide claims.[57] Turkish officials were not equipped to respond to questions about the issue, however, as many had little prior knowledge or awareness of it and few resources were available to help them defend or explain Turkey's position.[58] Consequently, international attention and references to the genocide continued to increase, bringing unwanted attention to the issue within Turkey and internationally.

Phase Two (1981–1993): "Tell[ing] the World the Truth"

On 12 September 1980, the Turkish military overthrew the civilian government, seeking to halt the political and economic turmoil and violence that had wracked Turkey in the late 1970s.[59] This third coup in twenty years dramatically altered the Turkish political landscape, ending the political paralysis and violence and returning Turkey's generals to power.[60] Although they brought stability, the new regime and constitution were conservative and undemocratic, and imposed tight controls on public life and discourse. Many leftists and intellectuals were purged from politics, and the military regime imprisoned and tortured thousands of leftists and Kurds.

The 1980 military coup marked a point of change in the official narrative, offering both the political opportunity and the motivation to rethink the official approach to better address the growing international attention. In the wake of the coup, Turkish officials in the ruling National Security Council (Milli Güvenlik Kurulu, MGK), the Foreign Ministry, and other agencies set out to revise the official narrative and develop strategies to get "the truth" out to Turkish citizens and international audiences.[61] Substantively, Turkey's narrative shifted from silence and denial to an actively defended position that involved mythmaking and relativizing. (For an overview of these changes, see Figure 2.1.) This shift involved substantial continuities in elements of the narrative, particularly the rejection of official intentionality in and responsibility for the deaths of Armenians and the silencing of the facts of the forced deportation and massacres of Armenians. It also entailed dramatic changes in the strategies to defend the narrative and in the arguments marshaled to rebut charges of genocide.

Both material concerns and legitimacy and identity concerns undergirded these changes. Regarding material concerns, Turkish officials viewed charges of genocide as a clear threat to the nation's territory. Reflecting this, Kamuran Gürün, a high-level official in the Foreign Ministry and one of the architects of the official narrative in this phase, referred in his memoirs to "the Armenian issue, the goal of which is to partition Turkey."[62] Similarly, in 1987 the Turkish president Kenan Evren, one of the generals who led the 1980 coup, warned a Turkish audience that in addition to seeking recognition, Armenians were "after something else. . . . There will be more demands. . . . I will tell you what sort of demands: They will say there used to be an Armenia in eastern Turkey at one time in history, so give those lands to the Armenians now."[63] And, in the midst of a discussion about the Armenian issue in a 1985 interview, PM Turgut Özal asserted: "I am of the opinion that no one has the right to claim even an inch of land from the Republic of

Turkey or to level any accusations."[64] Finally, PM Yıldırım Akbulut explicitly laid out these concerns in a February 1990 speech before the Turkish Parliament:

> In determining its stand on this matter, Turkey has attached importance, above all, to ascertaining the real aim of the resolutions that the Armenians are trying to extract from forums such as the UN Human Rights Commission, the European Parliament, and the U.S. Senate. Detailed assessments of this issue have led us to believe that the Armenians and other circles that support the resolutions view a U.S. Congressional resolution that legitimizes their allegations of so-called genocide as the first stage of a long-term political strategy. In actual fact, leaders of Armenian communities . . . have declared . . . at every opportunity that these resolutions will constitute the basis for their future claims for compensation and territory. . . . In view of these facts, Turkey has come to the conclusion that efforts to make the international community accept and confirm the so-called Armenian genocide must be stopped. . . . Consequently, it is out of the question to make concessions from our fundamental position.[65]

Officials also sought to defend the legitimacy of the state in the eyes of the Turkish public and the legitimacy of the Turkish nation in the eyes of the world. Many of the CUP leaders who planned the genocide and organized the national resistance movement had been members of the Turkish military. Subsequently, the military as an institution has been strongly committed to defining and protecting the memories of Atatürk and the national resistance movement and defending the unity of the Turkish nation and territory.[66] Unable to silence references to and questions about the genocide internationally, Turkish officials sought to defend the legitimacy of the Turkish nation from these charges. Illustrating officials' concerns about Turkish identity (along with concerns over territorial claims), in 1987 the Turkish Parliament argued that a resolution pending in the US Congress aimed "at having Turkey condemned in the eyes of the world public for a so-called massacre to prepare the ground for future claims on Turkey's territorial integrity."[67] Thus, as Bali notes, Turkish officials worked to replace the developing international view of Turkey as "a barbaric nation and state" with the image of "a civilized state" and a "virtuous" and humane nation.[68]

Given the depth of their concerns about territorial claims, Turkish identity, and the legitimacy of state institutions, officials took steps to centralize control over the official narrative, publish defenses of the official narrative, marshal evidence to support the official narrative, teach the official narrative to Turkish students and citizens, and gain international support for the official narrative.[69]

One of the first actions was to consolidate and coordinate the government's efforts in relation to the Armenian question, which had previously been dealt with in an ad hoc manner by different departments within the MFA. To centralize control, the Information and Planning Coordination Committee (İstihbarat ve Planlama Koordinasyon Kurulu) was established in 1981 under the direction of the MFA and headed by a retired military officer. At the same time, the Directorate General of Intelligence and Research (İstihbarat ve Araştırma Genel Müdürlüğü, İAGM) was created within the MFA to conduct research and produce scholarship on the Armenian question and coordinate policy with the National Security Council. Thereafter, the issue was handled centrally within the MFA and in coordination with the military, other government agencies, and a range of societal actors.[70]

Once the government's efforts were more centralized and coordinated, officials crafted a narrative that responded to charges of genocide and massacre with alternative labels and arguments. Instead of ignoring the term "genocide," Turkey's narrative rejected its application to the Armenian case with three broad arguments. One argument acknowledged that *something* had happened during WWI, but it was not a massacre of Armenians; rather, it was a "civil war" initiated by Armenians' armed uprising and massacre of Muslims. This theme revived explanations that had been advanced during WWI and in its immediate aftermath by Ottoman parliamentarians, former CUP officials, and Atatürk himself. In a letter to the editor of the *Washington Post* in April 1983, the Turkish ambassador to the United States, Şükrü Elekdağ, wrote: "The Ottoman state in 1915 was the scene of a civil war within a global war—the civil war stemming from an armed uprising of Armenians seeking to impose by force the establishment of an exclusively Armenian state in an area where the majority population was not Armenians."[71] Revised history textbooks similarly emphasized Armenian violence and treachery, portraying Armenians as a disloyal minority group that violently rose up against the Ottoman government and killed innocent Turks. They charged that the Russians had incited nationalism among Ottoman Armenians, who then rose up and massacred thousands of innocent Turks "with a brutality that has never been seen before" (*görülmemiş bir vahşet içinde*).[72] Related to this focus on the violence and barbarity of Armenians, Turkish officials argued that moves to recognize the Armenian Genocide would "legitimize terrorism" and "lend support to international terrorism."[73]

A second line of argument was that there was either insufficient or no reliable evidence to support allegations of genocide, or that such allegations were unfounded, baseless, or misrepresentations. For example, in 1986, Nihat Erman, the Turkish consul general in Los Angeles, argued in the *Los Angeles Times*: "No reliable evidence exists to justify the allegation that the Ottoman Empire either planned or carried out any systematic massacre of its Armenian population."[74] Statements directed at domestic audiences emphasized that Turkish officials were searching for documents and taking other steps to prove that Armenians' claims were baseless. For example, in January 1984, PM Özal noted that "a growing number of publications based on archive [sic] material show that all Armenian claims are baseless."[75]

The third contention in relation to the charge of genocide was that calling the Armenian case genocide would devalue the meaning of genocide and threaten the memory of the Holocaust. This argument drew on contemporaneous understandings of genocide. In the 1970s, a few scholars had begun to study genocide, but they tended to focus on single cases, especially the Holocaust. Beginning in the early 1980s, scholars began to study genocide comparatively and to develop a more general understanding of the phenomenon. At the same time, the Holocaust remained the primary focus of research on genocide, and many scholars and organizations argued that the Holocaust should not be compared to other cases.[76] Turkey's argument appealed to and defended a delimited understanding of genocide that equated the concept with the Holocaust. For example, in defending the Turkish government's strong opposition to the first international comparative conference on genocide in 1982, "a [Turkish] Foreign Ministry spokesman, Nazmi Akiman, said . . . , 'We are not against the conference in Tel Aviv but oppose any linkage of the Holocaust to the Armenian allegations of genocide.'"[77] In 1983, Elekdağ argued that calling the events of 1915 a genocide "dilutes the moral force that recollection of the Holocaust should generate for us all" and "deprive[s] the term of its meaning."[78] Several years later, opposing the US Senate's passage of a resolution that recognized the genocide, the deputy chief of the Turkish embassy argued: "Turks were deeply offended by a document that they believe 'morally equates Turks with Nazis.'"[79] These points were made mostly between 1982 and 1985, prior to the 1986 upgrade in diplomatic relations between Turkey and Israel, and around when Jewish American organizations began to lobby on behalf of Turkey's interests in US congressional debates over the Armenian Genocide. The insistence on distinguishing the Holocaust from the Armenian case, and the frequent assertion that Turkey was historically a "safe haven" for Jews fleeing from oppression, were part of Turkey's efforts to gain the support of Israeli and Jewish American political organizations (discussed below).[80] More generally, by crafting normatively resonant arguments, Turkish officials made it more legitimate and easier for actors to support its position. This *rhetorical adaptation* is "a strategy in which actors shape their rhetoric in response to understandings of an international norm in order to avoid charges of norm violation or resist pressures for compliance."[81]

Alongside these arguments about the label "genocide," Turkish officials ceased arguing that the Armenian issue should be left in the past. Instead, they argued that objective and unbiased analysis of the history was needed and that "the assessment of such incidents should be left to historians" who would, they implied, vindicate Turkey.[82] These calls first emerged in May 1985 and became a central element of the official narrative in May 1989, after the official opening of some of the Ottoman archives pertaining to the deportation of Ottoman Armenians (on which more follows). In a letter sent to the US president George H. W. Bush in October 1989, Özal "stated that such problems should be handled by historians, recalling that the Ottoman archives were made available to researchers toward this end." He further insisted "that it would be totally wrong for politicians to pass judgment on historical events at a time when academicians are in the process of studying the allegations."[83]

Despite these calls for openness and objective analysis, only a portion of the relevant archives were opened, and certain documents and collections were available only to scholars whose work supported the official narrative.[84] Moreover, the archives had likely been "cleansed" several times since the end of WWI.[85] This indicates that this argument was—at least in part—an adaptation to changing international expectations regarding past human rights violations. The early to mid-1980s marked the beginning of a shift in states' treatment of past human rights crimes, when some democratizing Latin American countries chose to establish commissions of inquiry to investigate, rather than repress, the human rights crimes of prior regimes. Amid these shifting normative expectations related to truth-seeking and truth-telling, states could no longer simply brush dark pasts under the carpet.[86]

Officials also began to point out that Turkey did not deny that there was suffering during WWI, without actually acknowledging the extent or causes of Armenian suffering. In 1988, Elekdağ declared in a letter to the editor of the *New York Times*: "Turkey has never denied that Armenians perished."[87] Two years later, in a letter to the editor of the *Washington Post*, the Turkish ambassador to the United States Nüzhet Kandemir asserted: "No one denies that all segments of the Ottoman population suffered during civil war—both Turks and Armenians."[88] These explicit assertions that Turkey was not denying human suffering are another sign that Turkish officials were rhetorically adapting to changing international expectations about how states should deal with past wrongs. This new theme joined the longer-standing relativization that everyone had suffered, but it shifted subtly to the claim that each side had suffered roughly equal losses and deaths. This included claims that "a large number of Turks were killed by Armenians," that "Turks as well as Armenians suffered terribly," that "more than 2 million Turks perished during the same period," and that there was "a heavy toll on all sides."[89]

Turkish officials also argued that Armenians had died from famine, epidemics, disease, and sickness. This theme first appeared in 1983 and was a frequent refrain in textbooks and official statements.[90] Textbooks did not mention the violence of the deportation, the scope of Armenian deaths, or the role of government agents in the deportation and massacres. However, some briefly alluded to, and then rationalized, the fact that some Armenians had died. For example, a 1983 textbook offered rationalizing, relativizing, and mythmaking explanations for the deaths of Ottoman Armenians, declaring: "During the migration, a portion of Armenians lost their lives because of lack of public security and from natural conditions. But this should also not be forgotten: At Sarıkamış alone, almost 100,000 Turkish soldiers died because of natural conditions and neglect. . . . In fact, thousands of Armenians reached Syria safe and sound and there continued their lives in the protection of the Turkish State."[91]

The deportation was largely left out of the official narrative, but the decision to "relocate" Ottoman Armenians, which was a euphemistic way of talking about the deportation, was occasionally mentioned. It was then typically rationalized with claims that violence and massacres by the Armenians led Ottoman authorities to conclude that "they had no alternative but to relocate the Armenians."[92] In a speech in Erzurum in July 1986, President Evren bluntly stated: "We sent them—the Armenians living here at the time—away for the atrocities they committed."[93] This claim echoed Ottoman officials' rationalizations during and after WWI, when officials argued that the deportation was necessary for the security and safety of the Ottoman army and the Muslim population.

The more fraught issue of responsibility for the virtual elimination of Armenians from Anatolia was almost never mentioned. A rare reference to responsibility appeared in a letter to the editor of the *New York Times* in May 1985, where Elekdağ argued: "Ottoman responsibility, if any, must lie in the empire's inability to protect its civilian population (both Moslem and Christian) from wide-scale civil war, famine and disease while fighting a world war on five fronts."[94] Textbooks that mentioned the deportation decision more clearly disavowed responsibility. A 1983 textbook stated: "The Turkish Nation is definitely not responsible for the things that happened during the Armenians' migration [*Ermenilerin göçü sırasında olanlardan Türk Milleti kesinlikle sorumlu değildir*]."[95]

Finally, Turkish officials' material concerns about territorial claims and demands for compensation became an explicit part of the official narrative. In statements to domestic audiences, leaders often called on the Turkish people to be on guard against threats to Turkish territory and to protect the unity of the Turkish nation. In a June 1981 speech, the Turkish leader General Evren declared: "Armenians outside the country . . . are demanding land from us. I ask you; why are they asking for land now? Why did they not ask for land during Ataturk's rule or even when the Ottoman Empire was at its weakest? The reason is that there was chaos and a threat of civil war in the country. Like vultures, they thought they might grab something from us."[96] In addition, Turkish high school history textbooks explicitly downplayed Armenians' presence in the Ottoman Empire, and some asserted that Armenians had not constituted a majority in any Ottoman province, so their claims to Ottoman territories were unfounded.[97] Some textbooks were even more direct, with one emphasizing: "Armenians did not constitute a majority in any province at any time. Accordingly then, Turkey will not cede an inch of its lands to the Armenians."[98]

"Determined Efforts to Enlighten the Public"

The reworked narrative was presented in speeches and public statements and in books and pamphlets published throughout the 1980s.[99] Beginning in 1981, Turkish officials encouraged and supported the publication of books that articulated this narrative, seeking to both present the Turkish government's position and undermine the charge of genocide.[100]

At first, the İAGM and the National Security Council encouraged Turkish historians to write about the Armenian question. When it became clear that this would not be possible—either because Turkish historians did not have the requisite knowledge to write on the topic or because they did not want to risk doing so—Turkish diplomats decided to write about it themselves.[101] One of the first and most important such books—*Ermeni Dosyası* (The Armenian file)—was written by Kamuran Gürün and was first published in Turkish in 1983. The book attempts to place WWI and the "relocation" of Armenians in historical context. Gürün presents the "relocation" as arising from the self-interested interventions of the great powers into the Ottoman Empire's minority affairs, terrorist activities of Armenian nationalists, widespread attacks and insurrection by Armenians at the beginning of WWI, and Armenians' traitorous cooperation with Turkey's enemy Russia. Gürün argues that the deportation was a "military requirement" and that "it was impossible to adopt a better solution under the circumstances."[102] He further contends that Armenians were at war with Turks and that "Armenians were forced to emigrate because they had joined the ranks of the enemy." He estimates that 702,900 Armenians were deported and claims that no more than 300,000 died during WWI.[103] The book closes with an assertion that reflects Turkish officials' concerns about territorial claims: "Today, no one has the right to make any kind of demand from Turkey about the events occurring before the signing of the Lausanne Treaty."[104]

Government officials also wrote a pamphlet about the Armenian question that presented basic information about the issue and refuted the charge of genocide. Called *The Armenian Issue in Nine Questions and Answers*, it was written by a group of diplomats and published by the Foreign Policy Institute (Dış Politika Enstitüsü) in 1982.[105] Of the nine questions addressed, three concern Armenian claims to Turkish territory, again signaling the centrality of this issue in Turkish officials' minds. Three other answers address the charge that Turks systematically massacred Armenians during WWI, arguing that no Armenians were massacred by Turks, that estimates of Armenians deaths are "highly exaggerated" because they exceed the prewar Armenian population, and that those deaths that did occur were due to "famine, sickness, contagious diseases, severe climatic conditions and actual combat."[106]

These publications were part of a broader effort to publish work articulating and defending the state's position. As shown in Figure 3.1, the number of official and quasi-official publications on the Armenian question skyrocketed in the early 1980s, from just one book published between 1976 and 1980 to twenty-one books published between 1981 and 1985. Publishing efforts involved more government agencies than in the 1970s, and many of the official and quasi-official publications were written in or translated into English (and often also French), indicating that they were aimed at least in part at foreign audiences.[107]

A parallel initiative supported archival research and the publication of archival documents related to the Armenian question. As Ömer Engin Lütem, a diplomat who was centrally involved in the government's strategizing on the Armenian question at the time, writes, "Since the claims of Armenians depend on mostly fake or misguided documents, it was important to publish the related documents."[108] The National Security Council and the MFA coordinated this effort. They instructed the director general of the Prime Minister's State Archives to find and publish archival documents that could support the Turkish government's position.[109] The MFA also brought in retired diplomats and officers who could read Ottoman Turkish, the language used by Ottoman officials and in the Republic of Turkey until 1928.[110] Under the leadership and with the support of the Foreign Ministry, this group—known as the Prime Minister's Archive Research Committee—looked for Ottoman archival documents related to the Armenian question.[111] Their efforts resulted in the publication of several books, including a collection of Ottoman documents and an English translation of Uras's seminal 1950 book.[112] This effort to locate and publish archival documents also extended abroad. In the early 1980s, Turkish diplomat and researcher Bilâl Şimşir researched the Armenian question in British archives, which resulted in a series of books published by the Turkish Historical Society.[113]

The MFA also pushed to have relevant archives cataloged and opened.[114] Officials believed that documents in the archives could be used to support the Turkish position, and that Turkey's narrative was less credible as long as the relevant archives were not open to researchers. Turkish officials hoped that this step would "defuse criticism abroad, and . . . improve relations with the United States and Western European countries."[115] Consequently, the goal of opening the Ottoman archives was announced with great fanfare in 1985, although they were not officially opened until 1989, after a team of Turkish archivists had organized and cataloged a portion of the available documents. The mere announcement that the archives would be opened decreased international pressures and gave Turkey credibility by appearing responsive to external criticisms. When the archives were officially opened in 1989, the Turkish foreign minister Mesut Yılmaz declared: "The issue of Armenian claims must no longer be a subject of political exploitation. This is not a matter for politicians to solve but for historians and we want to contribute to this effort."[116] However, the archives were not completely opened, nor were they open to all scholars who wished to conduct research on the Armenian question. Moreover, reports suggest that the cataloging of the archives involved the cleansing of documents inconsistent with the government's position.[117]

Another element of the state's strategy was to educate Turkish citizens and students about the official position, both in public speeches and other communications and at the primary, secondary, and tertiary levels of education. Government officials worked with universities, especially through the newly created Council of Higher Education (Yükseköğretim Kurulu, YÖK), to establish courses on the Armenian question and to encourage academic research into the issue among faculty and students. In 1983, the political scientist Türkkaya Ataöv offered the first university course on the Armenian question, at Ankara University.[118] Turkish academics—notable among them, Ataöv—also started to publish work that supported the Turkish government's position.[119] And between 1983 and 1991, ten academic conferences on the Armenian question were held in Turkey.[120]

Beginning in 1981, the MFA and the National Education Ministry (Milli Eğitim Bakanlığı) included the Armenian question in Turkish history textbooks.[121] By 1983, the representation of the Armenian question significantly differed from that of previous decades. Whereas silence had been the norm through the 1970s, high school history textbooks in the early 1980s acknowledged that something had happened to Ottoman Armenians in 1915, but rationalized authorities' decision to deport Armenians and relativized the violence by arguing that the deportation was not comparable to Armenian violence.[122] In 1982, the Education Ministry also instructed teachers on what to say about the Armenian question. According to Kaplan, the ministry directed teachers to "point out that we [Turks] had no problems with *Armenians*. . . . It must be explained that in recent times they have been supported by foreign powers and that bloody crimes have been perpetrated on our diplomatic representatives abroad. It must be made clear that the Turkish nation has been trapped into political intrigues with terrorist aims and that, as always, it patiently waits for the justice of its case to be accepted."[123] To reach the broader population, Turkish officials addressed the Armenian question and Armenian terrorism in domestic speeches and in television programs.[124]

Another important dimension of official efforts was diplomatic. Turkish officials sought to develop international sources of support, improve Turkey's international image, and suppress references to the genocide. The extent and intensity of Turkey's international public relations efforts differed both quantitatively and qualitatively from earlier efforts. According to Lütem, the MGK decided "to respond to any type of Armenian publication. . . . To this end, many letters were sent in reply to the Armenian claims which were published in foreign newspapers and periodicals. Furthermore, to counterbalance the Armenian claims, the Turkish perspective was to be voiced to the conferences, radio stations, and television programs organized in foreign countries where these Armenian claims were being made."[125]

The core goal, according to Özdemir, was "to pull Western countries to Turkey's side."[126] The United States was a particular focus, given its importance as an ally and that the genocide had become a persistent irritant in Turkish-US relations. Efforts were also made to win support in Israel, Australia, France, Canada, and Germany.[127] Alongside lobbying and soft power strategies, Turkish officials made threats and sometimes followed through with actions to pressure the United States and other countries to not recognize the genocide. For example, in conjunction with lobbying against a resolution before the US Congress in 1989, Bobelian writes that Turkey "raised the stakes by restricting U.S. military maneuvers and reconnaissance flights, halting visits to ports, suspending military cooperation meetings, and stopping the use of its training facilities."[128] As a result, while the US Congress considered resolutions that would have recognized the genocide in 1984–1985, 1987, and 1989–1990, all were strongly opposed by the White House and State Department, and none managed to pass both houses of Congress.[129]

Turkish officials also cultivated local advocates who could argue on Turkey's behalf in the US Congress, including key Jewish American organizations. The Turkish government sent delegations of Turkish Jewish businessmen to the United States to gain Jewish American support and pushed Turkish Jewish elites to develop strong connections with Jewish leaders in Israel and the United States.[130] In addition to the arguments discussed earlier, Turkish officials and advocates emphasized that good relations with Turkey were important for Israel. Bali suggests that the improvement of diplomatic relations with Israel was part of a tacit quid pro quo among Turkish officials, Turkish Jewish business and community leaders, some Jewish American groups, and Israeli officials.[131] Beginning in 1986, Turkey upgraded the level of its diplomatic relations with Israel. Five years later, in 1991, relations between Turkey and Israel were elevated again, this time to the level of ambassador. According to a retired Turkish diplomat, Turkey's decision to do so stemmed in part from its desire to maintain the support of key Jewish American interest groups in fighting genocide recognition efforts in the United States.[132]

Turkish officials also warned that if Israeli or Jewish organizations were to publicly recognize the Armenian Genocide, Turkey's relationship with Israel would suffer and Turkish Jews might be in danger.[133] In 1982, Turkish officials tried to pressure Israeli officials and scholars to cancel the first international and comparative academic conference on genocide, which was to be held in Tel Aviv. According to Elie Wiesel, who was on the conference organizing committee, Turkey threatened that if the conference took place, it might "sever diplomatic relations with Israel and take other measures against the lives and livelihood of Turkish Jews."[134] As a result of this combination of incentives and threats, a number of prominent Jewish American organizations supported Turkey's position. For example, when the US Senate was considering a resolution about the genocide in 1989, the Israeli embassy and some Jewish American organizations lobbied members of Congress on Turkey's behalf.[135]

Turkey also hired a series of Washington, DC–based public relations (PR) and lobbying firms to help improve its image in the United States, to suppress and defeat resolutions to recognize the genocide in the US Congress, and to promote its political and economic interests in the United States. The use of lobbying firms began in the late 1970s, as Turkish officials struggled to overturn the arms embargo imposed by the US Congress in the wake of Turkey's invasion of Cyprus.[136] Once the ban was lifted in 1978, and as it became clear that the Armenian question was not going to recede as a foreign policy issue, these PR firms increasingly focused on the Armenian issue. By the mid to late 1980s, Turkey employed several PR firms and had spent millions of dollars on lobbying efforts. These firms worked with the Turkish embassy, with Turkish organizations in the United States, and with other advocates in developing and coordinating their efforts.[137]

The Turkish embassy also expanded its focus into US society. Şükrü Elekdağ, who was the Turkish ambassador to the United States from 1979 to 1989, was instrumental in gaining support from US businesses (especially in the defense industry), the Turkish American community, and US-based academics. Elekdağ fostered the development of business associations for US companies with interests in Turkey and persuaded US defense firms and other businesses with interests in Turkey to lobby against congressional resolutions related to the genocide. Thus, when a resolution to recognize the genocide was introduced in Congress in 1990, Jørgensen reports, "letters from firms all over the USA poured in to Congress with warnings of the unfortunate consequences that would ensue for American exports if resolution 212 was accepted."[138]

Elekdağ also encouraged the establishment of pro-Turkish interest groups in a number of countries. According to Lütem, Turkish officials sought "to prepare the Turks living in foreign countries for answering Armenian claims," especially through "the counter activities of the Turks who became citizens of those countries."[139] In the United States, the Assembly of Turkish American Associations (ATAA), established in December 1979, was one of the main organizations reflecting this strategy. Bali reports that the ATAA's "purpose was to counter the lobbying efforts of Greek- and Armenian-American organizations and combat discrimination faced by Turks living in America."[140] The ATAA helped develop relationships with and win the support of Jewish American organizations. It also issued several booklets on the Armenian question in the early to mid-1980s that were aimed at US politicians and mirrored the content of Turkey's official narrative.[141] The ATAA also organized workshops across the country to teach members how to organize letter-writing and telephone campaigns. The result was that Turkish Americans and Turkish American organizations wrote numerous letters about the Armenian question (and other issues) to senators and representatives in Congress and to the editors of US newspapers.[142]

Elekdağ also cultivated support from academics specializing in Turkish and Ottoman studies, which lent legitimacy to claims that further historical research was needed to determine the nature of the events and the parties responsible. This support was often won indirectly, as individual academics calculated that if they worked on or wrote critically about the topic, they might lose access to archives in Turkey; hinder their chances of securing funding for research in Turkey; and threaten relationships with Turkish colleagues, contacts, family, and friends.[143] In 1982, the Turkish government established and funded (with $3 million) the Washington-based Institute of Turkish Studies (ITS), which supports academic research on modern Turkey and the Ottoman Empire.[144] According to a Turkish official, ITS was created "to facilitate greater knowledge of Turkey," because "there [wa]s a need for a better understanding of Turkey."[145] Since its inception, ITS has been one of the few sources of funding in the United States for research on Turkey. By offering funding and research opportunities for scholars working on Ottoman and Turkish subjects, ITS increased the costs of working on the Armenian question, since to do so effectively rendered a scholar ineligible for these funds.

Demonstrating its influence within US academic circles, in 1985 ITS asked US scholars of Turkish and Ottoman studies to add their names to an advertisement about the Armenian question that it would place in US newspapers. The ad was paid for by the ATAA and published in the *Washington Post*, the *Washington Times*, and the *New York Times*. Titled "Attention Members of the U.S. House of Representatives," the ad outlined "reservations" that the "undersigned American academicians who specialize in Turkish, Ottoman and Middle Eastern studies" had with the "use of the words 'Turkey' and 'genocide'" in House Joint Resolution 192, which was then under consideration. The ad asserted: "The Republic of Turkey bears no responsibility for any events which occurred in Ottoman times." While noting "the scope of Armenian suffering," it characterized the context as one of "inter-communal warfare" about which scholars, not politicians, needed to do further research.[146] Importantly, most of the sixty-nine scholars who agreed to sign their names to the ad were not experts on the genocide or the period, and many seem not to have understood how the ad would be used.[147] Nevertheless, Turkish officials and their advocates used the ad to persuade members of Congress (and others, both then and since) not to "politicize" the issue and to leave its evaluation to academics.

In addition, in the early to mid-1990s the Turkish government spent more than $3 million to endow chairs in Ottoman and Turkish studies at Princeton, Harvard, the University of Chicago, Indiana University, Georgetown, and Portland State.[148] By defining the terms of some of the most prestigious positions in the field, Turkey sought to shape the direction of Ottoman and Turkish studies in the United States. Hinting at this is a 1988 speech by Turkish foreign minister Mesut Yılmaz, who reported to the Turkish Parliament that the creation of academic chairs in Britain and the United States "aimed to influence scholarly opinion in those countries."[149] While this influence is generally subtle, this was not always the case. Notably, when the director of ITS, Heath Lowry, was selected in 1993 to fill the first endowed chair at Princeton, a coalition of academics, intellectuals, and Armenian Americans raised concerns about the independence of the chairs and the intentions of the Turkish government.[150] While Princeton stood by its hiring decision, this affair influenced UCLA's 1998 decision to turn down the Turkish government's $1 million offer to create an endowed chair in Turkish studies. The offer specified that the holder of the chair should be a scholar with "cordial relations with academic circles in Turkey" and "whose published works are based upon extensive utilization of archives and libraries in Turkey."[151] While these terms did not refer to the Armenian Genocide, prior to the mid-2000s, these conditions effectively excluded any scholar who worked on the topic.

Despite the success of Turkey's efforts to win support for its position and to counter charges of genocide, the trend toward international recognition of the Armenian Genocide continued throughout the 1980s. Notable instances of this were repeated attempts to recognize the genocide in the US Congress and the recognition of the genocide by the UN and the European Parliament.[152] Thus, despite the strenuous efforts undertaken by Turkish officials and their advocates, this issue continued to be a significant foreign policy problem for Turkey throughout the 1980s.

At the same time, legal constraints on freedom of speech, the continuing taboo on discussion of the "Armenian question," and the continued questioning of the loyalty of non-Muslim minorities prevented significant challenges to the official narrative from arising within Turkey. Together with the robustness of efforts to communicate the official narrative to Turkish citizens, these legal, political, and social pressures largely prevented challenges to and questioning of the official narrative within Turkey. Starting in the early 1990s, this began to change, setting the stage for the emergence of domestic counternarratives and contestation.

PLAYING HARDBALL (1994–2008)

If they want to establish good relations with Turkey, Armenia is in no position to place preconditions.

—Turkish ambassador to the United States Baki İlkin, October 1998

These Armenian efforts . . . are among those issues that Ankara has great sensitivities over. This is one of the important bases determining Turkey's relations with any other country.

—Foreign Minister İsmail Cem, May 2000

Between 1994 and 2008, there were major changes in Turkey's domestic politics and foreign relations, challenges to the official narrative from within the domestic sphere, and intensified pressure from continuing international recognition of the genocide. In response, Turkey's narrative shifted somewhat, no longer silencing and outright denying the events of the genocide, and coming to acknowledge some basic facts. At the same time, there were significant continuities in the narrative's content and in the strategies used to support and disseminate it, and the continued rejection of the label "genocide."

The third phase, which began in 1994, involved subtle changes in the tone and substance of the narrative. Despite major structural changes at the international level—notably, the establishment of an Armenian state—and the beginnings of domestic challenges to the state's narrative, its content was remarkably stable, highlighting the persistence of domestic constraints on change. The fourth phase, which began in 2001, involved some acknowledgment of Armenians' deaths and suffering, alongside continued relativization, rationalization, and mythmaking. The official narrative acknowledged basic facts about the genocide while rationalizing these new facts and continuing to reject the label "genocide." These changes were made primarily in response to increased international recognition of the genocide, and also reflected the broadening of domestic contestation questioning the official narrative.

The End of the Cold War and the Establishment of the Republic of Armenia

The end of the Cold War upended long-standing constants in Turkey's external relations. It prompted a shift in Turkey's foreign policy priorities and introduced two new states—Armenia and Azerbaijan—into the politics surrounding the Armenian question. Amid the reshuffling of alliances and borders, Turkish officials worried about the continued importance of NATO and Turkey's position in the constellation of US alliances. Another concern was that the European Community had rejected Turkey's application for membership in 1989. As Dağı points out, the coincidence of this rejection with the end of the Cold War prompted a questioning of the bases of Turkish foreign policy and the country's orientation toward the West.[1] Against this backdrop, Turkish elites and the press saw the potential for Turkey to act as a regional hegemon vis-à-vis the newly independent Central Asian states.

In the context of this unsettling and resetting of international relations, the Republic of Armenia gained independence in December 1991. This marked the first time in the history of the Republic of Turkey that an independent Armenian state existed.[2] Turkey recognized Armenia's independence, but Turkish officials were wary of the new state's intentions regarding the "Armenian question" and worried that Armenia might make claims on Turkish territory.[3] Illustrating officials' material concerns, in May 1991, in response to soon-to-be Armenian president Levon Ter-Petrosyan's observation that "the eastern Turkish township of Kars originally belonged to Armenia," the Turkish ambassador to the Soviet Union asserted: "Kars had always been a Turkish city, and none of its neighbors had any bit of territory to hand over to Armenia." He further warned, "Kars was always Turkish. [The] Armenian Government should understand this. It is in the benefit of the Armenian people to regulate its relations with its neighbors, respectful of their rights and interests. We hope common sense will prevail in the future."[4]

Once in office, Ter-Petrosyan and his party chose not to make the genocide a central element of Armenia's foreign policy. Instead, he explicitly *de*prioritized genocide recognition and acknowledged the existing borders with Turkey. Astourian argues that Ter-Petrosyan did this because he recognized Armenia's geopolitical weakness and sought to pursue "a realistic foreign policy unburdened by the weight of the past."[5] This logic was captured in a 1990 statement by the influential Armenian thinker Rafayel Ishkhanian, who said: "The steps of the Armenian people must be proportionate to the degree of our strength."[6] Gerard Libaridian, who was an adviser to Ter-Petrosyan, later explained that Armenia's strategy was driven by a desire to establish peaceful relations with neighboring countries, in part to avoid being forced into Russia's sphere of influence.[7]

While Ter-Petrosyan assured Turkish officials that Armenia acknowledged the borders established in the 1921 Treaty of Kars, other parties and politicians in Armenia questioned the borders and criticized Ter-Petrosyan for setting this issue aside. An early sign of these domestic tensions arose during the writing of Armenia's Declaration of Independence in the summer of 1990. Against Ter-Petrosyan's wishes, the declaration states: "The Republic of Armenia stands in support of the task of achieving international recognition of the 1915 Genocide in Ottoman Turkey and Western Armenia."[8] The parties that voted for this clause also pushed for Armenia to assert claims to Turkish territory. A leader of the Armenian Democratic Liberal Party, which is a long-standing diaspora party that was established in Armenia after its independence, stated: "The new Republic must include in its on-going agenda the recognition of the Armenian genocide and our historic territorial claims by the international community."[9]

Such inconsistencies in the messages from different actors within Armenia deepened Turkish officials' wariness. Not satisfied with Ter-Petrosyan's assurances that Armenia recognized the existing border, Turkish officials demanded an official statement to this effect. In spite of their stated position on the issue, Armenian officials refused to comply, on the grounds that the request was unreasonable and humiliating. As Mirzoyan explains, "Yerevan . . . insisted that the very fact of its proposal to establish diplomatic relations with Ankara constituted a de facto recognition of Turkey's territorial integrity."[10] Predictably, this response reinforced Turkish officials' material concerns. A retired Turkish diplomat characterized Armenia's refusal as a "rejection of the reaffirmation of mutual borders," arguing that "Armenia did not accept even a vague promise [to] stop its official activities for the recognition of the 'genocide' and refused a confirmation of the present borders, even by a reference to valid agreements and treaties."[11] Of course, this outcome might have been preferable to Turkish officials, since having normal relations with Armenia would have made it more difficult to ignore and dismiss any claims Armenian officials might have made for genocide recognition or restitution.[12]

Another stumbling block in Turkish-Armenian relations was the Nagorno-Karabakh conflict. The Nagorno-Karabakh region is situated within Azerbaijan, but its population was (and continues to be) primarily Armenian. The conflict began in early 1988, when Karabakh Armenians called for the region to join Armenia. This call was rejected by Soviet and Azeri officials, leading to pogroms against Armenians in several Azeri cities (notably, Sumgait and Baku). These pogroms galvanized the Armenian public and politicians to support the Karabakh leadership, and within the space of a year fighting broke out between Azeri and Armenian forces. Between 1991 and 1994, Azeri and Karabakh Armenian forces—with some support from the Republic of Armenia and diaspora Armenians—fought for control of the region, culminating in Karabakh forces gaining control of the enclave.[13] As the conflict escalated, Turkey became increasingly involved in supporting Azerbaijan's position, partially as a reflection of Turkey's focus on its Turkic neighbors and partially in response to pan-Turkic and anti-Armenian sentiments in Turkey.[14] Moreover, as Mirzoyan observes, "The Nagorno-Karabakh conflict only reinforced th[e] prevailing perception among the Turkish public and the military elite that Armenians pursued a similar goal of territorial revision in regards to Turkey."[15] Thus, Turkey first drew back from agreements with Armenia, and in April 1993 Turkey withdrew from negotiations over the establishment of diplomatic relations and closed the border with Armenia.

Since then, the issue of the genocide has been intertwined with the normalization of Turkish-Armenian relations and the resolution of the Nagorno-Karabakh conflict.[16] Within six months of the border closing, Armenia's foreign minister reported: "It is impossible to consider establishing a positive dialogue with Turkey before the Karabakh problem is resolved or at least a durable cease-fire agreement is reached with Azerbaijan. We are trying to defuse anti-Turkish sentiments, but the Turkish Government is not responding in kind."[17] Since then, Armenia has repeatedly stated that it sets no preconditions to the normalization of relations with Turkey. In contrast, Turkey insisted (at least until the mid-2000s) that before it would reopen discussions to normalize diplomatic relations, Armenia would have to make progress on the Nagorno-Karabakh conflict and recognize the 1921 border with Turkey.[18]

The Emergence of Domestic Contestation

Alongside these tectonic shifts in the international system and in Turkey's external relations, domestic developments also touched on Turkey's narrative of the Armenian question. Throughout the 1990s, Turkey's domestic politics were tumultuous, with the Kurdish conflict in Turkey's southeast at its height, human rights and the rule of law severely strained, and a series of weak coalition governments. The Kurdish conflict was characterized by high levels of violence, widespread torture and atrocities, endemic corruption, massive internal displacement and rural depopulation, and a wave of urbanization. Moreover, in response to the growing political weight of Islamic parties, the military reasserted its authority in a "soft" coup on 28 February 1997.

In response to these developments, as well as to the liberalization of the media and the lifting of key restrictions on freedom of speech, Turkish civil society began to tentatively challenge aspects of the state's policies toward the Kurds. Starting in the early 1990s, a few academics, publishers, activists, and journalists also began to draw attention to the genocide and to Armenians in the Ottoman Empire and contemporary Turkey. The limited nature of this initial activism reflected the deeply ingrained acceptance of the official narrative among the vast majority of the Turkish public. Tellingly, those who challenged the official narrative were often already involved in challenging the state's taboos and national narratives, particularly on the Kurdish question.

In the early 1990s, a few publishing houses began to release books on the genocide. In 1992, Taner Akçam's *Türk Ulusal Kimliği ve Ermeni Sorunu* (Turkish national identity and the Armenian question) was published in Turkey. This was the first book by a Turkish academic that was highly critical of Turkey's narrative.[19] In 1993, the human rights activist-owners of the publisher Belge Yayınları, Ayşe Nur and Ragıp Zarakolu, published a book titled *Ermeni Tabusu* (The Armenian taboo) on the history of the Armenian Genocide, which was a translation of historian Yves Ternon's 1977 book, *Les Armeniens: Histoire d'un Génocide* (The Armenians: History of a genocide).[20] The Zarakolus had published books that challenged the state's narrative of the Kurdish question, and they decided to publish something on the Armenian question because they saw it as being historically and rhetorically linked to the Kurdish question. Then in 1994, Peri Publications—which primarily publishes work on Kurdish history, politics, and literature—published the first book on the Armenian Genocide with the word "genocide" (*jenosid*) in its title.[21]

In 1993, a group of Turkish Armenians founded Aras Publishing with the aim of helping to "create background knowledge" about Armenians in Turkey, since at the time Turks knew nothing about Armenians other than propaganda and slander from the Turkish government and press.[22] Among Aras's publications are Turkish translations of Armenian literature, including the work of diaspora Armenian and Turkish Armenian writers. As Göçek notes, these translated works "present[ed] unauthorized remembrances of the past."[23] They also exposed gaps and inconsistencies in the state's narrative and demonstrated that Turkish Armenians' lives were part of Turkish history and society. Together with the books mentioned earlier, Aras contributed to the broadening of public discussion and knowledge of Armenians in Turkey.[24]

Activism related to the Armenian question also began to emerge in the early 1990s. In January 1994, activists in the Istanbul branch of the Human Rights Foundation of Turkey (İnsan Hakları Derneği, İHD) formed the Minority Rights Monitoring Commission (Azınlık Hakları İzleme Komisyonu).[25] The commission met once a month to discuss issues faced by minorities in Turkey. In addition to educating themselves, the commission's members prepared materials for the public. In 1994–1995, they prepared a report on the problems faced by ethnic and religious minorities in Turkey. In 1996, they organized the first exhibit in

Turkey on the 6–7 September 1955 pogroms of Greeks and other minorities, as well as an exhibition about the Turkish government's confiscation of properties from non-Muslim minority foundations.[26]

In the Turkish media, the Armenian question was first discussed critically in the mid to late 1990s. Yelda was one of the first Turkish journalists to write about Armenians and other minorities in ways that directly challenged the official narrative. In weekly columns published in several outlets between 1995 and 1997, Yelda frequently referred to the "Armenian genocide" (*Ermeni soykırımı*) without quotation marks and without a preceding "so-called" (*sözde*).[27] Critical articles also appeared in the pro-Kurdish newspaper *Özgür Gündem*, which was the only newspaper at the time that published articles challenging official narratives about minorities.[28] In 1996, the Turkish Armenian journalist Hrant Dink and several others founded the weekly newspaper *Agos*, which covers Turkish politics and society, as well as issues in and of interest to the small Turkish Armenian community. As Cheterian explains, "From the outset, *Agos* sought to convey the reality of the Armenian community to the Turkish public, one which stood in stark contrast to their portrayal in the smear campaigns of the Turkish media, and it also sought to express the problems the community, as well as those of other minorities, experienced on a daily basis."[29] Although its publication in Turkish and Armenian was unprecedented, *Agos* was not widely known and its readership was quite small in the 1990s. Nevertheless, its editor in chief Hrant Dink, who was one of the first Turkish Armenians to publicly draw attention to injustices faced by Armenians in Turkey, had a significant impact on public discourse in Turkey.[30]

Overall, however, these developments did not noticeably affect the official narrative until the early 2000s, in part because they were so limited in nature. More importantly, economic, legal, and ideological constraints meant that the mainstream Turkish media refrained from challenging the state's narrative.[31] Illustrating these constraints, *Agos* avoided using the term "genocide" throughout the 1990s, since as Dink explained in 2001, "If I use the word genocide, the next day *Agos* would stop publication."[32] In line with Dink's expectation, the initial activism outlined above did not go unsanctioned. The government banned Akçam's 1992 book immediately after it was published, along with Peri's 1994 book and the 1995 publication of a Turkish translation of an academic book on the genocide.[33] In addition, the author of the 1994 book was tried and convicted, and the Zarakolus were convicted under Article 8 of the antiterror law for publishing Ternon's book. Two years later, they were again tried but this time acquitted under Article 216 of the penal code for the publication of another book on the genocide.[34] In 1999, the Minority Rights Monitoring Commission's exhibition in Ankara about the state's confiscation of Armenian foundations' property was physically attacked and a court case was unsuccessfully brought against İHD.[35]

Tellingly, that no paper other than *Özgür Gündem* would publish articles about minorities reveals the self-censorship in the mainstream media, which derived from internalization of the official narrative, along with fear of prosecution and other sanctions that might arise from transgressing this taboo.

Even in spite of its limits, this initial contestation is notable for several reasons. First, some of these early activists had connections with actors in other countries, especially France, Germany, and the United States.[36] Second, some of the activists who worked on minority issues and the Armenian question in the 1990s did so because they saw connections between the Kurdish question and the Armenian question.[37] Likewise, some Kurdish activists began to draw connections between these issues, in some cases before the 1990s. The Kurdish publisher Recep Maraşlı began to compile a pamphlet about the Armenian Genocide in 1982, while he was imprisoned after the 1980 coup. He shared this pamphlet with fellow Kurdish inmates and expanded it over the years, many of which were spent in prison for his writing and activism on the Kurdish question. This process culminated in a 2008 book on the topic.[38]

Although the small group of activists and scholars who began to work on the Armenian question were at first primarily speaking to and educating each other, this was a crucial development. As one interviewee noted, whereas no one used to be interested in or know anything about the Armenian question or the problems of Armenians in Turkey, a group of activists concerned with this issue gradually emerged and coalesced. Very slowly, their activities got others interested in these issues.[39]

Phase Three (1994–2000): Continuity amid Changing Contexts

In spite of structural shifts in the international and domestic spheres, the third phase was characterized by strong continuities. There was a relative lull in international pressures, and Armenia's prioritization of stability over genocide recognition meant that its independence did not significantly alter the constellation of pressures on Turkey's narrative. In addition, domestic counternarratives had not yet gained traction within Turkey. Meanwhile, advocates within and outside Turkey reinforced the state's position, which highlights the role of societal actors in pushing for continuity. In particular, retired diplomats continued to work on and speak publicly about the Armenian question after leaving the Foreign Ministry, and Turkish American groups, academics, and many Jewish American organizations continued to support Turkey's position.

In the absence of new or significant pressures for change, and given Turkish officials' persistent material concerns about territorial claims, there was little change in existing strategies; mythmaking, relativizing, and denial continued to characterize the official narrative. A key, continuing theme was that what had happened was not genocide but a civil war. In a letter sent to members of the US Congress in 1994, the Turkish ambassador to the United States Nüzhet Kandemir "argued that 'what happened during the collapse of the Ottoman Empire in 1915 was a civil war—not genocide—during which both sides lost lives, due to Armenian collaboration with the invading Russian army and their intention to carve an autonomous Armenian state out of Anatolia.'"[40] In addition, official statements continued to argue that many Turks had also died and that to talk only of Armenian deaths was one-sided. An additional continuing argument was that historians, not politicians, should address the issue. Some statements went a step further, arguing that research had refuted these allegations or that documents in the Ottoman and other archives had shown that they were unfounded.[41]

Alongside these continuities was a renewed focus on the issue, which had waned following the end of Armenian terrorist attacks.[42] In the latter half of the 1990s, the numbers of both official publications and government agencies publishing books on the Armenian question doubled. As shown in Figure 3.1, between 1996 and 2000, six government offices published fifteen books on the topic. This is striking compared with the three government agencies that had published books on the topic and the average of six books published by government agencies in each of the three prior five-year periods (i.e., 1981–1985, 1986–1990, 1991–1995).

In addition, there were subtle shifts in the state's narrative. Given the increasingly comparative nature of genocide scholarship and evolving international jurisprudence related to the crime of genocide, arguments offered in opposition to the label "genocide" began to shift. Whereas Turkey's narrative had previously implied that an event should be comparable to the Holocaust to be defined as genocide, it now emphasized that a particular understanding of intent had to be proved for an event to qualify as genocide. This shift away from the academic understanding of genocide makes sense, given that by the early 1990s most scholars included the Armenian case in comparative studies of genocide. Moreover, the argument that the Holocaust was unique and could not be compared with other cases of genocide had become less salient by the mid-1990s, due in part to the 1994 Rwandan Genocide and the ethnic cleansing, massacres, and genocide during the Yugoslav Wars. Thus, Turkish officials stopped arguing that calling the deaths of Armenians "genocide" would devalue the term, and instead began to stress that Ottoman authorities had no *intention* to commit genocide, which is a necessary element of the international legal definition of genocide. For example, in May 1998 the Turkish Foreign Ministry issued a statement emphasizing that "it was a great tragedy but it also affected other populations of the Ottoman empire, including Turks. There never existed any plan for a genocide."[43] Retired Turkish ambassador Gündüz Aktan's September 2000 testimony before a US congressional committee highlights how Turkish officials were connecting evolving legal interpretations of genocide with their ongoing efforts to disavow official responsibility for the deaths of Ottoman Armenians. He stated:

> The crucial question is why the Armenians, not content with the word "tragedy" or "catastrophe", insist on genocide. . . . *What determines genocide is* not necessarily the number of casualties or the cruelty of the persecution but *the "intent to destroy" a group.* Historically the "intent to destroy a race" has emerged only as the culmination of racism, as in the case of anti-Semitism and the Shoah. Turks have never harbored any anti-Armenianism. Killing, even of civilians, in a war waged for territory, is not genocide. The victims of genocide must be totally innocent. In other words, they must not fight for something tangible like land, but be killed by the victimizer simply because of their membership in a specific group. Obviously, both Turks and Armenians fought for land upon which to build their independent states. Since genocide is an imprescriptibly crime [*sic*], Armenia has recourse to the International Court of Justice at the Hague and may therefore ask the court to determine, according to article IX of the Convention, whether it was genocide. But I know they cannot do it. They do not have a legally sustainable case. That is why they seek legislative resolutions which are legally null and void.[44]

At a time when international tribunals were grappling with how to define victim groups and intent, this argument attempted to reinterpret the norm against genocide by falsely claiming that genocide involves only "totally innocent" victims who are killed "simply because of their membership in a specific group."[45]

The deportation was also acknowledged more often in official statements, although references were still brief and oblique. In a 1998 letter to the French president, Turkish president Süleyman Demirel referred to "the settlement of Armenians in regions outside the war zone."[46] In April 1999, the Turkish consul general in Los Angeles reported: "Ottoman authorities took all the Armenians and sent them to Syria on foot. Many of them died along the way. This is what happened due to World War I and a civil war. It wasn't a genocide."[47] Moreover, the "deportation decision" was mentioned in all of the textbooks analyzed from this phase, in contrast to its mention in only half of the textbooks in the prior phase. It was also more strongly defended. For example, a 1995 textbook declared: "The Turkish nation definitely cannot be and should not be held responsible [*kesinlikle sorumlu tutulamaz ve tutulmamalıdır*] for what happened in the course of the Armenians' migration [*Ermenilerin göçü*]."[48]

Textbooks also emphasized the violence and the territorial ambitions of Armenians. A 1995 textbook described Russia's role in inciting nationalism in Ottoman Armenians, but then noted: "It was very easy to incite the Armenians; as a matter of fact, this is what happened. The leaders of the 'Armenian committees' that had been established were specially trained in Russia. With these armed gangs [*çeteler*], which were so crazed [*gözü dönmüş*] that they attempted to assassinate the Ottoman Sultan Abdulhamid II, the Armenian problem grew and continued."[49] Other official sources similarly emphasized Armenians' violence. For example, the introduction to a 1995 book of documents published by the Prime Minister's State Archives declared: "Armenians, under the influence of these states [i.e., Russia and England], first revolted, then later their uprising, while encompassing massacre, turned into genocide [*soykırım şekline dönüştürmüşlerdir*] intended to exterminate [*yok etmeye yönelik*] the Muslim-Turkish population living in Eastern Anatolia and the Caucasus. . . . These documents that are being published, demonstrate with utter clarity that Turks did not commit atrocities [*zulüm yapmadıklarını*] against Armenians, as the Armenians allege, but rather how Armenians committed genocide [*soykırım yaptıklarını*] against Turks."[50] In June 1998, President Demirel argued that "in 1915, the Armenians, provoked by outside forces, rebelled against the Ottoman state, resorting to extreme violence against the civilian population and the state forces."[51] The government's commemorative actions also reflected this emphasis on Armenian violence. Most strikingly, in October 1999 the Turkish government opened a museum and monument in the city of Iğdır that commemorated the "genocide" that Armenians had committed against Turks. A number of top officials attended and spoke at the opening ceremony, including President Demirel and Chief of the General Staff Hüseyin Kıvrıkoğlu.[52]

Textbooks also began to depict Armenians as traitors, accusing them of betrayal and noting that they tried to take advantage of the weakness of the Ottoman Empire and stabbed Turks in the back. A 1995 textbook stated: "Greeks and Armenians . . . took advantage of the bad situation into which the Ottoman State had fallen, cooperated with the occupying states and worked to break up our lands. . . . The Armenian Revenge Regiment, which had been established in Adana with the help of the French, started large-scale massacres. The goal of these massacres was to establish an independent State of Armenia in Eastern Anatolia."[53]

Finally, textbooks characterized the Armenian question itself as part of a set of lies and propaganda used to weaken Turkey and undermine its sovereignty. A 1994 textbook linked the Ottoman government's deportation decision to a series of imperialist provocations, games, and terrorism that extended from Armenian attacks during WWI, to Armenian terrorism against Turkish diplomats in the

1970s and 1980s, to Kurdish terrorism in the 1980s, and up to the Nagorno-Karabakh conflict.[54] A 1995 textbook cautioned that on the subject of Armenians, "there are baseless claims and propaganda directed against Turks and against the Turkish State."[55] Consistent with this contention, the government sent a letter to schools indicating that Greeks, Armenians, and Assyrians wanted to divide the country, and it created a program to prepare teachers to answer questions about allegations of massacres or genocide.[56]

Deepening Domestic Contestation and Renewed International Pressures

Although the changes in the late 1990s were limited, developments in the 1990s set the stage for later, more significant changes in the official narrative. Themes that emerged in the late 1990s became central to the narrative in the early 2000s, when Turkish officials redoubled efforts to defend the state's position. These changes came in response to a dramatic increase in international pressure, particularly around the year 2000. At the same time, the continued domestic contestation, along with shifts in Turkey's domestic politics, affected officials' decisions about the content and nature of the official narrative.

Between 1999 and 2001, developments in Turkish politics affected the legitimacy of the military and mainstream political parties. The Kurdish conflict, in which the Workers' Party of Kurdistan (Partiya Karkerên Kurdistan, PKK) had been engaged in a devastating civil war with the Turkish military since 1984, came to a conclusion with the February 1999 arrest of Abdullah Öcalan, the founder and head of the PKK. Then, in August 1999, a magnitude 7.4 earthquake hit near the industrial city of İzmit, an hour and a half outside of Istanbul. The earthquake killed an estimated thirty-five thousand people and destroyed thousands of shoddily constructed buildings and infrastructure. The slow and disorganized official response to the disaster, along with the fact that government officials had allowed contractors to erect so many buildings that did not meet safety codes, undercut the legitimacy of Turkish politicians and the state itself.[57] A year later, successive financial crises in November 2000 and February 2001 crippled the Turkish economy, forcing Turkey to secure two major loans from the International Monetary Fund and leading to a broad swath of reforms over the following two years. These crises further undermined the legitimacy of the governing parties.

Against the backdrop of these crises, the socially and religiously conservative AKP ran on a pro-EU platform and won a majority of seats in the Turkish Parliament in the November 2002 election. Unlike the CHP and the Nationalist Movement Party (Milliyetçi Hareket Partisi), the AKP was not beholden to traditional

power bases in Turkey, especially the military, and was not ideologically committed to Kemalism and its legitimating myths and narratives. This meant that legitimacy and identity concerns were potentially not as salient. Moreover, since
the 1970s, Turkey's Constitutional Court had closed most of the parties that
were AKP's predecessors in the Islamic political movement. Given this history, the
AKP sought to expand the scope of civil rights, especially religious expression,
and loosen the political power of the military and secular establishment.

These goals dovetailed with developments in Turkey's long pursuit of EU membership. In December 1999, Turkey was accepted as a candidate for EU membership. This was momentous, especially given that two years earlier the European
Council had decided not to open accession negotiations with Turkey when many
other countries' candidacies were approved. The announcement of Turkey's long-
sought EU candidacy, combined with the AKP's strategic prioritization of EU
membership, led to the passage in the early 2000s of reforms that expanded human
and civil rights and constrained the political role of the Turkish military. Although
the Turkish Parliament passed the first reforms before the AKP came to power,
once the AKP assumed power it passed a series of reforms to bring Turkish
laws further in line with the EU's *acquis communautaire*. By diminishing the role
of the military in political affairs and expanding minority rights and human rights
protections, the reforms expanded the space for debate on the Armenian question.

The reforms, in turn, led to the opening of EU accession negotiations in October 2005. Consequently, EU institutions' and member-states' statements and
actions on the Armenian question took on greater weight in the early 2000s.
Among EU institutions, the European Parliament and the European Commission
were the most influential. The European Parliament declared on several occasions
between 1987 and 2005 that Turkey's recognition of the Armenian Genocide was
a necessary precondition to joining the EU.[58] In contrast, the commission encouraged bottom-up and top-down reform efforts in Turkey while insisting that recognition of the genocide was *not* a precondition to joining the EU. Consistent
with the logic of the "boomerang model" of human rights influence, the commission amplified and gave weight to the voices of domestic advocates for minority and human rights.[59] It also funded a number of civil society projects, including ones that systematically track hate speech in the Turkish media, study
the role of education as a means to reconciliation on the Kurdish question, and
encourage the development of greater press freedom.[60] Consequently, the commission's use of conditionality and setting of clear expectations for reforms
introduced new calculations, a new actor, and additional funding into the domestic politics related to the Armenian question.

This coincided with and reinforced the expansion of Turkish civil society and
of public attention to the Armenian question. Building on developments in the

early 1990s, a small but growing number of activists, academics, and journalists began to discuss the Armenian question from a variety of perspectives. This work expanded public discussion of the issue and offered a different version of events for Turks to consider.[61] As a result, according to Ragıp Zarakolu, "holes were opened in the wall of silence."[62]

Since the release of Akçam's book in 1992, the publishers Belge, İletişim Yayınları, and Peri together published more than thirty books related to Armenians and the Armenian question. Meanwhile, Aras continued to publish Turkish translations of Turkish Armenian and diaspora Armenian literature, including more than thirty such works in the 2000s.[63]

Other publications challenged the official narrative in subtle but powerful ways, documenting the presence and stories of Armenians and other minorities in Anatolia prior to and after the genocide. In 2001, Osman Köker, who was a member of İHD's Minority Rights Monitoring Commission, started working on a project to educate people about life in Anatolia before WWI. Since then, his Birzamanlar Yayıncılık (Once Upon a Time Publishing) has published several books documenting the lives and presence of Armenians in the Ottoman Empire.[64] In 2004, Fethiye Çetin published a memoir about her grandmother, who was Armenian. Çetin learned this only toward the end of her grandmother's life, when the latter shared with her granddaughter the truth about her long-hidden identity and her experiences in the genocide and after. Çetin's book, *Anneannem* (My grandmother), was a best seller in Turkey. Other accounts of "secret or hidden Armenians" (*gizli Ermeniler*) have also been published.[65] Together, these books began "humanizing" Armenians for the broader Turkish population. As one civil society actor argued, work by Çetin, Köker, Dink, and others constituted "a sincere discourse" that stimulated more progress on the Armenian question than academic work and historical publications.[66]

Activism related to the Armenian question also expanded. The İHD commission remained active until around 2002.[67] Other nongovernmental organizations (NGOs) also began working on minority rights. Starting in the 1990s, the Turkish branch of the Helsinki Citizens' Assembly (Helsinki Yurttaşlar Derneği) nurtured Armenian-Turkish dialogue, jointly organizing (with the Yerevan branch) a June 2002 meeting titled "Civil Approaches to Turkish-Armenian Dialogue" and developing a summer school for Turkish and Armenian youths in 2003.[68] As Turkish civil society grew, a number of other groups pushed for free speech and human rights.[69] By the late 1990s, interest in the Armenian question had broadened beyond the small circle of human rights activists. Illustrating this, in 1997 a Turkish businessman and an Armenian businessman formed the Turkish-Armenian Business Development Council to develop and promote cross-border business opportunities. It has sought to build professional and business networks between Turkey and Armenia and to increase mutual understanding between Turks and Armenians.[70]

In addition, a small group of academics in Turkey, mostly from private universities in Istanbul, began to work on the Armenian question. Led by Akçam's pioneering work, a body of scholarship that Göçek has labeled the "postnationalist critical narrative" gradually developed.[71] An important part of this process was the establishment in 2000 of the Workshop for Armenian/Turkish Scholarship (WATS) by three academics at the University of Michigan–Ann Arbor: Göçek, historian Ronald Grigor Suny, and Armenologist Kevork Bardakjian. Seeking to build academic dialogue and improve scholarship on the Armenian question, WATS has organized an ongoing biennial academic conference and hosted a now-defunct e-mail Listserv. Through the workshops in particular, WATS helped build a transnational network of scholars and nurtured the development of an increasingly sophisticated body of scholarship on the Armenian Genocide.[72] Moreover, as the historian Halil Berktay noted, some of the Turkish scholars who attended the first WATS conference started thinking about how to engage in "scholarly activism" in Turkey, and many have been involved in related political and academic developments since 2000.[73]

Despite the significance of these developments, Necef reports that, in 2000, participants in domestic debates about the Armenian question who used the term "genocide" were a distinct minority. Alongside this tiny "genocide recognisers" group, Necef identified three other groups: "the 'mutual killings' group," the "'we are the real victims' group," which constituted the dominant view in public debates, and the "fourth group . . . [which] unabashedly defends the deportation and the massacres as a necessary measure which Turks should not feel any remorse over."[74] Thus, while it is important not to overstate the scope of critical discourse and contestation in this period, it contributed to the flourishing of public discussion on the Armenian question, challenged the official narrative from within Turkish society, and brought domestic and international attention to the state's narrative. And although Turkish officials did not change the official narrative in response to this contestation, when they did decide to update the official narrative, this contestation helped shape how they did so.

The trigger for change again came from international pressures. Between 1993 and 1998, Argentina, Bulgaria, Russia, Greece, and Belgium recognized the genocide, as did the Council of Europe's Parliamentary Assembly. In 1998, the US Congress considered a resolution to recognize the genocide and the French National Assembly passed a resolution recognizing the genocide. And between 2000 and 2001, several more states passed legislative resolutions recognizing the genocide.

These resolutions resulted in part from activism in the Armenian diaspora.[75] However, as noted in a report from the European Stability Initiative think tank, "Genocide resolutions have passed in countries with small Armenian populations" and with large Turkish populations, so Armenian activism was not the sole driver of these resolutions.[76] These resolutions have also been attributed to Armenia's changed policy after 1998, when Robert Kocharian replaced Levon Ter-Petrosyan as president. In contrast to Ter-Petrosyan, Kocharian made genocide recognition a foreign policy objective.[77] Even so, given Armenia's relative political weakness, it is unlikely that Armenia's policy change was a significant factor behind the passage of these resolutions.

Irrespective of their origins, this spate of recognitions disconcerted Turkish officials. In June 1998, the leader of the CHP, Deniz Baykal, declared in a speech to CHP parliamentarians: "'If the French Senate approves the bill, other countries' parliaments will inevitably follow suit and the issue may even be put on the United Nations' agenda.' . . . [He] warn[ed] that if the matter is internationalized, Armenian demands for restitution and repatriation may be raised as a result. The CHP leader also argued that a multitude of historians had refuted the claims of Armenian genocide in their research and had proved Turkey's position right. 'But in the prevailing circumstances, being right is not enough. We should initiate comprehensive activities to make the world accept that we are right.'"[78] Until 2001, however, Turkish officials responded to these pressures in an ad hoc fashion. Then, in the space of a few months in late 2000 and early 2001, the US House of Representatives considered a resolution to recognize the Armenian Genocide (H.Res. 596), the French Senate passed the resolution recognizing the Armenian Genocide that had been previously approved by the National Assembly, and the French resolution became law. These events were the proverbial final straws, in response to which Turkish officials began to reformulate the state's narrative and renewed efforts to defend it domestically and internationally.[79]

Phase Four (2001–2008): Rhetorical Adaptation and Renewed Defenses

In the fourth phase, the official narrative was characterized by continuities and shifts in emphasis and argumentation.[80] As in the early 1980s, international pressures triggered ambivalent responses, with greater acknowledgment coming alongside increased defenses. Given the increasing evidence available within Turkey that hundreds of thousands of Ottoman Armenians had died in the genocide, the official narrative shifted to acknowledge a higher death toll. At the same time, it rationalized this higher death toll and advanced new arguments for why the deportation of Ottoman Armenians did not fit the definition of genocide.

Turkish officials drew on the set of strategies developed in the 1980s and again sought the support of actors within and outside Turkey. Thus, despite early indications of AKP leaders' potential willingness to consider a different approach to the Armenian question,[81] bureaucrats, the military, the Turkish Historical Society (Türk Tarih Kurumu, TTK), and retired diplomats influenced the direction and nature of change. For example, when foreign researchers proposed to the TTK that they conduct joint research on the Armenian question—an approach the AKP promoted between 2005 and 2009—the efforts failed, particularly because of the grandstanding tactics of Yusuf Halaçoğlu, the TTK's head until 2008. This highlights the TTK's role as one of a set of institutionalized actors that imposed strong constraints on change in the state's narrative. In late 2002, the AKP's minister of culture, Hüseyin Çelik, alluded to these constraints in commenting on resistance to the proposed restoration of the Church of the Holy Cross, which is a medieval Armenian cathedral on Akhtamar Island in Lake Van. Çelik stated: "What we are up against is an undeclared policy by certain narrow-minded individuals, within the state. . . . The fear of these policymakers is that if Christian sites are restored, this will prove that Armenians once lived here and revive Armenian claims on our land."[82] As Çelik suggested, and in a striking example of feedback effects from earlier efforts to defend the state's narrative, state elites continued to shape the trajectory of the official narrative through their hold on the institutional mechanisms through which the narrative is reproduced and with rhetorical and other interventions in the public sphere, which rallied nationalist fears and served as warnings to the AKP and others of the risks of challenging the official narrative.

Bureaucratic and military elites' concerns were similar to those that shaped officials' responses in earlier phases. As Çelik's statement reveals, material concerns over territorial claims continued to predominate. A 2007 court ruling against two Turkish Armenian journalists who had used the term "genocide" also illustrates this concern. The ruling warned, "Talk about genocide, both in Turkey and in other countries, unfavorably affects national security and the national interest. . . . The claim of genocide . . . has become part of and the means of special plans aiming to change the geographic political boundaries of Turkey . . . and a campaign to demolish its physical and legal structure. . . . The acceptance of this claim may lead in future centuries to a questioning of the sovereignty rights of the Republic of Turkey over the lands on which it is claimed these events occurred."[83] Similarly, Üngör and Polatel report that the "archive of the land registers (*tapu kayıtları*) remains closed due to Turkish fears of potential Armenian material claims. These records, stored at the Land Register General Directorate (*Tapu Kadastro Genel Müdürlüğü*), contain the (presumably) highly detailed account books of confiscated Armenian property. In August 2005 Turkey's powerful Council for National Security . . . strongly and confidentially admonished the archive staff not to disclose their material because 'the data could be abused for the purpose of unfounded genocide and property claims.'"[84]

Alongside these material concerns, officials also sought to preserve the identity and legitimacy of the state and nation. As Turkish diplomat Yücel Güçlü explained in 2007, "If the entire world recognized Ottoman relocation policies and the massacres of 1915 as Turkish actions constituting genocide . . . it would be construed as character assassination and a violation of Turkish dignity. . . . [A] genocidal country is a shamed country . . . [and] Turkey should not be subject to this shame because the claims against it are patently false."[85] In a similar vein, in May 2005, PM Erdoğan declared to an audience of AKP politicians: "During its history, Turkey has never degraded itself to the vile cruelty of committing genocide. It's out of the question for us to accept this."[86] And in a 2007 interview, Erdoğan asserted: "Our history is not the history of genocides. Our religion would never allow this."[87] Finally, a 2001 article by Şükrü Elekdağ simultaneously highlights these material and identity concerns: "The charge of 'Armenian genocide' against Turkey is directly related to not only our national honor but also our foreign policy, economy, our image in the world, and our security. . . . Armenia, together with its diaspora, have declared war against Turkey. The objective of this war is to make Turkey pay reparations and then to put forward territorial claims based on charges of 'genocide.'"[88]

Finally, given that evidence about the genocide was increasingly available within Turkey, officials also sought to maintain a plausible and legitimate official narrative for domestic audiences. Ulgen emphasizes how in 2004, in response to the revelation that one of Atatürk's adopted daughters was Armenian, Turkish officials and the media rushed to counter this perceived threat to the nation's unity and Atatürk's memory. The chief of the general staff of the Turkish Armed Forces issued a statement arguing that the revelation "target[ed] our national unity and togetherness and national values" and asserting that "it is clear that defending the unity and togetherness of the Turkish nation . . . is an obvious duty to be undertaken by every Turkish citizen and by all institutions besides the Turkish Armed Forces."[89]

Defending the State's Story

Once international pressures reached a critical threshold in late 2000, officials acted to address them. Official efforts were first centralized, with the establishment in May 2001 of the Committee to Coordinate the Struggle with the Baseless Genocide Claims (Asılsız Soykırım İddiaları ile Mücadele Koordinasyon Kurulu, ASİMKK). Coheaded by the foreign minister and the secretary general of the National Security Council, this interagency committee included high-level representatives from key government ministries and organizations, including the Ministry of the Interior, the National Intelligence Organization, the Turkish

Historical Society, and the archives. ASİMKK's goals were to coordinate and execute a centralized strategy for responding to international pressures on this issue and to shape public opinion in Turkey and abroad. In announcing ASİMKK's establishment, the Directorate General of Press and Information stated that its purpose was "to dismiss—without causing negative effects on [the] country— efforts concerning the unjust and baseless genocide claims to which Turkey was exposed, and to eliminate their negative effects on [Turkey's] national interest."[90]

As in the early 1980s, think tanks and research groups were formed to aid in the production, defense, and maintenance of the official narrative. The most important of these was ERAREN, formed in late 2000/early 2001. This think tank was headed by the retired diplomat and founding head of İAGM, Ömer Lütem. Although nominally independent from the government, ERAREN was established with the involvement of YÖK, and many of its contributors were retired diplomats and former government officials. Until 2009, ERAREN was situated within the larger Eurasian Strategic Studies Institute (Avrasya Stratejik Araştırmalar Merkezi, ASAM), which also had researchers working on the Armenian question.[91] ERAREN published a quarterly journal in English and Turkish called *Armenian Studies/Ermeni Araştırmaları*, along with several books on the Armenian question, and it organized academic conferences to build networks among Turkish scholars working on the issue.[92] Another state-sponsored think tank established in this period was the Turkish-Armenian Relations National Committee (Türk-Ermeni İlişkileri Milli Komitesi, TEİMK). Established by YÖK in late 2002, TEİMK was active for about two years. The committee, whose members were academics, worked in conjunction with ERAREN to produce a handbook on the Armenian question that was intended for universities and was not sold publicly. ASAM subsequently published a larger reference book, which was an expanded version of the handbook.[93]

Also in 2001, a Track Two diplomatic initiative called the Turkish-Armenian Reconciliation Commission (TARC) was established. Whereas Track Two diplomacy typically refers to initiatives involving nonstate actors, TARC was a top-down, quasi-state-led effort: it was suggested and funded by the US State Department, and three of the four members of the Turkish delegation were retired high-level government officials who were reportedly in close contact with MFA officials throughout TARC's life.[94] Moreover, according to a member of the Turkish delegation, Turkish participation in TARC was an attempt to engage in dialogue to reduce the likelihood of another genocide resolution being introduced in the US Congress.[95] Thus, while TARC is generally considered a failure, from this perspective it was not, as Congress did not consider any genocide resolutions during the two years that TARC was active.

Updating the Official Narrative

With efforts more centralized and international pressures lessened for the duration of TARC's operation (2001–2003), officials reworked the content of the official narrative, introducing several notable changes alongside a number of continuities.

Although the overarching argument that what had happened was not a genocide continued, arguments for why the events should not be called a genocide shifted. The narrative continued to focus on the alleged massacres, uprisings, and rebellion of Armenians. For example, in 2005, Yusuf Sarınay, head of the Prime Minister's State Archives, announced that Armenians had massacred 523,955 Turks from 1910 through 1922. He argued that because Armenians wanted to establish a state of their own, in certain areas they committed systematic massacres (*belirli bölgelerde sistematik katliam yapmışlar*).[96] Textbooks more frequently mentioned Armenians' killing of Turks, albeit in less graphic terms than in the previous phase, and chronicled Armenians' plans to rise up against the Ottoman government in greater detail. This created a stronger overall impression of Armenians' disloyalty, without the textbooks using such strong language. For example, a 2005 textbook declared, "The Turkish Government is held to be responsible for these events, and there is talk of a so-called Armenian genocide. It should not be forgotten that a genocide was committed by the Armenians in Eastern Anatolia. Mass graves and discoveries, which are emerging with research and investigations that are being conducted today, document the massacres that Armenians carried out."[97] This less graphic language reflected a 2005 National Security Council decision to use more moderate language when referring to neighboring countries and to avoid expressions that would instigate animosity between peoples.[98] Related to this decision, Erdoğan announced in 2006 that the phrase "so-called Armenian genocide" (*sözde Ermeni soykırımı*) should not be used by government officials, who were instead instructed to use the more neutral phrase "the events of 1915" (*1915 olayları*).[99]

Several aspects of the official narrative were not changed: officials continued to emphasize that everyone had suffered during WWI and that "Armenian allegations" were only one side of the story. Official statements at times noted that the deportation was a decision that had to be taken to ensure the safety, security, and survival of Turks and Muslims. Similarly, textbooks continued to mention the passage of the Deportation Law. Instead of asserting that Turkey was not responsible for the outcome of the deportation, textbooks rationalized the decision as a "precautionary measure" to "ensur[e] the security of the army and the state."[100]

After 2005, several new themes were added to the official narrative. In particular, Turkish officials argued that allegations of genocide have never been legally or historically substantiated, thereby explicitly invoking international law. This new theme reflected Turkish officials' monitoring of international legal decisions related to genocide, and their conviction that genocide was primarily an international legal term and that a court should determine its applicability to the Armenian case.[101]

This rhetoric was a key part of official efforts to fend off charges of genocide. In 2002, the Turkish delegation to TARC requested that the International Center for Transitional Justice (ICTJ), which is a prominent transnational NGO, legally assess whether the UNCG was applicable to the Armenian case. Retired Turkish diplomat Gündüz Aktan, who was one of the Turkish delegates to TARC, believed that the ICTJ would conclude that the UNCG was not applicable because the events occurred several decades before the convention's passage and before the concept of genocide existed. Contrary to Aktan's expectations, the ICTJ's report, issued in February 2003, found that the case fits the UN definition of genocide, but that no legal claim could be made because it had occurred before the UNCG was established. This satisfied neither the Turks nor the Armenians on the commission and prompted TARC's dissolution.[102]

This argument—that the concept of genocide was not *legally* applicable to the Armenian case—became a key theme in official communications to international audiences. Illustrating this example of rhetorical adaptation, in a March 2007 op-ed in the *Washington Times*, Foreign Minister Abdullah Gül wrote: "With regard to the Armenian allegation describing the tragedy that befell them as genocide, the question, from the point of view of international law, is whether the Ottoman government systematically pursued a calculated act of state policy for their destruction in whole or in part. The answer to this question can only be established by scholars who have the ability to evaluate the period objectively, working with the full range of available primary sources."[103] In an October 2007 piece in the *Wall Street Journal*, Erdoğan wrote: "The truth is that the Armenian allegations of genocide pertaining to the events of 1915 have not been historically or legally substantiated. If the claim of genocide—the highest of crimes—can stand scrutiny and the facts are as incontestable as Armenian lobbies say, then the question must be asked as to why this issue has never been taken to international adjudication as prescribed by the U.N. Convention on the Prevention and Punishment of Genocide."[104]

The official narrative also began to emphasize the need for dialogue, Turkey's desire for reconciliation, and its readiness to face the past. This "norm signaling" reflects the fact that since 2000, the norm of truth-seeking has gained strength: calls have escalated for states and others to recognize and apologize for past wrongs, and public apologies for historic wrongs have increased.[105] In addition, transitional justice has been strongly endorsed by the UN, the EU, and international human rights organizations; and truth commissions and trials have become standard policies for countries emerging from authoritarian rule and conflict.[106] Since 2005, language reflecting this norm has been a key element of Turkish officials' statements to international audiences. In a 2007 article, Turkish ambassador Nabi Şensoy argued, "Our ultimate responsibility is to seek out the truth and engender reconciliation. We owe this to our past and future generations."[107]

This language of reconciliation and dialogue was accompanied by Erdoğan's 2005 invitation to Armenian president Kocharian to establish a "joint group consisting of historians and other experts . . . to study the developments and events of 1915."[108] The proposal for a joint historians' commission built on the longstanding theme that historians, not politicians, should address this issue. The narrative also emphasized that a full review of all the evidence was still needed and that the issue was still disputed or not yet fully grasped by historians, among whom—it was asserted—there was no consensus. For example, in the same 2007 article, Şensoy argued: "Many prominent historians have agreed with us that the world has yet to see a full review of the historical record."[109]

This shift acknowledged that by then a number of historians *had* looked into many of the historical details related to the events of the genocide. A notable indicator of this was the 2005 conference in Istanbul titled "Ottoman Armenians during the Decline of the Ottoman Empire." Dubbed the "Genocide Conference" in the Turkish press, this was the first time Turkish scholars had organized a conference in Turkey that focused on Ottoman Armenians—including on the genocide itself—and that challenged the official narrative. In so doing, the conference revealed that leading scholars in Turkey disagreed with the state's narrative.[110] The conference also challenged the official claim that the Armenian question should be "left to historians." On its surface, the conference was exactly what Turkish officials had long been calling for—qualified historians to look into the issue. In actuality, it was exactly what Turkish officials had long sought to avoid: Turkish historians challenging the official narrative and doing so using Ottoman and Turkish sources.[111] As a result, although the conference was originally supposed to take place in May 2005, the organizers postponed it because of ultranationalist threats and a court injunction. The most notable threat was from Minister of Justice Cemil Çiçek, who accused the conference participants of "stabbing the nation in the back."[112] At the same time, Foreign Minister Abdullah Gül offered behind-the-scenes encouragement to the conference organizers and sent a statement of support to be read at the opening of the conference.[113] Despite physical and legal threats, the conference was held several months later and without mishap at Istanbul Bilgi University. Given this conference and the emergence of a "critical postnationalist narrative," the official narrative shifted from arguing that historians needed to look into the events to claiming that further study of all of the relevant information was needed before accurate conclusions could be drawn.

Another new theme was the claim that other countries' efforts to legislate history would only do damage to Turkey's evolving relations with Armenia, as well as to Turkey's relations with the legislating country. For example, in response to a 2002 European Parliament resolution about the genocide, the *Turkish Daily News* reported, "The office of President Ahmet Necdet Sezer warned that such moves would not help stability in the Caucasus and efforts to improve ties between Turkey and Armenia."[114] And in May 2003, Minister of Education Hüseyin Çelik warned, "The Armenian societies in Europe and America should know that they are not doing good deeds for poor Armenia, struggling with a load of problems, instead they are giving harm."[115]

Turkish officials also questioned Armenia's own commitments to dialogue, truth, and reconciliation. They repeatedly called on Armenia to accept the invitation to establish a joint historical commission, hinting that Armenia's rejection of the proposal would indicate that it was afraid of what the evidence might show and implying that Armenia and Armenians did not want reconciliation and dialogue. In a May 2006 letter to the editor of the *New York Times*, Turkish ambassador to the United States Nabi Şensoy questioned why the Republic of Armenia had not accepted Turkey's offer to establish a joint historical commission, asking, "If the evidence is really there, why not accept this offer?" He then advised: "It is only through such a common dialogue that a process of reconciliation can begin. This may ultimately lead to closure for Armenians and Turks alike."[116] Striking a similar note in a March 2007 op-ed, Foreign Minister Abdullah Gül misleadingly claimed, "Turkey has no difficulties in facing its past. All Turkish archives, including the military archives of the period, are open to the entire international academic community. However, important Armenian archives are not." Gül closed with this call: "We are determined to save future generations from the hegemony of bitter rhetoric and outright hostility. . . . Self-examination is an inseparable part of any process of comprehension. In this regard, Turkey has been doing its share of soul-searching. It is high time for Armenians to do the same."[117]

Getting Out the Message

Along with the centralization of policymaking on the Armenian question and the retooling of the official narrative, officials redoubled efforts to disseminate the state's narrative. Replicating strategies initiated in the 1980s, officials focused on publishing books that countered arguments and evidence underlying claims of genocide. This led to a nearly twofold increase (from fifteen to twenty-eight) in the number of official publications between the late 1990s and the early 2000s. In particular, the state and military archives published a number of books of documents (nine and five, respectively, between 2001 and 2005; see Figure 3.1).[118]

The number of quasi-official publications also exploded. Beginning in 2002 and at the request of ASİMKK, the TTK refocused its efforts on the Armenian question, establishing an Armenian Desk and producing research that addressed the claim of genocide and drew from books and documents in foreign and domestic archives.[119] Hikmet Özdemir, the head of the Armenian Desk from 2002 to 2007, reports that he and three other TTK researchers conducted research in archives in England, Switzerland, the United States, and Germany.[120] Reflecting these efforts, the TTK published fifteen books on the topic between 2001 and 2005, compared with two books in each of the prior two five-year periods (1991–1995 and 1996–2000).[121] Official and quasi-official institutions also continued to encourage Turkish academics to work on the issue. The Turkish Historical Society supported Turkish academics working on the topic, and asked scholars to work on particular topics to address issues raised in publications that challenged the official narrative. If the resultant work was of good enough quality, the TTK then published it.[122] In addition, between 2001 and 2007, thirteen conferences on topics related to the Armenian question were held, compared with only six between 1994 and 2000.[123]

Turkish officials also sought to convey the official narrative to the next generation. Reflecting the importance of education in disseminating the state's narrative, one of ASİMKK's three working groups was the National Education Working Group.[124] Thus, the *Turkish Daily News* reported in 2002 that "the National Education Ministry . . . decided to teach issues related to so-called Armenian genocide claims . . . to elementary and high school pupils . . . to make students more aware of the issues and lobby activities related to 'Armenian Genocide Claims.'"[125] In 2003, the National Education Ministry required Turkish students in every grade, including those in Armenian schools, to write an essay refuting Armenians' genocide claims.[126] The ministry also directed the heads of schools to organize lectures and conferences that countered genocide claims and to hold "essay contests on the 'Armenian rebellion and activities during the First World War.'"[127] To comply, schools organized conferences and annual essay and poetry competitions.[128] The ministry also organized mandatory seminars to prepare teachers to answer questions about genocide claims, and distributed guidelines about points that should and should not be used in trying to shape public opinion on this issue.[129]

Internationally, Turkish diplomats actively cultivated support for the official narrative. This involved financially and administratively supporting organizations that backed the Turkish government's interests, financially supporting research that did not criticize official policies on sensitive topics such as the Armenian question, and employing PR firms and lobbyists to advocate on Turkey's behalf, especially in the US Congress.[130] Illustrating the commitment to such efforts, one observer estimated that "approximately 70 percent of the Turkish Embassy's time in Washington is spent trying to persuade leading Americans to support the Turkish position on the Armenian question."[131]

The close connection between the Turkish government and the ITS also continued. In a sign of this, in 2006 the historian Donald Quataert was pressured to resign as chair of ITS's board of governors because he had acknowledged the Armenian Genocide in a book review. In a letter of protest, the Middle East Studies Association wrote that Şensoy had "threatened to revoke the funding for the ITS if he [Quataert] did not publicly retract statements made in his review or separate himself from the Chairmanship of the ITS."[132] Efforts to suppress references to the genocide also took on a new, legal dimension. The Turkish Coalition of America (established in 2007) and other Turkish American groups launched several lawsuits against scholars and universities, including historian Keith Watenpaugh and the University of Minnesota's Center for Holocaust and Genocide Studies, claiming that references to the genocide had caused injury to particular parties.[133] Most of these lawsuits failed, but they increased the potential costs for those who work on and write about the genocide and have likely encouraged self-censorship in some scholars and continue to deter others from working on the issue.

Subsequent Developments

Alongside these changes in the official narrative, societal attention to the issue continued to evolve, partially in response to developments related to the official narrative, but also in response to more general trends in domestic politics. In particular, as Turkish society has become increasingly polarized, this issue has started to become a fissure *within* Turkey's domestic politics, not just an issue between Turkey and outside actors.

After 2005, the pace of EU-inspired reforms slowed significantly, the result in large part of deepening polarization in Turkey's domestic politics. The military and secular parties deployed increasingly vitriolic language and sought to discredit the AKP and mobilize the public against the party's feared Islamist agenda.[134] In this context, the Armenian question was used as an issue around which to rally support for nationalist groups and causes. Unfortunately, this was more than merely a rhetorical tool and led to serious violence and threats of violence against Armenians and Turks who challenged the official narrative. This included death threats against and the intimidation of Taner Akçam and other prominent journalists, academics, and writers,[135] along with the devastating January 2007 assassination of Hrant Dink by a seventeen-year-old acting on behalf of an ultranationalist group with suspected deep state connections.

In response to Dink's assassination, there was a huge outpouring of public support—including the participation of an estimated one hundred thousand people in his funeral procession in Istanbul—for his family and friends, as well as for the Turkish Armenian community. New efforts to fight hate crimes and challenge the official narrative were also launched in the wake of the assassination. A year after Dink's murder, members of his family along with a group of activists, academics, and journalists formed the International Hrant Dink Foundation (Uluslararası Hrant Dink Vakfı), which is dedicated to preserving his legacy by undertaking and supporting activities and projects that address the issues he worked on and advocated for during his life.[136]

Since 2008, a number of other civil society and human rights organizations have also begun to work on the Armenian question and related human rights issues. At the same time, groups that have long worked on the issue have gained more attention and support, both within and outside Turkey. Since 2005, the Istanbul branch of İHD has publicly marked and commemorated the anniversary of the Armenian Genocide each year on April 24.[137]

New academic efforts also emerged, most notably the annual Hrant Dink memorial workshop organized by academics at Sabancı University and a series of oral history projects led by the anthropologist Leyla Neyzi.[138] In addition, the Turkish Economic and Social Studies Foundation (Türkiye Ekonomik ve Sosyal Etüdler Vakfı, TESEV) has conducted several research projects that include discussion of the situation of minorities in Turkey, along with reports on the Armenian question and Turkish-Armenian relations.[139] Finally, four Turkish intellectuals launched an "Apology Campaign" in December 2008. This campaign, which was in part a response to Hrant Dink's assassination, consisted of a website with a simple message of apology directed at Armenians, to which individuals could add their names. The English text of the apology read: "My conscience does not accept the insensitivity showed to and the denial of the Great Catastrophe that the Ottoman Armenians were subjected to in 1915. I reject this injustice and for my share, I empathize with the feelings and pain of my Armenian brothers and sisters. I apologize to them."[140] The apology gathered more than thirty thousand signatures and generated discussion and debate in Turkey and responses from diaspora Armenian organizations and others. Although this campaign was significant, it also revealed differences of opinion among Turkish activists, since those that had pushed to include the word "genocide" in the apology were overruled by the organizers. Moreover, while the campaign received significant support within and outside Turkey, it elicited a much larger counterreaction from Turkish nationalists and diplomats, including two websites opposed to the campaign that gathered more than two hundred thousand signatures. And while President Gül was initially somewhat supportive of the campaign, he backtracked after being publicly criticized, and PM Erdoğan was dismissive of the campaign from the outset.[141]

Domestic contestation also extended to the political realm, where Kurdish politicians began to challenge the government's position, publicly calling for it to recognize and apologize for the genocide. In December 2008, for example, Osman Özçelik, a member of parliament from the ethnically Kurdish Democratic Society Party (Demokratik Toplum Partisi, DTP), brought up the deportation and killing of Ottoman Armenians in the Turkish Parliament and questioned his fellow parliamentarians' assertions that there was nothing to apologize for.[142] And in October 2009, Selahattin Demirtaş, the deputy chair of the DTP's parliamentary group, in the context of a discussion of Turkish-Armenian relations, called for the Turkish government to change its official policy, declaring: "In the last period of the Ottoman Empire, in the years 1915–1916, the Unionists, with the goal of Turkifying and Islamifying Anatolia, carried out a systematic policy of extermination (*tasfiye etme politikası sistematik bir şekilde uygulanmıştır*) of the non-Muslims and minorities who had lived for hundreds of years as a part of Ottoman society."[143]

These statements and developments highlight the broadening of domestic contestation around the Armenian question and the gradual loosening of some constraints on the discussion of the issue. This partial opening is attributable to the reforms and influence of Turkey's EU candidacy, the diminished influence of the military, and the influence and support of transnational connections among scholars, activists, and journalists within and outside Turkey.

And yet, polarization, nationalism, and violence have also dampened debate within Turkey on this issue.[144] The state continues to inconsistently sanction those who challenge the official narrative, and the topic remains a sensitive and "divisive" issue in Turkey.[145] Consequently, given the continued domestic constraints on information and speech, alongside the state's rhetorical adaptations, much of the Turkish public has been persuaded that the accepted, international definition of genocide is synonymous with understandings of the Holocaust. As Bakiner observed in 2013, "Most pundits in the mainstream media [in Turkey] refer to the mass killing of Armenians as a 'sad event,' a 'tragedy,' or a 'massacre.'"[146] Thus, while the official narrative is not the only reason why many in Turkey avoid the label "genocide" and question its applicability to the Armenian case, it has shaped the way that many Turks think and talk about genocide in general and the Armenian case in particular.

Against the backdrop of this increased domestic contestation and deepening nationalism, in 2008 Turkey and Armenia initiated a series of highly public and symbolic visits, accompanied by behind-the-scenes exchanges. This rapprochement was shaped by several factors. One was the AKP's "zero-problem neighborhood" approach, which led AKP leaders and the policy's architect, Foreign Minister Ahmet Davutoğlu, to work to improve ties with Turkey's neighbors. Second, the United States and the EU pushed Turkey to improve relations with Armenia. Third, rapprochement gained Turkey some respite from international pressures to recognize the Armenian Genocide, as states did not want to complicate or stall the possible improvement of Turkey's relations with Armenia. For example, in response to Turkey's stated commitment to dialogue and the thawing of relations with Armenia, the European Parliament changed its position on the issue in 2006. Whereas before the European Parliament had insisted that recognition of the genocide was a precondition to EU accession, since 2006 it has called on Turkey to work with Armenia to establish good "neighbourly relations" and to pursue a "process of reconciliation."[147] Fourth, Russia's invasion of Georgia in the summer of 2008 signaled to Turkish officials and others the risks of dependence on Russian energy, increasing the value of improving relations with Armenia, which could serve as an alternate transit country for oil and natural gas resources from the Caspian Sea.[148] This last factor, in particular, swiftly propelled Turkey and Armenia to more concrete steps. Thus in October 2009, the foreign ministers of Turkey and Armenia signed protocols agreeing to move toward the establishment of diplomatic relations between the two countries. Notably, one element included in the protocols was a commitment to create a subcommittee to look into the "historical dimension," which was understood to refer to the genocide.[149] Shortly after the signing of the protocols, however, the normalization process came to a standstill because of vociferous objections from Azerbaijan and from within Turkey.[150] Neither country ratified the protocols, and Armenia called for their termination in March 2018.

In the years since, domestic and international developments—including the Syrian civil war, the rise of the Islamic State of Iraq and Syria (ISIS), and the international refugee crisis, as well as deepening polarization and democratic erosion in Turkey—have drawn domestic and international attention to other issues. At the same time, legitimacy and identity concerns and material concerns have continued to militate against greater acknowledgment in the official narrative. With regard to legitimacy and identity concerns, a 2014 article in *Hürriyet* quotes Turkish ambassador Altay Cengizer, who refers to genocide claims as "claims that target its [Turkey's] own identity." Emphasizing the way in which such claims threaten the legitimacy of the Turkish nation, Cengizer explains, "Genocide is a political term, and Turkey does not deserve to be presented to the world as a nation that has committed genocide."[151] Given these concerns, the official narrative has not substantially changed since 2009 and officials have continued to work to minimize pressures for greater acknowledgment.[152]

THE NANJING MASSACRE AND THE SECOND SINO-JAPANESE WAR

The Second Sino-Japanese War was fought on the Chinese mainland between Imperial Japan and the Republic of China. The war unofficially began on 18 September 1931 with the Manchurian Incident, which served as a pretext for the Japanese military's invasion of Manchuria and its subsequent establishment of a puppet state in northeastern China. Although Japan's incursion into China began in 1931, the war officially began in the wake of the July 1937 Marco Polo Bridge Incident, which was a short battle between the Japanese Imperial Army and Chinese Nationalist forces over control of a bridge near Beijing. The Second Sino-Japanese War was fought within the context of the Asia Pacific War and was part of Japan's efforts to establish a colonial empire and regional hegemony in East Asia.[1] The war ended in 1945, when Japan surrendered to the Allied Powers and Japanese troops left the Chinese mainland.

During the fifteen-year period from the invasion of China to the end of the war, tens of millions of Chinese people were killed; many Chinese POWs were executed; tens of thousands of Chinese women were raped by Japanese soldiers, some in isolated incidents and others repeatedly in the "comfort women" system of forced prostitution organized by the Japanese military; approximately forty thousand Chinese men were forced into slave labor, during which about seven thousand died; and Japanese biological and chemical warfare programs— including those conducted by Unit 731 and others—killed more than one hundred thousand Chinese people.[2]

The Nanjing Massacre occurred within the context of the Second Sino-Japanese War. It began in December 1937, when the Japanese army invaded Nanking (as

Nanjing was then called and which was then the capital of the Chinese Nationalist forces), and extended into early 1938. During and after the capture of the city, Japanese soldiers burned much of the city, killed an estimated one hundred thousand to two hundred thousand civilians and POWs, and raped an estimated twenty thousand women.[3]

Several factors contributed to the occurrence and nature of the Nanjing Massacre. Longer-term causes include the dehumanization of Japanese soldiers by their own officers and by the fighting conditions in China, and the militarist and racist ideologies that were inculcated in the Japanese population by the wartime regime. As Eykholt explains, "Japanese military life created soldiers who . . . treated anyone beneath them with the same contempt that they experienced themselves." Moreover, according to the Japanese government's fascist ideology, "the Japanese were superior to all other peoples."[4] Together, these factors desensitized Japanese soldiers to brutality and dehumanized the Chinese people. Illustrating this, Yang points out that "the kind of brutality seen in Nanjing—wanton killing, raping, and looting—was by no means isolated, but rather characteristic of the war Japan was waging in China."[5] In addition, the Battle of Shanghai, which preceded the capture of Nanjing, was more difficult and prolonged than the Japanese side had anticipated, which contributed to a desire among Japanese officers and soldiers to exact revenge on the Chinese. Consequently, Eykholt explains, "when the soldiers reached Nanjing, their expectations of revenge, sex, and goods combined with the heightened desire to make an example of Nanjing and prove Japan's dominance. The results were atrocities against both civilians and prisoners of war."[6] Finally, the Japanese military's policy of taking no prisoners further contributed to the scope of the massacre.

In addition, the leaders of the Chinese Nationalist forces fled Nanjing as the Japanese military approached the city, leaving civilians defenseless and leaving Chinese soldiers without officers to organize the city's defense. Thus, Chinese soldiers attempted to blend in with the civilian population after the capture of the city, further contributing to the Japanese military's unlawful treatment of the civilian population.[7]

Although the Nanjing Massacre was a discrete event, it has become a symbol for the war as a whole and a lightning rod for debates over the Japanese Imperial Army's wartime conduct. By the late 1980s, Yoshida writes, "the Nanjing Massacre had become a part of Chinese national memory and a symbol of Japan's wartime atrocities and cruelty in China."[8] Because of this symbolism, debates over the nature of the broader war often focus on the Nanjing Massacre, and the official narrative of the massacre is entwined with the broader narrative of the Second Sino-Japanese War. As a result, official statements and actions about the Nanjing Massacre and the broader Second Sino-Japanese War are treated here as a single narrative.[9]

Disputed Elements of This History

As might be expected of an event that is often seen as a symbol for the conduct of an entire war, key aspects of the Nanjing Massacre are contested, including the death toll, the temporal and geographic scope of the massacre, the naming and nature of the event, and responsibility for it.

Estimates of the number of Chinese civilians and POWs killed by Japanese soldiers in the Nanjing Massacre extend from the claim that there was no massacre, which has been argued by Japanese revisionists from the "Illusion School"; to intermediate assessments, for example, by conservative historian Hata Ikuhiko, who estimated that there were approximately forty thousand deaths; to the figure of two hundred thousand deaths advanced in the Tokyo Trial's majority judgment in 1948; to estimates of one hundred thousand to three hundred thousand by Japanese historians from the "Great Massacre School," such as Hora Tomio and Kasahara Tokushi; to the official Chinese figure of three hundred thousand; to journalist Iris Chang's suggestion that the death toll could reach "into the 300,000 or even 400,000 range."[10]

Assessments of the temporal and geographic scope of the massacre influence the variation among these estimates. Some scholars narrowly define the time frame of the massacre, typically limiting it to the three-week period following the Japanese army's invasion and occupation of the city. For example, legal scholar David Askew defines the "Nanjing Incident" as "the killing and raping of large numbers of Chinese over a relatively short period of time by the Japanese military *after* the city of Nanjing was captured on 13 December 1937."[11] This geographic and temporal delimitation leads to a lower estimate of the death toll. In contrast, others more broadly define the temporal and geographic scope of the massacre and arrive at a higher death toll. Some include the area outside the city walls, while others include up to six counties in the surrounding countryside.[12] For example, journalist Honda Katsuichi defines the "Nanjing Massacre" as "the atrocities that occurred after the initiation of all-out war from the first Japanese advances to the time of the occupation of Nanjing, a three-month period of atrocities that included massacres, arson, rape, looting, and indiscriminate bombing."[13] Similarly, historian Joshua Fogel writes, "A great massacre occurred in and around Nanjing from December 1937 through February 1938."[14] In these examples, the massacre is argued to have started *before* the Japanese army entered the city walls of Nanjing, leading to higher death toll estimates. Not all discrepancies in death toll estimates can be explained by differences in the scope conditions by which scholars define the event, however.

In addition to the "Nanjing Massacre," the event is also known as the Rape of Nanking, the Nanjing Atrocity, and the Nanjing Incident. As with the naming of the broader conflict, the nomenclature used signals the interpretation of the nature of the event. As Yang explains, "'the Rape of Nanking' has been used primarily in the West. Since the end of the war, the Chinese have always referred to it as *Nanjing datusha*, which they have translated as the Nanjing Massacre. In Japan, *dai gyakusatsu* (great massacre) or *gyakusatsu* (massacre) tends to confirm the magnitude of an atrocity, as do *dai zangyaku* (great atrocity) and *Nankin atoroshitisu* (the Nanjing atrocities). *Nankin jiken* (Nanjing incident) clearly lacks these connotations, but it is occasionally used interchangeably with other terms."[15]

Understandings of the nature of and responsibility for Japan's conduct in the broader war have also been vigorously debated since 1945, both within Japan and in Japan's relations with other countries. Within Japan, a fundamental debate has been over the question of whether Japan's actions were "aggressive" and whether the war was one of "aggression." Other issues include whether the Japanese government was officially responsible for the comfort women system; the degree of official responsibility for the biological and chemical warfare programs, as well as for the suffering of slave laborers; the nature of Japan's colonization of Korea and other Asian countries; and official responsibility for Japanese forces' treatment of POWs, an estimated 27 percent of whom died as prisoners.[16] These debates have often been tied in with Japanese experiences and suffering in the war, including the atomic bombing of Hiroshima and Nagasaki by the United States and the Allied firebombing of Japanese cities, and the fairness of the International Military Tribunal for the Far East (known as the Tokyo Trial).

Establishing an Official Narrative, 1945–1952

The United States occupied Japan from its surrender at the end of the war until April 1952. During this period, central elements of the official narrative took shape, including the neglect of Asian victims, the emphasis on Japanese victimhood, and the contention that a small group of military leaders and civilians was responsible for the war and Japan's defeat.

Before the US Occupation authorities arrived in Japan, Japanese officials took steps to begin reshaping postwar views of Japan's actions. Fourteen days after the emperor announced the country's surrender, the caretaker PM called on the Japanese people to "repent" for their collective "sins" that were responsible for defeat. This call, referred to as "the repentance of the one hundred million," implied that the emperor was not responsible for the war.[17] Then, in early November 1945, the Japanese cabinet issued an official statement that explicitly disavowed the emperor's responsibility for the war.[18]

The US Occupation began in early September 1945 and was headed by General Douglas MacArthur, the Supreme Commander for the Allied Powers (SCAP). Several policies enacted during the occupation had a significant impact on the narrative in subsequent decades: key clauses in Japan's postwar constitution; evidence and arguments presented at the Tokyo Trial, along with MacArthur's decision to allow the emperor to remain in office; the US decision not to demand reparations from Japan; and the empowerment of conservative politicians and bureaucrats in the context of the emerging Cold War rivalry.

The "Peace Constitution" drafted by US Occupation authorities established lasting understandings of Japan's war legacy. Articles 1 and 4 of the constitution removed the emperor's divine status and circumscribed his role to ceremonial duties. Keeping the emperor in office helped construct the view that the emperor was a victim of the militarism and adventurism of the civilian and military leadership. It also complicated postwar discussions of war responsibility, since who could be called responsible for the war and Japan's atrocities if not the person in whose name the war was fought? In addition, decreeing that the emperor's role be ceremonial and apolitical led to persistent questions about whether it was constitutional for the emperor to apologize for Japan's wartime aggression. Also of consequence, Article 9 of the constitution declared: "The Japanese people forever renounce war as a sovereign right of the nation and the threat or use of force as means of settling international disputes." The renunciation of the use of force has been a fundamental issue in Japanese politics and foreign policy since Japan regained its sovereignty in 1952, with debate polarized along political lines and intertwined with issues of war guilt and responsibility. Conservatives have long advocated revising this clause and recognizing and expanding the role of Japan's military, known as the Japan Self-Defense Forces (JSDF). In contrast, leftists have opposed the revision of Article 9, fearing that such action would threaten Japan's neighbors and spark a revival of militarism. Finally, Article 20 stated: "The State and its organs shall refrain from religious education or any other religious activity."[19] This clause has framed debates over the constitutionality of Japanese politicians' visits to the Yasukuni Shrine, whose long-standing ties to the state were severed on 15 December 1945, when SCAP abolished State Shinto and the state's sponsorship and control of Yasukuni.

Postwar trials of Japanese officials and soldiers also helped establish key themes. The most significant postwar trial was the Tokyo Trial, which lasted from 1946 to 1948 and at which twenty-eight accused "Class A" war criminals were tried for playing leading roles (in military or civilian capacities) in violating the peace and waging war against the Allies. Of those tried, twenty-five were convicted and seven were sentenced to death.[20] The Tokyo Trial helped establish the idea that a small group of military and civilian leaders was responsible for the war. According to this "myth of the military clique," as Yinan He puts it, the Japanese people were victims of a small group of military leaders who had recklessly led the nation into war and were responsible for the destruction and brutality of the war.[21] This myth was bolstered by the fact that Emperor Hirohito remained in office and was absolved of all responsibility for the war.[22] In addition, the tribunal primarily focused on Japan's aggression against the United States, overlooking crimes against Asian victims and nations, which contributed to the neglect of non-Japanese victims in official and popular narratives of the war.[23]

One of the few atrocities for which defendants were prosecuted at the Tokyo Trial was the Nanjing Massacre, which was framed as representative of the Japanese army's war crimes. Among the twenty-five defendants convicted by the tribunal, two were found guilty and hanged for their failure as military leaders to prevent or mitigate the Nanjing Massacre.[24] The tribunal's majority judgment also established that "approximately 20,000 cases of rape occurred within the city [i.e., of Nanjing] during the first month of the occupation [i.e., from 13 December 1937]" and "the total number of civilians and prisoners of war murdered in Nanking and its vicinity during the first six weeks of the Japanese occupation was over 200,000."[25] According to Yoshida, this "set in place the standard understanding of the event in Japanese postwar historiography."[26]

In addition to information that came out in this and other postwar trials, the Civil Information and Education Section of the US Occupation Authority sought to educate the Japanese public about Japan's war crimes and atrocities, including the Nanjing Massacre.[27] Illustrating this, a 1946 elementary school history textbook characterized the Japanese army as "ravaging Nanjing."[28] Although such references were typically quite brief, Nozaki emphasizes, "they represented the view that the event took place in the context of Japan's aggression, involving atrocities committed by the Japanese Army."[29] More generally, and like the Tokyo Trial, textbooks published during the occupation blamed the war on a small group of militarists, rather than on the emperor or the Japanese people.[30] For example, a 1946 textbook declared: "Our citizens suffered terribly for a long time during the war. This unhappiness was caused by the militarists who suppressed our citizens and led us into a useless war."[31]

In early 1948, US policies in Japan underwent a "reverse course." Prior to this reversal, the United States aimed to rehabilitate Japan as a democratic and pacifist nation; to purge wartime leaders, conservatives, and nationalists from politics and the bureaucracy; and to have Japan pay reparations to the victims of its wartime aggression. As the Cold War took shape and tensions developed on the Korean peninsula, however, the United States reversed many of its occupation policies to ensure that Japan would be a strong, stable, and reliable ally in East Asia. Consequently, most of the nearly two hundred thousand wartime politicians, officials, and bureaucrats who had been arrested, charged, or fired in the first years of the occupation were released and/or permitted to hold public office, while more than twenty thousand leftists were removed from office in the 1950 "Red Purge."[32] As a result, many conservative politicians who had been arrested or banned from politics resumed positions of power. Prominent examples include Shigemitsu Mamoru, who had been minister of foreign affairs from April 1943 until the end of the war and who was deputy PM between 1952 and 1956; and Kishi Nobu-suke, who was a cabinet minister and Diet member in the early 1940s and was PM between 1957 and 1960. Both had been charged as Class A war criminals and yet both rose to the highest levels of power in the postwar years.

Over the longer term, this reversal contributed to a striking continuity in political leadership, which has been a source of stability in Japan's narrative. In particular, many members of the long-dominant and conservative Liberal Democratic Party (LDP) are the second or third generation in a family to be a Diet member. For such politicians, questions of war memory and guilt are not only political or moral issues but also personal ones concerning the actions of their fathers and grandfathers. Furthermore, for those politicians whose family businesses used forced labor during the war, admitting Japan's responsibility could mean *personally* having to pay compensation. Consequently, this continuity has meant that many politicians have had personal and material—in addition to political—incentives to avoid acknowledging the nature and extent of Japan's war crimes.[33]

Also as part of this policy reversal, US officials decided that to facilitate Japan's economic recovery and its establishment as a strong ally in East Asia, Japan should not have to pay reparations. In April 1946, before the "reverse course," the US government's mission on Japanese reparations had called for Japan to pay repa-rations to China and other Asian countries.[34] By May 1949, this proposal had been scrapped and the United States instead argued that the signatories of the San Fran-cisco Peace Treaty should waive Japan's responsibility to pay war reparations.[35] Consequently, the treaty—which was signed by Japan and the Allied Powers in September 1951 and went into effect on 28 April 1952—noted that Japan "should pay reparations to the Allied Powers for the damage and suffering caused by it during the war," but its resources were "recognized" as "not presently sufficient." Article 14 of the treaty then declared: "The Allied Powers waive all reparations claims of the Allied Powers, other claims of the Allied Powers and their nationals arising out of any actions taken by Japan and its nationals in the course of the prosecution of the war, and claims of the Allied Powers for direct military costs of occupation."[36] In an exception that arose from the Philippine government's strong protests, the treaty stipulated that those states whose "territories were oc-cupied by Japanese forces and damaged by Japan" could seek reparations from

Japan.[37] Consequently, Japan ended up paying reparations to four countries: Burma, the Philippines, Indonesia, and South Vietnam.

Since the signing of the San Francisco treaty and bilateral treaties with former victim states in the 1950s, 1960s, and 1970s, Japanese officials have argued that the issue of compensation is settled and that claims of individual compensation would not be considered. This position has been vigorously disputed by Korean, Chinese, and other claimants in political fora and in Japanese, Korean, and US courts. Nevertheless, alongside arguments about the statute of limitations and sovereign immunity, this agreement has been a nonnegotiable position for Japan and a bulwark against potentially vast claims. While Japanese and other courts have ruled in different ways on this issue, an April 2007 ruling by the Japanese Supreme Court definitively affirmed the government's position on this issue, finding "that the Chinese plaintiffs [in a forced labor compensation case and a "comfort women" case] did not have individual rights to claim compensation in the court."[38]

Finally, whereas Article 9 of Japan's constitution renounced war, after the reverse course and in the context of the Korean War, the United States pushed Japan to rearm. In early 1952 the Japanese government reluctantly established the "defensive" National Security Force, which became the Self-Defense Forces in 1954. As a result of this and the other policy reversals outlined above, Pyle observes that by the end of the occupation, Japan "was transformed from bitter wartime enemy to the lynchpin, the key ally, in the new U.S. security structure in Cold War Asia."[39]

As in the Turkish case, these early policies set forth themes that remained central to the official narrative in the ensuing decades.

The Trajectory of the Official Narrative, 1952–2008

Since 1952, Japan's narrative has moved from a baseline of mythmaking, relativizing, and silencing that was quite similar to Turkey's, to gradually acknowledging the Nanjing Massacre and Japan's aggression against China, acknowledging the harm suffered by Chinese victims in the massacre and in the broader war, and admitting Japan's responsibility for this harm. Since the mid-1990s, Japan's narrative has included general apologies for its past aggression and crimes, including the Nanjing Massacre. Alongside these steps toward greater acknowledgment and contrition, Japan's narrative has also exhibited increased mythmaking and relativization. The six phases in the trajectory of Japan's narrative from 1952 to 2008 are outlined below and shown in Figure 5.1.

The first phase lasted from 1952 through 1971 and was characterized by silencing, mythmaking, and relativizing. The international context—which was

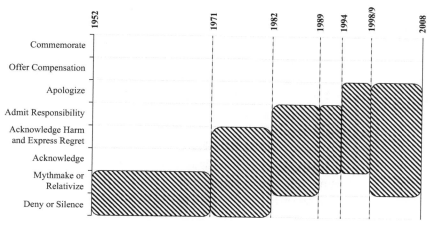

FIGURE 5.1.   Trajectory of Japan's narrative, 1952–2008

characterized by the Cold War prioritization of stability over ideals, and the lack of international expectations related to truth-telling—did not encourage truth-seeking. In addition, Japan's alliance with the United States and former victim states' need for political recognition and economic development meant that there were few international calls for greater contrition or acknowledgment of Japan's war crimes. Consequently, textbooks included scant coverage of war crimes and atrocities, especially in the 1950s and early 1960s, and official statements, commemorations, and other actions focused on Japanese victims and victimhood.

The second phase of the narrative began in 1971, as Japan and the People's Republic of China (PRC) began to reestablish diplomatic relations, and extended through 1982. The normalization of relations brought some demands for increased acknowledgment, but the continuation of the Cold War and the lack of international normative expectations related to truth-telling meant that these demands were relatively limited. As a result, official statements changed only minimally when Japan and China normalized diplomatic relations in September 1972. Japan expressed "deep remorse" and "deep regret" for having caused China "much trouble," and issued a statement that Japan was "keenly feeling responsibility."[40] At the same time, China gave up its right to claim war reparations or compensation from Japan, and commemorative actions continued to focus on Japanese victims. Meanwhile, domestic contestation led to shifts in textbook coverage in this phase, but conservatives' continued hold on power domestically meant that there was little other change in the state's narrative.

The third phase began in 1982 and extended through Emperor Hirohito's death in early 1989. Overall, the official narrative expressed greater remorse and more explicit acknowledgment, although the general tenor of acknowledgment was still vague. These shifts were reflected in official statements and in textbook coverage, which increased beginning in 1984. At the same time, new undercurrents relativized and mythologized the massacre and the broader war. In particular, between 1982 and 1987, PM Nakasone Yasuhiro pushed to instill more pride in being Japanese and regularly declared that it was time for Japan to "close the books" on the past and "settle political accounts."

The fourth phase began in 1989 and extended until 1994. In this period, the narrative ceased mythmaking about and relativizing the events, while official statements more strongly acknowledged wrongdoing and explicitly acknowledged a broader set of victims. In addition, non-Japanese victims were acknowledged in an official commemoration for the first time in 1993, and textbooks' coverage of the Nanjing Massacre and other war crimes increased.

The fifth phase began in late June 1994, when Murayama Tomiichi became PM, and extended until the end of 1998. The changes in this period included the issuance of the first official apology by a PM, increased textbook coverage of the Nanjing Massacre and Japan's war crimes, and the first explicit acknowledgment of the Nanjing Massacre in official statements.

Finally, the sixth phase began in 1999 and continued through 2008. In this phase, the narrative resumed mythmaking and relativizing, alongside the continued issuance of official apologies. The frequent apologies were accompanied by signals that officials were tiring of the perceived need to repeatedly apologize for Japan's past actions. These ambivalent signals included decreased coverage of war crimes in Japanese textbooks, increased resistance to international pressures to express greater contrition for Japan's past actions, and PM Koizumi Junichirō's annual visits to the highly controversial Yasukuni Shrine.

Explaining Changes in Japan's Narrative

Since the early 1980s, Japan's narrative has been the focus of international contestation and an issue in Japan's relations with China, South Korea, and other Asian countries. At several junctures, international pressures prompted Japanese officials to consider changing the state's narrative.[41] In each of these moments, however, domestic political constraints and pressures played important roles in shaping whether change occurred and the form(s) it took.

While this basic dynamic parallels the Turkish case, two differences have prompted greater and more frequent changes in Japan's narrative. First, as China's power increased, Japanese officials' interest in addressing Chinese demands deepened due to the increasing economic and political stakes of maintaining good relations. In contrast, ignoring Armenia's demands has been much less costly for Turkey, given the continued economic and political weakness of the Republic of Armenia. Second, Japan has faced pressures for change from a number of victim states, often at the same time. In contrast, Turkey faces a single victim state that has been independent only since the end of the Cold War.

In further contrast to the Turkish case, domestic pressures have triggered some changes in Japan's narrative, although international pressure has been a more significant trigger for change. In contrast to Turkey, where challenging the state's position on the Armenian question long risked prosecution or other sanctions, Japan has not had formal constraints on the discussion of history issues. As a result, the nature of and responsibility for the war have been contested, debated, and investigated within Japanese society since the early 1950s.[42] A second factor that has contributed to the greater degree of domestic contestation over Japan's past is that views about the past have often aligned with the left-right divide in Japanese politics. Consequently, conservative and nationalist domestic groups have pushed for diminished coverage of and contrition for the Nanjing Massacre and other atrocities, while leftists have pushed for greater acknowledgment and contrition. This push and pull of domestic political contestation has generated both constraints on and pressures for change.[43]

Turning to the sources of continuity, the decades-long dominance of the LDP and Emperor Hirohito's long reign—both of which the United States had a strong hand in establishing—sustained and reinforced continuities in Japan's narrative for its first several decades. As these structures have shifted—with Hirohito's death in 1989, the end of the Cold War, and the end of the LDP's dominance in 1993— they have facilitated changes in the state's narrative.

In terms of motivations, material concerns have not militated quite as strongly against change in Japan as they have in Turkey, which also helps account for the greater degree of change in Japan's narrative. Whereas Turkish officials have feared having to pay reparations and give up territory, Japanese officials have argued that the issue of compensation was settled in the San Francisco Treaty and in individual treaties with former victim states. Specifically, the Japanese government has argued that these treaties, which included *states'* waivers of reparations claims (or reparations agreements in four cases), also extended to *individual* compensation claims. While this position has been challenged, the Japanese government's maintenance of this claim has to some extent mitigated officials' fears of potential material costs. In addition, the territories that have been in dispute with China, South Korea, and Russia are largely uninhabited islands that are not part of Japan's main islands. The disputes over these islands revolve around national identity, diverging historical memories and interpretations, and the potential economic rents from natural resources and fishing rights.[44] While these issues are by no means inconsequential, they are not as serious as the potential territorial claims feared by Turkish officials, which amount to vast swathes of eastern Turkey and myriad valuable properties, homes, and businesses that were confiscated from Armenians in the context of the genocide.

Electoral-political concerns have been consequential for Japanese officials, often operating as a constraint on change. When considering changes in the state's narrative, Japanese officials have often sought to balance external pressures with the demands of right-wing politicians and activists, who advocate for the maintenance of the status quo or for *less* contrition and acknowledgment. Moreover, right-wing ultranationalists' threats, intimidation, and violence have deterred many civil society actors and politicians from supporting or calling for greater contrition and acknowledgment.[45] These ultranationalists have reinforced continuity in the official narrative, even against the views of the Japanese public, a majority of which supported greater official contrition for WWII-era crimes and atrocities from the early 1990s until the late 2000s.[46]

Legitimacy and identity concerns have also been salient, although they have been somewhat weaker in Japan than in Turkey. Most importantly, Japan's crimes were not genocide, as there was no intention to destroy the Chinese people. As a result, in contrast to Turkish officials, Japanese officials have not had to worry about the stigma of genocide. A notable exception was the journalist Iris Chang's characterization of the Nanjing Massacre as a "holocaust" in her best-selling 1997 book; however, her use of the label "holocaust" has not been more widely adopted.[47]

In spite of this legal distinction, identity concerns have importantly shaped Japanese officials' as well as societal actors' considerations vis-à-vis history issues. Japanese officials—and some parts of the public—have at times resisted labeling Japan's actions as "aggressive" and have attempted to elide the military's agency in war crimes and atrocities in order to defend a more "heroic" and less "masochistic" view of Japanese identity. In contrast, politicians and activists on the left have pushed for greater acknowledgment and contrition for Japan's wartime actions to reinforce the country's identity as a pacifist and democratic nation. Moreover, over time, as Japan became one of the world's leading economies and its leaders sought an international political role commensurate with the country's economic status, they realized that, given shifting international expectations about truth-telling, it might be necessary to address external demands for greater apology, recognition, and compensation to strengthen Japan's international political reputation. Thus, legitimacy and identity concerns have played an important role in shaping domestic contestation over history issues and in framing officials' attitudes toward the state's narrative.

"HISTORY ISSUES" IN THE POSTWAR PERIOD (1952–1989)

It is an unfortunate fact that, throughout Japan's history, it has never been possible for the people to alter the nation's power structure on their own: all the important transformations have come about through *galatsu*, or "outside pressure." Even the sketchy descriptions of the Nanjing Massacre in Japanese textbooks came about through external pressure from China and the government's grudging acknowledgment.

—Journalist Honda Katsuichi

Phase One (1952–1971): Cold War Realpolitik and Japanese Victimhood

The first phase of Japan's narrative was characterized by silencing, mythmaking, and relativizing and lasted from the return of Japan's sovereignty in 1952 until the beginning of negotiations to normalize relations with the PRC in 1971. The narrative included a broad silence and lack of acknowledgment of the Nanjing Massacre and other aspects of Japan's aggression, with little coverage in textbooks, especially in the 1950s and early 1960s. Symbolic actions by state leaders silenced and minimized these events, focusing instead on Japanese victims and victimhood.

International and domestic structural factors—namely, the Cold War, Japan's lack of diplomatic relations with China, and the dominance of the LDP—shaped the political context and reinforced these silences in the official narrative. Former victim states prioritized economic growth and stable relations with Japan, while the alliance with the United States emphasized stability over introspection. In addition, truth-telling and truth-seeking were not yet seen in terms of human rights, so international normative expectations along these lines were nonexistent. As a result of this confluence of factors, there were few international pressures for greater contrition and acknowledgment, and history issues were mainly debated and discussed at the domestic level. Within Japan, conservative and leftist social movements developed around issues of war memory and responsibility, but conservative groups were more powerful and effective. Consequently, over the course of this phase, textbook coverage of atrocities diminished and war criminals were destigmatized and honored.

Given Japan's place in the Cold War power structure and the economic and political disparities between Japan and former victim states, realpolitik principally governed how Japan dealt with questions of reparations and apologies in the first couple of decades after the war. Japan's foreign policy was dominated by its security relationship with the United States, which dictated a lack of relations with China and minimized external pressure on Japan regarding its wartime behavior. The development of markets and opportunities for trade was also central to Japan's decisions to issue statements of apology and regret, and to offer development aid (or, in a few cases, reparations). Thus, when PM Kishi toured fifteen Southeast Asian countries in 1957, in part to "make amends for the suffering she [Japan] caused in World War II," the underlying motivation was to restore relations with Japan's neighbors to secure its importance within the region.[1]

Official statements of contrition, which typically accompanied the normalization of relations, were highly circumscribed in the first two decades after the war. Japan expressed sorrow, regret, and remorse—but not apology—to several former victim states with which it normalized relations. In 1952, Japan signed a peace treaty with Taiwan, in which the latter received neither reparations for nor recognition of its wartime suffering, despite the fact that Taiwan had pushed for reparations in the treaty negotiations.[2] Instead, Japan expressed "'regret' (*ikan*) for 'unfortunate events' (*fukōna jiken*)."[3] And in 1965, after several failed negotiations and under strong pressure from the United States, Japan normalized relations with South Korea.[4] South Korea had sought an official apology, but Japanese diplomats refused because of political concerns about domestic backlash in Japan and also because of material concerns that an apology could lead Korea to press harder for reparations.[5] Instead, Japanese foreign minister Shiina Etsusaburō stated: "In our two countries' long history there have been unfortunate times (*fukō na jiki*), it is truly regrettable (*makoto ni ikan*) and we are deeply remorseful (*fukaku hansei*)."[6] As Yamazaki notes, "The terms 'remorse (*hansei*)' and 'regret (*ikan*)' as well as 'unfortunate past' in these early statements establish[ed] the basic vocabulary for apologies that follow."[7] Korea also gave up its right to claim reparations from Japan and in exchange received economic development aid.[8] (Note that, at the time, South Korea was under a military regime, which meant that domestic mobilization related to history issues was unlikely to arise to challenge the treaty's terms.[9])

Most other countries similarly subordinated reparations claims to their need for political recognition and economic aid. Consequently, the only countries to which Japan paid reparations were Burma, the Philippines, Indonesia, and South Vietnam, to which Japan paid a total of 3.643 billion yen (about 10 million USD) in reparations.[10]

Aside from these developments, in the first two decades after the war, debates over history issues were primarily contained within the bounds of domestic politics in Japan, falling along the left-right divide and revolving around the treatment of war criminals, the content of and control over textbooks, and official worship at the Yasukuni Shrine. As with its foreign affairs, Japan's alliance with the United States similarly influenced its domestic politics. The "reverse course" had reinstated conservatives in power and facilitated the further consolidation of their power. Under the "1955 System," the conservative LDP controlled the Diet and Japanese politics from its formation in 1955 (from the joining of the Liberal and Democratic Parties) until 1993.[11] This structural feature of Japan's domestic politics shaped continuities in the content of the state's narrative, via both LDP politicians' influence in the executive and legislative branches and conservative administrators' dominance of bureaucracies such as the Ministry of Education.

Alongside this structural feature of domestic politics, domestic contestation was characterized by a back-and-forth dynamic between conservative and leftist activists focused on the commemoration of the war, compensation for veterans and war-bereaved families, and textbook coverage of Japan's war crimes. Even before Japan regained sovereignty, a movement led by war criminals and citizens emerged to advocate for lenient treatment and the release of imprisoned war criminals, arguing that treating them as criminals was a form of victor's justice and unfairly punished soldiers' and officers' families.[12] Within a few years, the movement shifted the public's understanding of accused Class A, B, and C war criminals from "war criminals" to "war victims," and in some cases to "war heroes." The movement also gathered the signatures of millions of Japanese citizens on a petition for the parole of imprisoned war criminals.[13] In response, "in August 1953, the Diet unanimously revised the law so those executed after the [Tokyo] trials were regarded as war casualties. Further revisions in 1954 and 1955 also saw time spent in Allied-controlled prisons as time served performing official duties. As a result, all Class A prisoners still held were released in March 1956, while all Class B and C prisoners were freed in May 1958."[14] This movement reinforced the myth that responsibility for the war was held by a small group of militarists, which was a form of mythmaking, and relativized Japan's war crimes and atrocities by labeling Japanese war criminals as victims. Another, more concrete consequence of this movement was that several accused Class A war criminals went on to hold high political offices in the 1950s and 1960s, including Kishi Nobusuke, who served as foreign minister and then PM.

At the same time, but coming from a very different perspective, an alliance of organizations began to advocate in the early 1950s for the establishment of diplomatic relations with China and the development of trade and economic contacts. The alliance was led by the Japan-China Friendship Association (Nihon

Chūgoku yūko kyōkai), which was formed in Japan in October 1950 by a group of leftist intellectuals, Socialist politicians and activists, and businessmen, many of whom had long-standing ties to China. From its beginning, the group argued for the normalization of relations with China and official recognition of Japan's war crimes. This and other groups, working separately and together in the Committee for Mourning the Martyred Chinese Prisoners (Chūgokujin horyo junansha irei jikkō iinkai), which was established in 1953 by the Friendship Association, also pushed for Japan and Japanese citizens to remember Chinese victims of the war.[15] In 1957, the Liaison Society for Returnees from China (Chūgoku kikansha renrakukai, known as Chūkiren) was established by about one thousand Japanese soldiers who had fought in China during the war and who were held in China as POWs until 1956. Until its dissolution in 2002, Chūkiren members spoke out about their experiences and actions during the war, including atrocities they had personally committed, and encouraged the development of friendly relations with China.[16]

In spite of this advocacy, Japanese victims and victimhood remained a central focus in the state's narrative as well as in public discourse, while Chinese and other victims of Japan's actions were largely unacknowledged (and thus silenced). Alongside the themes established in the occupation period, another factor contributing to the narrative of victimhood was the devastating and unprecedented atomic bombing of Hiroshima and Nagasaki by the United States. In the mid-1950s, in response to the Lucky Dragon Incident, in which the crew of a Japanese commercial fishing boat was exposed to fallout from a US thermonuclear test at Bikini Atoll, an activist movement opposing the use of nuclear weapons took shape in Japan. While the movement was pacifist and leftist, the unique suffering of Japanese victims of the bombings of Hiroshima and Nagasaki was a central focus of its activism.[17]

This focus on Japanese victimhood was particularly evident in commemorative activities, notably official worship at the Yasukuni Shrine in Tokyo. Yasukuni is a Shinto shrine at which the spirits (*kami*) of Japanese soldiers killed while fighting in the name of the emperor are symbolically interred. It was state-funded and state-controlled until the end of the war, but the occupation authorities ended the state's support for the shrine. Shortly after the end of the occupation, the issue of the state's relationship to the shrine was reopened. In 1946 and 1947, the Association of Shinto Shrines (Jinja Honchō) and the Japan League for the Welfare of the War Bereaved (Nihon izoku kōsei renmei) were established, the latter by war-bereaved families. In 1953, the Japan League for the Welfare of the War Bereaved was renamed the Japan War-Bereaved Families Association (Nihon Izokukai). These conservative interest groups lobbied politicians to renew state funding for the shrine, pushed government officials and the emperor to worship

at the shrine, and helped bureaucrats in the Ministry of Health and Welfare identify soldiers killed in the war so their spirits could be enshrined at Yasukuni.[18]

These efforts quickly bore fruit. In 1955, the Military Pension Law of 1953 was
revised to make convicted war criminals and their families eligible for compensation as war veterans, making it possible for war criminals to be enshrined at
Yasukuni.[19] Within a few years, the Ministry of Health and Welfare began giving
the names of Class B and C war criminals to Yasukuni Shrine officials for enshrinement, and in 1966 the ministry sent the names of fourteen Class A war criminals
to the shrine. As Breen explains, "The Ministry's position . . . was that the war only
ended with the departure of the American Occupation in 1951. [Therefore, t]he
war criminals were executed during 'war time' and were technically 'war-dead.'"[20]
At the time, Yasukuni's head priest opposed the enshrinement of Class A war
criminals, apparently out of consideration for the emperor, who opposed this
step, and because it might have generated opposition to the reinstatement of
state support for the shrine.[21] Consequently, the Class A war criminals' spirits
were not enshrined at Yasukuni until late 1978, when a new head priest was in-
stated. Thus, while four of the six PMs in this period visited the shrine, as did
Emperor Hirohito seven times between 1952 and 1975, none of these visits provoked international protests, primarily because shrine visits had not yet become
politicized in Japan's relations with neighboring countries.[22]

The focus on Japanese victims—and the concomitant silencing of the existence
of non-Japanese victims—was further manifested in the National Memorial Service for the War Dead, first held on 15 August 1963. This annual service, which
was created in response to Izokukai's demand for a public commemoration of
the war dead, "is dedicated 'to the war dead (soldiers; civilian employee families;
those who died an unnatural death outside Japan; those killed by warfare in
Japan; others) in the wars following the China Incident.'"[23] Until 1993, the only
victims acknowledged at the service were Japanese.[24]

The Japanese government also offered compensation and support for war victims and their families, but primarily for Japanese soldiers and the families of
soldiers killed in the war. Again as a result of Izokukai's lobbying, fourteen victims' aid laws were passed in the 1950s and 1960s. Four were explicitly restricted
to Japanese citizens, and the rest focused on groups mostly composed of Japanese citizens, such as soldiers and their families and victims of the atomic bombings in Hiroshima and Nagasaki.[25] Seraphim reports that "the [1952] War-injured
and War-bereaved Families Support Act . . . regarded the war bereaved explicitly
as *victims of war* and constituted the basis on which the government awarded a
one-time condolence payment and, beginning in August 1953, annual pensions."[26]
Every ten years since then, the Japanese government has offered bonds to survivors and families of deceased Japanese veterans.[27]

Along with the silencing inherent in the non-acknowledgment of non-Japanese victims, the government took steps in this period to silence and downplay Japan's war crimes. In a striking example of this, in the late 1940s and early 1950s, the Japanese government—particularly the Ministry of Foreign Affairs (MOFA)—actively suppressed information about the wartime slave labor program.[28] In addition, Japanese textbooks said little about the Nanjing Massacre and other war crimes. According to a textbook editor, "From the 1950s until the early 1970s, high-school textbooks referred briefly to a war between Japan and the United States, but gave students no hint that Japan had invaded neighbouring countries."[29] Nozaki reports that although the Nanjing Massacre was sometimes mentioned in history textbooks, references were brief and did not include the number of people killed or other details. A 1952 high school textbook stated: "The occupation of Nanjing resounded throughout the world because of the notoriety of 'the violent incident of Nanjing,' so called because of the Japanese Army's destruction of the city, its pillaging, and its assaults." And a 1954 social studies textbook reported: "At the time [of capturing Nanjing], the army, entering the fortress Nanjing in triumph, inflicted severe acts of violence on the civilians. Because of this, the people of the world increasingly denounced Japan and sympathized with China."[30] This limited coverage partially resulted from the fact that, starting in 1953, primary and secondary school textbooks had to be approved by the Ministry of Education (MOE), which thus influenced what and how much was said about the war. For example, Nozaki reports, "In the 1955–56 textbook screening, the MOE commented: 'Do not write bad things about Japan in [describing] the Pacific War. Even though they are facts, represent them in romantic [language].'"[31]

Despite textbooks' limited coverage of the Nanjing Massacre and other war crimes, in 1955 conservatives within and outside the LDP launched the first textbook "offensive." They charged that textbooks featured too much negative coverage of Japan's wartime actions and that they should instead encourage patriotism and morals.[32] Illustrating this, in May 1962 PM Ikeda Hayato declared: "In order to build a superior nation, a nation that will be trusted throughout the world, it is necessary for all of the Japanese people to love their homeland and their nation's culture and history, to attain sound judgment and superior technique, and to cultivate a character that will be respected by people throughout the world."[33] The campaign succeeded, reducing textbooks' already scant references to Japan's wartime atrocities, in part by further centralizing the MOE's control over textbook curricula and approval. Thus, by the early 1970s, a textbook editor noted, "We couldn't even mention the Nanjing incident in a footnote."[34]

In response to this campaign, in 1955 a countermovement led by the influential left-wing Japan Teachers' Union (Nihon kyōshokuin kumiai, known as

Nikkyōso) emerged. Nikkyōso opposed textbook revisions that attempted "to beautify the aggressive war in the past, accentuate the position of the Emperor, glorify the policy of the Government, give weight to people's duties rather than their rights, and regard countries of Asia and Africa as underdeveloped countries."[35] These efforts attracted national attention beginning in 1965, when the historian Ienaga Saburō launched the first of three lawsuits against the MOE's textbook approval process. In 1957, Ienaga had written a history textbook called *A New History of Japan*, which the MOE approved only after Ienaga had made many revisions. When Ienaga submitted this textbook for reapproval in 1962, the MOE requested hundreds of revisions, particularly to descriptions of wartime atrocities such as the Nanjing Massacre.[36] Ienaga later reported that in one place "the [ministry's textbook] examiner insisted that: 'If atrocities by Japanese troops are described, similar actions by Soviet forces should also be included or the text will be biased. And what about the Americans?'"[37] According to contemporaneous reporting, "The official reason for rejection was that . . . Ienaga's textbook departed far from the goals of history education, which calls for greater recognition of our ancestors' endeavors, enhancement of our self-awareness as Japanese and fostering a love for the nation."[38] In response, Ienaga's lawsuit "charged that the textbook certification process was illegal and a violation of four constitutional rights: the freedoms of thought (Article 19) and expression (Article 21), plus academic freedom and the freedom of children to an education (Articles 23 and 26, respectively)."[39] This case, combined with two more filed in 1967 and 1984, marked the beginning of a three-decade-long legal challenge to the MOE's textbook approval process and its relativizing and silencing of Japan's war crimes.[40]

Phase Two (1971–1982): Normalization and Acknowledgment

The second phase began in 1971, as Japan was in the process of reestablishing diplomatic relations with China, and extended through 1982. Alongside a continued focus on Japanese victims, the official narrative shifted to include a general acknowledgment of the events and the harm suffered, along with vague expressions of regret. These changes were driven by domestic activism and expectations and pressures that arose in the context of the normalization of relations between Japan and China. The normalization of relations with China prompted stronger statements of contrition, but these statements were limited by the Cold War context that prioritized realpolitik over idealpolitik, the lack of international expectations related to truth-telling, and China's relative weakness. In addition, domestic contestation led to increased and then decreased acknowledgment in

Japan's textbooks, but prompted little other change in the official narrative. At the same time, Japan's strategic alliance with the United States and the LDP's continued hold on power reinforced continuities in the official narrative.

Japanese politicians and diplomats began to think seriously about normalizing relations with China in the late 1960s, but they held back from doing so because the United States opposed it.[41] Within a few years, however, both the United States and Japan established relations with China. In July 1971, the United States announced that President Richard Nixon would visit China in February 1972 to formalize a rapprochement between the two countries. This "Nixon shock," so called because Japan was notified only shortly before the announcement, caught Japanese leaders off guard and prompted a questioning of Japan's alliance with the United States and a rush to normalize relations with China.

As this process began, Japanese officials acknowledged that Japan had committed wrongs against China during the war and argued domestically that Japan would need to apologize to China for those wrongs. In an October 1971 Diet committee meeting, PM Satō Eisaku stated: "Japanese militarism in China has left deep wounds which cannot easily be healed, and I recognize fully what we have done in the past." At the same time, Foreign Minister Fukuda Takeo declared, "It was a mistake to send a Japanese army to the mainland and victimize the Chinese, for which we must apologize."[42] A few months later, in December 1971, Fukuda told a Diet committee: "Mutual reliance is a prerequisite for normalization of diplomatic relations between Japan and the People's Republic of China. In order to attain this, it is necessary for the Japanese Government to apologize to the Chinese people for what Japan did during the war."[43] And in a Diet committee meeting a few months later, cabinet minister and soon-to-be PM Tanaka Kakuei opined that "the first precondition for the normalization of diplomatic relations with China is our understanding that Japan caused China enormous trouble and that we truly want to offer an apology from the bottom of our hearts. This belief of mine is now unshakable and will never change in the future."[44]

When Japan and China normalized diplomatic relations in September 1972, however, neither Japanese leaders' statements nor the joint communiqué issued by the two countries included an expression of apology.[45] Instead, Japanese officials' statements were limited to expressions of "deep remorse" and "deep reproach" for having caused China "huge trouble" and "serious damage." Thus, in September 1972, PM Tanaka told Chinese premier Zhou Enlai: "I would like to express my deep remorse for the huge trouble [*meiwaku*] which Japan caused to the Chinese people."[46] And the joint communiqué announcing the normalization of diplomatic relations noted: "The Japanese side is keenly conscious of the responsibility for the serious damage that Japan caused in the past to the Chinese people through war, and deeply reproaches itself."[47] This retreat from Japanese leaders' earlier assertions of the need for an apology was largely due to the fact that China did not demand an apology, which stemmed in part from Chinese leaders' desire to normalize relations and to increase trade and economic relations with Japan. In the absence of pressure to apologize, Japanese leaders elected not to do so at this juncture.

Official statements of regret and remorse were, thus, relatively isolated. Illustrating this is a speech by PM Fukuda marking the signing of the 1978 Treaty of Peace and Friendship with China.[48] Fukuda emphasized the long history of positive relations between Japan and China, and then deftly skimmed over the first part of the twentieth century, stating: "But in this century, they [Japan and China] experienced hardships due to unfortunate relations. This should never be allowed to happen again. This is exactly what the two countries have pledged in the Japan-China peace and friendship treaty."[49] Emperor Hirohito also issued a vague statement about the war in the wake of normalization. Addressing Chinese premier Deng Xiaoping, he vaguely declared: "At one time, there were unfortunate events."[50] While this statement did not advance the official language of contrition, the fact that the emperor said *anything* about the war was new. Typically, Hirohito avoided the topic. As Dower reports, "When a journalist . . . ask[ed] Hirohito his thoughts about 'war responsibility' in a famous press conference in 1975, . . . the emperor's response was revealing. 'Concerning such a figure of speech,' he said, 'I have not done much study of these literary matters and so do not understand well and am unable to answer.'"[51]

China also waived its right to war reparations, even though Japan was reportedly prepared to pay up to $10 million in reparations.[52] According to Wan, Chinese officials made this decision "(1) to express friendly intentions to Japanese people; (2) to avoid a repeat of the situation like that in which the Nazis came to power in Germany partly due to the economic difficulties resulting from huge reparations; and (3) because some governments, including Taiwan, had already given them up."[53] In exchange, Koga points out, China expected "that Japan not forget its past and never again resort to militarism and that it keep that promise by becoming a good neighbor and economic partner."[54] In lieu of formal reparations, in 1979 Japan began granting low-interest yen loans and Official Development Assistance (ODA) to China. The first yen loan, in the amount of 330.9 billion yen (about 1.38 billion USD), was announced in late 1979.[55] This was followed by subsequent low-interest loans and foreign aid, making China one of the top recipients of Japanese aid. Crucially, these loans and aid were mutually understood as an unofficial form of reparations.

Confirming this understanding, Whiting writes that "in . . . interviews, Japanese officials asserted, 'We owe it to China. We must help after all the damage we did to them.'"[56] The ODA and loans also gave Japanese firms valuable access to China's growing domestic market.[57]

The agreements that marked the normalization of relations with China reinforced dominant aspects of the official narrative, notably the myth that a small group of militarists was responsible for the war. As Wan reports, "Mao and Zhou explained China's decision not to demand reparations on the ground that the Japanese people, who had also suffered from the acts of Japanese militarists, should not be burdened with reparations and that China wanted to have friendly relations with them."[58] Crucially, since China waived its right to reparations, Japanese officials have argued that issues of reparations and compensation, both for states *and for individuals*, were settled in this and other postwar treaties. Officials have held to this position—which they have invoked in court cases, in international negotiations, and in public and private communications—in the conviction that agreeing to pay compensation to even a single victim could quickly snowball into thousands of demands for compensation.[59]

While the normalization of relations was an important trigger for change in Japan's narrative, domestic contestation played an important role in shaping the content of official discourse about the Nanjing Massacre and the Second Sino-Japanese War. In response to the thaw in Sino-Japanese relations, Japanese journalist Honda Katsuichi traveled to China in the summer of 1971 to investigate Japanese atrocities committed during the war.[60] He interviewed many Chinese citizens who had experienced Japan's invasion, including survivors of the Nanjing Massacre. Honda also interviewed Japanese soldiers who had fought in China. Based on these interviews, and on observations and evidence from the trip, Honda published a series of articles in late 1971 titled "A Journey in China" (Chūgoku no tabi) in the *Asahi Shimbun*, Japan's major left-of-center national newspaper. The four-part series covered the suffering of Chinese villagers and forced laborers at the hands of the Japanese army, including during the Nanjing Massacre.[61] A turning point in domestic debates over history issues, the series broke the taboo on discussion of this issue in the Japanese media and sparked widespread discussion about Japan's conduct during the war.[62] As Wakabayashi put it: "More than anyone else, Honda forced Japan to confront Nanking as an ethical issue for the first time since the IMTFE [International Military Tribunal for the Far East, known as the Tokyo Trial]."[63] A year or so later, historian Hora Tomio—who a few years earlier had published the first academic book that seriously addressed the Nanjing Massacre—began to publish primary documents about the massacre. Aside from Hora's work, however, little research was published on the topic in the 1970s.[64]

Honda's series also prompted a vigorous response from a small group of conservatives and nationalists who opposed the official expressions of remorse that had been made to China. Their response focused on the Nanjing Massacre and triggered a debate between a handful of intellectuals on the left and right. In this debate, Nozaki reports, those on the right "began to openly deny the Nanjing Massacre by disseminating a theory that characterized the Nanjing Massacre as an illusion."[65] Together, this debate and Honda's series expanded the Japanese public's interest in and knowledge of the massacre and led to a shift in popular consciousness from identifying Japan's role in the war as a "victimized" party to that of a "victimizer."[66] Nozaki reports that "approximately 95 percent . . . [of *Asahi* readers' responses to Honda's series] were positive, expressing the view that Japan had made a huge mistake, and that the nation must admit it as fact."[67]

The textbook "battles" between conservatives and leftists also continued. Ienaga's ongoing legal cases against the MOE gradually led to changes in textbook coverage. In particular, a 1970 ruling in Ienaga's favor found that the MOE's censorship of textbook content was unconstitutional. In response to this ruling, the ministry backed off somewhat in its requests for changes and publishers realized they might be able to get more critical passages through the screening process.[68] As one textbook editor explained: "From 1973 onwards we began including references to the 'Nanjing Incident' in texts submitted to the Education Ministry. . . . But we couldn't cite numbers or use the word 'massacre.'"[69] Consequently, several textbooks that referred to the massacre were approved in the 1972–1973 and 1973–1974 screenings. However, the references were brief and the few details were often relegated to footnotes. For example, Nozaki reports that a high school history textbook "referred to the Japanese occupation of Nanjing in its main text, and included a footnote, which read: 'Because at that time a large-scale massacre of civilians took place, the consciousness of Chinese people to resist (Japan) escalated further.'"[70] A junior high social studies textbook also mentioned the Nanjing Massacre in a footnote: "At the time [it occupied Nanjing], because there were those [Chinese] who attacked and shot [the Japanese Army] outside the battle lines, the Japanese Army killed 42,000 civilians, including women and children. There were numerous small-scale incidents similar to this."[71]

By 1975, half of the junior high school textbooks approved by the ministry mentioned the Nanjing Massacre, and textbooks' references to the massacre increased in subsequent years.[72] For example, Nozaki reports, a footnote in a 1978 junior high school history textbook stated: "Immediately after entering the city of Nanjing, the Japanese Army killed and wounded an enormous number of Chinese people, including women, children, and soldiers who were either no longer armed or wearing civilians clothes. For its actions in this incident, [Japan] met with criticism from various foreign countries, which denounced [the incident] as the Nanjing Massacre, but ordinary Japanese were not informed of the facts [of the event]."[73] Nevertheless, textbook coverage of the Nanjing Massacre remained vague or silent on details, actors, and responsibility, and the little information provided was often in footnotes.[74]

Moreover, the increased coverage of Japan's war crimes elicited a counterreaction from conservative politicians in the late 1970s and contributed to a nationalist revival in the early 1980s. In 1979, the second textbook "offensive" was launched by conservative politicians in the LDP, with the cooperation of bureaucrats and officials in the MOE. LDP politicians publicly criticized textbooks, several LDP publications and Diet committees took up the issue in 1980, and education reform was a central plank of the LDP's 1982 platform.[75] In July 1981, the MOE requested that writers and publishers of high school textbooks for the 1983–1986 period "soften their approach to Japan's excesses during World War II."[76] Nozaki reports that "one of the items the MOE . . . attempted to erase entirely from textbooks was . . . the Nanjing Massacre. When its attempt met with resistance from textbook authors and publishers' staff members, the MOE attempted to represent the massacre as something that had occurred by chance during the 'chaos.'"[77] Illustrating this, Ienaga reports that the MOE requested that he water down the description of the Nanjing Massacre in a textbook submitted in 1981. He explains:

> I had also written: "Immediately after the occupation of Nanjing, Japanese forces killed a large number of Chinese soldiers and civilians. This is known as the Nanjing atrocities." The examiner objected: "How can you tell it was 'immediately after'? Furthermore, this wording could be misinterpreted as indicating that the army officially sanctioned it. . . . One could say 'During the confusion of the occupation of Nanjing many Chinese soldiers and civilians were killed.' Although embarrassing to Japan, it is a fact. If you would write the sentence this way, it would be within the guidelines. Please reconsider the wording. The present construction, particularly the words 'Japanese forces,' suggests that [the killings] were systematically carried out by the Japanese army."

Ienaga stood firm, however, and the final text read: "Japanese forces crushed the staunch Chinese defense and occupied Nanjing. Enraged by their heavy casualties, the troops killed a large number of Chinese soldiers and civilians. This is known as the Nanjing atrocities."[78] Even so, as a result of the second textbook offensive, many passages about the Nanjing Massacre that had passed the 1977 high school history textbook screening process were not approved in 1981.

Commemorative actions continued to focus on Japanese victims, with all five PMs in this period paying visits to the Yasukuni Shrine. In 1975, Miki Takeo was the first post-WWII PM to visit the Yasukuni Shrine on 15 August, which was the anniversary of Japan's surrender and the date on which the war and its victims are commemorated each year. Miki announced that he was visiting as a private citizen, which initiated ongoing debates about the "private" or "official" nature of PMs' visits, and about the constitutionality of such visits.[79] However, debates over politicians' visits to the shrine were still contained within the domestic sphere, with the more powerful conservatives advocating for officials' visits and some leftists arguing against them.

In a step that would contribute to the internationalization of debates over such visits, in late 1978 the new head priest of the Yasukuni Shrine secretly enshrined the spirits of the fourteen Class A war criminals whose names had been passed to shrine officials a decade earlier. This step became public knowledge a few months later, in early 1979. It was immediately criticized by domestic groups and by Chinese authorities, the latter of whom thought that they had had a tacit understanding with Japanese officials that the country's wartime aggression would be blamed on a small group of militarists (i.e., on the group of Class A war criminals whose souls had just been enshrined at Yasukuni).[80]

Finally, throughout the 1970s, Japan's economy grew tremendously. Between 1972 and 1981, Japan's gross domestic product (GDP) grew threefold, from less than $500 million to more than $1 billion, while its overall trade volume increased sixfold, from approximately $50 billion to about $300 billion.[81] Toward the end of the decade, Japanese leaders began to seek an international political role commensurate with the country's dominant economic position. The Fukuda Doctrine, which was announced by PM Fukuda Takeo in August 1977, was a major statement of Japan's shifting foreign policy. Fukuda reaffirmed Japan's commitment to peace and rejection of militarism, and declared that Japan would develop relations with Southeast Asian countries on the basis of cooperation and friendship, rather than just on economic self-help.[82] Then in January 1980, Foreign Minister Ōkita Saburō gave a Diet speech outlining Japan's foreign policy goals for the coming decade. He declared: "Against the backdrop of the great strides in its economic power, our country in recent years has gained an increasingly important world position. . . . In the 1980s, our country must assume responsibility [in international society] and a role suitable to its international status."[83] While these statements signaled a new direction for Japan's foreign policy, Japan's wartime actions—and domestic and regional attitudes toward those actions—would continue to complicate the pursuit of this goal.

Phase Three (1982–1989):
The Internationalization of "History Issues"

The third phase began in 1982 and extended until Emperor Hirohito's death in early 1989. Overall, the official narrative more explicitly identified the Nanjing Massacre and Japan's aggression, although the general tenor of acknowledgment remained vague. And while the official narrative began to admit some responsibility for the massacre, other statements and actions communicated a desire to move beyond this history, thereby both relativizing and mythmaking about the past. International pressures primarily triggered these changes, although their substance was shaped by domestic contestation and attempts by Japanese leaders to move out of the "shadow of the past."

In this period, China's and Japan's economies grew and bilateral trade expanded. China's GDP grew at a rate of about 10 percent per year throughout the 1980s, but its economy continued to be dwarfed by Japan's. The 1980s marked the apex of Japan's "economic miracle," with its economy the second largest in the world. Over the course of the decade, Japan's GDP nearly tripled, growing from just above $1 billion in 1982 to more than $3 billion in 1990.[84] Sino-Japanese trade also continued to develop, exceeding $20 billion in 1985 and then dropping below that mark in subsequent years. According to Whiting, by the mid-1980s, Japan represented about 25 percent of China's trade, while China constituted less than 5 percent of Japan's.[85] Japan also continued to extend generous yen loans to China.

Japan and China's deepening economic relationship was complicated by the emergence of more nationalist policies in both countries. Beginning in 1982 Chinese textbooks, official propaganda, and scholars began to emphasize Japan's aggression and war crimes during the Second Sino-Japanese War, marking the start of a strategy of "aggressive nationalism."[86] Chinese leaders sought to bolster the regime's legitimacy—which was threatened by the economic reforms begun in 1978—by strengthening Chinese citizens' feelings of nationalism and patriotism. In addition, Mitter notes, Chinese officials "felt that reminding Japan of its wartime record . . . was a good way to soften up the Japanese government into giving loans and investment to China at preferential rates."[87] In this context, Chinese officials began to react more strongly and publicly to statements and actions that were perceived to "whitewash" Japan's wartime behavior, thereby sending signals both to Japanese leaders and to Chinese citizens about the importance of this issue.

As China's attitude toward Japan changed, so did Japan's political ambitions. Japan's new foreign policy, which had begun to emerge in the late 1970s, was more fully articulated and developed under PM Nakasone Yasuhiro, who was in office from late 1982 to 1987. Nakasone sought to shift Japan's postwar national identity from one constructed around Japan's economic "miracle" to a "normal" identity that included pride in Japan's history and culture. Nakasone regularly declared that it was time for Japan to "close the books" on the past and to "settle political accounts," and he pushed to instill more pride in being Japanese and for the "reconstruction of a Japanese identity."[88] A few months before taking office, Nakasone explained the thinking underlying this strategy in a July 1982 speech: "After Japan's defeat in the war, . . . there spread throughout Japan a self-torturing belief that our country was to blame for everything. This thinking persists even today. It was fashionable to blame Japan alone and condemn everything prewar. I'm against this. . . . Casting disgrace aside, advancing forward in the pursuit of glory—this is the essence of the nation and of the people. We must look critically at Japan's actions in the past and establish our country's identity from this point of view."[89] In October 1983, the MOFA announced that "Japan should play a greater role in the international community and pursue a more active, independent foreign policy."[90]

Nakasone's vision was also reflected in domestic policies, including attempts to reform the educational system to embrace "moral education."[91] A 1982 LDP statement declared: "School education should 'cultivate the Japanese spirit and foster national pride.'"[92] Reflecting this goal, a senior MOE official stated in 1985: "For 30 years, we have criticized ourselves severely. This should pass. There is no need for continuous cleansing now. We must see history from a more neutral point of view."[93]

Aware of the risks inherent in this nationalist revival, which sought to relativize and elide Japan's dark past, Nakasone attempted to preempt and assuage international concerns by repeatedly emphasizing Japan's peaceful intentions and its continued rejection of militarism. In the spring of 1983, Nakasone reiterated Japan's commitment to peaceful relations in meetings with other Asian leaders, and when he visited China in November 1983, he "promise[d] that Japan w[ould] never again resort to war with China as a means of solving bilateral problems."[94] In February 1984, Nakasone declared that "Japan will not become a military power that threatens neighboring nations."[95] In a seeming contradiction to these assertions, however, in January 1987 Japan announced that defense expenditures would exceed 1 percent of GDP, which had long been the symbolic ceiling on the country's military budget. In response, Chinese officials began to worry more seriously about the potential military threat posed by Japan.[96]

The 1982 Textbook Controversy

A few months before Nakasone became PM, an international controversy erupted over Japanese textbooks' representations of aspects of Japan's WWII conduct. In response to the LDP's focus on educational reform, along with the MOE's increased scrutiny of history textbooks in the 1980–1981 screening process, Japanese newspapers in turn closely scrutinized the textbooks that the MOE approved in the spring of 1982.[97] In June 1982, Japanese newspapers reported that the MOE had changed the guidelines for coverage of the Second Sino-Japanese War. Among several changes reported, two received particular attention. According to Yang, "The most controversial point . . . was the change from '*shinryaku*' (invade and plunder) to '*shinkō*' (enter and assault), or even to the neutral '*shinshutsu*' (advance into), in the description of pre-1945 Japanese activities on the Asian continent."[98] In an internal document, the ministry reasoned "that invasion or advance, rather than aggression, [was] more historically objective in describing the events leading to the seven-year war. The document also said the term 'advance' conform[ed] with historical descriptions of the China invasion by European powers as found in European textbooks."[99] Even though it was quickly revealed that these guidelines had actually been in place for more than a decade, domestic criticisms continued to build.

As a result of unrelenting domestic attention and scrutiny in the summer of 1982, the issue developed into a regional controversy, with China and South Korea officially protesting to Japan, and the Chinese and South Korean press lambasting the Japanese government.[100] At first, Japanese officials dismissed these protests as unwarranted interventions in Japan's internal affairs.[101] Illustrating this, Yang writes, "A member of the government Textbook Examination Council was quoted as calling it 'unfair to describe the Nanjing Massacre in three to five lines while mentioning Soviet or American atrocities against the Japanese [during the war] in only one line or two.' The government examiner further suggested that it was blasphemy to the Japanese troops to emphasize their atrocities."[102] Within a month, however, the vehemence of protests from China and South Korea, and their escalation into street protests in South Korea, led Japanese PM Suzuki Zenkō to intervene. In a press conference on 23 August 1982, Suzuki emphasized the importance of history issues in Japan's relations with Asian countries, declaring:

> I think that the textbook issue has its roots in the deep national sentiments of the peoples not only of China and the ROK but also of other neighboring Asian countries. This leads me to conclude that the issue has a vitally important aspect. It relates to the ties of friendship, cooperation and mutual trust which we have endeavored so much to develop

with neighboring countries. It would be a disaster if these international ties should be damaged and hurt. Thus, I take a very serious view of the issue and its impact. I believe that Japan should deeply reflect on the sacrifices, damages, losses, injuries and pains it inflicted upon the peoples of neighboring countries in the past war, that it should humbly listen to their complaints and criticisms about Japan, and that it should redouble its effects to forge relations of true friendship, cooperation and mutual trust with them.[103]

Several days later, Chief Cabinet Secretary Miyazawa Kiichi issued an official statement that signaled the government's reversal on the issue. Miyazawa's statement opened by acknowledging that "the Japanese Government and the Japanese people are deeply aware of the fact that acts by our country in the past caused tremendous suffering and damage to the peoples of Asian countries, including the Republic of Korea (ROK) and China, and have followed the path of a pacifist state with remorse and determination that such acts must never be repeated."[104] Noting Japan's previous statements of acknowledgment and regret, he declared: "These statements confirm Japan's remorse and determination . . . and this recognition has not changed at all to this day." He further observed: "This spirit . . . naturally should also be respected in Japan's school education and textbook authorization," promising that the textbook guidelines would be revised accordingly. China and South Korea accepted this statement and Japan's commitment to resolve the points of contention, officially ending the controversy.

Later that fall, the MOE introduced the Neighboring Countries Clause (Kinrin shokoku jōkō), according to which: "Proposed texts should 'show the necessary consideration for international understanding and . . . harmony in their treatment of the events of modern and contemporary history between [Japan and its] Asian neighbors.'"[105] As Nozaki explains, "The MOE also noted that it would not ask authors to replace the term 'aggression' with 'advancement,' or add phrasing suggesting that the Nanjing Massacre occurred as the result of a moment of chaos. With respect to authors' references to the number of victims of the Nanjing Massacre, the MOE announced it would only ask authors to provide citations."[106] Interestingly, while significant and persistent international pressures from China and South Korea had prompted these changes, if it had not been for the initial and sustained *domestic* media scrutiny, this controversy would likely not have arisen in the first place.

Although the new guidelines did result in changes in textbooks' coverage of the massacre and the broader war, such changes were not immediate, as the MOE did not agree with the policy reversal and was reluctant to change approved textbooks or its approval procedures.[107] Despite this bureaucratic opposition, within a year or so of the controversy, textbooks' coverage of the Nanjing Massacre increased. Many of the textbooks published in 1983–1984 and most of those published in 1987–1988 mentioned the massacre, although the references were quite brief.[108] The MOE also began allowing publishers to include more details about the massacre and specific and higher death toll figures, but ministry reviewers continued to carefully monitor these issues.[109] Dierkes explains that "references [to the Nanjing Massacre in middle school social studies textbooks] generally did not include estimates of the number of victims until the mid 1980s; even then they gradually rose from estimates of 10,000 to 200,000 victims until the 1992 edition . . . that acknowledged that Chinese estimates ranged up to 300,000 victims."[110] Testimony and documents filed in Ienaga's third lawsuit further revealed that the MOE was still unwilling to accept descriptions of the Nanjing Massacre that implied that "Japanese forces carried out a systematic killing."[111] It also would not approve descriptions that referred to Japanese forces raping Chinese women during the massacre. The MOE contended that "rape in times of war by military officers and soldiers is 'a common, customary practice all over the world since ancient times,' so that 'it is inappropriate to refer only to the rape committed by the Japanese forces, because to do so gives too much emphasis to a specific matter,'" arguing further that "the data determining whether the frequency of that rape was extreme was inconclusive."[112]

Nevertheless, textbook coverage of the Nanjing Massacre and Japan's wartime actions clearly increased. A textbook editor explained, "Since the Miyazawa document was issued, it has become permissible to say 'aggression' about Japan and 'advance' about other countries, . . . and most textbooks do."[113] Thus, whereas middle school social studies textbooks published through 1982 typically referred to the start of the Sino-Japanese War by saying that China "claimed" that Japan had invaded the country, from 1983 on textbooks referred to Japan's "invasion" as the start of the war.[114]

Following this controversy, history issues also took on greater importance in Japan's foreign relations and domestic politics. Domestically, the debate over Japan's war memory was continued by scholars and activists on the left and right, who searched for new evidence to support the positions they argued, published new work, and kept the domestic debate active. In particular, the 1982 textbook controversy inspired action among societal groups on the left and the right in Japan. Over time, these responses had both positive (i.e., supporting and reinforcing) and negative (i.e., challenging or undermining) feedback effects on the official narrative and on the broader political context.

In the wake of the controversy, the right-wing National Conference to Defend Japan (Nihon o Mamoru Kokumin Kaigi) decided to write a history textbook that would minimize coverage of wartime aggression and atrocities and would instead cover more positive aspects of Japan's history. The project was announced in 1982 and the resulting textbook, *A New History of Japan*, was submitted for MOE approval in 1985. The textbook's tentative approval in the beginning of 1986 prompted a second international textbook controversy, renewing both international and domestic attention to and pressure on the government's narrative. This time, the textbook had strong support from conservative politicians and from PM Nakasone. As a result, despite the fact that "some members of the [MOE's textbook screening] council felt the . . . manuscript was . . . 'distasteful,' 'biased,' and 'lacking in consideration for neighbouring countries,'" and in spite of vociferous domestic and international protest, it was approved.[115] While the MOE ended up requesting that the publisher make additional revisions as a concession to international pressure, the textbook was nevertheless approved. Moreover, in notable contrast to the resolution of the 1982 controversy, the government did not apologize for its approval.[116]

Also in response to the 1982 textbook controversy, in late 1983 the conservative veterans' organization Kaikōsha asked members to send personal accounts of the capture of Nanjing to its monthly magazine to disprove allegations of a massacre. Instead, and to the surprise of Kaikōsha and the magazine's editors, many of the approximately one hundred submissions actually confirmed the massacre. To its credit, the magazine published many of these accounts over the course of eleven issues, and the series ended with an open statement of acknowledgment and apology by the editor. Notably, these eyewitness testimonies and two subsequent books provided invaluable primary data that have since been used by scholars.[117]

Progressive efforts were also initiated in response to the 1982 textbook controversy. In January 1984, Ienaga filed his third lawsuit. This case sought to "put history on trial" by challenging the MOE's resistance to the coverage of eight historical points, including "the use of the term 'aggression' (*shinryaku*) to describe the Japanese invasion of China, the description of the Nanjing Massacre, the reference to Japanese soldiers' rape of Chinese women (in Nanjing as well as in northern China), [and] the reference to Unit 731."[118] Shortly after the suit was filed, a group of academics and journalists founded the Society for Investigation and Research into the Nanjing Incident (Nankin jiken chōsa kenkyūkai, known as Nankin ken). The initial aim of Nankin ken was to publish evidence and analyses of the Nanjing Massacre to help Ienaga's case. Over time, the group's members discovered new information about the massacre, authored a number of important scholarly works, and published English and Chinese primary sources in Japanese. One of Nankin ken's most notable discoveries was the diary of Lieutenant General Nakajima Kesago, who had commanded one of the divisions that captured Nanjing. Nakajima's diary, which was published in 1985, confirmed that one of the army's policies following the invasion of Nanjing was to execute Chinese POWs. Like the testimonies gathered by Kaikōsha, this and other publications by members of Nankin ken made it difficult to deny all wrongdoing in the capture of Nanjing or to dismiss the massacre as an "illusion" or "fabrication."[119]

In 1984, the *Asahi Shimbun*'s weekly journal published another series of articles by Honda Katsuichi, who was also a founding member of Nankin ken. Titled "The Road to Nanjing," the series "told of more stories of Japanese atrocities between Shanghai and Nanjing."[120] Then, in the summer of 1986, the *Asahi Shimbun* asked its readers to send in accounts of their wartime experiences. As Gibney reports, "*Asahi* received an unprecedented flood of letters—over 4,000— and continued to print selections for more than a year! Some 1200 of the letters were later published as a book."[121] This book, called *The War* (*Sensō*), added to the growing number of firsthand testimonies and accounts, many of which recounted crimes committed by the Japanese army. Around the same time, Azuma Shirō, a Japanese veteran who had fought in Nanjing, provided another firsthand testimony of the massacre. In 1987, Azuma decided to speak publicly about crimes he had committed and witnessed in Nanjing, and to publish his diary from the time. Azuma's diary and testimony received significant attention and support in Japan and China, and again brought the Nanjing Massacre to the attention of the Japanese and Chinese governments.[122]

Finally, an important international response to the 1982 controversy was the Chinese government's decision to build the Memorial for the Compatriot Victims in the Nanjing Massacre by the Japanese Invading Troops, which was completed in time for the fortieth anniversary of the end of the war in 1985. The official Chinese figure for the massacre's death toll—three hundred thousand— is written in huge numbers on the building's facade. Since its completion, the memorial has shaped Chinese perceptions of the scope and nature of the massacre, and has committed Chinese actors (and others) to this figure.[123]

As these varied responses highlight, political and societal actors across Japan's political spectrum responded to the 1982 textbook controversy. Some objected to foreign intervention in Japan's domestic affairs and to the government's accommodation of such pressures, while others opposed the government's attempts to relativize Japan's dark past.

A few years after the 1982 textbook controversy, the issue of official visits to the Yasukuni Shrine similarly metastasized into an international problem. Nakasone made an official visit to the shrine on 15 August 1985, which was the fortieth anniversary of the war's end. While this was the sixth year in a row that a PM had visited the Yasukuni Shrine on that date, the 1985 visit provoked outcries from China, Korea, and other Asian countries, and student protests in Beijing and other Chinese cities.[124] Interpreted as honoring the Class A war criminals whose spirits were enshrined at Yasukuni, the visit was seen as a sign of Japan's lack of contrition for its wartime actions. The strength of international reactions in 1985, compared with previous years, was due to a concatenation of factors, including the date (the fortieth anniversary) and nature (official) of the visit, the two recent textbook controversies, Nakasone's other statements about the past, and the effects of China's new nationalism. In response to the protests, especially from China and Korea, Nakasone canceled another planned visit to the shrine, and despite strong pressure from fellow LDP Diet members and from influential right-wing groups, he did not visit the shrine again for the remainder of his tenure in office. Thus, in August 1986, Whiting reports, "Chief Cabinet Secretary Gotoda Masaharu announced that 'after careful and independent consideration' Nakasone had made a 'prudent and independent' decision not to visit the shrine. Referring to the 'criticisms of neighboring countries,' he added, 'We must stress international ties and give appropriate consideration to the national sentiments of neighboring countries.'"[125]

Against the backdrop of—and often in response to—this accommodation and the changes in textbooks' coverage of war crimes, in the late 1980s several Japanese politicians made revisionist statements denying the existence of the Nanjing Massacre, disavowing that Japan's behavior in the war was aggressive, or lauding aspects of Japan's colonization of Korea or fighting in China. These "gaffes," or "anti-apologies" as Yamazaki terms them, began in 1986 and were taken as troubling signs of elite opinion in Japan.[126] "Gaffe" is a misnomer, as most of the statements do not seem to have been accidental, and some view them as intentional efforts by nationalist politicians to counter international criticisms and domestic left-wing views.[127] However, because these statements were primarily by officials who did *not* speak for the state on history issues, they are not counted as official. Rather, the government's reactions to these statements signaled the official position.

The first gaffe was by Education Minister Fujio Masayuki, who in a 1986 interview "argued that Japan 'did nothing to be ashamed of' during the war."[128] Nakasone asked Fujio to recant, and when he refused to do so, Fujio was fired from his post as education minister. His firing was followed by a statement from Chief Cabinet Secretary Gotoda, who noted: "Fujio's remarks were 'deeply regrettable because . . . (they) gave birth to doubts over our country's policy to pursue peace and friendly foreign relations, based on the grave reflections of the last war.'"[129] Also in response to Fujio's comments, Nakasone made a Diet speech in which he acknowledged Japan's "aggression" in the war.[130] Two years later, in the spring of 1988, Cabinet Minister Okuno Seisuke asserted that "Japan 'had no intention' of invading China," that "Japan fought the war in order to secure its safety," and that "it [wa]s nonsense to call Japan the aggressor or militaristic."[131] Japanese officials initially tried to make light of Okuno's statements, but as criticism mounted and Okuno refused to recant or apologize, PM Takeshita Noboru forced him to resign.[132] Thus, both Fujio and Okuno were fired, signaling that their statements did not reflect the government's position. However, in a sign that such views were not isolated, in 1985 an LDP committee published a book about the war that more or less denied that there were atrocities in the Nanjing Massacre.[133]

Consequently, just as Japanese officials sought to move out of the shadow of history, its shade instead darkened and lengthened, in part due to efforts by Nakasone and other conservatives within and outside the government to normalize—and in some cases, deny—the dark parts of Japan's past.

7

UNFREEZING THE QUESTION OF HISTORY (1998–2008)

> **We need a Japanese leader who can help us come to terms with the past and forge a consensus about how we view our history. The question is: do we have one?**
>
> —Retired senior Japanese government official, August 1994

> **We know we have to make a sincere apology, but at the same time we are sort of bored with making these statements.**
>
> —Mine Yoshiki, Japanese official at the Asian Women's Fund, August 1995

Over the twenty-year period from mid-1989 through 2008, the official narrative came to include apologizing and then backtracked to resume mythmaking and relativizing, while continuing to include apologizing. External pressures from China and South Korea, along with transnational activism, contributed to the shift to apologizing and deepening acknowledgment. At the same time, political dynamics within Japan were, in many cases, the most important determinants of the timing and content of changes in the state's narrative. Interestingly, and in contrast to Turkey's narrative, which has tended toward patterns of strong continuity followed by relatively abrupt and wide-reaching change, different elements of Japan's narrative—particularly textbooks and official statements—have tended to shift in a disaggregated fashion in reaction to discrete pressures and controversies.

Phase Four (1989–1994): Moving toward Apology

The fourth phase began in mid-1989 and extended until June 1994. Japanese officials issued the first apologies for WWII-era war crimes, but they were not offered to China or Taiwan and did not refer to the Nanjing Massacre or the Second Sino-Japanese War. Rather, the first apologies were made to Korea for the colonization of the Korean peninsula and the "comfort women" system. Other official statements expressed deeper remorse and acknowledged a broader set of victims.

129

Structural changes, international pressures, and domestic activism shaped the timing and content of these changes. The changes reflected continuing concerns about material and identity costs and changing legitimacy concerns, while the timing of the most significant changes reflected the loosening of long-term structural constraints.

Given the long-running domestic and international scrutiny of textbooks' coverage of the Nanjing Massacre and Japan's war crimes, and the commitments for greater acknowledgment made in the wake of the first textbook controversy, textbook coverage of Japan's war crimes continued to increase. Curriculum changes announced in 1989 included "forthright statements about the exploitation of neighboring Asian countries and wartime aggression."[1]

As a consequence of these changes, and of textbook publishers' perceptions of more permissive attitudes at the MOE, the Nanjing Massacre—including estimates of the massacre's death toll—appeared in the majority of junior and high school history textbooks published in this phase.[2] Textbooks also more openly and critically described Japan's aggression and war crimes.[3] For example, a 1994 high school history textbook stated that in Nanjing, the Japanese army committed a "great slaughter against the Chinese military and civilians" and "large-scale plundering, arson and massacre."[4] For high school history textbooks authorized in 1992, Rose reports,

> the word "invasion" or "aggression" (*shinryaku*) replaced advance or incident (*shinshutsu* or *jiken*), and phrases such as "Chinese and Japanese troops clashed" were changed to "Japanese troops fought with Chinese troops" so that in general Japanese behaviour was no longer using the passive voice, and responsibility was seen to lie with Japan. All the textbooks took up the Nanjing Massacre. . . . The word "rape" was not always allowed by the Ministry of Education but on the issue of casualties it was acceptable to state the figures accepted at the Tokyo trial. Unit 731 was mentioned in most of the textbooks (previously reference to this had not even been allowed in footnotes) and details of the sort of experiments that took place there appeared in most books. Reference to the use of forced labour and comfort women also began to appear in texts.[5]

While deepening acknowledgment was evident in textbooks from the beginning of the phase, changes in other indicators did not occur until later. However, two structural changes at the beginning of the period shook up support for the status quo, creating conditions in which further change was more likely.[6]

The first was the January 1989 death of Emperor Hirohito. Since the war's end, Hirohito had not visited China and had issued only vague statements about "unfortunate events" at a "certain point in time." Moreover, that the emperor had been allowed to remain in office and had not been labeled or tried as a war criminal had complicated and hindered discussions in Japan about individual and collective war responsibility. His death, therefore, had direct and indirect effects on the state's narrative. In direct terms, his son, Emperor Akihito, who succeeded him, expressed regret for and made slightly less vague statements about the war in the ensuing years. In addition, leading up to and after Hirohito's death, actors across the domestic political spectrum began openly questioning the emperor's responsibility for the war, which had been symbolically waged in his name. Over time, this discussion broke the taboo on the question of the emperor's war responsibility and contributed to deepening acknowledgment and contrition.[7]

In spite of the unprecedented nature of this discussion, it also revealed the persistence and strength of important domestic constraints on change. This was most evident when, in December 1988, a month before the emperor's death, Nagasaki mayor Motoshima Hitoshi stated that the emperor "must bear some of the responsibility for the Second World War."[8] This statement prompted a domestic uproar. While Motoshima received numerous expressions of support, his statement was intensely criticized on the political right and Motoshima was expelled from the LDP for his remarks. A month later, he was shot in the back by a right-wing extremist.[9] Motoshima survived, but the attack and the LDP's and conservatives' responses to his statement underscored the domestic considerations— including the threat of right-wing violence—that reinforced continuities in the official narrative.

Further illustrating the LDP's resistance to change, shortly after the emperor's death, PM Takeshita Noboru declared "the war 'broke out in spite of his [i.e., Hirohito's] wishes,'" which reflected the myth of the emperor's lack of responsibility that had been perpetuated since the occupation.[10] Takeshita also commented that the determination of whether the war was one of aggression should be left to historians, thereby indirectly denying its aggressive nature.[11] In response to domestic and international anger, Takeshita quickly retracted his observations, stating, "The 'militaristic aggression' (*gunjishugi ni yoru shinryaku*) of our country cannot be denied."[12] This swift backpedaling signaled international audiences' increasing scrutiny of Japanese officials' pronouncements about history issues.

The end of the Cold War was the second major structural change. As PM Miyazawa Kiichi noted in a January 1993 Diet speech, this international turning point "induced major changes in the circumstances affecting Japanese foreign policy and Japan's own position within the international community."[13] The end of the Soviet-American rivalry removed the guarantee of US support for political stability above other concerns, creating space for such concerns to be voiced, both within Japan and internationally. The end of the Cold War also triggered new conflicts that shifted international attention to issues of human rights and international justice and contributed to the deepening of normative expectations related to truth-seeking and truth-telling for past wrongs.

Amid the shifting balance of power and the emergence of new international issues and priorities, the first Gulf War exposed the limitations of Japan's "Peace Constitution," which prevented Japan from contributing troops to the war, and its implications for Japan's international political position and stature. Japan contributed $13 billion to the US-led Gulf War effort, but did not contribute any personnel, which was harshly criticized as "checkbook diplomacy." Japan's legal and political inability to send personnel also raised serious concerns among US policymakers about whether Japan would be able to help if a conflict were to break out in East Asia.[14] This international reaction and criticism shocked, embarrassed, and worried Japanese leaders, bringing into stark relief the gap between the country's economic and political status. As Soeya, Tadokoro, and Welch put it: "Not being able to participate militarily in the liberation of Kuwait in 1991—instead writing a cheque to cover much of the costs incurred by the U.S.-led international coalition—at a time when Japan was by far the largest developed-country importer of Persian Gulf oil, was an embarrassment."[15] In response, Japanese politicians sought to loosen some of the legal and bureaucratic constraints on the country's foreign policy. The first step in this direction was the 1992 passage of the PKO Bill, which allowed Japanese forces to participate in international peacekeeping missions (within defined constitutional limits).[16] This crisis also prompted the influential politician Ozawa Ichirō to initiate a still-ongoing discussion about the need for Japan to become a "normal country" that would be able to fulfill "its rightful international responsibilities" in cooperation with other states.[17]

More generally, with the removal of the common Soviet threat and the 1996 Taiwan Strait Crisis, China gradually became more wary of the US-Japan security alliance. This occurred in conjunction with tectonic shifts in the relative economic balance of power between China and Japan, and with Japan's efforts to alter the nature of Sino-Japanese relations from a "special relationship," in which Japan was careful to help and not offend China, to a more "normal" relationship.[18] The changing balance of power was also driven by the bursting of Japan's housing bubble in 1990, which ushered in a decade-long domestic recession, and by China's continued shift from a state- to a market-led economy.

At roughly the same time, civil society activists in the United States, South Korea, China, and Japan began to draw attention to Japan's war crimes. In the late 1980s and early 1990s, groups in China, South Korea, and Taiwan mobilized domestically and transnationally to demand compensation and an apology from Japan for former slave laborers and comfort women, for victims of germ and biological warfare and experiments, and for atrocities such as the Nanjing Massacre.[19] In 1989, surviving former Chinese slave laborers announced that they were seeking an apology and compensation from the Kajima Corporation,[20] and "in 1990 a group of South Koreans sued the Japanese government for being forced to perform hard labor in Japanese mines and factories."[21] Then in December 1991, three South Korean former comfort women filed a lawsuit against the Japanese government.[22] This case drew significant attention, especially in Japan and Korea. Women's groups in South Korea and Japan that had mobilized to support these and other former sex slaves pressed the Japanese government to acknowledge its organization of the comfort women program and to compensate these women. In 1992, the Committee for Chinese Civilians Seeking Compensation against Japan was established in China, with help from Japanese lawyers and activists. This group called on the Japanese government to apologize and compensate Chinese victims for their suffering and filed one of the first cases demanding compensation for Chinese war victims in a Japanese court.[23] At the same time, in response to the increasing incidence of Japanese officials' "gaffes" in the late 1980s and early 1990s, as well as the successful end to the long campaign for redress for Japanese Americans forcibly interned during WWII, Chinese Americans and Taiwanese Americans began to mobilize to publicize and demand an apology for Japan's WWII-era crimes.[24]

Within this context of uncertainty, shifting power, and heightened scrutiny, Japanese politicians and bureaucrats increasingly recognized that if they wanted Japan to have a more prominent international political role, they would have to do more to address persistent criticisms of the state's position on the issue of war responsibility.[25] Given Japan's desire for greater international legitimacy and prominence, and the coincidence of a series of major war-related anniversaries in the early to mid-1990s, a number of Japanese politicians and elites began to propose that Japan express greater contrition for its war crimes.[26]

The first war-related official apology, which was issued to the people of South Korea, was made in May 1990. That this first apology was made to South Korea reflects pressures from the South Korean government and activists, as well as a clearer sense of wrong on the part of Japanese officials for the country's colonization of Korea. As the first official apology using the word *owabi*, which is a direct and informal word for "apology," this step was also a sign of changes to come. During a visit to South Korea, PM Kaifu Toshiki stated: "During a period in the past, the people of the Korean peninsula experienced unbearable grief and suffering because of the actions of our country. (We) are humbly remorseful (*kenkyo ni hansei*) and wish to note our frank feelings of apology (*owabi*)."[27] In the same visit, Emperor Akihito declared: "I think of the sufferings your people underwent during this unfortunate period, which was brought about by my country, and cannot but feel the deepest regret [*makotoni ikan*]."[28] However, because the Korean government had pressed Japanese officials for an apology from the emperor, they were disappointed with both Kaifu's apology and Akihito's statement of regret.[29]

A year later, Kaifu made a statement that went further than previous statements about the broader war, but was still not an apology. (To be clear, at that point, Japan had apologized only to Korea, which, officials argued, was "a former colony and thus a special case."[30]) At a May 1991 ASEAN meeting in Singapore, Kaifu expressed "our sincere contrition at Japanese past actions which inflicted unbearable suffering and sorrow upon a great many people of the Asia-Pacific region. The Japanese people are firmly resolved never again to repeat those actions which had tragic consequences." He also stated his determination to teach the next generation of Japanese about the country's dark past.[31] Despite the fact that this statement was not an apology, compared with previous statements it acknowledged a much broader range of victims, namely the "people of the Asia-Pacific region." In so doing, the statement ceased eliding and silencing the existence and suffering of non-Japanese victims.

Six months later, prompted in part by the fiftieth anniversary of the bombing of Pearl Harbor, the MOFA came up with a new official formulation, but it was not much different from Kaifu's earlier statement. The "new" formulation, as stated by Foreign Minister Watanabe Michio, was: "We feel a deep remorse (*fukaku hansei*) about the unbearable suffering and sorrow Japan inflicted on the American people and the peoples of Asia and the Pacific during the Pacific War." Identity concerns again limited the extent of change, with officials avoiding the word "apology" out of concern that if they had done so, "some people in our country [might have argued] that we had totally negated our entire past history."[32] Consequently, the main difference between Kaifu's ASEAN statement and this formulation was that the latter also included "the American people."

Another factor accounting for Japan's continued lack of apology to China was the relative lack of pressure from China in the early 1990s. Whereas pressure from South Korea and from transnational activists helped push Japanese officials to issue the first apologies for the comfort women program and Japan's colonization of the Korean peninsula, China was more concerned in the early 1990s with regaining its international legitimacy in the wake of the June 1989 Tiananmen Square massacre of unarmed democracy activists in Beijing. In response to the massacre, the international community shunned the Communist regime. Chinese officials were thus grateful when in August 1991, Japan's PM was the first leader of a democratic country to visit China following the massacre.[33] Several months later, in negotiations over Emperor Akihito's October 1992 trip to China, Chinese leaders agreed not to mention history issues during his visit. Consequently, even though most of the major Japanese newspapers saw the emperor's visit as an opportunity for him to express contrition for the past, and "a clear majority of Japanese [55 percent] believe[d] Emperor Akihito should apologise for Japanese wartime atrocities in China," Akihito did not do so.[34] Rather, the emperor expressed his "deep sorrow" for the "unfortunate period in which my country inflicted great sufferings on the people of China."[35]

Although this was not an apology, it went further than statements made by his father, demonstrating one effect of Emperor Hirohito's death on the official narrative. The main reason the emperor's statement was so limited was that the Japanese government was concerned that nationalist and conservative Diet members within the ruling LDP, powerful conservative interest groups such as Izokukai, and sometimes-violent ultranationalists in Japan would negatively react to any statement that shifted the official narrative too much in the direction of apology.[36] That this concern was valid is evidenced by the fact that "the announcement [of Akihito's visit] immediately drew protests from right-wing nationalists in Japan," with "one extremist steer[ing] a burning truck towards the official residence of Japanese Prime Minister Mr Kiichi Miyazawa."[37] Moreover, the constitution prohibits the emperor from making political statements or actions, so his statements are carefully considered and planned by the PM and cabinet. Miyazawa and his cabinet negotiated and deliberated for several months before deciding to accept China's invitation for the emperor to visit the country, and they did so only after securing promises from Chinese officials that the emperor would not experience any pressure to apologize for past wrongs and would not be put "in an awkward position" in any way.[38] This outcome represented Japanese officials' attempt at a compromise between China's desire for the emperor to visit in the anniversary year of normalization and the demands of ultranationalists and conservatives in the LDP that he not visit China at all. Thus, when the emperor's visit was publicly announced in Japan, Japanese officials stated that he would neither apologize nor visit Nanjing during the trip.[39]

As the debate and compromise over Akihito's China visit reveal, key domestic constraints on change persisted. Conservative politicians and bureaucrats were reluctant to issue apologies, both because of their own views and interests and because of the likely negative political repercussions among important nationalist constituencies. These electoral-political concerns muted the impact of the structural shifts discussed above and militated against deepening domestic pressures for greater contrition and acknowledgment, which are described below. In addition, material concerns about individual compensation claims remained a significant factor behind the government's opposition to lawsuits and individual compensation, as well as its reluctance to issue clear apologies.

At the same time, domestic research and activism related to Japan's war responsibility deepened, and public opinion supported greater contrition and acknowledgment. Over the course of the 1990s, a number of public and private "peace museums" were established in Japan. By 2004, Yoshida notes, "Japan ha[d] at least 200 museums that, in whole or part, examine[d] the wars that Imperial Japan waged between 1868 and 1945."[40] By including non-Japanese victims and by including or featuring Japan's war crimes, these museums differed from existing museums and exhibits addressing WWII.[41] Paralleling this trend, a majority of the Japanese public believed that the government should express greater contrition for its past wrongs, and public opinion surveys indicated support for increased compensation for non-Japanese victims. For example, "in 1993, . . . 78 percent [of twenty- and thirty-year-olds polled] wanted to see the government pay compensation to countries in which Japanese forces had committed atrocities."[42]

In terms of domestic contestation, academics, lawyers, and citizen-activists uncovered new evidence of Japan's wartime atrocities and launched efforts to document and publicize Japan's past wrongs. One of the most notable developments was the discovery and publication of evidence confirming the Japanese government's role in the comfort women program. Historian Yoshimi Yoshiaki found this evidence in the National Institute for Defense Studies library, and his discovery was announced in early January 1992, a few days before PM Miyazawa was scheduled to visit South Korea.[43] Together with intense pressure from the South Korean government, victims, and activists in Korea and Japan, this discovery led to the Japanese government's acknowledgment of and official apology for its involvement in the comfort women program. Within days, the cabinet issued an official statement acknowledging that the Japanese military had been involved in the "comfort stations" and expressed "sincere apology and remorse to all those who have suffered indescribable hardship as so-called 'wartime comfort women.'"[44] The statement was followed by PM Miyazawa's visit to Korea, during which he expressed "remorse (*hansei*) and apology (*owabi*)" to the Korean people and explicitly referred to the "military comfort women."[45] The most explicit and detailed official apologies to date, they were again directed toward the Korean people.

A year and a half later, in August 1993, the Japanese government completed an official investigation into the comfort women system. On the basis of the results of this investigation, Chief Cabinet Secretary Kōno Yōhei issued official remarks (*danwa*) on behalf of the government, acknowledging that the "Japanese military was, directly or indirectly, involved in the establishment and management of the comfort stations and the transfer of comfort women," and expressing "sincere apologies and remorse to all those . . . who suffered immeasurable pain and incurable physical and psychological wounds as comfort women."[46] Notably, the *danwa* was issued just before the LDP left office (and were out of power for the first time in thirty-eight years), a sign that in the wake of the party's momentous loss the winds were changing domestically and internationally.

Not all discoveries had such effects. In many cases, the government tried to suppress or cover up evidence of Japan's war crimes, while citizens' groups fought against these efforts. Perhaps the most shocking example of this was the discovery of human bones buried under what had been the location in Tokyo of the Imperial Army Medical School, where medical and biological "experiments" had been conducted on prisoners during the war. The bones, which were discovered in 1989, apparently bore many indications of such experiments. Despite this, or perhaps because of it, the Japanese government "declared the bones of no historic interest" and argued that they should be destroyed.[47] A group of citizens opposed this, leading to a lawsuit that progressed all the way to Japan's Supreme Court. In December 2000, the group lost, and in June 2001 the Ministry of Health, Labor, and Welfare declared that it had found no evidence of torture or atrocities in its study of the bones.[48] Similarly, a groundbreaking 1993 Japan Broadcasting Corporation (Nihon Hōsō Kyōkai, NHK) documentary revealed that the Japanese government had long suppressed documentation and knowledge of the wartime slave labor program, but no apology or acknowledgment followed this revelation.[49]

Thus, despite growing domestic and international pressures for change, domestic constraints continued to prevent moves toward deeper acknowledgment or broader apologies.

The LDP out of Power

Such change became possible only after a momentous shift in Japan's domestic politics: between August 1993 and April 1994, the LDP was out of power for the first time since 1955, replaced by a multiparty, anti-LDP coalition government headed by Hosokawa Morihiro.[50] This watershed in Japanese politics displaced a fundamental obstacle to change in the state's narrative. Shortly before taking office, the incoming coalition released a statement indicating "its readiness to cooperate in promoting peace and development in Asia and the world with repentance for involvement in World War II," while the incoming Deputy PM and Minister of Foreign Affairs Hata Tsutomu made similar comments.[51]

A few days before taking office, Hosokawa boldly declared that the war had been "a war of aggression, a mistaken/wrong war."[52] This statement went further than previous official assessments, particularly in calling the war a "mistake" and using the term "aggression," rather than simply calling Japan's wartime conduct "aggressive."[53] As Yamazaki explains, the difference between the word "aggression" and the phrase "acts of aggression" was quite significant. She reports that "an opposition legislator explained the difference in terminology . . . as follows:

'When you say "acts of aggression," you are indicating individual or regimental actions, acts that were against policy, specific instances of wrongdoing that can be considered "illegal," whereas when you say "war of aggression," you are criticizing the war as a whole. It's a completely different dimension.'"[54] Hosokawa was aware of this distinction, notes Wakamiya, and explicitly chose to go "one step further, using the balder nominal form, 'aggression.'"[55] Hosokawa also declared that Japan should "clearly express our remorse at and atonement for our past history."[56]

In response, 72 percent of Japanese surveyed in a national poll indicated their support for Hosokawa's statement, while nationalists and ultranationalists reacted negatively.[57] As a leftist academic and activist put it, "All of the right wing stood up to respond to Hosokawa's statement."[58] Hosokawa was strongly criticized by Diet members, including the powerful future PM and head of the Japan War-Bereaved Families Association Hashimoto Ryūtarō, and the right-wing newspaper *Sankei Shimbun*. Their criticisms centered on material and identity concerns, namely that such statements exposed Japan to individual compensation claims, besmirched the memories and sacrifices of Japanese soldiers, and threatened Japan's national identity.[59]

These criticisms also took concrete form. In August 1993, more than one hundred LDP Diet members—including a number of the party's most prominent leaders and three future PMs—formed the Committee to Examine History (Rekishi kentō iinkai), whose goal "was to absolve the war dead of disgrace and to teach the correct historical view to other Diet members."[60] Over the subsequent two years, the group organized panel discussions and expert talks on the Nanjing Massacre, the comfort women system, and other history issues.[61] Then, in August 1995, the group published a book called the *Summary of the Greater East Asia War* (*Daitōa Sensō Sōkatsu*), which characterized the war as "one of self-defence and liberation" and the Nanjing Massacre as a "fabrication."[62] This marked the emergence of a multifaceted and powerful nationalist movement that opposed greater pressures for acknowledgment and deepening official expressions of acknowledgment and contrition.

Despite these criticisms, less than two weeks after Hosokawa's first statement, he and speaker of the Diet's lower house Doi Takako explicitly acknowledged non-Japanese war victims in speeches at the annual 15 August commemoration ceremony. Hosokawa stated: "We take this opportunity to go beyond our national boundaries in stating our feelings of sincere sympathy toward all victims of war, starting with Asian nations and their families." At the same ceremony, Doi, who was the chair of the traditionally leftist and pacifist Japan Socialist Party (JSP), recognized "the people on both sides who were made wretched (*itamashii*) victims in the last war." In a Diet speech a week later,

Hosokawa expressed "profound remorse (*hansei*) and apologies (*owabi*)" for "past Japanese actions, including aggression and colonial rule."[63] Despite being a more general statement of apology, this was perceived as backtracking from statements of the prior two weeks, both because it did not refer to the entire war as a "war of aggression" and because it did not explicitly mention particular victims.[64] Nevertheless, taken together, Hosokawa's statements marked important shifts in the official narrative, identifying a broader set of victims and more clearly marking Japan's actions as wrong.

Alongside—and in response to—this deepening acknowledgment, high-level politicians continued making revisionist statements about Japan's actions. Part of the nationalist movement that was taking shape at this time, these "gaffes" highlighted two facts. First, many conservative politicians, typically members or former members of the then-out-of-power LDP, rejected and actively resisted the shift toward greater acknowledgment of Japan's war crimes. At the same time, these gaffes did not represent the official position, since, as in the previous phase, two of the three politicians were forced to apologize and one was forced to resign his cabinet position. For example, in May 1994 Justice Minister Nagano Shigeto, who was a former LDP member and former chief of staff of the army, denied Japanese aggression and the Nanjing Massacre, which he called a "hoax." In response, PM Hata, under pressure from China and South Korea, forced Nagano to apologize, retract his statements, and resign.[65] Arguably, the government disavowed and distanced itself more strongly from this gaffe, compared with the two revisionist statements made in 1990, because the LDP was out of power (albeit not for long), because China and other Asian countries protested more strongly than they had in 1990, and because the official narrative had come to acknowledge greater remorse for Japan's wrongdoing.

Societal actors also mobilized in response to these gaffes. The most notable response was from the Japan Democratic Lawyers' Association (Nihon Minshu Hōritsuka Kyōkai), which in the wake of Nagano's remarks began to look into and gather evidence of Japan's war crimes and atrocities during the Second Sino-Japanese War. Its investigations led the group to decide to help Chinese victims seek compensation in Japanese courts, which had an impact beginning in the late 1990s.[66]

These responses from both the right and the left marked the beginning of another round of intense domestic contestation over official war memory and responsibility. As we will see in the next phase, this emergent nationalist mobilization would prompt renewed international pressures on Japan while at the same time constraining the degree of change in the state's narrative. Meanwhile, the bottom-up legal mobilization would bring new domestic and international pressures to bear on the official narrative.

Phase Five (1994–1998): Apology and Acknowledgment

The fifth phase began in June 1994, when JSP leader Murayama Tomiichi became PM in a three-party governing coalition that returned the LDP to power, and extended until the end of 1998. The most notable changes in the official narrative in this phase were the official apology by PM Murayama, increased coverage of the Nanjing Massacre and war crimes in textbooks, and the explicit acknowledgment of the Nanjing Massacre in official statements.

These changes were made in response to several factors. First, there were escalating calls from within and outside the country for Japan to apologize for its war crimes and compensate victims. The most important of these were diplomatic protests from former victim states, particularly China and South Korea, which were increasingly frustrated with gaffes by high-level Japanese officials and with growing nationalism in Japan. Throughout this phase, China and South Korea protested against repeated gaffes, revisionists' efforts to reduce textbook coverage of Japan's war crimes, and other statements and actions that signaled that some elites did not accept Japan's responsibility for war crimes.

The emergence of an anti-Japanese nationalist movement in China contributed to this increasing pressure on Japanese officials for compensation and a formal statement of apology. To bolster its domestic legitimacy in the aftermath of the 1989 Tiananmen Square massacre and subsequent crackdown, the Chinese government launched the Patriotic Education Campaign. The campaign emphasized China's past humiliations and victimization at the hands of Japan and Western powers in order to inculcate patriotism and support for the Chinese Communist Party.[67] As a result, Yoshida explains, "popular accounts of the [Nanjing] massacre became widely available to the [Chinese] public, and the Japanese revisionists became notorious among the general public."[68] In response to this campaign, Chinese activists began to agitate for compensation and greater contrition from Japan. Although Chinese authorities tried to prevent this activism from negatively affecting Sino-Japanese relations, they were only partially successful, with Chinese nationalists pressuring the government to take a tougher line on history issues and putting direct pressure on Japan with massive protests and boycotts of Japanese products.[69] At the same time, redress movements in Japan, Korea, and the United States further increased pressure on Japan to apologize and compensate victims.

Second, Japanese officials' and politicians' continued desire for the country to play a more prominent international role led Foreign Ministry officials to conclude that achieving this goal would require new steps with regard to history issues, particularly given that international pressures were escalating and were likely to continue. Complicating this desire was that by the mid-1990s, the drawn-out economic recession had taken its toll on Japan's economy. At the same time, the bounding growth of China's economy meant that international attention to the rise of China had begun to supplant interest in Japan's "economic miracle." This shifting locus of power affected Japanese leaders' assessments of Japan's international role. Consequently, since Japan's stunning economic resurrection had been a core element of Japan's postwar national identity, these developments led some in Japan to begin to search for other bases for Japan's national identity, contributing to an increase in nationalist sentiment.[70]

Given these considerations, Japanese leaders decided that the fiftieth anniversaries of war-related events would be an appropriate time to deepen the degree of official contrition. Officials, especially in the MOFA, decided that a broad apology that went further than Hosokawa's statements might reduce the potential for history issues to more seriously impact Japan's foreign relations. This decision was reinforced by PM Murayama's long-standing commitment to the view that Japan should do more to acknowledge its war responsibility.

At the same time, domestic contention over history issues complicated the realization of this goal. In particular, the increasingly vocal and organized nationalist movement in Japan strongly opposed further expressions of acknowledgment and contrition. Consequently, while international pressures and expectations shaped the perceived need for further contrition and acknowledgment, domestic politics again influenced the timing and the content of changes in the state's narrative.

Japan's first postwar Socialist PM, Murayama Tomiichi, took office on 30 June 1994 at the head of a coalition that included the JSP, the LDP, and the New Party Sakigake. Although this coalition signaled the LDP's return to power, that Murayama held the office of PM had important implications for Japan's narrative. The leading opposition party for much of the postwar period, the leftist and pacifist JSP had long been committed to more honestly addressing Japan's wartime aggression. As part of the negotiations to form the coalition, Murayama demanded—and the other two parties agreed—that the Diet pass a parliamentary resolution on the fiftieth anniversary of the war's end "to repent Japan's past military actions and to declare that it will never again invade its neighbours."[71]

Within a month of taking office, Murayama announced that the government would launch a Peace, Friendship, and Exchange Initiative to mark the fiftieth anniversary of the war's end the following year. The initiative involved spending 100 billion yen (about a billion USD) over several years "to support historical research" and "exchange programs to promote dialogue and mutual understanding."[72] In announcing the initiative, Murayama reiterated the government's recognition of and apology for its involvement in the comfort women program and offered his own "profound and sincere remorse and apologies." In addition, he stated: "Japan's actions in a certain period of the past not only claimed numerous victims here in Japan but also left the peoples of neighboring Asia and elsewhere with scars that are painful even today. I am thus taking this opportunity to state my belief, based on my profound remorse for these acts of aggression, colonial rule, and the like [that] caused such unbearable suffering and sorrow for so many people, that Japan's future path should be one of making every effort to build world peace in line with my no-war commitment."[73] Although his statement did not advance the content of the official narrative, it hinted at the changes that would come the following year. At the same time, the initiative highlighted a long-standing and continuing aspect of Japan's narrative: the refusal to pay compensation to individual, non-Japanese victims. The program focused on developing and enhancing "mutual understanding" between Japan and "the peoples of neighboring Asia and elsewhere," but it conspicuously avoided compensating actual victims of Japan's actions.

As Murayama's statements and actions signaled deepening acknowledgment and contrition, conservatives and nationalists mobilized in opposition. An overt sign of opposition were two gaffes by prominent politicians. In an August 1994 press conference immediately following a cabinet meeting to discuss the proposed Peace, Friendship, and Exchange Initiative, Sakurai Shin declared: "I don't think Japan fought with the aim of waging a war of aggression" and "I don't think we should take the position that Japan was the only one that was wrong."[74] In October of that year, cabinet minister and future PM Hashimoto Ryūtarō demurred in answering a question about whether Japan had fought a war of aggression, saying: "Whether Japan actually launched a war of aggression against its neighbours in Asia is a delicate question of definition," and "it is still questionable whether the war Japan launched in those years was a war of aggression."[75] While Sakurai was forced to retract his mythmaking and relativizing statements and resign, the powerful Hashimoto only apologized.[76]

Within the Diet, two committees formed to oppose the issuance of a formal apology for the war. The Diet Members League for the Fiftieth Anniversary of the End of the War, which was established in December 1994 with more than two hundred LDP members, sought "to revise the 'masochistic understanding' of wartime and prewar Japanese history."[77] A few months later, members of the opposition New Frontier Party (Shinshintō) formed the Diet Members League for the Passing on of a Correct History.[78] Meanwhile, the Japan War-Bereaved Families Association and the National Conference to Defend Japan, which were two of the most influential right-wing, nationalist interest groups in Japan, together established the National Committee for the Fiftieth Anniversary of the End of World

War II. This committee gathered signatures on a national petition opposing the resolution and successfully pressured Diet members to vote against it.

This intense mobilization against the proposed resolution succeeded in limiting the extent of change, despite the significance of both the fiftieth anniversary and Murayama's leadership. An important reason for the influence of right-wing interest groups was the March 1994 reform of electoral and campaign finance rules.[79] Although conservative groups such as the Japan War-Bereaved Families Association and the Association of Shinto Shrines had long been influential within the LDP, their clout increased in the latter half of the 1990s, especially among conservative and nationalist politicians and within the MOE and the Ministry of Health and Welfare. As restrictions on campaign fund-raising were tightened, interest groups that could bring attention to individual politicians and get out the vote in individual districts were even more important. Moreover, the economic recession had reduced campaign donations, so politicians were more reliant on those interest groups that continued to support them.[80]

Although the Diet resolution did not pass until June, the constraining effects of the political right were signaled in May 1995, when Murayama visited the Marco Polo Bridge outside Beijing. As a symbolically important first visit by a Japanese PM to the site of the "incident" that had officially started the Second Sino-Japanese War, it was notable that Murayama did not apologize during his visit. This was even more notable given that Murayama and his party, the JSP, had long advocated for greater contrition for and acknowledgment of Japan's war crimes. Analysts interpreted this omission as an attempt to balance Murayama's and the JSP's inclinations (on one hand) and nationalists' demands (on the other).[81]

A month later, when the Diet passed the much-debated Resolution to Renew the Determination for Peace on the Basis of Lessons Learned from History, the success of domestic opposition to the resolution was evident. A range of conservative politicians and right-wing groups had vehemently opposed the issuance of an apology, arguing that doing so would "desecrate the honor of Japanese soldiers killed in action," "erode pride in the nation among youths," affirm "the distorted interpretation of history that has prevailed in the postwar period," "become an obstacle to Japan's future," and "mean that the Japanese would be eternally labeled a cruel and inhuman people."[82] In addition to these identity concerns, conservative politicians also had electoral-political concerns that gave them further incentive to oppose the proposed apology resolution. As Benfell explains, the Izokukai-backed National Committee for the Fiftieth Anniversary of the End of World War II had "threatened to withdraw electoral support from conservative politicians who supported (or even refused to oppose) the resolution."[83] Together, the national petition campaign, the political pressure put on individual candidates by Izokukai and others, and the organized opposition within the LDP and the New Frontier Party resulted in a significantly diluted resolution that was barely passed by the Diet.

The resolution, which merely expressed "deep remorse," did not meet the original goal of issuing an apology. It also relativized Japan's wartime actions by contextualizing them in relation to other countries' "colonial rule and acts." The key part of the resolution reads: "Solemnly reflecting upon many instances of colonial rule and acts of aggression in the modern history of the world, and recognizing that Japan carried out those acts in the past, inflicting pain and suffering upon the peoples of other countries, especially in Asia, the Members of this House express a sense of deep remorse."[84] As Yamazaki writes, "By enlarging the scope, by introducing the much larger scene of international wrongdoing, the resolution attempts to dwarf the wrongdoing of Japan."[85] As Wakamiya further notes, the use of the phrase "acts of aggression," rather than the unqualified term "aggression" that Hosokawa had used, "was clearly a step backward."[86]

Chinese officials shared these perceptions. When former PM and Diet member and Shinshintō party leader Kaifu visited China at the end of June and asked the Chinese leader Jiang Zemin to support Japan in its bid for a permanent UNSC seat, Jiang's response indicated his displeasure with the Diet resolution. Noting that "the idea was 'complicated by Japanese perceptions of the war,'" Jiang advised: "When it comes to perceptions of the war, the Germans have shown how to win credibility."[87]

In addition to the Diet resolution, in July 1995 the Japanese government announced that it was setting up the Asian Women's Fund to compensate surviving former comfort women.[88] Although the fund offered "atonement money" "from the Japanese people" and a letter of apology signed by the Japanese PM, it was widely criticized because it was made explicit that the compensation should *not* be considered reparations or compensation from the Japanese government.[89] To maintain this distinction, the government contributed only 500 million yen (about 5.7 million USD), which was intended to support the running of the fund and the payment of welfare and medical expenses for surviving comfort women. The "atonement money" itself was to come from private donations from Japanese citizens and firms. This arrangement reflected Japanese officials' continued material concerns, manifested in their reluctance to compensate individual victims of Japan's war crimes. As a former senior Foreign Ministry official explained, although Murayama wanted individuals to be directly compensated by the Japanese government, the LDP and the MOFA feared that such a step would undermine the legal framework of Japan's postwar settlements and open the door to myriad individual claims against the Japanese government.[90] Consequently, when the fund officially closed in March 2007, it had disbursed "approximately

565 million yen from citizen donations," and "approximately 750 million yen from government funds went to medical welfare support."[91] Notably, also in 1995, the Japanese government offered "bonds worth 400,000 yen ($4,545) to each of the 1.51 million war-bereaved families and living veterans who sustained injuries during the war—a $6.8 billion gesture."[92]

Around the same time, the Japanese government announced plans to establish the Japan Center for Asian Historical Records (Ajia rekishi shiryō sentaa) as part of the Peace, Friendship, and Exchange Initiative that Murayama had announced the year before. The center opened in 2001 and was intended (in part) as an alternative to the Shōwa Hall museum.[93] The Japan War-Bereaved Families Association had originally proposed Shōwa Hall to the Ministry of Health and Welfare in 1979, and by 1995 its planning had devolved into controversy. According to Jeans, whereas Izokukai envisioned the museum as a "memorial hall for the war dead" that would "focus on the sufferings of Japanese civilians and soldiers in the war," critics argued that the plans for the museum would present a "one-sided" and "'unbalanced' impression of Japan's role in the war."[94] The Ministry of Health and Welfare, which was in charge of the Shōwa Hall project and seems to have sympathized with Izokukai, attempted to skirt the political problem of having to decide which view to present in the museum by focusing on the lives of Japanese civilians and soldiers during the war. In contrast, Jeans reports, the Japan Center for Asian Historical Records was intended to "exhibit a more comprehensive history of the war than the Showa Hall and, most importantly, recognize the suffering caused by Japan during the war."[95]

The most significant change in the state's narrative came in the form of a statement of heartfelt apology and acknowledgment made by Murayama on 15 August 1995. Moving beyond both the "standard formulation" developed by the MOFA in 1991 and Hosokawa's 1993 statements, Murayama worked with the MOFA to come up with a new formulation that included an explicit apology.[96] In addition to Murayama's personal commitment to greater acknowledgment and contrition, MOFA officials viewed the fiftieth anniversary as an appropriate time to address the issue anew. They hoped both to fend off the growing clamor of international calls for Japan to apologize and to counter the right-wing nationalist movement in the Diet, which MOFA officials believed was threatening relations with Japan's neighbors.[97] As a former senior MOFA official noted, crafting the statement was challenging, because it needed to reflect the current state of public opinion in Japan on the issue. This official further opined that if an LDP politician had been PM at the time, it would have been much more difficult to make such an apology, because an LDP politician might not have felt that he could make such a statement for fear of criticism from within the party.[98] Thus, while Murayama, his cabinet, and the MOFA sought to respond to international pressures and dissatisfaction with a step in the direction of greater acknowledgment and contrition, domestic contestation, identity concerns, and electoral-political concerns shaped the form of that response.

Despite these considerations and constraints, Murayama's speech states (in part):

> During a certain period in the not too distant past, Japan, following a mistaken national policy, advanced along the road to war, only to ensnare the Japanese people in a fateful crisis, and, through its colonial rule and aggression, caused tremendous damage and suffering to the people of many countries, particularly to those of Asian nations. In the hope that no such mistake be made in the future, I regard, in a spirit of humility, these irrefutable facts of history, and express here once again my feelings of deep remorse and state my heartfelt apology. Allow me also to express my feelings of profound mourning for all victims, both at home and abroad, of that history.[99]

The most important part of the speech is the phrase "heartfelt apology" (*kokoro kara no owabi*).[100] Whereas Japanese officials had made statements of apology for the government's involvement in the comfort women program, prior to this there had been no official apology for the war as a whole or for the full range of victims of Japan's aggression. In addition, by referring to "a mistaken national policy," Murayama repeated Hosokawa's characterization of the war as "mistaken." Evidencing its importance and status as the new standard formulation, this statement has since been reaffirmed by PMs, Japanese officials, and the MOFA.

The statement was not received as positively as Japanese officials might have hoped. Most notably, China's lukewarm response included a warning that "some people in Japanese society, including political circles, are still unable to adopt a correct attitude toward the history of that period."[101] One sign of this "incorrect" attitude was conservative and nationalist Diet members' and cabinet ministers' continued visits to the Yasukuni Shrine. While each year some politicians and cabinet ministers visited the shrine on 15 August, on the day that Murayama issued his apology, ten cabinet ministers and about sixty parliamentarians visited the shrine. As Lai explains, "Some critics associate such visits with the revival of chauvinistic nationalism and Japanese militarism, while others perceive them as a sign of 'historical amnesia' representing Japan's enduring inability to reflect on its wartime responsibility and actions."[102] Neither interpretation was consistent with the spirit or aims of Murayama's statement. The following year, moreover, the new PM Hashimoto Ryūtarō made the first visit to the shrine by a PM since Nakasone's visit a decade before.[103] Although Hashimoto insisted his visit was private (i.e., not official), and despite the fact that it was not made on 15 August, it elicited strong protests from China, South Korea, and other countries, along with popular protests in China.[104] As a result, Hashimoto did not visit Yasukuni again as PM. And yet, although Hashimoto recognized the importance of bending to international pressure on this symbolic issue, like his predecessors he sought to balance such demands with those of domestic nationalist groups. Thus, when he visited China in 1997 on the twenty-fifth anniversary of the normalization of Sino-Japanese relations, Hashimoto explicitly avoided visiting Nanjing, despite pressure from China to do so. According to a newspaper report at the time, he refused because "an implicit act of contrition on such a major issue would incite a right wing backlash from within his own country."[105]

Another indication of "incorrect" attitudes was the increased frequency of revisionist statements by high-level officials and politicians. Moreover, in this phase only some of the ministers who made such statements were forced to resign, eliciting consternation from Japan's neighbors and former victims. For example, in August 1995, Education Minister Shimamura Yoshinobu was not forced to resign—although he did apologize—for saying, "It makes little sense to keep harping on the past and apologizing for one particular incident after another" and "Whether Japan pursued a war of aggression depended on 'how you think about it.'"[106] This and similar earlier statements—by Hashimoto, Sakurai, and others—underscored the resistance among some high-level politicians to the trend toward deepening acknowledgment and contrition.

Domestic contestation also focused on textbooks' coverage of Japan's WWII atrocities. The official commitment to greater acknowledgment was also apparent in increased textbook coverage of Japan's war crimes and atrocities. The Nanjing Massacre was included in almost every junior high and high school history textbook, and MOE reviewers allowed higher death toll estimates, including "more than 100,000 deaths" and estimates of "200,000 or above."[107] Yoshida reports, "Six out of seven junior history textbooks available in 1997 stated that the Japanese military killed between 100,000 and 200,000 Chinese during and after the Battle of Nanjing. Four of them also gave the Chinese official estimate of 300,000."[108] Textbooks also expressed stronger judgments of the Nanjing Massacre, referring, for example, to the Japanese military's "hideous" actions.[109] Additional changes in textbooks' coverage included references to the "war of aggression" and to Japan's chemical and biological warfare and use of slave labor, and acknowledgment that "some of Japan's war compensation problems have not been resolved."[110]

In response to these trends, and related to the broader nationalist mobilization, the "third textbook offensive" began in mid-1996. In reaction to the news that all of the junior high school history textbooks approved by the MOE included references to the comfort women program, education professor Fujioka

Nobukatsu and literature professor Nishio Kanji established the Society for the Creation of New History Textbooks (Atarashii Rekishi Kyōkasho o Tsukuru-kai, known as Tsukurukai). Highlighting the identity concerns that motivated them, Fujioka stated: "If the Japanese do not learn of a history that they can be proud of, they will lose their national identity, leading to the spiritual breakdown of Japan."[111] Advocates of textbook revision further argued that the "anti-Japanese" textbooks approved by the ministry "could undermine children's faith in their country."[112] Importantly, Tsukurukai was supported by the National Conference to Defend Japan, a powerful conservative interest group, and by prominent nationalists. In 1997, the National Conference to Defend Japan and the Association to Defend Japan (Nihon o Mamoru Kai) merged to form the Japan Conference (Nippon Kaigi). One of the most powerful right-wing political groups in Japan, the Japan Congress played an important role in this revisionist textbook offensive. Although Tsukurukai and Nippon Kaigi did not have formal ties, representatives of both acknowledge that the two organizations "worked together" on the textbook issue.[113]

As part of this "offensive," Diet members in the LDP and the New Frontier Party formed separate committees focused on the revision of history textbooks.[114] Echoing Tsukurukai's rationale, former education minister and LDP Diet member Shimamura Yoshinobu stated: "We need to seek ways how we can restore our glorious history, tradition and pride."[115] Within a couple of years, this movement succeeded in scaling back history textbooks' coverage of Japan's war crimes.

In response to this revisionist movement, domestic and international groups mobilized to counter their efforts and push for greater acknowledgment and contrition in both textbooks and other domains. Within Japan, leftist groups mobilized in opposition to Tsukurukai et al.'s efforts, thereby demonstrating the back-and-forth movement of domestic contestation over history issues. One such group was Children and Textbooks Japan Network 21 (Kodomo to Kyōkasho Zenkoku Netto 21), which was founded in June 1998 by three hundred activists who had been in Ienaga's support organization.[116]

Outside Japan, the transnational redress movement continued to raise awareness of Japan's war crimes and put pressure on Japan to more fully acknowledge and apologize for them. Led by a group of Chinese American activists, the Global Alliance for Preserving the History of World War II organized academic conferences and exhibits on the Nanjing Massacre and other aspects of Japan's war crimes and supported efforts to bring lawsuits seeking compensation for victims of Japanese atrocities in US courts and elsewhere. Although the Global Alliance first emerged in California, within several years it had expanded to include at least thirty NGOs. Interestingly, there have been a number of connections between this movement and groups working to maintain the memory of the Holocaust and bring to justice those guilty of involvement in it.[117] Moreover, lawyers and activists involved in the transnational Japanese war crimes redress movement borrowed inspiration and ideas from efforts to preserve the memory of the Holocaust and to push for compensation for Holocaust victims from firms and governments, and also shared ideas across different issue areas (e.g., forced labor and comfort women).[118]

Within the United States, these efforts led to two consequential developments at the governmental level. In December 1996, the US Justice Department's Office of Special Investigations added the names of sixteen Japanese war criminals to its watch list of those banned from entering the country. Although this list had existed since 1979 and included the names of more than sixty thousand Nazi war criminals, this was the first time Japanese war criminals were added to it.[119] And in July 1997, a resolution calling on Japan to apologize and pay reparations for its war crimes—including the Nanjing Massacre—was proposed in the US House of Representatives, although it later died in a House subcommittee.[120] Whereas such resolutions have been an important form of international pressure on Turkey since the mid-1970s, this was the first such resolution addressing Japanese crimes. As in the Turkish case, the State Department actively resisted this and other such efforts to pressure Japan on history issues.

The most significant outcome of this movement was the 1997 publication of what was billed as the first English-language nonfiction account of the Nanjing Massacre. Written by Chinese American journalist Iris Chang, *The Rape of Nanking: The Forgotten Holocaust of World War II* was a best seller in the United States and gained tremendous attention in China and Japan.[121] Despite being widely criticized by historians, the book was influential in several respects. It brought public and academic attention to the Nanjing Massacre in the United States, where the event had previously been relatively unknown, and further galvanized the growing US-based redress movement, from which Chang had emerged and which strongly promoted her book.[122] In addition, the book prompted a widespread debate about the massacre within Japan. Unfortunately, because the book had numerous factual errors, it also provided "evidence" for revisionists to claim that the massacre was a "fabrication" and a "lie."[123] More generally, the book's publication and the attention it received led revisionists to focus more strongly on efforts to downplay and deny the Nanjing Massacre.[124]

In terms of the official narrative, Chang's book elicited Japanese officials' first explicit acknowledgment of the factuality of the Nanjing Massacre and the Japanese military's involvement in it. Remarkably, up to this point the Nanjing Massacre had not been explicitly acknowledged in an official statement. Of course, numerous official statements had acknowledged the suffering of the Chinese people, Japanese textbooks had included basic references to the Nanjing

Massacre since the mid-1980s, and Japan had officially accepted the verdict of the Tokyo Trials—in which two defendants were convicted and executed for failing to prevent the massacre—in the San Francisco Treaty.[125] That said, it was only in response to the debate and controversy over Chang's book that Japanese officials finally explicitly acknowledged—in statements, rather than just in textbooks—the Nanjing Massacre and the military's involvement in it. These acknowledgments emerged over the course of a year, with the help of pressure from China. The first acknowledgment came in late 1997, on the sixtieth anniversary of the Nanjing Massacre, when the Japanese ambassador to China stated: "The Nanjing incident must be remembered clearly. We should not repeat such history."[126] Later, in response to mounting criticism in the international media that stemmed from charges in Iris Chang's book, Japanese ambassador to the United States Saitō Kunihiko rejected accusations that the Japanese government had denied, covered up, or refused to apologize for the Nanjing Massacre. This was in a tele-vised debate with Iris Chang, in which Saitō also noted that the Japanese govern-ment had expressed remorse and apology to China. He further stated: "'We do recognize a really unfortunate thing happened and acts of violence were commit-ted by members of the Japanese military' in Nanjing."[127] This statement recog-nized the involvement of the Japanese military in "acts of violence" in Nanjing but avoided acknowledging the event as a massacre or the responsibility of the government for its outcome. A few weeks later, in response to Chinese diplo-matic complaints over a Japanese civil ruling in a libel case related to the Nan-jing Massacre, the MOFA officially acknowledged that the event was a massacre that Japanese troops had perpetrated. Ministry spokesman Numata Sadaaki declared: "Our historical perception remains unchanged . . . about the fact the massacre of civilians occurred." He further stated: "The Japanese government be-lieves it was an irrefutable fact that after entering Nanjing, the Japanese troops in those days killed non-combat personnel and committed robberies."[128] These statements finally directly and explicitly acknowledged the Nanjing Massacre and the Japanese government's role in it.

Also in the mid to late 1990s, a handful of court rulings in Japan recognized the Nanjing Massacre and other war crimes as historical facts. Rulings in Ienaga's third lawsuit against the MOE recognized the Nanjing Massacre as a historical event, first in a 1993 decision by the Tokyo District Court and then in a 1997 de-cision by the Supreme Court. The Supreme Court ruling also affirmed the existence of Unit 731, which (as noted earlier) was one of several secret medical units that had developed biological and chemical weapons and conducted "scientific" experi-ments on live Chinese prisoners and POWs during the war. This ruling was the first time that the Japanese government recognized this program's existence.[129]

In addition to Ienaga's cases against the MOE, between 1995 and 2005 more than three hundred lawyers in the Lawyers Team for Chinese War Victims Demanding Compensation helped file more than twenty cases on behalf of Chinese victims.[130] A key development in this process came in March 1995, when the Chinese Foreign Ministry announced that Chinese war victims would be permitted to make individual compensation claims against the Japanese government.[131] This announcement came as opposition to a Diet resolution was building in Japan, so it might have been an attempt by Chinese officials to put pressure on Japanese officials to stick to the announced plan to issue a formal apology. Following this policy change, Japanese lawyers intensified their efforts to help Chinese victims of war crimes (and their families) file lawsuits in Japanese courts seeking compensation from the Japanese government and firms for their suffering.[132]

Although most of the plaintiffs lost their cases, the lawsuits had an indirect impact on Japan's official narrative, since the courts affirmed all of the historical facts brought up in the cases and found that the Japanese Imperial Army's conduct in WWII was illegal.[133] Over the longer term, these cases have contributed to the information that is publicly available in Japan.[134] Notably, as courts have confirmed various events as historical facts, textbook authors and publishers have had a stronger basis for including them in textbooks, since the MOE requires textbook authors to cite scholarship and evidence that firmly establish events as facts. These rulings thus contributed to the increasing coverage of war crimes—especially the Nanjing Massacre and the comfort women program—in textbooks throughout the 1990s.

In response to the multifaceted deepening of official acknowledgment and contrition in this phase, conservatives and nationalists within and outside the government intensified their efforts to halt and reverse these changes. They scored a significant victory in this regard in the context of the symbolic first visit to Japan of a Chinese premier. In the approach to Jiang Zemin's November 1998 visit, Japanese officials signaled that they were considering issuing a written apology during his visit, particularly as Japan had proffered a written apology to South Korean leader Kim Daejung when he had visited Japan that October.[135] Despite these early indications, the MOFA and the PM ended up refusing to issue a formal written apology to China. A key factor behind this decision was the electoral-political concern that doing so would threaten the stability of the coalition government and the position of PM Obuchi Keizō within the LDP, since many conservative Diet members strongly objected to this step. This decision also highlighted differences in Japanese officials' perceptions of China and South Korea. One official noted that Japan had a larger historical debt to Korea because of Japan's colonial rule of the Korean peninsula.[136] In addition, officials were concerned that China would not stop using "history issues" as a "diplomatic trump card" and source of political leverage.[137] As Wakamiya explains, "The Chinese side refused to have 'reconciliation' expressly stated in the text of the Joint Declaration, hinting that China, unlike Korea, would continue to be concerned with problems of the past."[138] Thus, despite intense pressure from China and last-minute negotiations, Japan refused to issue a written apology. Instead, Obuchi verbally apologized—using the language of Murayama's 1995 apology— but both sides considered this to be less significant than a formal written apology. This unexpected outcome soured the remainder of Jiang's visit, during which he repeatedly and insistently brought up history issues.[139] It also signaled the continued contentiousness of history issues, both within Japan and in its foreign relations.

Phase Six (1999–2008): Attempting to Break the Spell of History

The sixth phase began in 1999 and continued through the end of my analysis in 2008.[140] This phase featured frequent apologies, some of which went further than Murayama's 1995 apology, alongside signals that Japanese officials and politicians were tiring of apologizing. Even so, officials continued to express their "heartfelt apology" for Japan's past aggression and for the suffering of victims of its war crimes. These apologies were issued in response to pressure for greater contrition from China, South Korea, and other states, and were intended to reassure these states and their citizens that Japan remained committed to past statements of apology and acknowledgment. In addition, Japanese officials explicitly acknowledged the Nanjing Massacre at several junctures. These statements went further than previous ones by explicitly acknowledging that the Japanese army had killed civilians in Nanjing. Thus, on the face of things, official rhetoric shifted slightly in the direction of greater contrition.

Victims and victim states often perceived these apologies as perfunctory and insincere, however, because they were contradicted by other statements, actions, and policies. Thus, alongside more frequent apologies and increased acknowledgment, the narrative was also characterized by increased mythmaking and relativizing, including diminished coverage of Japan's war crimes in textbooks and the resumption of prime ministerial visits to the Yasukuni Shrine. High-level officials also continued to make gaffes, but in this phase politicians who spoke *with* the official voice of the state made many of them. In addition, the officials who made such statements were not asked to resign or apologize, signaling that the government was not distancing itself from the statements.

Escalating protests by and pressures from China and South Korea drove the continued issuance of official apologies by Japanese officials. In addition, China's patriotic education policies and Japanese responses to the shifting relative balance of power fueled the growth in China of anti-Japanese nationalism. Thus, as Japanese officials wearied of being pressed to apologize for past wrongs, and as signs of this "apology fatigue" undermined perceptions of Japanese officials' sincerity, Chinese nationalists increasingly protested Japan's actions. Over time, this nationalism constrained Chinese officials' ability to compromise in dealing with "history issues" in the context of bilateral relations with Japan. At stake for Chinese officials was their legitimacy in the eyes of Chinese nationalists and the broader public, which had been socialized by years of anti-Japanese propaganda and by the narratives pushed in the state's patriotic education policies.[141] Consequently, this nationalism contributed to a dangerous hardening of official positions on both sides of the Sino-Japanese relationship.

Alongside these external pressures for greater acknowledgment and contrition, societal actors, interest groups, and politicians in Japan continued to push for the revision of textbooks and other steps to reduce attention to Japan's war crimes. In this phase, the ascendance of more nationalist politicians in the Diet, along with the demise of the political left, meant that the locus of the revisionist movement shifted from Japanese society to the government itself.[142] Moreover, given that both the JSP (later the Social Democratic Party of Japan) and the Japan Communist Party had pushed for greater contrition and for improving relations with China, their diminished relevance in national politics by the late 1990s meant that there was no strong, clear institutional voice to argue against the increasingly visible and powerful revisionists.[143] Nationalists were leading figures in the LDP, and a series of politicians with nationalist and revisionist views served as PM, notably Abe Shinzō, Asō Tarō, and Mori Yoshirō. As a result, politicians and elected officials themselves were often the motivating forces behind revisionist statements and actions.[144] At the same time, violence and its ever-present threat by nationalists on the far right quieted voices of dissent within Japan—including influential ones in the political and economic realms. Consequently, the revisionist movement succeeded in militating against external pressures for greater contrition and acknowledgment and in shifting some aspects of the narrative toward mythmaking and relativizing.

At the beginning of this phase, both China and South Korea refrained from bringing up history issues in their relations with Japan, albeit for slightly different reasons. In October 1998, South Korean president Kim had promised that the historical acrimony related to Japan's colonization of Korea would be put to rest by PM Obuchi's written apology, and in the early part of this phase, Korean officials upheld this promise. In contrast, Chinese officials' reticence was due to perceptions among Chinese and Japanese officials that Chinese premier Jiang Zemin had overplayed the "history card" in his November 1998 visit. Chinese officials sought to repair the perceived damage to the bilateral relationship by avoiding history issues in the beginning of this phase. This was evident during Obuchi's June 1999 visit to Beijing and in Chinese premier Zhu Rongji's October 2000 visit to Japan.[145]

Alongside this intention, the shifting balance of power between China and Japan was destabilizing long-standing givens in Sino-Japanese relations. Highlighting China's waning economic dependence on Japan, a March 2005 article in the state-run *China Daily* noted, "China now trades more with the European Union and the United States than it does with Japan, which had been China's largest trade partner for 11 consecutive years before 2003. In terms of foreign direct investment in China, Japan was also replaced by the Republic of Korea for the first time in 2004, dropping from the third to the fourth in foreign investment [in China]."[146] And yet, trade between the two countries continued to deepen, increasing more than 25 percent between 2003 and 2004, and Japanese businesses increasingly viewed China's economic growth as an opportunity rather than a threat.[147]

Japan's relative decline attenuated the identity crisis that had been triggered by the abrupt end of the Japanese economic "miracle" in 1990. In the first four decades after the war, Japanese nationalism had been constructed around pride in the country's remarkable economic growth. As this was undercut by the economic recession, Japanese elites attempted to construct alternative bases for national identity, including efforts to reclaim Japan's history and past as sources of pride. Japanese officials and politicians also sought to bolster Japan's international status and to make Japan a more "normal" nation, including in its relations with China. According to Samuels, these "normal nation-alists," as he labels them, believe that "the statute of limitations for Japan's mid-twentieth century aggression expired long ago; it is time for Japan to step onto the international stage as an equal of the United States."[148] As Soeya further explains, "Conservative politicians . . . strongly believe that China uses the 'history card' to keep Japan down and to check Japan's move toward 'independence.'"[149] Signs of these identity concerns—along with the increased mythmaking and relativizing in Japan's narrative, and the impact of China's "patriotic education" policies on Chinese views—put Chinese officials on guard, fed anti-Japanese sentiment in China, and contributed to the deterioration of Sino-Japanese relations.

Early signs of these dynamics came at the beginning of the phase. Aiming to restore pride in Japan's history, conservative politicians and bureaucrats in the MOE, along with revisionist groups within Japanese society, sought to reduce or remove references to war crimes in history textbooks. In January 1999, the MOE requested that publishers make sure that textbooks were "more balanced." In response to this request, and possibly also to behind-the-scenes pressure on textbook publishers from government officials, "when the final drafts . . . were actually submitted to the MOE in the spring of 2000," Nozaki writes, "many descriptions concerning Japanese wartime atrocities had been cut back or removed altogether."[150] Compared with earlier textbooks by the same publishers, "two of the seven textbooks had changed the phrase 'Nanjing massacre' to 'Nanjing incident.'"[151] Moreover, of the six textbooks that included the Nanjing Massacre, "only one put a concrete figure—200,000—on the number of casualties. . . . The others either described the number of casualties as 'many' or said there is no accepted count or that the tally is still in debate."[152]

Other signs of revisionism around the same time prompted Japanese officials to repeatedly restate the government's acknowledgment of the Nanjing Massacre. In April 1999, former LDP Diet member Ishihara Shintarō—who had previously questioned the existence of the Nanjing Massacre—was elected mayor of Tokyo. In response to Chinese concerns over his election, Chief Cabinet Secretary Nonaka Hiromu clarified the Japanese government's position, stating: "It cannot be denied that civilians were killed and looting took place when Japanese troops conquered Nanjing and entered the city."[153] A month later, in response to Chinese protests over new statements by Ishihara, Foreign Ministry spokesman Numata Sadaaki "reiterated Japan's apology and remorse for the suffering and damage inflicted on other Asian people during the war" and stated, "It can't be denied the imperial Japanese army massacred civilians and engaged in looting after the fall of Nanjing."[154] This time Numata acknowledged the role of the Imperial Japanese Army in massacring civilians.

Several months later, Japanese officials again felt compelled to confirm the factuality of the Nanjing Massacre. In September 1999, a Tokyo District Court judge ruled against the plaintiffs in a compensation case brought against the Japanese government on behalf of victims of the Nanjing Massacre and Unit 731, finding that they did "not have the right to directly ask the Japanese government to compensate them for even the most inhuman of actions."[155] Alongside this core finding, the ruling also stated: "The atrocity known as the Nanjing Massacre definitely happened, although the exact scale of the devastation is not known."[156] The ruling, which called on the Japanese government to apologize to the Chinese people, was an important acknowledgment of the existence of the Nanjing Massacre and Unit 731, and of the Japanese military's responsibility for both. In response to Chinese protests that the ruling denied the plaintiffs' compensation claims, Nonaka declared: "It cannot be denied that killings of non-combatants and plunder occurred after Japanese troops entered Nanjing city walls."[157] While these statements acknowledged the massacre, the events that prompted their issuance sent mixed messages about Japanese sentiments.

A similar dynamic played out a few months later. In January 2000, as part of an ongoing struggle between progressive and conservative groups in Japan, a revisionist group held a conference titled "The Biggest Lie in the Twentieth Century: Complete Verification of the Massacre in Nanjing" at the Osaka International Peace Center.[158] Despite diplomatic protests from China, the Japanese government did not intervene to stop the conference, arguing that to do so would violate freedom of speech. In explaining the government's nonintervention, Numata again stated: "We do feel it is an undeniable fact that after the Japanese army entered Nanjing in 1937, there were noncombatants who were killed, and looting and other acts."[159] This assertion did little to blunt Chinese dissatisfaction. The conference was strongly criticized by Chinese agencies and media outlets. A few days later, Chinese hackers attacked a number of Japanese government websites, replacing their content with accusations of glossing over the country's war crimes.[160] This was a harbinger of growing popular protests in China related to history issues.

In addition to this conference, revisionist groups in Japan launched other efforts, particularly focused on the Nanjing Massacre. The most notable initiative was the junior high school history textbook that Tsukurukai prepared and submitted for review in early 2000. Even though this textbook—known as the *Fusōsha* textbook—minimized coverage of Japan's war crimes, it received strong support from within the Diet and the MOE. Later that year, one of the founders of Tsukurukai, Fujioka Nobukatsu, together with the academic Higashinakano Osamichi, established a research group called the Japan Association for "Nanjing" Studies (Nihon "Nankin" Gakkai), which, according to Yoshida, focused on publishing reports and books arguing that "the Nanjing Massacre was not historical truth, but an illusion resulting from political manipulation."[161] At the same time, the powerful, right-wing interest group Japan Conference published a book titled *The Alleged "Nanking Massacre": Japan's Rebuttal to China's Forged Claims*, which argued that increasing attention to the massacre was a Chinese strategy to undermine US-Japan relations.[162]

In a sign of feedback effects from the push and pull of domestic contestation, these revisionist efforts inspired and occurred alongside continued counterefforts by progressives in Japan and activists elsewhere. Over the course of the 1990s, redress movements in South Korea and the United States expanded and became more visible, and transnational connections between groups developed. These networks often involved societal groups in Japan, such as the progressive Japanese educators and textbook activists who collaborated with Chinese and

Korean counterparts to develop a joint supplementary textbook on modern Asian history.[163] Japanese lawyers also continued to help Chinese victims bring lawsuits in Japanese courts. Wan reports, "As of March 2005, Chinese citizens had filed 26 lawsuits against the Japanese government and Japanese companies in the Japanese courts. . . . Three categories of victims have brought the suits: victims of forced labor (16), victims of war atrocities (6), and comfort women (4)."[164] While most of these cases were unsuccessful, several rulings affirmed the facts of the Nanjing Massacre and other war crimes. For example, the Nanjing Massacre was affirmed in a May 2002 Tokyo District Court ruling in a libel case brought by a survivor of the Nanjing Massacre against the author and publisher of a book that questioned the event.[165] This was also the case in the Japanese Supreme Court's 2007 ruling that foreclosed the possibility of individual compensation for victims of Japanese war crimes. As Koga notes, "Despite its firm rejection, the court acknowledged in unprecedented, strong language the violence and injustice committed by the Japanese government and corporations during the war."[166]

At the governmental level, official protests from China, Korea, and other countries increased as revisionists' efforts led to changes in the state's narrative. In contrast to the previous phase, however, China's and South Korea's demands went largely unheeded. Illustrating this, in January 2001, PM Mori referred "to the Pacific War as the 'Greater East Asia War,' and to the Sino-Japanese War as the 'China Incident.'"[167] Both terms are widely understood as revisionist, and yet the only official response was a statement by the chief cabinet secretary that "the terms were inappropriate."[168]

Around the same time, it was reported that, despite earlier warnings from China and South Korea, the MOE was going to approve the *Fusōsha* textbook, which characterized the Nanjing Massacre as contested and in doubt. Moreover, the coverage of war crimes was notably reduced in all the textbooks the MOE approved for use beginning in 2002. As the Associated Press reported, "Only one of the eight [approved textbooks] mentioned sex slaves, and none mentioned the scale of the Nanjing massacre."[169]

In response, China, South Korea, and other countries lodged strong diplomatic protests. South Korea issued a statement expressing "deep regret" and recalled its ambassador to Japan, and Koreans protested in Seoul and boycotted Japanese products.[170] Meanwhile, Chinese officials warned that the textbook "could 'damage the friendship' between the two countries" and recalled their ambassador to Japan, and Taiwan and North Korea expressed their displeasure.[171] But, in a sign of Japan's decreasing receptivity to such criticism, newly elected PM Koizumi acknowledged these criticisms but refused to intervene. Consequently, after a number of minor revisions were made, the ministry approved the *Fusōsha* textbook in

April 2001. Despite the ministry's approval, Park reports that the *Fusōsha* text-book "was adopted by fewer than 0.04 per cent of middle schools in 2002."[172] This is because decisions about textbook use are made at the local level, either by school boards or by schools themselves.

The limited adoption notwithstanding, the trend toward diminished acknowledgment continued, driven by identity concerns and electoral-political concerns stemming from contestation by right-wing nationalist groups. These efforts were led by Tsukurukai, with strong support from conservative Diet members and MOE officials, and with the tacit (and in some cases, active) support of the cabinet and PMs. Thus, Japan's relationships with China and Korea declined in the face of the tide of nationalism in Japan and the protest movements that arose in response in China, Korea, the United States, and elsewhere.

Despite the fact that Koizumi was not regarded as particularly nationalist, while in office he exacerbated regional tensions over history issues. One of the main factors was his insistence on visiting the controversial Yasukuni Shrine. Starting in August 2001, Koizumi paid an official visit to the shrine in each of the five-plus years that he was PM, in contrast to the single visit by a sitting PM in the entire prior decade. Koizumi argued that he was *not* visiting the shrine to honor the fourteen enshrined Class A war criminals. Furthermore, until his last year in office, Koizumi avoided visiting the shrine on the 15 August anniversary of the war's end and did not fully comply with the shrine's Shinto rites. These tactics did not placate the escalating chorus of international and domestic criticisms.[173]

Several factors account for Koizumi's intransigence, with electoral-political concerns prominent among them. First, Koizumi wanted to keep his campaign promise to Izokukai to visit the shrine annually, both to restore the public's trust in government officials and to strengthen the power of the executive in Japanese politics.[174] Second, Koizumi wanted to establish a stronger, more independent Japan, and he saw his shrine visits as a way to send China the message that it could not continue to use history issues to elicit economic and political concessions from Japan. According to a 2005 *Financial Times* article, Koizumi explained his visits to a Foreign Ministry official, saying: "Don't you understand? Unless I keep visiting the shrine, China will forever bring up this issue. By continuing to go, I can put a stop to this once and for all."[175] Koizumi refused to accede to domestic and international pressures, and his annual visits, along with those of conservative Diet and cabinet members, contributed to the dramatic deterioration of Japan's relations with its Asian neighbors.

A few months after his first shrine visit, in October 2001, Koizumi visited the Marco Polo Bridge, where the Second Sino-Japanese War officially began. During the visit, Koizumi "expressed his 'heartfelt apology and condolences (*kokoro kara owabi to aitō*) to the Chinese people who fell victim to aggression.'"[176] Koizumi further stated his desire to develop Sino-Japanese relations on the basis of "wholehearted sincerity" and "considerateness."[177] While Chinese president Jiang Zemin indicated his appreciation of this "meaningful action," over time such apologies and arguments that the government's position had not changed could not erase the gradually mounting signals to the contrary.[178]

This occurred within the broader context of increased nationalism in Japan, and against the backdrop of Japan's reevaluation of aspects of its foreign policy and its relations with China. Domestically, there were efforts to move toward the LDP's long-held desire to revise Article 9 of the constitution, and education policies were revised, in part to encourage patriotism among Japanese citizens. Internationally, Koizumi sought to increase Japan's stature. In 2003, the Diet passed a law allowing the JSDF to deploy to Iraq to participate in the postwar reconstruction effort. While the JSDF's participation was extremely limited, this was the first time since WWII that Japanese soldiers were sent into a live war zone.[179] It was also a significant step toward conservatives' long-cherished goal of revising the constitution to eliminate the "unnatural" restrictions on Japan's military. For these reasons, the decision was negatively perceived by Chinese officials, as well as by progressives in Japan.

With regard to Japan's China policies, two major changes occurred during Koizumi's tenure, both reactions to the shifting relative balance of power and a reflection of Japanese officials' desire to "normalize" relations with China. In 2002, Japan began to reduce its ODA to China, which had been a key feature of its foreign policy toward China since relations were normalized in 1972 and had been tacitly understood as being in lieu of reparations. Then in late 2004, Japan identified China as a security concern, "break[ing] a long tradition of pretending that China posed no military problems."[180] This latter shift reflected the fact that Japanese politicians and officials increasingly felt that the "special relationship" with China should come to an end.

Sino-Japanese diplomatic relations more or less ground to a halt during Koizumi's tenure from 2001 to 2006, while Japan's relations with South Korea similarly stagnated in the context of important changes in Korean politics and in South Korea's relationships with North Korea and China. When Hu Jintao became president of China in 2003, he tried to recalibrate relations with Japan, but to little effect.[181] By 2004, after three straight years of shrine visits, Koizumi was unwelcome in China and Chinese officials refused to hold formal bilateral meetings with him. Bilateral and transnational civil society efforts to repair the widening breaches in Japan's relations with South Korea and China had little effect on the deteriorating situation. Such efforts included an advisory panel that explored the possibility of creating an alternative to the Yasukuni Shrine as a site of commemoration, a joint Japan–South Korea history committee launched in 2002, and a similar bilateral committee to look into history issues between China and Japan that was established a few years later.[182]

A consequence of Japan's retrenchment on history issues was that the majority of Asian countries, including China and South Korea, refused to support Japan's 2005 bid for a permanent UNSC seat. The US-based redress movement organized a petition opposing Japan's bid that gathered more than 40 million signatures and helped trigger widespread popular protests in China.[183] In April 2005, anti-Japanese sentiments erupted into massive street protests in many Chinese cities, violent attacks on Japanese businesses and stores in China, and angry protests outside the Japanese embassy in Beijing and the Japanese consulate in Shanghai. Organized against Japan's bid for a permanent UNSC seat, these protests were fueled by anger over the MOE's reapproval of the *Fusōsha* textbook and the continuing decline in textbooks' coverage of Japan's war crimes.[184]

With relations with China and South Korea at a nadir, Koizumi made a strong statement of apology before leaders of one hundred countries at the Asian-African summit in Indonesia in April 2005. This statement was notable because of the audience, which included leaders of many states that had been victims of Japan's aggression and crimes in the war.[185] However, as the historian Arai Shinichi explained at the time, "The problem is that only the words were repeated, but Japan has never done anything to prove it really regretted its past."[186]

Other signals also undercut the perceived sincerity of this apology in the eyes of target audiences. In June 2005, Education Minister Nakayama Nariaki accused teachers and the influential Japan Teachers' Union of having "overemphasized that Japan is a bad country." Instead, he asserted, "We need to educate children so that they can live to be proud and confident as Japanese."[187] He then declared "that 'comfort women' were fiction and that this 'non-existent' issue should be removed from history textbooks." Although both Nakayama and the chief cabinet secretary subsequently acknowledged that comfort women did exist, Nakayama remained in office and did not apologize.[188] Then, on the sixtieth anniversary of the end of the war, the Diet again passed a commemorative resolution. The August 2005 resolution differed from the 1995 one in subtle but important ways. Most notably, "the resolution omitted the references to 'invasion' and 'colonial rule' that were in the version passed on the 50th anniversary."[189] The resolution was, thus, another indication of backtracking.

After Koizumi left office in late September 2006, China and Korea sought to repair relations with Japan. Koizumi's successor, Abe Shinzō, was an avowed nationalist and the grandson of former PM and accused Class A war criminal Kishi Nobusuke. Despite these facts, both China and South Korea were willing to improve relations so long as Abe took an "ambiguous" position on the Yasukuni issue by not publicly stating whether he would visit the shrine.[190] As a former

Foreign Ministry official opined, this indicated that China was dealing with the history issue much more carefully after Koizumi.[191]

And yet, while Abe took steps to less blatantly antagonize neighboring countries on history issues, he was pragmatic about the nature of Sino-Japanese relations. As a foreign diplomat reported, Abe believed that China and Japan could never have really great relations, but neither can they have really bad relations. This is because two factors pull in opposite directions on the relationship: on the one hand, the economic relationship between China and Japan is too important for both sides for either to truly put it in jeopardy. On the other hand are history issues. These two factors lead to a situation that is never too good, but also never too bad.[192] Thus, while both sides were not eager for history issues to again derail bilateral relations, China's patriotic education policies made it difficult for officials to overlook "incorrect attitudes," for fear of the domestic political repercussions vis-à-vis the increasingly nationalist population.[193]

Subsequent Developments

As one journalist emphasized in 2008, even though more than sixty years have passed since the end of the war, war history is not at all settled in Japan.[194] In the years since then, this has continued to be true. The "nationalist resurgence" in Japan has been further strengthened by Abe's return as PM and his remarkably long second tenure in office, and history issues have become even more prominent in Japanese politics.[195] With strong support from right-wing nationalist interest groups, Abe has articulated and pursued more avowedly nationalist positions on a range of issues related to Japan's war responsibility. Moreover, as the Japanese public and especially younger generations have been socialized to more nationalist views via public discourse and education, public opinion has shifted to the right on history issues. Illustrating this, Evans reports that "in a Jiji Press opinion poll conducted in January [2013], 56.7 per cent of those surveyed believed that Abe should visit Yasukuni now—up significantly from 2006, when 43 per cent took a similar position."[196] Against this backdrop, identity concerns and electoral-political considerations arising from the entrenched influence of nationalist interest groups and the long-term decline of the left in Japanese politics have reinforced continuities in Japan's narrative and deepened the retrenchment that began in the late 1990s.

Conclusion

THE POLITICS OF DARK PASTS

In a 2005 commencement address at Spelman College, the historian Howard Zinn drew on his experiences in the US civil rights movement to reflect on the power of truth and the possibility of change. He declared: "The lesson of that history is that you must not despair, that if you are right, and you persist, things will change. The government may try to deceive the people, and the newspapers and television may do the same, but the truth has a way of coming out. The truth has a power greater than a hundred lies."[1] In contrast to this promise, however, the truth does *not* necessarily emerge from "rightness" or persistence. Nor does it necessarily prevail over lies. Rather, struggles over truth and history are more complex and contingent than this statement suggests.

Outing the truth is a long, uncertain, and highly political process. Rather than simply changing with the passage of time, persistence, and rightness, interactions between political factors at the domestic and international levels together influence states' narratives of dark pasts. Changes and continuities arise from political decisions made by state agents, but their decisions are shaped by the intersection of a variety of factors. The multifaceted and contingent nature of these political processes thus eludes simple explanations and predictions. The argument developed in this book acknowledges the inherent complexities of the politics of memory while highlighting the relative importance of international pressures over domestic pressures in triggering change and the relationship between international and domestic considerations in shaping the content of changes and continuities. It further identifies the domestic considerations that are most consequential in officials' decisions about whether and how to change the state's narrative, the limits that structures and institutions impose on agents of change, and the ways in which agents can both challenge and reinforce the status quo.[2]

Accounting for the Diverging Trajectories of Turkey's and Japan's Narratives

The previous chapters traced and analyzed changes and continuities over time in Turkey's and Japan's narratives, demonstrating that international pressures increase the *likelihood* of change, while domestic considerations determine the *content* of such change. While both Turkey's and Japan's narratives have exhibited strong degrees of continuity over time, Turkey's narrative has been much more resistant to change. Differences in the nature and degree of international pressures, along with the higher degrees of material, legitimacy, and identity concerns for Turkey and the more sustained nature of domestic contestation in Japan, together account for this divergence in the two narratives' trajectories.

Four key differences in the nature and extent of international pressures help account for the varying degrees of change in the trajectories of the two narratives. First, international pressures on Japan's narrative have come more from victim states, whereas pressures on Turkey's narrative have been more from third-party states and nonstate actors. Second, the key victim state in Japan's case—China—is much more powerful than Armenia. Thus, the economic and political consequences of refusing to accede to China's demands have been much higher than the consequences for Turkey, since Armenia is a poor, isolated, and relatively powerless country. Third, a chorus of former victim states have protested the content of Japanese textbooks' coverage of the country's actions in the war, as well as Japanese officials' statements about history issues. In contrast, the only victim state from which Turkey has faced calls for greater acknowledgment and contrition is Armenia, and it has been an independent state only since the end of the Cold War. Finally, the absence of normal diplomatic relations between Turkey and Armenia for most of the period since the genocide has meant that Armenia's ability to pressure Turkey on this issue has been limited. In contrast, within the first couple of decades after the end of WWII, Japan reestablished diplomatic relationships with most of the Asian countries it had victimized. Most of those countries were weaker and poorer than Japan, and many—but not all—prioritized official recognition and development aid from Japan over reparations or an apology. Despite the fact that history issues were often reduced to a bargaining chip in these early diplomatic negotiations, the first changes in Japan's narrative arose in the process of normalizing relations with China and subsequent shifts followed diplomatic normalization. Together, these differences in the nature and extent of international pressures have meant that, over time, Japan has experienced more serious and sustained pressures than Turkey.

The other half of the story stems from differences in the existence and strength of the domestic considerations identified in my argument. Turkish officials have had stronger material concerns and deeper legitimacy and identity concerns than have Japanese officials, which helps account for the stronger continuities in Turkey's narrative. In addition, domestic contestation in Turkey has been much more limited, and has tended more toward status quo–reinforcing positions, which has contributed to the more limited degree of change in Turkey's narrative.

Regarding material concerns, both Japanese and Turkish officials have been concerned that change in their respective narratives could lead to material demands for compensation or territory, which helps account for the continuities in each narrative. However, the perceived extent and likelihood of material costs have been much higher in the Turkish case, which has contributed to the higher degree of continuity in Turkey's narrative.

One reason for this is that Japanese officials have been able to rely on legal defenses that do not exist in the Turkish case. This is because Taiwan and China gave up their rights to claim compensation in 1951 and in 1972, respectively. Although these treaties are not clear on the issue of individual compensation, Japanese officials have interpreted them to mean that the compensation issue—both with states and, crucially, with individuals—has been "settled." Consequently, while both Japan and Turkey have been able to argue that they should not have to face claims for reparations or compensation in foreign courts because of the doctrine of sovereign immunity, and both have also been able to argue for decades that the crimes in question have surpassed applicable statutes of limitations, Japan has also argued that relevant victim states gave up their rights to compensation in bilateral and multilateral treaties.

The other difference with regard to material concerns arises from the fact that the territories that might be claimed from Japan are neither as monetarily valuable nor as geographically central as is the case for Turkey. Turkish officials have long been concerned about potential territorial claims from the state of Armenia and from descendants of Ottoman Armenians. In the past couple of decades, moreover, the descendants of victims and survivors of the genocide have initiated cases in Turkey and in the United States seeking compensation for and/or restitution of properties that were confiscated in and after the genocide. For example, in 2010, three Armenian Americans filed a civil lawsuit in US federal court against the Republic of Turkey, the Central Bank of Turkey, and the Turkish state-owned Ziraat Bankası (Agriculture Bank). The plaintiffs—who possessed land deeds for properties in the province of Adana, including part of the strategically valuable Incirlik Air Base—sought more than 60 million USD for the confiscation and ongoing use of those properties.[3] As this case illustrates, the territories and properties potentially at stake for Turkey are extensive and valuable, including the former presidential residence in Ankara and significant portions of Turkish territory. In contrast, while territorial disputes from the war persist in Japan's relations with China, the ROK, and Russia, and have recently grown more serious, they concern small, largely uninhabited islands.[4] The disputed islands do involve potential economic rents from natural resources, fishing rights, and maritime control; but the crucial point is that they are not part of Japan's main islands.[5]

Turning to legitimacy and identity concerns, while such concerns have factored into officials' considerations in both countries, Turkey's narrative is more fundamentally connected with the ideology of the Turkish state, the founding national narrative, and the legitimacy of state institutions. In contrast, while societal actors and elites in Japan have long connected the state's degree of acknowledgment of and contrition for its WWII-era crimes with contemporary understandings of the nation, the legitimacy and identity of the nation are not centrally tied in with the state's narrative as is the case in Turkey. Consequently, Turkish officials have been much less willing to change the state's narrative, since doing so stands to undermine the state's identity and legitimacy.

This difference in the depth of perceived legitimacy and identity concerns also helps account for the different *patterns* of change in the two cases. Turkey's narrative has tended toward stretches of continuity followed by relatively abrupt and wide-reaching moments of change, whereas Japan's narrative has tended to shift in a disaggregated fashion, primarily in response to discrete pressures and controversies. The deeper identity stakes for Turkish officials have meant that when they have responded to international pressures, they have done so in a more systematic and defensive manner. Because of the relatively lower identity stakes for Japanese officials, they have responded to international pressures more frequently and less systematically, resulting in a more disaggregated and reactive pattern of change.

The final difference between the two cases is in the extent and direction of domestic contestation. There has been a much higher degree of domestic contestation in Japan than in Turkey, and domestic activism has trended at several points toward calls for greater acknowledgment of Japan's war crimes. This contrasts strongly with the Turkish case, in which domestic contestation emerged much more recently and has been more limited.

One reason domestic contestation arose earlier and has been more robust in Japan than in Turkey is because of differences in the formal and informal constraints on freedom of expression. In Turkey, legal constraints have deterred most people from publicly talking about or looking into the Armenian question. The most prominent of these constraints has been a series of broadly written laws that have made it dangerous to make public statements at odds with the official narrative on the Armenian question, since doing so risked being prosecuted and possibly jailed for insulting the nation, the military, or Atatürk's memory. In addition, the taboo surrounding this issue muted discussion in the Turkish media until the early 2000s, while academics interested in studying the Armenian question were long made to understand that doing so would damage their careers in serious ways. In Japan, a domestic taboo initially limited discussion of the Nanjing Massacre in the media and in academia, but this taboo began to break down much earlier than in the Turkish case, with the first challenges coming in the early 1970s. Even so, a small but highly vocal and intimidating right-wing nationalist fringe, and social pressures that discourage many people from studying or looking into Japan's war crimes, have together limited domestic challenges to Japan's narrative. That said, these constraints are informal, whereas those in Turkey have been both formal and informal.

The different levels of domestic contestation also derive from how the narratives have been framed in each country. In Japan, differing views of the war have fallen along the domestic political fault line between conservatives (on the one hand) and leftists (on the other hand). As a result, domestic activists in Japan have had greater incentives to contest history issues, both because these narratives relate to other political issues within Japanese politics, and because the dominant perspectives on history issues correspond with domestic political divisions on other salient issues in Japan's domestic politics. As Yang observes, "The debate over the Nanjing Massacre is a microcosm of the clashes between larger ideological undercurrents in postwar Japan in terms of evaluating the past and making choices for the future."[6]

In contrast, Turkey's narrative has been framed along the fault line between the domestic and international spheres. Turkey's founding narrative emphasizes that the country was established in the face of external attempts by Britain, Russia, Greece, Italy, and France to carve up Ottoman territories. A key lesson of this history, it is argued, is that Turkey is a nation that is surrounded by enemies, both internally and externally, that Turks have no friends and can rely on no one but themselves. As an observer of Turkish politics writes, "Turks are taught, and most believe, that their country is under continual external and internal threat, both from other countries plotting to divide or acquire Turkish territory and from internal forces seeking to change the constitutional status quo."[7] The narrative of the Armenian question has reflected and supported this foundational narrative, arguing that Armenian nationalists rose up against their Muslim neighbors and threatened the security of the Ottoman Empire and the safety of Ottoman citizens. As a result, compared with the situation in Japan, societal actors in

Turkey have had fewer political incentives—and more numerous and serious disincentives—to challenge the state's narrative of the Armenian question.

Overall, these different degrees of domestic contestation have two broad implications. First, domestic contestation has been a source of pressure for change in Japan, which has not been the case in Turkey. And second, at moments when Japanese officials have considered changing the state's narrative, domestic contestation has at times pushed officials toward greater change. This has also not been the case in Turkey, where public debate and societal activism in relation to the Armenian question were long taboo and where public opinion has largely aligned with the state's narrative.

In sum, higher material and identity concerns have given Turkish officials greater incentives to resist change than has been the case for Japanese officials. In addition, differences in the nature and extent of international pressures and in the degree of domestic contestation further account for the greater degree of change over time in Japan's narrative.

The analysis of Turkey's and Japan's narratives more broadly contributes to scholarship on Turkish politics and the Armenian Genocide, as well as to understandings of the politics of "history issues" in Japan and East Asia. With regard to the Turkish case, the analysis uncovers the agents of the state's narrative of the "Armenian question," sheds light on the range of strategies through which the official narrative has been supported and defended, and highlights the evolving relationship between normative expectations and Turkey's denial of the genocidal nature of the events. In addition, by locating the genocide within the historical trajectory of Turkish politics, this research has the potential to help better historicize the Armenian Genocide within Turkish politics. Meanwhile, the analysis of Japan's narrative goes beyond conventional treatments in two key ways. First, the book's conceptual framework is used to analyze the composite official narrative, rather than the more common and narrower analyses of apologies, commemorations, and textbooks.[8] Second, the conceptual framework allows for a more nuanced identification of points of change and continuity in Japan's overall narrative, especially when compared with the broader categories used in other studies of Japan's remembrance.[9]

The Complex Impact of International Norms

While the central argument focuses on the international pressures and domestic considerations that shape patterns of change and continuity in states' narratives, these factors are situated within structures of meaning that are shaped (in part) by international norms. The empirical chapters refer to these normative structures, and here I focus on unpacking the ways in which international norms of human rights, accountability, and justice have influenced the politics through which official narratives of dark pasts are shaped and contested.

Many scholars have noted the escalation of calls for states (and other institutions) to recognize, come to terms with, and apologize for past wrongs.[10] Moreover, international relations scholars have specified a range of ways in which human rights norms emerge and spread among states, focusing in particular on the agency of nonstate actors and on processes through which states adopt and comply with norms.[11] While I find evidence of these dynamics, the analysis also underscores the complexities of norms' impact and of actors' responses to normative expectations. Contrary to often-implicit characterizations of norms' influence as univalent and progressive, the analysis demonstrates that norms have complex and multivalent effects on actors' preferences and behavior, and that state and societal actors respond to and use international norms in diverse ways.

One indication of the influence of norms of truth-telling and legal accountability is the increased involvement of third-party states in recognizing other states' past crimes. For example, the dramatic acceleration of third-party states' recognition of the Armenian Genocide in the late 1990s and early 2000s is partially attributable to the increased strength of these norms over time. At the same time, other factors, most notably international and transnational activism by Armenian groups in the wake of the fiftieth anniversary of the genocide, have also influenced this trend.

International normative expectations and developments related to truth-seeking and legal accountability have also served as a resource for state and nonstate actors. In line with work on "naming and shaming," increased attention to dark pasts has given activists some leverage in attempts to hold public actors accountable, especially in calling politicians to stand by their moral pronouncements.[12] For example, in the late 1970s Armenians in a number of countries protested the elimination of a reference to the Armenian Genocide in a UN report, in part by "publicly invoking the human rights declarations of several member states of the UN Human Rights Commission."[13] As a result of this campaign and this use of what Keck and Sikkink call "accountability politics," the UN Human Rights Commission appointed a special rapporteur to investigate and prepare a report on the Armenian Genocide.[14] Overall, however, the success of such strategies has been mixed, with realpolitik often trumping idealpolitik. For example, despite the fact that as candidates for US president, George H. W. Bush, Bill Clinton, George W. Bush, and Barack Obama all acknowledged that the Armenian Genocide was a genocide and promised Armenian American organizations to continue to do so if elected, none used the word "genocide" once in office.

Attention arising from the strengthening of relevant international human rights norms has also introduced new language, actors, and sources of funding, thereby altering incentives and the balance of power on these issues. Again considering the Turkish case, some domestic activists became more attentive to the issue of minority rights, in part from international discourse and criticism of Turkey, while civil society organizations in Turkey have, over time, increasingly framed their claims in the language of international human rights.[15] Since the early to mid-2000s, international organizations have closely followed and supported domestic initiatives in Turkey that have focused on human rights education (UNICEF), hate speech (the EU Commission Delegation in Turkey), minority rights (the Open Society Institute), and freedom of expression (the European Union). This has not necessarily changed actors' positions, but it has increased the voice and influence of particular perspectives. Meanwhile, many of the Turkish activists and academics who have challenged the official narrative had or subsequently developed strong connections with activists and researchers outside Turkey (especially in Armenia, France, Germany, and the United States), which offered sources of legitimacy for counternarratives, along with new information and opportunities.[16]

The demands of Armenian and Chinese diaspora groups have also been shaped by learning about the actions taken by other victim groups and perpetrator states.[17] Progressive scholars and activists in Japan, Korea, and China have looked to and learned from German, French, and Polish experiences with joint history textbook projects and the arduous process of trying to get to "thick" reconciliation.[18] Meanwhile, lawyers representing Armenian American descendants of victims and survivors of the genocide have learned from and adopted strategies employed in the Holocaust redress movement in their pursuit of restitution, compensation, and acknowledgment from Turkey.[19]

At the same time, state actors have exhibited their own learning. While activists in Turkey, Japan, and elsewhere learned and gained support from international human rights networks and from the development of the norms of truth-telling and legal accountability, officials in Turkey and Japan have also been attentive to expectations stemming from these norms. Turkish officials have monitored international legal decisions related to genocide with an eye toward learning from them in their efforts to reject the charge of genocide, and Japanese officials have attended to international developments related to accountability and reparations.[20]

These norms have also influenced the costs and benefits of truth-seeking and truth-telling. In particular, as the norm of truth-seeking gained strength, the costs of impunity and denial increased.[21] Thus, as Japan's economy reached its apex in the 1980s, Japanese officials sought to align the country's international political role with its international economic status. To achieve this goal, Japanese officials realized that they might need to take steps toward greater recognition and contrition. Twenty or thirty years earlier, it is unlikely that this would have been an obvious path to greater international credibility. Turning to the Turkish case, as international expectations shifted from the view that dark pasts were "better left buried in the past" to the current emphasis on the importance of truth-telling and truth-seeking, officials shifted from silencing the genocide to rationalizing and relativizing what had happened.[22] Further reflecting this shift in normative expectations, Turkish officials stopped arguing that the Armenian issue should be left in the past and instead began to point out that Turkey did not deny that there was suffering at the time. As the norm of truth-seeking further strengthened, Turkish officials began to emphasize that they are "ready to face the past," would like to engage in "dialogue" with Armenia, and are committed to "reconciliation." These rhetorical adaptations reflect an awareness of and attempts to adapt the state's narrative to rhetorically (if not substantively) meet international normative expectations.[23]

Likewise, as the norm against genocide has strengthened, Turkish officials have paid increasing attention to the concept of genocide and to rejecting the application of the label "genocide" to the events of 1915–1917. In particular, Turkish officials have been increasingly willing to accept characterizations of the event that would have been strongly disputed in the past, as long as they do not include the term "genocide." Thus, while some might argue that Turkey's denial of the Armenian Genocide derives primarily from the perceived stigma of genocide, the word "genocide" has not been the only or even the most significant obstacle to change in Turkey's narrative.[24] Instead, the continuities in Turkey's narrative have been driven more by officials' concerns that acknowledging the genocide will lead to territorial and compensation claims, and by the concern that changing the state's narrative would fundamentally threaten the legitimacy of the state and its founding narrative. Over time, however, Turkish officials and supporters of the state's narrative have been increasingly motivated (in part) by normative concerns about what it would mean for the identity of the Turkish nation to acknowledge that the Ottoman state and the ancestors of some Turkish citizens and officials committed *genocide*. Reflecting this concern, aspects of the state's narrative have shifted over time in ways that paralleled changes in the content and strength of the norm against genocide.

Overall, this diversity of responses to international normative expectations underscores the agency of so-called norm takers and points to the range of actions and rhetoric that falls outside the categories of norm adoption, compliance, and violation.

Politics and the Past

While the analysis of these two narratives sheds light on the ways in which norms operate as structures that shape costs for and constraints on, as well as opportunities and resources available to actors, it also suggests new approaches to the study of memory and transitional justice. In particular, the book's overall approach and the analysis of the cases move beyond prevailing approaches to the study of memory and transitional justice in several important ways.

First, by emphasizing contingent interactions between a variety of factors, the book avoids the tendency to focus on a single domain or variable. Changes and continuities in states' narratives of dark pasts are not primarily determined by structures, such as generations or the international distribution of power, or by agents including "memory activists," "carriers" or "agents" of memory, or state actors.[25] Likewise, focusing on either domestic or international factors, as is typically the case in studies of particular countries' politics of memory, is insufficient to account for the trajectories of such narratives.[26] As the analysis of the two cases demonstrates, the timing and content of changes in states' narratives are shaped by interactions between international pressures and domestic considerations.

Second, this book employs a broad time frame, analyzing Turkey's and Japan's narratives far beyond their initial formulation in periods of transition. This widened lens illuminates the politics inherent in official historiography and the ways in which historical accounts—as instantiated in official narratives—themselves affect politics. In other words, states' narratives are a function of political decisions and compromises, which in turn affect subsequent political decisions in relation to both memory politics and other issues. This insight underscores the need to go beyond periods of transition to understand the nature of struggles to come to terms with dark pasts, as well as the ways such struggles bleed into and color other aspects of society and politics. In addition, some of the themes in Turkey's and Japan's narratives were developed as the violence in question unfolded, while the motivations behind some of the resistance to greater acknowledgment and contrition in both countries lie in institutions and ideologies that can be traced back to power arrangements in place during and shortly after the violence occurred. This further suggests the importance of broadening the time frame and resisting the tendency to treat the transition to democracy or from violence as an analytical *Stunde Null* (zero hour).

Finally, by focusing explicitly on the *politics* by which states' narratives are shaped and contested, I demonstrate that narratives of dark pasts are politicized from the very beginning. In contrast to accounts of truth-seeking and justice-seeking that characterize such processes as "depoliticized," this book analyzes the politics that shape the construction, contestation, and maintenance of official narratives.[27] Moreover, by tracing the ways in which officials seek to resist and defend against pressures for greater acknowledgment and contrition, I uncover subtle strategies and forms of denial.[28]

Thus, while rightness and persistence are often not enough to prompt change in a state's narrative, this book offers insights that should travel beyond the cases at hand, and should interest not only scholars but also policymakers and activists who want to better understand the likely effects of different types of pressure on such narratives.

RESEARCH CONDUCTED

Interviews

Over the course of more than eight months of fieldwork, I conducted seventy-five elite interviews, primarily in Turkey and Japan.[1] I interviewed current and past government officials, civil society actors, journalists, academics, and political analysts. All interviewees have been involved in observed or contested decision making related to the state's narrative. Interviews were semistructured and generally lasted an hour, although some were longer. In each interview, I asked open-ended and more specific questions that were tailored to interviewees' experiences and expertise. Interview questions addressed specific instances of change in the state's narrative, as well as potential factors that might have influenced specific changes. I did not ask interviewees about their personal views about the historical events in question, although some chose to share their opinions with me. Given the sensitive nature of these issues in Turkey and Japan, interviewees' names are not provided.

On Turkey's Narrative

My analysis of Turkey's narrative is based on interviews and research conducted in Istanbul and Ankara between June 2007 and April 2009, along with a handful of interviews conducted in the United States.

I conducted approximately fifty semistructured elite interviews in the spring of 2008 and the spring of 2009.[2] I interviewed a range of elites across the political spectrum, including journalists, academics, retired government officials, high-level bureaucrats, foreign diplomats, publishers, activists, and think-tank researchers.

The interviews were with individuals whose work, activism, or research relates to the "Armenian question," Turkish-Armenian relations, Armenian affairs in Turkey, and/or human rights in Turkey. These interviews helped identify when and why policy decisions were made, and assess the impact of international pressures and domestic activism on societal and official actions in relation to the state's narrative.

In Turkey, I collected and analyzed books and articles published by government agencies, high school history textbooks, educational curricular announcements, and newspaper articles on the Armenian question. I analyzed the representation of the Armenian question in two series of high school history textbooks: *Tarih Lise III* (High School History III), published between 1951 and 1990, and *Türkiye Cumhuriyeti İnkılâp Tarihi ve Atatürkçülük* (The History of the Revolution of the Turkish Republic and Atatürkism), published between 1981 and 2007.[3] The processes of writing curricula and approving textbooks are centralized at the national level, under the auspices of the Ministry of National Education and the Instruction and Education Board (Talim ve Terbiye Kurulu). As a result, the content of these textbooks reflects the official narrative. To analyze publication trends (see Figure 3.1), I compiled a comprehensive list of books published on the Armenian question in Turkey between 1950 and 2009. I assembled the list by searching the online catalogs of the Turkish Historical Society and the Turkish Parliament; bibliographies on the Armenian question on the websites of the Prime Minister's Office, the Office of the President, the state archives, the military archives, the Turkish Armed Forces, the Ministry of National Education, the Ministry of Foreign Affairs, and the Institute for Armenian Research; published bibliographies on the topic; and the bibliographies of several books published by the Turkish Historical Society.[4] Finally, I analyzed hundreds of English-language newspaper articles capturing official speeches, statements, and actions related to the state's narrative.

Drawing on this range of sources, along with relevant secondary sources, I developed a detailed timeline of Turkey's narrative over the past sixty years, traced changes in the content of and strategies supporting the official narrative, and identified factors that shaped changes and continuities in the state's narrative.

On Japan's Narrative

My analysis of Japan's narrative is based on information gathered from primary and secondary sources, along with twenty semistructured interviews conducted in Japan.

To identify the content of and changes in the state's narrative, I constructed a detailed timeline of statements, events, and other information over the sixty-year period of my analysis. To create this timeline, I conducted searches in the Factiva and FBIS databases, from which I gathered and analyzed several thousand newspaper articles that captured statements and actions about the Nanjing Massacre by a range of actors within and outside Japan. I also surveyed the chronicles of the quarterly political news magazines *Japan Quarterly* (between 1954 and 2001) and *Japan Echo* (between 2001 and 2008), and analyzed official statements released by the Japanese government and by relevant societal groups.

Finally, I spent two months in Tokyo in the summer of 2008 interviewing key individuals working on history issues, including conservative and liberal activists; journalists from the *Asahi Shimbun*, the *New York Times*, and the *Yomiuri Shimbun*; academics who work with and/or have advised the Japanese government on history issues; and diplomats.[5] These interviews provided insights into the motivations behind and factors that have influenced official and societal actions in relation to history issues.

Drawing on these varied sources, along with relevant secondary sources, I traced and analyzed the evolution of Japan's narrative over the past sixty years, identifying points of change, periods of continuity, and the factors that shaped both.

TURKISH HIGH SCHOOL HISTORY TEXTBOOKS ANALYZED

Ekrem İnal and Nurettin Ormancı, *Tarih: Lise III Yeni ve Yakın Çağlar* (İstanbul: Ders Kitapları Türk Ltd. Şti., 1951).

Niyazi Akşit, *Lise Kitapları Tarih III Yeni ve Yakın Çağlar* (İstanbul: Remzi Kitabevi, 1951).

Emin Oktay, *Lise Kitapları Tarih III Yeni ve Yakın Çağlar* (İstanbul: Remzi Kitabevi, 1952).

Niyazi Akşit, *Lise Kitapları Tarih III Yeni ve Yakınçağlar* (İstanbul: Remzi Kitabevi, 1956).

Emin Oktay, *Lise Kitapları Tarih III Yeni ve Yakınçağlar* (İstanbul: Remzi Kitabevi, 1956).

Niyazi Akşit, *Lise Kitapları Tarih III Yeni ve Yakınçağlar* (İstanbul: Remzi Kitabevi, 1961).

Emin Oktay, *Tarih Lise III Yeni ve Yakınçağlar* (İstanbul: Atlas Yayınevi, 1961).

Emin Oktay, *Tarih Lise III Yeni ve Yakın Çağlar* (İstanbul: Atlas Yayınevi, 1966).

Emin Oktay, *Tarih Lise III Yeni ve Yakın Çağlar* (İstanbul: Atlas Yayınevi, 1967).

Niyazi Akşit, *Lise Kitapları Tarih III Yeni ve Yakınçağlar* (İstanbul: Remzi Kitabevi, 1970).

Emin Oktay, *Tarih Lise: III* (İstanbul: Atlas Yayınevi, 1971).

Niyazi Akşit, *Lise Kitapları Tarih III Yeni ve Yakınçağlar* (İstanbul: Remzi Kitabevi, 1980).

Kemal Ertürk, *Türkiye Cumhuriyeti İnkılâp Tarihi Dersleri Lise I* (Ankara: Felma Yayınları, 1981).

Mükerrem K. Su and Ahmet Mumcu, *Lise Türkiye Cumhuriyeti İnkılâp Tarihi ve Atatürkçülük* (İstanbul: Milli Eğitim Basımevi, 1983).

Emin Oktay, *Tarih Lise: III* (İstanbul: Atlas Yayınevi, 1984).

İsmet Parmaksızoğlu, *Ortaokul Türkiye Cumhuriyeti İnkılâp Tarihi ve Atatürkçülük* (İstanbul: Milsan Basın Sanayi A.Ş., 1988).

Güler Şenünver, H. Samim Kesim, Rıfat Turgut, and Aliye Akay, *Orta Okullar İçin Türkiye Cumhuriyeti İnkılâp Tarihi ve Atatürkçülük III* (Ankara: Türk Tarih Kurumu Basımevi, 1989).

Nurer Uğurlu and Esergül Balcı, *Tarih Lise 3* (İstanbul: Serhat Yayınları A.Ş./Örgün Yayınları Ltd., 1989).

Niyazi Akşit, *Tarih Lise III* (İstanbul: Remzi Kitabevi, 1990).

Mükerrem K. Su and Ahmet Mumcu, *Lise ve Dengi Okullar İçin Türkiye Cumhuriyeti İnkılâp Tarihi ve Atatürkçülük* (İstanbul: Milli Eğitim Basımevi, 1991).

Kenan Kalecikli, *Türkiye Cumhuriyeti İnkılâp Tarihi ve Atatürkçülük 1* (İstanbul: Gendaş A.Ş., 1994).

Ahmet Bekir Palazoğlu and Osman Bircan, *Türkiye Cumhuriyeti İnkılâp Tarihi ve Atatürkçülük 1* (İstanbul: Koza Eğitim ve Yayıncılık Ltd. Şti., 1995).

Ahmet Mumcu and Mükerrem K. Su, *Lise ve Dengi Okullar İçin Türkiye Cumhuriyeti İnkılâp Tarihi ve Atatürkçülük*, edited by Güler Şenünver, Nilay Işıksalan, and Hamiyet Bican (İstanbul: Millî Eğitim Basımevi, 2000).

İdris Akdin, Muhittin Çakmak, and Mustafa Genç, *Türkiye Cumhuriyeti İnkılâp Tarihi ve Atatürkçülük Lise 3* (İstanbul: Ilıcak Matbaacılık A.Ş., 2005).

Kemal Kara, *Lise Türkiye Cumhuriyeti İnkılap Tarihi ve Atatürkçülük* (İstanbul: Önde Yayıncılık, 2007).

Notes

INTRODUCTION

1. The euphemistic phrase "Armenian question" dates to the late nineteenth century. It was initially used to refer to the status of Armenians in the Ottoman Empire and Western states' actions on their behalf. Since 1915, it has come to focus on the controversy over the Armenian Genocide.

2. MFA (Ministry of Foreign Affairs, Republic of Turkey) 2014. For praise of this statement, see Zaman 2014; Yardley and Arsu 2015. For criticism, see Akçam 2014.

3. For Davutoğlu's statement, see Prime Minister of the Republic of Turkey 2015.

4. Quoted in *New York Times* 2015.

5. MFA 2015.

6. A *dark past* is a large-scale or systematic human rights atrocity that occurred in the past and for which the state bears at least partial responsibility.

7. Wakamiya 1998, 20. The phrase "history issues" refers to controversies related to Japan's official position regarding the state's responsibility for WWII-related atrocities and aggression.

8. See National Diet of Japan 1995.

9. Wakamiya 1998, 180. I follow the practice of listing family names first when writing Japanese, Chinese, and Korean names, except when citing English-language publications that do not follow this practice.

10. Brooks 1999; Nobles 2008; Sikkink 2011; Ben-Josef Hirsch and Dixon 2017.

11. On the "age of apology," see Gibney et al. 2008. See also Barkan and Karn 2006; Torpey and Burkett 2010.

12. Ben-Josef Hirsch 2014.

13. Australian Government 2008.

14. An *official narrative* is a state's characterization of an event, including the nature and scope of the event, and the state's characterization of the role and responsibility of government officials and institutions in the event. For a critique of the idea of "coming to terms with the past," see Adorno 1986 [1959]. See also Olick 1998.

15. The analysis of Turkey's narrative begins in 1950, when single-party rule ended, whereas the analysis of Japan's narrative begins two years later, in 1952, when the US occupation of Japan ended and Japan regained its sovereignty. The Nanjing Massacre and the Second Sino-Japanese War are analytically intertwined in official rhetoric, such that it is not possible to study the official narrative of the massacre independent from the broader war. For clarity and consistency, I refer to Japan's narrative in the singular.

16. A large body of evidence has documented the genocidal nature of these events. For historical scholarship, see R. G. Hovannisian 1992, 1999b, 2003; Dadrian 1995a; Bloxham 2005; Akçam 2008, 2012; Kévorkian 2011; Suny, Göçek, and Naimark 2011; Üngör 2011b; Üngör and Polatel 2011; Suny 2015. For primary sources, see Davis 1989; Miller and Miller 1993; Sarafian 1993a; Morgenthau 2000; Bardakçı 2008; Dadrian and Akçam 2011; Gust 2014. In addition, the majority of genocide scholars have categorized this violence as genocide, along with the scholar who coined the term. See Lemkin 1946, 227; Kuper 1981; Staub 1989; Chalk and Jonassohn 1990; Fein 1990; Melson 1992; Charny 1994; Rummel 1994; Valentino 2004; Bloxham 2005; Levene 2005; Mann 2005; Midlarsky 2005; Straus

2007; Schaller and Zimmerer 2009. On legal succession from the Ottoman Empire to the Republic of Turkey, see E. Öktem 2011; Avedian 2012.

17. Göçek 2011, 55, 151.

18. Estimates of the number of Chinese civilians and POWs killed by Japanese soldiers in the Nanjing Massacre vary widely and are intensely debated, extending from lows of very few to several thousand, which have been argued by Japanese revisionists from the "Illusion School" (see, e.g., Tanaka M. 1984; Higashinakano 2005); to intermediate assessments, for example, by the conservative historian Hata Ikuhiko, who estimated that there were forty thousand deaths (Hata 1998); to the figure of two hundred thousand deaths advanced in the Tokyo Trial's majority judgment in 1948 (Boister and Cryer 2008a, 535–39); to estimates of one hundred thousand to three hundred thousand by Japanese historians from the "Great Massacre School," such as Hora Tomio (1967) and Kasahara Tokushi (Kasahara 1997, 228, cited in Yoshida 2000, 104); to the official Chinese figure of three hundred thousand; to journalist Iris Chang's suggestion that the death toll could reach "into the 300,000 or even 400,000 range" (I. Chang 1997, 101, 102).

19. For these figures, see Rose 2005, 5, 88; Wan 2006, 305, 312. On chemical and biological warfare programs, see Y. Tanaka 1996, 135–65; Tsuchiya 2008. On the comfort women system, see Hicks 1995; Yoshimi 2000; Y. Tanaka 2002; Hayashi 2008; Soh 2008. On slave labor, see Underwood 2005, 2006a, 2010; Umeda 2008.

20. The quoted text is from Pierson (2000, 260). On rhetoric as a constraint and an opportunity, see Cruz 2000; Krebs 2015.

21. B. Anderson 1983; Gellner 1983; Hobsbawm and Ranger 1983; Brand 2014.

22. On citizenship and belonging, see Weiner 2005; Nobles 2008. On public discourse, see Olick and Levy 1997; Art 2006. On the quality of democracy, see Morlino 2010; Bernhard and Kubik 2014b, 289–93.

23. Van Evera 1994; Kaufmann 2004; Krebs and Lobasz 2007.

24. Kaufman 2006; Sémelin 2007; Straus 2012, 2015.

25. Mendeloff 2001, 2008; Müller 2002; Lind 2008; Langenbacher and Shain 2010; Gardner Feldman 2012; Miller 2013.

26. Ekmekçioğlu 2016; Suciyan 2016.

27. Analysts and observers of Turkish politics often distinguish between the elected government and the "deep state," which, Gingeras explains, "refers to a kind of shadow or parallel system of government in which unofficial or publicly unacknowledged individuals play important roles in defining and implementing state policy" (2010, 152).

28. Quoted in McNeill and Selden 2005.

29. Quoted in Edwards 2005.

30. Blight 2001; Weiner 2005; Nobles 2008; Madley 2016.

31. King 2014; Fegley 2016.

32. Burgis 2010.

33. King 2010.

34. On narratives in the Israeli-Palestinian conflict, see Ben-Josef Hirsch 2007b, 2017; Nets-Zehngut 2011. On memories of past violence in the Congo Wars, see Prendergast and Smock 1999; Straus 2006.

35. On sites of memory, see Nora 1989; Winter 1995. On collective memory, see Halbwachs 1980; Olick, Vinitzky-Seroussi, and Levy 2011. On apologies, see Tavuchis 1991; Brooks 1999; Yamazaki 2006; Gibney et al. 2008; Lind 2008; Nobles 2008.

36. On memory and foreign policy, see Berger 1998; Müller 2002; Miller 2013. On memory and threat perception, see Lind 2008. On reconciliation, see He 2009. On nationalist myths and conflict, see Van Evera 1994.

37. For work that treats memory as a dependent variable, see Lebow, Kansteiner, and Fogu 2006; Berger 2012; Bernhard and Kubik 2014a; Nets-Zehngut and Bar-Tal 2014.

38. For foundational work on transitional justice, see Kritz 1995; Minow 1998; Teitel 2000; Hayner 2001; Elster 2004; Roht-Arriaza and Mariezcurrena 2006. For second- and third-generation work, see Subotić 2009; Nalepa 2010; Leebaw 2011; Stan 2012; Ben-Josef Hirsch 2014; Buckley-Zistel et al. 2014; Teitel 2014; Bakiner 2015a.

39. For an exception, see Kim 2014. See also Aguilar 2008.

40. On the establishment of narratives via transitional justice processes, see Maier 2000; Wilson 2007; Leebaw 2008, 2011; Savelsberg 2013; Buckley-Zistel 2014; Bakiner 2015b.

41. Leebaw 2011.

42. Loyle and Davenport 2016, 126. For additional critiques of early transitional justice advocates, see Mendeloff 2004, 2009; Leebaw 2008; Subotić 2011; Ben-Josef Hirsch, MacKenzie, and Sesay 2012.

43. Fletcher, Weinstein, and Rowen 2009.

44. Schuman and Scott 1989; Schuman and Rodgers 2004; Lebow, Kansteiner, and Fogu 2006. Against generational arguments, see Art 2006; Cheung 2010.

45. Aguilar 2008; Encarnación 2014.

46. Katzenstein 1996, 5. See also Wendt 1998, 1999.

47. See, e.g., Finnemore and Sikkink 1998; Risse, Ropp, and Sikkink 1999, 2013; Checkel 2001, 2005; Kelley 2004; Zürn and Checkel 2005; Simmons 2009.

48. Sikkink 2011; Subotić 2014; Ben-Josef Hirsch and Dixon 2017.

49. On domestic public debate, see Maier 1988; Art 2006. On bottom-up mobilization, see Yoshida 2007; Nobles 2008; Kim 2012, 2014; Arrington 2016. On memory activism and agents, see Seraphim 2006; Bernhard and Kubik 2014a; Sierp and Wüstenberg 2015; Gutman 2017; Wüstenberg 2017.

50. On the agency of nonstate actors, see Keck and Sikkink 1998; Price 1998; Carpenter 2007, 2011; Sikkink 2011.

51. On norm localization and translation, see Acharya 2004; Capie 2008, 2012; Zimmermann 2016, 2017. On norm resistance, see Subotić 2009; Badescu and Weiss 2010; Deitelhoff and Zimmermann 2013; Cloward 2014; Sanders 2014, 2016; Cronin-Furman 2015; Bloomfield 2016; Búzás 2017, 2018; Dixon 2017; Erickson 2017.

52. For institutional and processual approaches to memory, see Herwig 1987; Schudson 1992; Olick 1999, 2007; Krebs 2015. On historical institutionalism, see Thelen 1999; Pierson 2004; Fioretos 2011.

53. Krebs (2015) similarly emphasizes the interaction between structure ("context") and agency in relation to national security narratives.

54. On the instrumental uses of norms, see Dixon and Erickson 2017. See also Greenhill 2010.

55. On the effects of international pressures on domestic policies, and the interactions between international and domestic political dynamics, see Risse-Kappen 1991, 1994; Risse 1999; Risse, Ropp, and Sikkink 1999, 2013; Cortell and Davis 2000; Cardenas 2004, 2007; Schimmelfennig 2005, 2008; Dai 2007; Subotić 2009; Schrad 2010.

56. On entrenchment, see Hassner 2006/7.

57. See appendix 1 for a detailed discussion of the research conducted.

1. CHANGING THE STATE'S STORY

1. Finney (2014, 447) speaks of this "semantic promiscuity," and Kansteiner (2002, 181) notes the "terminological profusion" in the field of memory studies.

2. Among political science work, see, e.g., He 2009; Berger 2012.

3. Related concepts include historical injustices, historic wrongs, and traumatic historical events. For definitions of each, see Barkan 2000, xxx; Marrus 2007, 83–84; and Art 2006, 3 (respectively).

4. On political narratives, see Autesserre 2012; Berger 2012; Subotić 2013. On social narratives, see Shenhav 2015.

5. On memory, see Olick and Robbins 1998; Olick, Vinitzky-Seroussi, and Levy 2011; Bernhard and Kubik 2014a. On remembrance, see Winter 2008.

6. On "reparations politics," see Torpey 2001. On restitution, see Barkan 2000. On the "politics of regret," see Olick 2007. Other terms include "historical consciousness" (Saaler 2005) and "coming to terms with the past."

7. Berger (2012) similarly analyzes a range of "policy dimensions" to assess the state's official narrative. Curricula or textbooks written or approved by the government are valid indicators of an official narrative. In both Turkey and Japan, the education ministries write curricula and approve textbooks for use in schools. In Turkey, the ministry also writes some textbooks.

8. Berger (2009, 11) and Bakiner (2013) also make this point.

9. This contrasts with characterizations of states' narratives as ideal types, e.g., Berger 2012; Dian 2015.

10. Reconciliation and forgiveness are omitted because they are *two-way* processes that include a responsible party and an injured party. On reconciliation, see He 2009; Verdeja 2009; Tang 2011; Gardner Feldman 2012. On forgiveness, see Löwenheim 2009.

11. While denial and silencing are distinct phenomena, they are combined because they often co-occur and are frequently driven by the same logic.

12. This definition parallels Cohen's concept "literal denial" (2001, 7).

13. C. Smith 1989, 4. See also Lipstadt (1993) and Charny (2003) for broader conceptualizations of denial.

14. Winter 2010. I prefer "silencing" to "forgetting," since forgetting implies a cognitive process, whereas silencing focuses on the action(s) undertaken. On forgetting, see Connerton 2008.

15. These definitions draw in part on Charny (1991, 13–15; 2003, 30–32). While mythmaking and relativizing are distinct phenomena, they are combined in a single element because they typically co-occur. This element is akin to what Cohen (2001, 7–8) calls "interpretive denial."

16. For a broader definition of mythmaking, see He 2007b, 44. See also Van Evera 1994; Mendeloff 2001. On myths and rumors, see Greenhill and Oppenheim 2017.

17. National Diet of Japan 1995.

18. See King (2010, 294) for a broader understanding of acknowledgment. This and the next three elements draw in part from B. O'Neill (1999, 187).

19. B. O'Neill (1999, 185–86) also makes this distinction.

20. B. O'Neill 1999, 185. See also Tavuchis 1991; Yamazaki 2006; Lind 2008; Nobles 2008.

21. This requirement also draws on B. O'Neill (1999, 178).

22. On commemoration, see Gillis 1994.

23. Torpey (2007) and Zarakol (2010) also compare historical memories in Turkey and Japan, but both emphasize continuity.

24. On the strengthening and institutionalization of the norms of truth-seeking and legal accountability, see Ben-Josef Hirsch and Dixon 2017.

25. These cases thus represent a most similar systems design. See Levy 2008, 10.

26. To better isolate pressures and changes in each state's narrative, I have chosen to focus on a single, dominant narrative within each complex of narratives. As a result, I do not systematically analyze Japan's narratives of the colonization of the Korean peninsula and the "comfort women" program. Nor do I systematically analyze Turkey's narratives of the genocide of Assyrians or of the violence against and relocation of Kurds in and after WWI. On violence against Assyrians and Kurds in the context of WWI, see Gaunt 2006; Üngör 2011b; Akçam 2012, 63–123.

27. Valentino 2004, 10.

28. On the ways in which the trajectory of Turkey's narrative reflects shifts in the norm against genocide, see Dixon 2017.

29. There continues to be a small Armenian community in Turkey. Since the genocide, however, the community has been weak and threatened. See Ekmekçioğlu 2016; Suciyan 2016.

30. On the Western orientation of both Turkey and Japan, see Zarakol 2011.

31. On the confiscation of Armenian properties in the genocide, see Der Matossian 2011a; Üngör and Polatel 2011; Akçam and Kurt 2015.

32. *TRT Television Network* 1990a.

33. On the "norm of border fixity" in the post-WWII period, see Atzili 2012.

34. The compensation fund that, in late 2015, the Japanese government agreed to set up and fund for former South Korean sex slaves is a striking exception to this position.

35. Moreover, since a 2007 ruling by the Japanese Supreme Court, the government's argument has been legally accepted and upheld domestically.

36. See, e.g., B. Anderson 1983; Gellner 1983; Hobsbawm and Ranger 1983; Brand 2014. Following Hurd (1999, 381), legitimacy is defined as "the normative belief by an actor that a rule or institution ought to be obeyed."

37. Heisler 2008, 20. See also Herf 1997; Cruz 2000; Zarakol 2010; Bernhard and Kubik 2014a; Göçek 2015.

38. Krebs (2015, 44) emphasizes that national security narratives need to be consistent with "deeper identity narratives." See also work on ontological (in)security, e.g., Mitzen 2006; Zarakol 2010.

39. Akçam 2004; Göçek 2007, 2015.

40. Ulgen 2010a; Der Matossian 2011a; Üngör and Polatel 2011; Akçam and Kurt 2015; Kurt 2015.

41. Göçek 2015, 504–50. See also Zürcher 1984; Kaiser 2003; Üngör 2008a, 2011b.

42. Göçek argues that the Armenian Genocide constituted "foundational violence" for the Turkish state, which, she further argues, is more likely to be "silenced and denied" (2015, 18).

43. Saaler 2005, 11. See also Seraphim 2006; Yoshida 2006b, 129; Nozaki 2008, 150.

44. Baldwin 1978, viii.

45. Interview with political analyst [J-1], Tokyo, July 2008.

46. Kubik and Bernhard (2014, 22) make an observation along these lines.

47. Yoshida (2007) similarly emphasizes the impact of bottom-up domestic activism.

48. Göçek 2006, 121–22.

49. Kubik and Bernhard (2014, 24) make a similar observation.

50. Krebs (2015, 46) makes a similar point.

51. On Turkish public opinion on the Armenian question, see Centre for Economics and Foreign Policy Studies 2015.

52. Schickler 2001; Pierson 2004; Streeck and Thelen 2005. Bernhard and Kubik (2014a) and Göçek (2015) also discuss layering in the politics of memory. In addition, Germany's remembrance of the Holocaust has been similarly characterized by layering (Olick 2007).

53. Yamazaki 2006, 95.

54. Kubik and Bernhard (2014, 25) hint at potential feedback effects in the politics of memory, while Berger (2012, 3) argues that, over time, historical narratives have independent and unexpected effects on actors' interests and political outcomes. Krebs (2015, 46) makes a similar point regarding national security narratives.

55. On such efforts, see, e.g., Şenay 2011, 2013.

56. Yoshida similarly emphasizes the back-and-forth and ongoing nature of contestation over the past, referring to feedback effects as "spillover effects" (2014, 162, inter alia).

57. Lind (2008) warns of this. See also Göçek 2007; Langenbacher 2010, 20.

2. THE ARMENIAN GENOCIDE AND ITS AFTERMATH

Epigraphs: Holstein quoted in Üngör 2011b, 94; Evren quoted in Gültekin 1989.

1. On demographic engineering policies, see Dündar 2008, 2010; Üngör 2008a, 2011b; Akçam 2012, 227–85. On the broader context, see Levene 1998; Gingeras 2009; Schaller and Zimmerer 2009. On policies toward Assyrians, Greeks, and Kurds, see Gaunt 2006; Bjørnlund 2008; Üngör 2008a, 2011b; Akçam 2012, 63–123.

2. Ulgen 2010a, 160.

3. Ulgen 2010a, 201–2, 212–13; Üngör 2011b, 36, 43–50; Göçek 2015.

4. Göçek 2011, 112–13.

5. Üngör 2011b, 41, 49–50, 54, 61; Akçam 2012, xvii–xviii.

6. Melson 1992; Bloxham 2003b; Winter 2004; Suny 2015.

7. On initial deportations, see Üngör 2011a, 297; Akçam 2012, 175–82. On labor battalions, see Üngör 2011b, 60; Akçam 2012, 159.

8. Akçam and Kurt 2015, 19.

9. Üngör 2011b, 70.

10. Mann 2005, 149; Üngör 2011b, 76, 85. Because the genocide was a process that bled into later events, scholars variously date its end as 1916, 1917, or 1918. The end of the genocide is sometimes marked as late as 1923, but this dating is mostly found in popular histories and memoirs.

11. On local party officials' involvement, see Akçam 2004, 171. On the Special Organization, see Dadrian 1995a, 237–39; Mann 2005, 163–66; Üngör 2011b, 58, 72–74; Akçam 2012, 410–23; Göçek 2015, 194–204. On the military's role, see Dadrian 1992. See also Üngör 2012.

12. On the gendered nature of the violence, see Sarafian 2001; Derderian 2005; Bjørnlund 2009; Ekmekçioğlu 2013, 2015; Watenpaugh 2013.

13. Kévorkian 2011; Akçam 2012, 254, 261, 272–83; Mouradian 2015, 2016.

14. Der Matossian 2011a; Üngör and Polatel 2011; Akçam 2012, 341–71; Akçam and Kurt 2015; Göçek 2015, 276–77.

15. R. G. Hovannisian 1999a, 217–19; Bloxham 2005, 10; Mann 2005, 140; Akçam 2012, 258–61; Göçek 2015, 216.

16. Sonyel 1972, 53; 1990, 768; 2001, 122; Gürün 1985, 217; Halaçoğlu 2002, 103–7.

17. Ekmekçioğlu 2016, 4. See also Sarafian 2001; Ekmekçioğlu 2013; Watenpaugh 2013.

18. On this issue, see R. G. Hovannisian 2007. Those who argue that the genocide was planned in advance include Dadrian 1993, 1995a; Balakian 2003. Those who argue that the genocide was the result of more "contingent" processes include Bloxham 2003b; Mann 2005, 140; Üngör 2011b; Akçam 2012, 126–29; Göçek 2015, 204–26; Suny 2015.

19. On sources, see Der Matossian 2011b; Üngör 2011b, xi–xiv; Akçam 2012, 1–27; Philliou 2015.

20. Üngör 2011b, 95; Akçam 2012, 287–339, 373–83, 399–410.

21. Akçam 2012, 228.

22. Akçam 2012, 158–70.

23. Akçam 2012, 182.

24. Naimark 2001, 29–30; Bloxham 2003a, 42–43; Mann 2005, 146, 149; Kaligian 2014.

25. Nalbandian 1963, 183–84; Suny 1993, 99–100; R. G. Hovannisian 1997, 212–18; Kaligian 2009.

26. Mann 2005, 136. For the memoir of an Ottoman Armenian officer in WWI, see Aktar 2012.

27. Göçek 2015, 216. See also Mann 2005, 143.

28. National Archives and Records Administration 1915. See also Holquist n.d.

29. For international coverage of the deportations, see Kloian 1985; Elbrecht 2012; see also M. Anderson 2011. For official Ottoman responses to such criticism, see *Aspirations et Mouvements* 1915; *Aspirations et Agissements* 1917.

30. Kaiser 2003, 4.

31. Quoted in Guroian 1986, 141, citing Osmanlı Devleti 1916.

32. Shortly before doing so, they destroyed many incriminating documents (Akçam 2006b, 129–32).

33. Figures from Kramer 2006, 446; Akçam 2012, 4. See also Dadrian 1997; Bass 2000, 106–46; Dadrian and Akçam 2011; Göçek 2015, 354–73.

34. R. G. Hovannisian 1986, 116.

35. Talât's memoirs, which were first published in 1921, made similar arguments (Adak 2007).

36. Aktar 2007, 254.

37. Aktar 2007, 258.

38. Aktar 2007, 266.

39. Ulgen 2010a; Üngör 2011b.

40. Quoted in Akçam 2012, xi, citing *T. B. M. M. Gizli Celse Zabıtları* 1985, 177.

41. Akçam and Kurt 2015.

42. Treaty of Sèvres 1920, Art. 89, 142. Note that the Treaty of Sèvres was supplanted by the 1923 Treaty of Lausanne. On the Paris Peace Conference, see Cheterian 2015, 102; Ekmekçioğlu 2016, 6.

43. Zürcher 1984; Kaiser 2003; Akçam 2006a, 127–30; Göçek 2006, 112; Üngör 2011a, 305. Not all of the leaders of the resistance movement were involved in the genocide. In particular, Mustafa Kemal, who became the leader of the movement and the founder of the Republic, was not involved in the massacres and deportations (Ulgen 2010a, 263; 2010b, 373).

44. Zarakol 2010, 15.

45. Ulgen 2010b, 378–82.

46. Quotes in Ulgen 2010a, 277–78, 280, 284 (respectively). On the phrase "shameful act," see Akçam 2006a.

47. Quoted in Ulgen 2010a, 282.

48. Ulgen 2010b, 390.

49. Tusan 2014, 62–69.

50. Quoted in Bobelian 2009, 71. See also Marashlian 1992; Ekmekçioğlu 2014.

51. Göçek makes this point in several publications (e.g., Göçek 2006). An exception is Atatürk's famous *Nutuk* [Speech] in 1927, in which he referred several times to the Armenian deportations and the Armenian question (Ulgen 2010a, 289–99; 2010b, 383–89).

52. Kurban 2004/5; İçduygu, Toktaş, and Soner 2008; Üngör 2011b, 107–217; Bali 2012, 2–11; Suciyan 2016, 126–68.

53. Suciyan 2016, 126–42.

54. Kouymjian 1985, 173. See also K. Öktem 2008; Nişanyan 2011. On "administered forgetting" in the early Republican years, see also Özyürek 2007, 3–6.

55. Cheterian 2015, 40.

56. Üngör 2011c, 17; Suciyan 2016, 126–42.

57. R. G. Hovannisian 1986, 120–21; Ulgen 2010a, 309–64. See also Foss 1992.

58. Göçek 2011, 230.

59. Olson 1986.

60. Bobelian 2009, 77; R. G. Hovannisian 1986, 113. In Soviet Armenia, the issue rarely came up (Marutyan 2009, 38; de Waal 2015, 109).

61. Minasian 1986–87.

62. "Official" actors include the president; the PM; the ministers of foreign affairs, national education, justice, and the interior; the secretary general of the National Security Council; the National Security Council as a whole; the Parliament as a whole; ambassadors and diplomats; and spokespersons for these ministries and offices.

63. Akçam 2004; Ulgen 2010a; Akçam and Kurt 2015.

64. Kaplan 2006, 202.

65. Bazyler 2011; Tacar 2013. Examples of cases brought in the United States include *Bakalian v. Republic of Turkey* and *Davoyan v. Republic of Turkey*. See also Armenian Genocide Reparations Study Group 2015. On the norm of border fixity, see Atzili 2012.

66. Akçam 2004, 39, 50; Göçek 2011, 35. See, e.g., *Ankara Domestic Service* 1987a; Üngör 2011b, 149, 161.

67. Akçam 2004, 22; Ulgen 2010a, 105; Göçek 2011, 41, 132. For an example, see Üngör 2011b, 229.

3. FROM SILENCING TO MYTHMAKING (1950–EARLY 1990S)

Epigraphs: Bakkalbaşı quoted in Davidian and Ferchl 1982; Turkish embassy official quoted in Adams 1983.

1. In addition, many Armenian survivors were denaturalized and expelled from Turkey in the 1920s and 1930s (Tachjian 2006).

2. Aktar 2000; Kurban 2004/5; Vryonis 2005.

3. Polatel et al. 2012.

4. Quoted in Bali 2012, 99, citing Karabağlı 2003. See also Hofmann 2002, 14; Bali 2012, 110, 114–15, 152, 192.

5. Göçek 2011, 191. See also Suciyan 2016, 200–201.

6. Interview with political scientist [T-i], Istanbul, March 2009.

7. Kaiser 2003, 12–14; Ulgen 2010a, 366–76; Üngör 2011b, 36–37.

8. Jørgensen 2003, 206.

9. Kaiser 2003. See also Göçek 2015.

10. Lemkin 1944, 79.

11. UN 1948.

12. Lemkin 1946, 227. In contrast, Armenians did pay attention to the new term and to the UNCG's ratification (Mouradian 2009, 129–33).

13. *United Nations Treaty Series* 1951, 278. There might have been some official concern about the UNCG, as Talât's memoirs were published in Turkish in the immediate wake of WWII. According to Adak, his memoirs "exonerated the Unionists from responsibility in the events of 1915–1916, . . . claiming that the Ottoman government had only the most *peaceful* of intentions" (Adak 2007, 166, emphasis in original).

14. Frieze 2013, 201. Thanks to Khatchig Mouradian for pointing me to this source.

15. Suciyan 2016, 142–68. See also de Waal 2015, 113–18.

16. Suciyan 2016, 164.

17. Interview with political scientist [T-l], Ankara, May 2008. See also Gürün 1985, 296–97.

18. Bobelian 2009, 111. In the United States, the field of Armenian studies began to develop in the late 1950s. The National Association for Armenian Studies and Research was established in 1955, and academic chairs in Armenian studies were created at Harvard in 1959 and UCLA in 1969 (Mamigonian 2012–13).

19. Bakalian 1993, 97–99; Panossian 1998, 157–60; Bobelian 2009, 107–12.

20. R. K. Hovannisian 1994; Bobelian 2009, 123.
21. R. Smith 1989, 26. See, e.g., Attarian 1997, 61n6; Bobelian 2009, 127–34.
22. Bobelian 2009, 130.
23. Bobelian 2009, 132.
24. Özdemir 2008, 10.
25. Kılıç 1957. For another example, see Kılıç 1965.
26. Kılıç 1965.
27. Van Boven 1985, 169.
28. Aktar 2007, 254.
29. Ben-Josef Hirsch 2007a, 191.
30. Kılıç 1965.
31. Dixon 2010a, 109–10. This point is based on my analysis of eleven high school history textbooks published between 1951 and 1980. See Appendix 2 for the textbooks analyzed.
32. Dadrian 1967.
33. De Waal 2015, 142.
34. Marutyan 2009, 39.
35. For example, *Washington Post* 1971; Donabedian 1977; Armenian National Committee 1978.
36. Mouradian 2009, 133.
37. R. G. Hovannisian 1986, 122. In this context, the Armenian Assembly of America was established in 1972.
38. Bobelian 2009, 1–5, 141–63.
39. Dugan et al. 2008; Lütem 2008; Cheterian 2015, 123–31. See also Tololyan 1987.
40. Interview with foreign diplomat [T-g], Ankara, April 2008. See also Şimşir 2000.
41. Quoted in Davidian and Ferchl 1982.
42. Lütem 2008, 37; interview with retired Turkish diplomat [T-d], Ankara, May 2008; interview with political scientist [T-l], Ankara, May 2008.
43. UN 1982, 257, para. 25.
44. Göçek 2011, 152.
45. Interview with political scientist [T-l], Ankara, May 2008.
46. Faik 1981. On the questioning of Armenians' loyalty, see Elmas 2016; Suciyan 2016.
47. ECOSOC 1973, 10.
48. ECOSOC 1973, 5.
49. ECOSOC 1978, 1–4. On the political pressures that led to the passage's deletion, see *Armenian Weekly* 1979; ECOSOC 1984, 27; Attarian 1997, 63–71; interview with retired Turkish diplomat [T-e], Istanbul, April 2009.
50. ECOSOC 1985, 1. On these protests and mobilizations, see Attarian 1997, 67–83.
51. ECOSOC 1985, 9. On Turkish diplomatic efforts, see Attarian 1997, 85–93.
52. House Joint Resolution 148 designated 24 April 1975 as a "National Day of Remembrance of Man's Inhumanity to Man" (Library of Congress 1975). There were earlier attempts to pass a resolution in 1968 and 1974 (Bobelian 2009, 166, 277). See Congressional Record 1968, 5458; 1974, 18354.
53. Also beginning in the late 1970s was a debate over the scope of the proposed US Holocaust Memorial Museum. Armenian groups in the United States and Turkish officials and their US advocates pushed for the inclusion/exclusion (respectively) of the Armenian Genocide in the proposed museum, with the latter prevailing in the end (Bali 2012, 203–7, 251–56, 286–95). See also Osman Olcay Papers, Folder 33, International Institute of Social History, Amsterdam, the Netherlands.
54. The title for this section comes from Gürün's reference to the "passive" nature of Turkish efforts prior to the early 1980s. He wrote: "The propaganda activity of Turks has

been restricted to refuting articles and erroneous assertions; thus it has been nothing more than a passive effort to defend the Turkish position. This attitude enabled the opposite side to act freely in portraying Turks as being guilty" (Gürün 1985, 36).

55. Quoted in Bali 2012, 195, citing *Milliyet* 1975.

56. In 1974, the Greek military government supported a coup on Cyprus and announced the island's unification with Greece. In response, the Turkish military invaded and established control of the northern part of the island. The attempted coup and the international community's condemnation of Turkey's actions reinforced the perception, especially among the Turkish military, that Turkey was surrounded by enemies and had to vigilantly protect its interests in the face of ever-present threats to Turkish unity and territory. In the late 1970s, a series of short-lived coalition governments in Turkey made little progress in addressing a growing financial crisis and increasing violence between leftists and right-wing paramilitary groups in Turkey's cities. Economically, the oil crises of the 1970s, combined with failed import-substitution policies of the 1960s and 1970s, led to skyrocketing inflation and looming financial collapse. See Zürcher 1998, 276–82.

57. Interview with political scientist [T-a], Ankara, April 2008; interview with retired Turkish diplomat [T-e], Istanbul, April 2009. De Waal reports that Turkish diplomats discussed the issue with Armenian representatives from the diaspora, but these efforts got hung up on the issue of territorial claims (2015, 159–63). See also R. G. Hovannisian 1984, 92–95; Lütem 2008, 37–38; Bali 2012, 202–7.

58. Interview with retired Turkish diplomat [T-e], Istanbul, April 2009. See also Özdemir 2008, 60; Göçek 2011, 53; Bali 2012, 192.

59. The title for this section comes from a speech given by Turkish president Kenan Evren in Erzurum in July 1986. He argued that the reason why Turkey was being characterized as "a nation that has committed massacres" was that "we have not been able to tell the world the truth" (*Ankara Domestic Service* 1986).

60. The Turkish military had previously ruled from 1971 to 1973.

61. Lütem 2008, 38–39; Özdemir 2008, 66.

62. Quoted in Bali 2012, 244, citing Gürün 1995, 428–29.

63. *Ankara Domestic Service* 1987a. See also *Ankara Domestic Service* 1984; *Reuters News* 1989a.

64. Quoted in *Güneş* 1985.

65. *TRT Television Network* 1990a. During the same session, Turkish politician Erdal İnönü expressed similar concerns, warning: "If the bill passes, the affair will not end there. The militant Armenian groups who are behind the bill will immediately ask Turkey for indemnities and territory to repair the damages of the injustice suffered by their ancestors" (*TRT Television Network* 1990b). In addition, in the 1980s a former Turkish diplomat explained "that if his country recognized the Genocide, the Turkish authorities were afraid that they would have to face compensation claims by the relatives of the victims and perhaps territorial claims by the Armenian SSR" (Chrysanthopoulos 2002, 28). For similar statements by retired diplomat Ömer Lütem, see de Waal 2015, 174.

66. One academic emphasized that the policy changes in the early 1980s are in part attributable to the fact that the military, which was in power from 1980 to 1983, was more sensitive about this issue than other institutions (interview with political scientist [T-a], Ankara, April 2008).

67. *Ankara Domestic Service* 1987a.

68. Bali 2012, 314. Zarakol (2011) emphasizes the importance for Turkish officials of being perceived and treated as a "civilized" and "modern" state.

69. Elsewhere I refer to these strategies as a "repertoire of action" (Dixon 2010b).

70. İAGM's first head was Ömer Engin Lütem, and its work was closely overseen by Deputy Foreign Minister Kamuran Gürün until his retirement in September 1982. Infor-

mation in this paragraph is from the following: interview with retired Turkish diplomat [T-d], Ankara, May 2008 and March 2009; interview with retired Turkish diplomat [T-e], Istanbul, April 2009; anonymous interview [T-h], Istanbul, April 2009; interview with retired Turkish diplomat [T-f], Istanbul, April 2009. See also Gürün 1995, 375–434; Lütem 2008, 38; Özdemir 2008, 67.

71. Elekdağ 1983a. See also Elekdağ 1983c.

72. Uğurlu and Balcı 1989, 229. This characterization is based on my analysis of eight high school history textbooks published between 1981 and 1991 (Dixon 2010a, 110–12). See appendix 2 for the textbooks analyzed.

73. *New York Times* 1984. For another example, see Bali 2012, 291. Although Armenian terrorist attacks had ended by the mid-1980s, the Turkish government continued to argue that recognizing the genocide would be a concession to terrorists, claiming that Kurdish terrorism (which began in 1984) was related to Armenian terrorism. See Owen-Davies 1989; *Reuters News* 1989b.

74. Erman 1986. See also *San Francisco Chronicle* 1985.

75. *Ankara Domestic Service* 1984. See also *Ankara Anatolia* 1985.

76. For early comparative work on genocide, see Fein 1978; Kuper 1981; Charny and Davidson 1983. On debates over the exceptionality of the Holocaust, see Kansteiner 1994.

77. Quoted in *New York Times* 1982a. On the conference, see Charny 1983.

78. Elekdağ 1983a, 1983b (respectively). For similar examples, see Howe 1982; Elekdağ 1983c, 1985. Elsewhere, Turkish officials disregarded these concerns about the sanctity of the term "genocide." For example, in July 1983 Foreign Minister İlter Türkmen declared: "The Turkish nation's retaliation will be as heavy as its patience has been great. . . . Armenian organizations are committing the worst example of genocide, but they will pay heavily for these crimes" (quoted in *New York Times* 1983).

79. Quoted in *New York Times* 1989. R. Smith (1989, 16–18) also argues that acknowledging the Holocaust was a tactic used to deny the Armenian Genocide.

80. For an example of such safe-haven arguments, see Elekdağ 1982.

81. Dixon 2017, 84.

82. Quoting from *Ankara Domestic Service* 1987b. See also Erman 1986.

83. Paraphrased in *Ankara Domestic Service* 1989. See also Lowry 1989.

84. Sarafian 1993b, 1999.

85. Akçam 2012, 9–27. See also Barsoumian 2011a.

86. Ben-Josef Hirsch 2007a, 186. On the norm of truth-seeking, see Ben-Josef Hirsch and Dixon 2017.

87. Elekdağ 1988.

88. Kandemir 1990.

89. Quoting from Elekdağ 1983a, 1983b, 1988; Erman 1986.

90. For example, Ludington 1983.

91. Su and Mumcu 1983, 118. See also Uğurlu and Balcı 1989, 229. Sarıkamış was an Ottoman military campaign in WWI, during which the Ottoman army suffered a great loss. Note that the last sentence of the quoted passage is a myth; on the massacres in Der Zor and other refugee camps, see Kévorkian 2011; Akçam 2012, 264–72; Mouradian 2016.

92. Elekdağ 1983c. For this point in textbooks, see Dixon 2010a, 111.

93. *Ankara Domestic Service* 1986.

94. Elekdağ 1985.

95. Su and Mumcu 1983, 118.

96. *Ankara Domestic Service* 1981. Evren is likely referring to the domestic turmoil in the late 1970s, implying that Armenians saw Turkey's domestic political weakness as an opportunity.

97. Dixon 2010a, 112.

98. Parmaksızoğlu 1988, 115. See also Su and Mumcu 1983, 118; Şenünver et al. 1989, 89. On the roots of this framing in the Paris Peace Conference negotiations, see Ekmekçioğlu 2013, 542–44.

99. The title for this section comes from a statement made by Turkish PM Bülent Ulusu in a 16 October 1982 press conference. Reporting on official efforts to combat Armenian terrorism, he stated: "Those who had been content to believe in unilateral claims are beginning to have more objective views on the issue as more and more historical facts, based on documents, begin to surface. We will continue our determined efforts to enlighten the public on the issue" (*Ankara Domestic Service* 1982).

100. Gürün 1985, 209; Lütem 2008, 39; Özdemir 2008, 66–67.

101. For example, Şimşir 1982a. I thank Seyhan Bayraktar for suggesting the latter rationale. Lütem 2008, 39; Özdemir 2008, 69–70; interviews with retired Turkish diplomat [T-d], Ankara, May 2008 and March 2009.

102. Gürün 1985, 214, 216 (respectively).

103. Gürün 1985, 215, 216, 217 (respectively).

104. Gürün 1985, 295.

105. Lütem 2008, 39; Özdemir 2008, 73; interview with retired Turkish diplomat [T-d], Ankara, March 2009.

106. Foreign Policy Institute 1982, 24, 29, 30 (respectively).

107. Gürün 1983 was translated into English and French (Gürün 1984, 1985). *The Armenian Issue in Nine Questions and Answers* was published in French, English, and Turkish. The Foreign Policy Institute published another pamphlet in Turkish, English, French, and German; see *Setting the Record Straight on Armenian Propaganda against Turkey* 1982.

108. Lütem 2008, 40.

109. Sarafian 1999; interview with retired Turkish diplomat [T-d], Ankara, March 2009.

110. Ottoman Turkish and modern Turkish have completely different orthographies, differences in grammar, and vocabularies that have become more distinct over time. As a result, most Turks cannot read, speak, or write Ottoman Turkish, and history written prior to the language reform is inaccessible to most Turks.

111. Gürün 1995, 388–89; Özdemir 2008, 81, 83; interview with historian at Turkish Historical Society [T-k], Ankara, March 2009; interview with retired Turkish diplomat [T-e], Istanbul, April 2009.

112. See Ökte (1989) and Uras (1988), respectively. See also Orel and Yuca 1983, 1986.

113. See Şimşir 1982b, 1983, 1989, 1990. Interview with retired Turkish diplomat [T-d], Ankara, May 2008; interview with retired Turkish diplomat [T-e], Istanbul, April 2009.

114. Sarafian 1999; Özdemir 2008, 73; interview with retired Turkish diplomat [T-d], Ankara, May 2008; interview with retired Turkish diplomat [T-e], Istanbul, April 2009; interview with retired Turkish diplomat [T-f], Istanbul, April 2009.

115. Howard 1989.

116. Quoted in Gurdilek 1989.

117. See references in note 85.

118. Anonymous interview [T-h], Istanbul, April 2009.

119. For example, Ataöv 1984a, 1984b, 1985a, 1985b, 1986.

120. Özdemir 2008, 74–75.

121. Interview with retired Turkish diplomat [T-d], Ankara, May 2008; interview with retired Turkish diplomat [T-f], Istanbul, April 2009.

122. Dixon 2010a, 110–12.

123. Kaplan 2006, 198, emphasis in original.

124. For example, *Ankara Domestic Service* 1981, 1986; *Ankara Anatolia* 1986.

125. Lütem 2008, 40.

126. Özdemir 2008, 67.

127. Gürün 1995, 406; Auron 2003; Bali 2012, 241, 285–86; Şenay 2013.

128. Bobelian 2009, 185.

129. King and Pomper 2004, 7–8; Bali 2012, 272–74, 276–84. Bobelian further reports: "In a little known 1987 agreement with Turkey, the United States had apparently promised to block such Genocide resolutions" (2009, 179).

130. Vryonis 1991, 79–118; Gürün 1995, 375–434; Bobelian 2009, 180–83; Bali 2012, 196–201, 310–29.

131. Bali 2012, 242–43, 266–67, 269, 277, 279.

132. Interview with retired Turkish diplomat [T-c], Ankara, May 2008. For other motivations, see Inbar 2009, 228–36.

133. It was suggested that the Turkish public might react badly—and perhaps violently—if Israeli or Jewish groups publicly supported efforts to recognize the Armenian Genocide.

134. Howe 1982. See also Charny and Davidson 1983.

135. Blitzer 1989; Shalev 1989; Frucht and Jerozolimski 2000. Former Turkish diplomats emphasized that Jewish American groups' lobbying on behalf of Turkey helped defeat genocide resolutions in the US Congress (interview with retired Turkish diplomat [T-c], Ankara, May 2008; interview with retired Turkish diplomat [T-f], Istanbul, April 2009). Of course, only some Jewish and Israeli organizations and leaders supported Turkey's position (Charny and Davidson 1983; Bobelian 2009, 183).

136. Bali 2012, 200.

137. Nesmith and Alexander 1987; Vryonis 1991, 88; Bobelian 2009, 181; Bali 2012, 271–72, 335.

138. Jørgensen 2003, 217. See also Bali 2012, 237.

139. Lütem 2008, 40.

140. Bali 2012, 235.

141. For example, United Turkish Americans 1985; ATAA 1986; McCarthy and McCarthy 1989.

142. For example, Ali 1982; Kuzay 1983; Gurun 1985; Basol 1986; Ozer 1986; Sevin 1991. See also ATA-USA 1983. On the ATAA's activities, see R. G. Hovannisian 1986, 129; I. Kaya 2004, 298; 2009, 625.

143. On such considerations, see Quataert 2006; Gingeras 2009, vii–viii; Akçam 2012, xxv; M. Anderson 2013, 464; Reynolds 2013, 473; Göçek 2015, xiv–xviii; Philliou 2015.

144. ITS is a registered nonprofit foundation based at Georgetown University. Until 2015, most of its funding came from the Turkish government, and it had a close connection with the Turkish embassy in Washington. ITS has received donations from US defense manufacturers and US and Turkish companies. See Vryonis 1991, 91–118; Jørgensen 2003, 211; Matossian 2008b. On the 2015 withdrawal of the Turkish government's support, see Redden 2015.

145. Quoted in Rubin 1995.

146. *Washington Post* 1985.

147. *Journal: Armenian Assembly of America* 1987, 8; Vryonis 1991, 98–102, 110–15; Charny and Fromer 1998; Bali 2012, 274.

148. Lowry 2000, 114.

149. Quoted in Bali 2012, 268. The Turkish government also helped fund the Chair in Contemporary Turkish Studies at the London School of Economics and Political Science.

150. Honan 1996.

151. Quoted in *Associated Press Newswires* 1997. See also Lim 1997; K. Weiss 1997.

152. ECOSOC 1985; *Official Journal of the European Communities* 1987.

4. PLAYING HARDBALL (1994–2008)

This title is a spin on a 2007 statement by foreign policy adviser Egemen Bağış: "Yesterday, some in Congress wanted to play hardball, . . . I can assure you, Turkey knows how to play hardball" (quoted in Holthouse 2008). Epigraphs: Turkish ambassador quoted in Morrison 1998; Cem quoted in *BBC Monitoring Service* 2000.

1. Dagi 1993, 60–62.

2. An independent Armenian state briefly existed in the immediate aftermath of WWI, but it was defeated in a war with Turkish nationalist forces and then subsumed into the Soviet Union. These events preceded the establishment of the Republic of Turkey. See R. G. Hovannisian 1967; Suny 1993, 124–32.

3. De Waal 2015, 202–3.

4. Quoted in *Ankara Anatolia* 1991.

5. Astourian 2000, 2. See also Kaligian 2008, 75–77.

6. Quoted in Astourian 2005, 83.

7. Sarafian 1998.

8. Government of the Republic of Armenia 1990, Art. 11.

9. Quoted in Astourian 2000, 20. See also Astourian 2005, 84.

10. Mirzoyan 2010, 67. See also Chrysanthopoulos 2002, 25; Görgülü 2008, 17; 2009, 21; de Waal 2015, 200–203.

11. Alp 2001.

12. Astourian (2016, 33–34) makes a similar point.

13. See Astourian 1994; Herzig 1999, 65–73; Cheterian 2008, 87–154.

14. Astourian 1994, 101–4. Turkey threatened to invade Armenia and massed fifty thousand troops on the border (Astourian 2005, 89; Mirzoyan 2010, 74).

15. Mirzoyan 2010, 88–89. See also Astourian 2000, 29–30; Görgülü 2008, 10–11; Mirzoyan 2010, 66–68.

16. For many Armenians, the conflict over Nagorno-Karabakh evoked memories of the genocide, which accounts for the strong support for the enclave's independence (Astourian 2000, 22; 2005, 85–86; Marutyan 2007). Armenian American groups also linked the Nagorno-Karabakh issue to the genocide (Paul 2000; King and Pomper 2004).

17. Nazaryan 1993, quoted in Mirzoyan 2010, 75.

18. Migdalovitz 1996, 9–10. See also de Waal 2015, 209, 221, 228–29.

19. See Akçam 1992.

20. See Ternon 1993.

21. See Kalman 1994. The other Turkish word for "genocide" is *soykırım*.

22. Cheterian 2015, 11–12.

23. Göçek 2011, 192.

24. Göçek 2011, 185–210; interview with civil society actor [T-v], Istanbul, May 2008.

25. Founded in 1986, İHD focuses on human rights and freedom of expression, particularly—but not only—in relation to the Kurdish question.

26. Köker 1995; Hofmann 2002, 22; interview with civil society actor [T-n], Istanbul, May 2008; interview with civil society activist [T-p], Istanbul, May 2008; interview with civil society actors [T-w], Istanbul, March 2009. For a book on the latter exhibition, see *Tuzla Ermeni Çocuk Kampı* 2000.

27. See Yelda 2000, 27–31, inter alia. See also Günaysu 2008b, 2013; interview with researcher [T-j], Istanbul, April 2009; interview with civil society actor [T-x], Istanbul, April 2009.

28. See, e.g., Yüce 1993. Interview with civil society activist [T-p], Istanbul, May 2008.

29. Cheterian 2015, 14–15.

30. On Dink's influence, see Eraslan 2007; Ozel 2009; Cheterian 2015, 36; interview with civil society activist in Turkey [T-p], Istanbul, May 2008.

31. Bayraktar 2010; Göçek 2011, 180.

32. Quoted in Cheterian 2015, 24.

33. See Dadrian 1995b. The original is Dadrian 1995a.

34. Hofmann 2002, 33; Zarakolu 2008c, 249, 251–58; interview with civil society actor [T-x], Istanbul, April 2009; Ragıp Zarakolu, comments on panel at "Armenian Genocide in the Ottoman Empire during World War I, 1915–2015" conference, Paris, 28 March 2015.

35. Interview with civil society activist [T-p], Istanbul, May 2008.

36. Zarakolu 2008b, 19–22.

37. Interview with civil society activist [T-p], Istanbul, May 2008; interview with civil society actor [T-x], Istanbul, April 2009. See also Günaysu 2008a.

38. See Maraşlı 2008. See also Ayata 2009, 2015; Günaysu 2009c.

39. Interview with civil society actor [T-v], Istanbul, May 2008.

40. Quoted in Morrison 1994.

41. For example, Morrison 1995; *BBC Monitoring Service: Central Europe and Balkans* 1998; *Turkish Daily News* 1998a, 1999.

42. Lütem 2008, 42.

43. Quoted in *Agence France-Presse* 1998.

44. MFA 2000, emphasis added. Although Aktan was retired at the time of his testimony, his statement is considered official because of its inclusion on the MFA's website.

45. Dixon 2017, 89–90. On victim groups, see ICTR 1998; ICTY 1999. On intent, see ICTR 1998, 1999. Note that genocide typically occurs in the context of war, civil war, or revolution and that the actions of members of a victim group are irrelevant to the determination of whether an event constitutes genocide.

46. Quoted in *BBC Monitoring Service: Central Europe and Balkans* 1998.

47. Quoted in Condon 1999.

48. Palazoğlu and Bircan 1995, 145. The discussion of textbooks is based on my analysis of three high school history textbooks published between 1994 and 2000. See appendix 2 and Dixon 2010a, 113–15.

49. Kalecikli 1994, 134.

50. Tuncer 1995, VI. Note that the Turkish text uses the word "genocide" (*soykırım*) twice in reference to Armenians' actions, whereas the English text does not (see Tuncer 1995, VIII).

51. Quoted in *BBC Monitoring Service: Central Europe and Balkans* 1998.

52. Türkdoğan 1999. See also Uzundere 2002.

53. Palazoğlu and Bircan 1995, 40.

54. Kalecikli 1994, 136–37.

55. Palazoğlu and Bircan 1995, 144.

56. *Özgür Politika* 2003; interview with civil society actor [T-y], Ankara, April 2008.

57. K. Öktem 2011, 114.

58. This was first declared in 1987 and was repeated in 2000, 2004, and 2005 (European Parliament 1987, 2000, 2004, 2005).

59. Keck and Sikkink 1998.

60. Interview with EU diplomat [T-s], Ankara, March 2009; interview with civil society actors [T-w], Istanbul, March 2009.

61. Interview with civil society activist [T-p], Istanbul, May 2008; interview with civil society actor [T-v], Istanbul, May 2008.

62. Zarakolu 2008b, 30.

63. Göçek 2011, 269–71.

64. Köker 2005; Natanyan 2008.

65. Altınay 2006; Altınay and Türkyılmaz 2011.

66. Interview with civil society actor [T-z], Istanbul, May 2008. See also Açar and Rüma 2007, 459–60; de Waal 2015, 235–47.

67. The committee was revived in 2007, after Hrant Dink's assassination (interview with civil society activist [T-p], Istanbul, May 2008).

68. Tunçay 2008, 241; Zarakolu 2008b, 23.

69. Interview with civil society activist [T-ff], Istanbul, May 2008; interview with civil society actor [T-x], Istanbul, April 2009.

70. Görgülü 2008, 26–28; interview with civil society actor [T-r], Ankara, March 2009; interview with businessman [T-o], Ankara, March 2009; anonymous interview [T-gg], Ankara, March 2009.

71. Göçek 2006, 121–22. Üngör (2008b, para. 16) refers to a fourth developing narrative, which he labels the "minority memorial narrative."

72. For example, Suny, Göçek, and Naimark 2011.

73. Halil Berktay, comments on panel, Hrant Dink Memorial Workshop, Istanbul, 1 June 2013. On WATS, see Göçek 2008; Suny 2009; Suny and Göçek 2011. See also Bayraktar 2008, 7–8; Kaligian 2008, 87–91. Note that the use of the term "genocide" was not a condition of participation in the workshop (Suny 2009, 944–45).

74. Necef 2003, 230. See also Açar and Rüma 2007; Bayraktar 2010.

75. Panossian 1998, 180.

76. European Stability Initiative 2009, 19.

77. Toumani 2004, 42; Astourian 2005, 97; Giragosian 2005, 12; Mirzoyan 2010, 89–93; de Waal 2015, 207–8.

78. Quoted in Turkish Daily News 1998b.

79. Interview with political scientist [T-a], Ankara, April 2008; interview with retired Turkish diplomat [T-d], Ankara, May 2008. See also Mirzoyan 2010, 92.

80. My analysis ended in 2008, thus the end date of 2008. That said, a new phase has not begun since then.

81. Interview with civil society actor [T-b], Istanbul, May 2008; interview with civil society actor [T-r], Ankara, March 2009.

82. Quoted in Zaman 2002.

83. Quoted in Akçam 2012, xii.

84. Üngör and Polatel 2011, ix–x, quoting from Hürriyet 2006.

85. Paraphrased in Cannon 2009, 239. See also Zarakol 2010.

86. Quoted in Turkish Weekly 2005.

87. Quoted in The Times 2007.

88. Elekdağ 2001.

89. Quoted in Ulgen 2010a, 131–32, citing from Hürriyet 2004.

90. T. C. Başbakanlık Basın-Yayın ve Enformasyon Genel Müdürlüğü 2002. Many officials I interviewed claimed not to know about ASİMKK, but other interviewees referred to the committee or mentioned that it had made certain decisions. Interview with retired Turkish diplomat [T-d], Ankara, March 2009; interview with historian at the Turkish Historical Society [T-k], Ankara, March 2009; interview with academic [T-cc], Ankara, March 2009. For references to ASİMKK, see Özcan 2002; Zarakolu 2008b, 16.

91. Interview with political scientist [T-a], Ankara, April 2008. Ünlü (2006, 195–98) details the connections of ASAM board members to the Turkish military and security establishment, highlighting how this think tank was effectively an extension of the state. In 2009, ASAM was closed and ERAREN was folded into the new Center for Eurasian Studies (Center for Eurasian Studies 2016, 9).

92. Özdemir 2008, 80–81; interview with retired Turkish diplomat [T-d], Ankara, March 2009.

93. Interview with retired Turkish diplomat [T-d], Ankara, March 2009. The books are Kantarcı et al. 2002 and Lütem 2007. See also Kasım and Laçiner 2003.

94. Phillips 2005, 32–33, 40, 62; interview with civil society actor [T-b], Istanbul, May 2008. See also Cheterian 2015, 169–76. The Armenian delegation was similarly composed of carefully selected representatives from the Armenian diaspora and the Republic of Armenia (Kaligian 2008, 81).

95. Interview with civil society actor [T-b], Istanbul, May 2008; Phillips 2005, 62.

96. *Akşam* 2005.

97. Akdin, Çakmak, and Genç 2005, 106. For this phase, I analyzed two textbooks published in 2005 and 2007. See Dixon (2010a, 115–17) and appendix 2.

98. *Taraf* 2009.

99. This decision was made by ASİMKK (interview with academic [T-cc], Ankara, March 2009).

100. Akdin, Çakmak, and Genç 2005, 106.

101. Interview with political scientist [T-a], Ankara, April 2008; interview with retired Turkish diplomat [T-c], Ankara, May 2008. For a piece by a retired Turkish diplomat on the ICTY's 2001 verdict on Srebrenica, see Aktan 2001. According to a 2007 newspaper article, "Turkish legal experts have . . . been examining, among other things, whether the ICJ [International Court of Justice] decision on Serbia could bring Turkey closer to clearing it of Armenian genocide allegations" (Sarıibrahimoğlu 2007). For a retired Turkish diplomat's arguments that genocide is a legal concept, see Tacar 2007; Tacar and Gauin 2012.

102. ICTJ 2003; Phillips 2005, 91, 99–100, 109; interview with civil society actor [T-b], Istanbul, May 2008. For Aktan's response, see Aktan 2003. For critiques of TARC, see Kaligian 2008, 80–7.

103. Gül 2007.

104. Erdoğan 2007. For another example, see Robinson 2010. This theme also appeared in textbooks (see Akdin, Çakmak, and Genç 2005, 39; Kara 2007, 57).

105. "Norm signaling involves expressing support for values or practices that are part of a norm, while not changing relevant behaviors" (Dixon 2017, 86).

106. On these trends, see Nobles 2008; Subotić 2009; Sikkink 2011; Ben-Josef Hirsch 2014.

107. Şensoy 2007. See also Logoglu 2005.

108. Erdoğan 2005. For Erdoğan's letter and Kocharian's response, see Görgülü 2008, 43–44.

109. Şensoy 2007.

110. Halil Berktay made this point at the Hrant Dink Memorial Workshop, Istanbul, 1 June 2013. See Aral 2011 for many of the conference papers. On the conference, see Boğa 2006; Kaligian 2008, 88–9; Cheterian 2015, 179–82.

111. Thanks to Margaret Lavinia Anderson for this observation.

112. Quoted in Toumani 2008.

113. Interview with Turkish academic [T-bb], Istanbul, July 2007; interview with Turkish intellectual [US-3], Boston area, February 2010.

114. *Turkish Daily News* 2002a.

115. Quoted in *Turkish Daily News* 2003. For another example, see Gül 2007.

116. Şensoy 2006.

117. Gül 2007.

118. For example, *100 Soruda Ermeni Sorunu* (The Armenian question in 100 questions) 2001; *Ermeniler Tarafından Yapılan Katliam Belgeleri (1914–1919)* (Documents on massacres committed by Armenians) 2001; Karacakaya 2001; Demirbaş 2002; *Arşiv Belgeleriyle Ermeni Faaliyetleri 1914–1918* (Armenian activities in archival documents,

1914–1918) 2005. The increase in archival publications was coordinated by ASİMKK (interview with retired Turkish diplomat [T-d], Ankara, March 2009; interview with high-level bureaucrat [T-dd], Ankara, March 2009). The TTK worked with the archives to publish archival materials related to the Armenian question so that materials would be ready if and when a historians' commission is formed (interview with historian at the Turkish Historical Society [T-k], Ankara, March 2009).

119. Interview with historian at the Turkish Historical Society [T-k], Ankara, March 2009.

120. Özdemir 2008, 4, 78.

121. See Halaçoğlu 2001; Özdemir et al. 2004; Çiçek 2005; Özdemir 2005.

122. For example, Ata 2005; Karaca 2005; Dilan 2005–6. Interview with historian at the Turkish Historical Society [T-k], Ankara, March 2009.

123. Özdemir 2008, 75–76. ERAREN organized several conferences open only to Turkish scholars (interview with retired Turkish diplomat [T-d], Ankara, March 2009).

124. Zarif 2003.

125. *Turkish Daily News* 2002b. For the decisions, see Ministry of National Education 2002a, 2002b.

126. Armenian schools did not comply with this (N. Kaya 2009, 27).

127. Zarif 2003.

128. For example, Çakır 2003.

129. *Özgür Politika* 2003.

130. Thompson 2007; Holthouse 2008; Edmonds and Giraldi 2009; Gunter 2011, 96–97. For scholarly developments, see R. G. Hovannisian 2015; Mamigonian 2015.

131. Bengür 2009, 45. On efforts in other countries, see Şenay 2011, 1624–25.

132. Middle East Studies Association 2008, 1–2. For the book review, see Quataert 2006. See also Matossian 2008a, 2008b; Bobelian 2009, 192.

133. On the former, see Barsoumian 2011b; Jaschik 2011. On the latter, see Jaschik 2010a. For another lawsuit, see Jaschik 2010b.

134. See Gürsoy 2012, 745–47.

135. See, e.g., Akçam 2007; European Stability Initiative 2009.

136. Interview with civil society actor [T-ee], Istanbul, May 2008; interview with civil society actors [T-w], Istanbul, March 2009.

137. See Zarakolu 2008b, 28; Keskin 2011; Günaysu 2013. For the text of İHD–İstanbul Şübesi's 2005 press release, see Zarakolu 2008a, 207–9.

138. For example, Neyzi and Kharatyan-Araqelyan 2010.

139. On TESEV's projects, see Görgülü, Iskandaryan, and Minasyan 2010, 5. See, e.g., Oran 2004; Kurban 2007; Görgülü 2008; Görgülü et al. 2009; Kurban and Hatemi 2009.

140. Quoted in Erbal 2012, 62–63.

141. On the apology campaign and responses to it, see Bayraktar 2008; Ulgen 2010a, 194–96; Erbal 2012.

142. Türkiye Büyük Millet Meclisi 2008, 961–62; see also *Atılım* 2008.

143. Türkiye Büyük Millet Meclisi 2009, 198; see also Günaysu 2009c. On Kurds' calls to recognize the genocide, see Ayata 2008, 2009, 2015; Günaysu 2009b; Lubbock 2015.

144. Interview with civil society actor [T-n], Istanbul, May 2008; interview with civil society actor [T-x], Istanbul, April 2009.

145. See Kentel and Poghosyan 2005, 42–43; interview with civil society actor [T-r], Ankara, March 2009; Keskin 2009–10.

146. Bakiner 2013, 702–3.

147. Quoting from European Parliament 2007, E.23.

148. Babalı 2009; Görgülü et al. 2009, 10; Kurt and Coşkun 2013, 3–4.

149. On the protocols, see Phillips 2012; de Waal 2015, 214–34.

150. Çelikpala 2009, 2–3; Göksel 2009; Görgülü, Iskandaryan, and Minasyan 2010, 10–11, 18–19; İşeri and Çelik 2013, 278–79.

151. Quoted in Çamlıbel 2014.

152. For example, in a 2012 letter to the editor of the *New York Times*, the Turkish ambassador to the United States, Namık Tan, wrote: "Turkey does not deny this tragedy. Our intention is to attain a just memory through an impartial and fair dialogue that will ultimately normalize Turkish-Armenian relations" (Tan 2012).

5. THE NANJING MASSACRE AND THE SECOND SINO-JAPANESE WAR

1. The broader war is known by several monikers, which vary in temporal and geographic scope. The "Greater East Asian War" is typically used by Japanese conservatives and encompasses a range of events, including the colonization of Korea. Terms used by moderates and leftists in Japan include the "Fifteen-Year War," which refers to the period from 1931 through 1945, and the "Pacific War," which refers to the part of WWII that was fought in the Pacific theater between 1941 and 1945. "World War II" refers to the period from 1939 to 1945 and includes all of the theaters of conflict. See A. Hashimoto 2015, 8–9.

2. Rose 2005, 5, 88; Wan 2006, 305, 312. Unit 731 was one of several secret medical units that developed biological and chemical weapons and conducted "scientific" experiments on live Chinese prisoners and POWs. For additional references, see note 19 in the introduction.

3. Kasahara 1997, 228, cited in Yoshida 2000, 104; Eykholt 2000, 15; Fogel 2000a, 6; Yoshida 2006b, 181. For primary sources and accounts, see Rabe 1998; Brook 1999; Honda 1999. For historical and historiographical work and discussions of the death toll, see Hora 1967; Yang 1990, 1999, 2001, 2011; Kasahara 1997; Hata 1998; Fogel 2000b; Yamamoto 2000; Askew 2002, 2007; Yoshida 2006b; Wakabayashi 2007b.

4. Quotes from Eykholt 2000, 17.

5. Yang 2000, 154.

6. Eykholt 2000, 18.

7. Yang 2011, 641–42, 645.

8. Yoshida 2006b, 35, 113. See also Eykholt 2000, 57–58; Brook 2001, 673; Bush 2007.

9. "Official" actors include the emperor; the PM; the chief cabinet secretary; the cabinet as a whole; the Diet as a whole; the ministers of education, foreign affairs, and justice; ambassadors and diplomats; and spokespeople for these ministries and offices. Note that the statements and actions of politicians who are not entitled to speak with the state's voice on these issues are not considered official.

10. See Hora 1967; I. Chang 1997, 101, 102; Hata 1998. For the Tokyo Trial judgment, see Boister and Cryer 2008a, 535–39. For revisionist positions, see Tanaka M. 1984; Higashinakano 2005. Here "revisionist" refers to a person or view that seeks to silence, relativize, rationalize, or deny Japan's war crimes. For discussions of the death toll, see Gibney 1999, xiii; Yang 1999; Askew 2002, 5; Tohmatsu 2011; Schwartz 2012. The most reliable estimates are in the range of one hundred thousand to two hundred thousand deaths (Eykholt 2000, 15; Fogel 2000a, 6; Yoshida 2006b, 181).

11. Askew 2002, 2, emphasis added.

12. Yang 2000, 149; Yoshida 2006b, 181.

13. Honda 1999, xxv.

14. Fogel 2000a, 5.

15. Yang 2001, 78.

16. Y. Tanaka 1996, 2.

17. Wakamiya 1998, 102–3; Kersten 2004, 499; Seraphim 2006, 1.

18. He 2009, 125–26.

19. This and above quote from the Constitution of Japan 1947.

20. Dower 1999, 452. See also Minear 1971; Awaya 1991, 2006; Brook 2001. The Japanese government officially endorsed the Tokyo Trial's findings in the 1951 Treaty of Peace with Japan (known as the San Francisco Treaty). See *United Nations Treaty Series* 1952a, 56. On the indictment and the selection of those tried, see Supreme Commander for the Allied Powers 1946; Boister and Cryer 2008b. "Class A" war criminals are those accused by the Allies of having committed "crimes against peace."

21. He 2009. See also Fujitani, White, and Yoneyama 2001, 7; Orr 2001; Y. Tanaka 2006, 6.

22. On SCAP's protection of the emperor, see Dower 1999, chap. 11.

23. Benfell 2002; Rose 2005, 35, 36; Nozaki 2008, 7. On victim consciousness, see Orr 2001.

24. Brook 2001, 677; Rose 2005, 35; Boister and Cryer 2008a, 535–39.

25. Boister and Cryer 2008a, 536, 537.

26. Yoshida 2006b, 51. In addition, between 1945 and 1951, war crimes trials were held in China, Taiwan, and elsewhere, including a trial in Nanjing that "found four men guilty of participating in the Nanjing massacre" (Rose 2005, 139).

27. Yoshida 2014, 10–15.

28. Quoted in Yoshida 2005, 61.

29. Nozaki 2008, 8.

30. Yoshida 2005, 61.

31. Quoted in Morris-Suzuki 2013, 15, citing Koshida 2002, 267.

32. Yoshida 2000, 73, 75; Seraphim 2006, 54.

33. Interview with political analyst [J-1], Tokyo, July 2008; interview with *New York Times* journalist [J-2], Tokyo, July 2008; interview with leftist historian [J-9], Tokyo, July 2008. See also Yang 2001, 57; Saaler 2005; Yoshida 2006b, 93. There were also strong continuities among bureaucratic elites (Seraphim 2006, 317–18).

34. Pauley 1946.

35. Dower 1999, 82; Rose 2005, 41–42. See also Ohno 1975.

36. *United Nations Treaty Series* 1952a, 60, 64.

37. *United Nations Treaty Series* 1952a, 62. See also Rose 2005, 43.

38. Koga 2013, 499. For a legal analysis of the ruling, see Levin 2008. See also Arakawa 2001; Umeda 2008, 18–29; Shin 2011, 11. For a critique of this position, see ECOSOC 1996.

39. Pyle 2007, 225.

40. Quoted in Field 1995, 413.

41. On *gaiatsu*, or external pressure in Japanese politics, see Schoppa 1993.

42. Honda 1999; Seraphim 2006; Yoshida 2006b, 2014; Nozaki 2008.

43. Yang (1990) and Yoshida (2000, 2006b, 2014) also emphasize the back-and-forth nature of domestic contestation over the past.

44. Arai, Goto, and Wang 2012; S. Smith 2015.

45. Interview with *New York Times* journalist [J-2], Tokyo, July 2008; interview with leftist historian [J-9], Tokyo, July 2008; interview with leftist activist [J-16], Tokyo, July 2008; interview with political scientist [J-19], Tokyo, June 2008.

46. On public opinion in the 1990s, see Seraphim 2006, 276; Seaton 2007, 25–26. On public opinion in the 2000s, see Gluck 2009, 99; Evans 2013.

47. I. Chang 1997.

6. "HISTORY ISSUES" IN THE POSTWAR PERIOD (1952–1989)

Epigraph: Katsuichi 1999, xxvi–xxvii.

1. *Japan Quarterly* 1958, 132.

2. *United Nations Treaty Series* 1952b, 1(b); Rose 2005, 44–45.

3. Rose 2005, 101.

4. "Japan-Korea Treaty on Basic Relations" 1965.

5. Wakamiya 1998, 237–39.

6. Quoted in Yamazaki 2006, 140.

7. Yamazaki 2006, 34.

8. Agreement between Japan and the Republic of Korea, Art. I and II. See also Berger 2003, 73; Seraphim 2006, 204.

9. H. Tanaka 1996, 14; Piper 2001, 158; Berger 2003, 68–69.

10. H. Tanaka 1996, 10. This and other yen-to-dollar conversions calculated using figures from the Board of Governors of the Federal Reserve System, available at research .stlouisfed.org/fred2/data/EXJPUS.txt.

11. On the 1955 System, see Samuels 2001.

12. Y. Tanaka 2006, 8. See also Dower 1999, 508–21.

13. Awaya 2006.

14. Ho 2005b.

15. Seraphim 2006, 10, 110–13, 124; Yoshida 2006b, 56.

16. Rose 2005, 36–37; Yoshida 2006b, 56–57; 2014, 35–40; Takahashi, Kaneko, and Inokuma 2008, 2; interview with leftist activist [J-10], Tokyo, July 2008.

17. Orr 2001. In addition, the Hiroshima Peace Memorial Museum, which commemorated the atomic bombing of the city and emphasized Japan's victimhood, was opened in 1955 (Yoshida 2014, 25–27). On the politics of victimhood and redress in Japan, see Arrington 2016.

18. H. Tanaka 1996, 11; Seraphim 2006, 9, 37, 61, 245.

19. Seraphim 2006, 79.

20. Breen 2008, 8.

21. Rose 2005, 149; Wakamiya and Watanabe 2006; Breen 2008, 8–10.

22. Seraphim 2006, 237, 242.

23. Quoted in Wakamiya 1998, 254. See also Rose 2005, 109.

24. Yoshida 2006b, 132.

25. Seraphim 2006, 80.

26. Seraphim 2006, 78–79, emphasis in original. See also H. Tanaka 1996.

27. Barr 1995a. In another form of this "inverted compensation," as Koga terms it, in 1946 the Japanese government paid "financial compensation to . . . Japanese corporations for 'losses' incurred through the wartime use and postwar loss of Chinese labor, rather than to the Chinese laborers whom they enslaved" (Koga 2013, 498). This compensation "amounted to approximately 57 million yen" (Koga 2016, 407).

28. Underwood 2005, 2006b; Koga 2013.

29. C. Smith 1994c, 26.

30. Both excerpts quoted in Nozaki 2008, 15, brackets in original. Dierkes (2010, 150–51) found no references to the Nanjing Massacre in middle school social studies textbooks from this period.

31. Quoted in Nozaki 2008, 21, brackets in original.

32. Rose 2005, 55–56; Lind 2008, 184.

33. Quoted in Beauchamp and Vardaman 1994, 156.

34. Quoted in C. Smith 1994c, 26. On textbook coverage, see *Japan Quarterly* 1968, 276–77; Dore 1970–71; Ienaga 1993–94, 124; Beauchamp and Vardaman 1994, 239; Dierkes 2010, 117.

35. Quoted in Beauchamp and Vardaman 1994, 239. On this movement, see *Japan Quarterly* 1956, 126; Nozaki 2008, 29–31. On Nikkyōso, see Aspinall 2006.

36. Ho 2005a.

37. Ienaga 1993–94, 125.

38. Obata 1970, 96.
39. Murdo 1996.
40. See Nozaki 2008.
41. *Japan Quarterly* 1970, 226; 1971, 121.
42. Both statements quoted in *Japan Quarterly* 1972a, 113.
43. Quoted in *Japan Quarterly* 1972b, 242.
44. Quoted in Wakamiya 1998, 250.
45. See Ministry of Foreign Affairs of Japan 1972.
46. Quoted in Wakamiya 1998, 251.
47. Quoted in Yamazaki 2006, 140.
48. *United Nations Treaty Series* 1978.
49. Quoted in *JOAK Television* 1978.
50. Quoted in Yamazaki 2006, 141.
51. Quoted in Dower 2012, 125.
52. Wan 2006, 88, 379.
53. Wan 2006, 88. See also Whiting 1989, 123.
54. Koga 2013, 498.
55. Whiting 1989, 122; Wan 2006, 265.
56. Whiting 1989, 123.
57. Wan 2006, 264.
58. Wan 2006, 88.
59. Wan 2006, 319–20; interview with former senior Japanese Foreign Ministry official [J-3], Tokyo, July 2008.
60. Honda 1999, 293–94.
61. Yoshida 2006b, 82. See Honda 1999.
62. Interview with *Yomiuri Shimbun* journalist [J-11], Tokyo, July 2008; interview with political scientist [J-13], Tokyo, July 2008; interview with conservative historian [J-17], Tokyo, July 2008.
63. Wakabayashi 2007a, 121.
64. On Hora's book and research, and the dearth of similar work, see Yang 1990, 18; Wakabayashi 2007a, 119, 143; Coox 2008, 89; Nozaki 2008, 52–53.
65. Nozaki 2008, 54. See also Yoshida 2006b, 87.
66. Boyle 2001; Yoshida 2006b, 88; Wakabayashi 2007a, 117.
67. Nozaki 2008, 53.
68. Nozaki and Inokuchi 2000, 111; Nozaki 2008, 46; interview with leftist textbook activist [J-5], Tokyo, July 2008.
69. Quoted in C. Smith 1994c, 26.
70. Quoted in Nozaki 2008, 63.
71. Quoted in Nozaki 2008, 64, brackets in original.
72. Yoshida 2000, 84, 124. Dierkes (2010, 150–51) found that the first reference to the massacre in the middle school social studies textbooks he analyzed was in 1977, and it was consistently referenced thereafter.
73. Nozaki 2008, 64, brackets in original.
74. Dierkes (2010, 152–53) reports that middle school social studies textbooks generally did not identify the number of victims until the mid-1980s.
75. Nozaki 2002, 604–5; 2008, 72.
76. Quoted in Murdo 1996, quoting from Beer 1984, 271. See also He 2009, 211.
77. Nozaki 2008, 72.
78. This and prior quote from Ienaga 1993–94, 126–27, brackets in original.
79. *Yomiuri Shimbun* 2005; Seraphim 2006, 242–43; Seaton 2007, 52; Lai 2014, 119.

80. *Japan Quarterly* 1979, 434; Yanada 1979, 414–16; *Japan Today* 2003; Seraphim 2006, 226–27; Breen 2008, 2–4; interview with foreign diplomat [J-4], Tokyo, July 2008; He 2009.

81. Wan 2006, 206.

82. "Speech by Takeo Fukuda" 1980. See also *Sekai* 1991; Lam 2012.

83. Quoted in *NHK Television Network* 1980.

84. Wan 2006, 205–6.

85. Whiting 1989, 99.

86. Whiting 1983, 914. See also Gries 2004; Wang 2012.

87. Mitter 2005, 19.

88. Quoted in Nozaki 2008, 82. See also *NHK Television Network* 1983; Nakasone 2002; C. Park 2011, 106–8.

89. Quoted in Wakamiya 1998, 171–72.

90. *Japan Quarterly* 1984a, 116.

91. *Japan Quarterly* 1983, 223; 1985a, 222; Nozaki 2002, 609.

92. Quoted in He 2007b, 53.

93. Quoted in Reston 1985.

94. *Japan Quarterly* 1984a, 117.

95. *Japan Quarterly* 1984b, 231.

96. Whiting 1989, 9, 134, 184.

97. Nozaki 2008, 75–80.

98. Yang 2001, 62.

99. *Kyodo* 1982.

100. While China and South Korea were the most vocal and persistent, they were not the only countries to protest. There was also criticism in the North Korean official media and official protests from Vietnam and Taiwan (Nozaki 2002, 606; Yoshida 2006b, 90).

101. Couturier 1982; *New York Times* 1982b.

102. Quoted in Yang 2001, 63, brackets in original.

103. Quoted in *NHK Television Network* 1982.

104. This and the next two passages quote from the Ministry of Foreign Affairs of Japan 1982.

105. Quoted in Jeans 2005, 185, brackets in original, citing Irie 1997, 35–36.

106. Nozaki 2008, 81.

107. Nozaki 2002, 607–8.

108. Whiting 1989, 50; Hirano 2009, 204–6.

109. Nozaki 2002, 608; Rose 2005, 142; Yoshida 2005, 63–64.

110. Dierkes 2010, 152.

111. Nozaki 2008, 99.

112. Quoted in Nozaki 2008, 100. See also Ienaga 1993–94, 127–28.

113. Quoted in C. Smith 1994c, 27.

114. Dierkes 2010, 150–51. See also Hirano 2009, 204–6.

115. Quoted in Nozaki 2002, 610. See also Rose 2005, 128; Shibuichi 2008. For domestic criticism, see *Asahi Evening News* 1986.

116. Whiting 1989, 60.

117. Yang 1990, 22; 2001, 65; Fujiwara A. 2007.

118. Nozaki 2008, 125, see also pp. 85–86.

119. Honda 1999, 194–96, 291–92; Yang 1999, 854; 2001, 65; Yoshida 2006b, 97–100, 137–39; Kimura 2007, 334; interview with leftist historian [J-9], Tokyo, July 2008.

120. Yang 1990, 21.

121. Gibney 1999, x.

122. Hua 2000.

123. Yang 1999, 858; Eykholt 2000, 34–36.

124. *Japan Quarterly* 1985b, 452; Reston 1985; Fukatsu 1986; Whiting 1989, 6, 67–68; Shimokoji 2003, 28–29; Seraphim 2006, 242, 244; Weiss 2014, 82–103.

125. Whiting 1989, 62.

126. Yamazaki 2006, 91.

127. Yoshida 2000, 109–10; interview with *Asahi Shimbun* journalist [J-12], Tokyo, July 2008.

128. Quoted in D. Jenkins 1992a.

129. Quoted in Moosa 1986. See also Wakamiya 1998, 15, 200. Because Fujio was the minister of education, his statements were official. However, that he was fired signaled that his comments did not reflect the official position.

130. Eykholt 2000, 39.

131. Quoted in Haberman 1988; *New York Times* 1988; Wakamiya 1998, 11 (respectively).

132. *Chicago Sun-Times Wires* 1988; *New York Times* 1988.

133. Saaler 2008, 140.

7. UNFREEZING THE QUESTION OF HISTORY (1998–2008)

The chapter title is a spin on a statement by *Asahi Shimbun* political correspondent Miura Toshiaki in an August 2001 roundtable discussion. Miura stated: "In [E]ast Asia the Cold War froze the question of history, and now for the last decade it has come up as a big issue" (Gordon et al. 2001). Epigraphs: Retired senior Japanese government official quoted in Smith 1994b; Mine quoted in Barr 1995b.

1. Burress 1995, quoting anthropologist Geoffrey White. See also C. Smith 1994c.

2. Nozaki 2002, 613; 2008, 129.

3. Rose 2005, 58; Dierkes 2010, 152.

4. Quoted in Murdo 1996. See also Nozaki 2008, 129.

5. Rose 2005, 58.

6. See Samuels 1990.

7. Seraphim 2006, 274.

8. Oberman 1989.

9. Field 1993, 177–266.

10. Quoted in Chira 1989.

11. Joseph and Sampson 1989.

12. Quoted in Seaton 2007, 88.

13. *NHK General Television* 1993.

14. Shinoda 2007, 5, 50–55.

15. Soeya, Tadokoro, and Welch 2011a, 8.

16. See *NHK General Television Network* 1991, 1992b.

17. Soeya, Tadokoro, and Welch 2011a, 4. See Ozawa 1994. See also Soeya, Tadokoro, and Welch 2011b.

18. Wan 2006, 84–85, 117–18, 202–3.

19. On transnational connections between activists, see Piper 2001; Arrington 2014; Koga 2016.

20. Rose 2005, 79; Wan 2006, 304–6.

21. *Asian Political News Kyodo News International* 1993.

22. *Asian Political News Kyodo News International* 1993.

23. M. O'Neill 1995; Wan 2006, 304.

24. Dao 1998; Dobbs 2000.

25. See *Chuo Koron* 1992; *NHK General Television Network* 1992b. See also Soeya, Tadokoro, and Welch 2011b.

26. *Kankai* 1991; *Kyodo* 1991; Yamazaki 2006, 94; interview with leftist historian [J-9], Tokyo, July 2008; interview with historian and leftist activist [J-14], Tokyo, July 2008.

27. Quoted in Yamazaki 2006, 42.

28. Quoted in *South China Morning Post* 1992b. See also D. Jenkins 1992b. *Makotoni ikan* could also be translated as "truly regrettable." I thank Shigehiro Suzuki for advice on this point.

29. D. Jenkins 1992b.

30. D. Jenkins 1992b.

31. *Kyodo* 1991.

32. This and prior sentence quoting from D. Jenkins 1992a, italics added. *Fukaku hansei* could also be translated as "deeply remorseful." I thank Shigehiro Suzuki for help with this. For repetitions of this formulation, see *Kyodo* 1992b; *NHK General Television Network* 1992a.

33. On the MOFA's reasoning behind Japan's muted response to the massacre, see *Kyodo* 1989; Weiss 2014, 106.

34. Crabb 1992. See also *Kyodo* 1992a.

35. Quoted in Sun 1992.

36. Crabb 1992; McCarthy 1992.

37. *South China Morning Post* 1992a. More generally, Shibuichi (2017, 185) reports that right-wing groups in Japan organized a "Movement to Oppose the Emperor Visiting China."

38. Wakamiya 1998, 283.

39. Rafferty 1992; *Straits Times* 1992.

40. Yoshida 2014, xvii.

41. Yoshida 2006b, 135–36.

42. Seraphim 2006, 276. See also Yoshimi 2000, 27–28.

43. Yoshimi 2000, 35, 58–59.

44. Ministry of Foreign Affairs of Japan 1992.

45. Quoted in Yamazaki 2006, 60.

46. Ministry of Foreign Affairs of Japan 1993.

47. Nickerson 1992.

48. McGill and Akagawa 1998; *Japan Times Online* 2002.

49. Underwood 2006b.

50. On the long-term drivers of this "regime shift," see Pempel 1998.

51. Quoted in *Asian Political News Kyodo News International* 1993. For Hata's comments, see *Kyodo* 1993.

52. Quoted in Yamazaki 2006, 74.

53. Wakamiya 1998, 180; Yamazaki 2006, 74–75.

54. Quoted in Yamazaki 2006, 81.

55. Wakamiya 1998, 180.

56. Quoted in Jones 1993.

57. Masumi 1995, 422.

58. Interview with historian and leftist activist [J-14], Tokyo, July 2008.

59. Rafferty 1993; Benfell 2002, 5; interview with *Asahi Shimbun* journalist [J-12], Tokyo, July 2008.

60. Yoshida 2006b, 141.

61. Saaler 2005, 77–80; Yoshida 2006b, 141; Nozaki 2008, 142.

62. Quoted in Rose 2005, 53. See also Saaler 2016, 4–5.

63. This and prior two statements quoted in Yamazaki 2006, 76, 78, 80–81 (respectively).

64. Rafferty 1993; Yamazaki 2006, 80–84; Seaton 2007, 89.

65. *Kyodo* 1994; C. Smith 1994a.

66. Anonymous interview [J-8], Tokyo, July 2008. See also Koga 2016, 417.

67. Gries 2004, 46, 57; He 2007b, 56–59; Wang 2012, 95–117.

68. Yoshida 2006b, 154.

69. See J. Weiss 2014.

70. McCormack 2002; interview with *Asahi Shimbun* journalist [J-12], Tokyo, July 2008.

71. Kwan 1995.

72. According to Hatano (2018), approximately 90 billion yen was ultimately spent on historical research projects.

73. This and above quotes from Ministry of Foreign Affairs of Japan 1994.

74. Quoted in *Agence France-Presse* 1994. See also Hills 1994.

75. Quoted in *BBC Monitoring Service: Asia-Pacific* 1996.

76. *Shukan Jiji* 1994; Dawkins and Cramb 1995.

77. Yoshida 2006b, 141.

78. McCormack 2000, 56; Yoshida 2006b, 141.

79. On these reforms, see Christensen 2000; Kaihara 2007.

80. Kattoulas 2001; interview with political analyst [J-1], Tokyo, July 2008.

81. Eckert 1995; Mufson 1995; Howell 1997, 84–85.

82. Quoted in Seraphim (2006, 277) and Masumi (1995, 423).

83. Benfell 2002, 10. See also Wakamiya 1998, 22; Shibuichi 2017, 185.

84. National Diet of Japan 1995.

85. Yamazaki 2006, 94.

86. Wakamiya 1998, 180.

87. Quoted in Wakamiya 1998, 26.

88. Ministry of Foreign Affairs of Japan 1995a.

89. For the letter, see R. Hashimoto 1996. On the state's position, see Asian Women's Fund 1996. On the controversy over the fund and "atonement money," see Soh 2001.

90. Interview with former senior Japanese Foreign Ministry official [J-3], Tokyo, July 2008.

91. Asian Women's Fund 2007.

92. Barr 1995a. Hiroshi Tanaka compared the total amount of compensation payments to Japanese victims with the reparations and other payments to non-Japanese victims and found that "the 40 trillion yen paid out to Japanese for suffering during the war comes to 40 times what Japan has paid in reparations" (1996, 11).

93. This paragraph draws from Jeans (2005). On Shōwa Hall, see Yoshida 2014, 186–92.

94. Jeans 2005, 158–59.

95. Jeans 2005, 162.

96. Wakamiya 1998, 28; Rose 2005, 103.

97. Interview with former senior Japanese Foreign Ministry official [J-3], Tokyo, July 2008; interview with historian and leftist activist [J-14], Tokyo, July 2008.

98. Interview with former senior Japanese Foreign Ministry official [J-3], Tokyo, July 2008.

99. Ministry of Foreign Affairs of Japan 1995b.

100. Yamazaki 2006, 103.

101. Quoted in Desmond 1995. For more on responses to the Murayama statement, see Togo 2013.

102. Lai 2014, 117.

103. That is, aside from Miyazawa's secret visit of a few years earlier.

104. Soh 1996; Ogawa 2000, 45.

105. Marshallsea 1997. See also Yang 2001, 67.

106. Quoted in Wakamiya (1998, 13) and Ishimura (1995), respectively.

107. Quoted in Amaha (1998) and *Mainichi Daily News* (1998), respectively.

108. Yoshida 2006a, 4. See also Yoshida 2005.

109. Quoted in Amaha 1998.

110. *Asian Political News Kyodo News International* 1994. See also *Wilson Quarterly* 2005.

111. Quoted in *Straits Times* 1997.

112. Quoted in Donnet 1997.

113. Saaler 2005; interview with Japan Conference representative [J-6], Tokyo, July 2008; interview with revisionist textbook activist [J-7], Tokyo, July 2008; interview with leftist historian [J-9], Tokyo, July 2008. On Nippon Kaigi, see also Shibuichi 2017.

114. Rose 2005, 59; interview with revisionist textbook activist [J-7], Tokyo, July 2008.

115. Quoted in Yamaguchi 1997.

116. Interview with leftist textbook activist [J-5], Tokyo, July 2008. Note that support groups are a common and often central feature of social movement activism in Japan (Steinhoff 1999).

117. Ishii 1999; Dobbs 2000.

118. McLaughlin 1993; I. Chang 1998; Arrington 2016.

119. Hicks 1997, vii; Feigin 2006, 500–506.

120. See Library of Congress 1997.

121. See I. Chang 1997.

122. Yoshida 2006b, 171–73, 179.

123. Yoshida 2006b, 146. On Chang's book, see Fogel 1998, 2000a; Yang 1999; Kasahara 2007.

124. Interview with Japan Conference representative [J-6], Tokyo, July 2008.

125. Brook 2001.

126. Quoted in Lee-Young 1997.

127. Quoted in *Japan Economic Newswire* 1998.

128. Quoted in *BBC Monitoring Asia Pacific—Political* 1998a, 1998b, respectively.

129. Crabb 1993; Y. Chang 1997a, 1997b.

130. Wan 2006, 315; Yoshida 2006a, 3; 2006b, 134.

131. Tan 1995; He 2007a, 10.

132. Anonymous interview [J-8], Tokyo, July 2008; interview with leftist activist [J-15], Tokyo, July 2008; interview with leftist activist [J-16], Tokyo, July 2008. See also Rose 2005, 69–98. Note that the lawyers worked pro bono and a support organization helped publicize the cases in Japan and supported the Chinese victims.

133. Underwood 2006a.

134. Koga 2013.

135. Snyder 1998; Wakamiya 1998, 259.

136. Holland 1998.

137. Interview with former senior Japanese Foreign Ministry official [J-3], Tokyo, July 2008.

138. Wakamiya 1998, 259.

139. Wakamiya 1998, 259.

140. The title for this section comes from "a report produced in late 2002 by Prime Minister Koizumi's 'Task Force on Foreign Relations' [that] identified China as Japan's top foreign policy concern in the immediate future. . . . It stated that 'it is important that both countries, while learning from history, must break the "spell of history" (*rekishi no jubaku*) and build a future-oriented (*mirai shikō*) relationship'" (Rose 2005, 27).

141. Gries 2005. See also Gries 2004, 116–34; Wang 2012; J. Weiss 2014.

142. On the demise of the JSP and traditional pacifism in post–Cold War Japan, see Samuels 2007, 117–19.

143. Interview with *New York Times* journalist [J-2], Tokyo, July 2008.

144. Fujiwara K. 2005; interview with *New York Times* journalist [J-2], Tokyo, July 2008; interview with political scientist [J-13], Tokyo, July 2008.

145. Ito 2000; Kakuchi 2000; Okazaki 2000.

146. Zhou 2005. See also Wan 2006, 205.

147. Dickie and Pilling 2005; Zhou 2005.

148. Samuels 2007, 112, see also pp. 5, 124–27.

149. Soeya 2011, 78.

150. Nozaki 2002, 616. See also Children and Textbooks Japan Network 21 2000; Nozaki 2002, 616–17; Rose 2005, 60; interview with leftist textbook activist [J-5], Tokyo, July 2008.

151. *Times of India* 2000.

152. *Japan Economic Newswire* 2000. See also Yoshida 2005, 65–68; Nozaki 2008, 144–45.

153. Quoted in Kwan 1999.

154. Quoted in *BBC Monitoring Service: Asia-Pacific* 1999.

155. Quoted in *Japan Economic Newswire* 1999.

156. Quoted in *Daily Yomiuri/Yomiuri Shimbun* 1999.

157. Quoted in *Japan Economic Newswire* 1999.

158. Jeans 2005, 176–77; Yoshida 2014, 172–80.

159. Quoted in Y. Chang 2000.

160. *Agence France-Presse* 2000; French 2000.

161. Yoshida 2006b, 150.

162. See Takemoto and Ohara 2000.

163. Mutsuko 2003; Yoshida 2006b, 152; S. Park 2011.

164. Wan 2006, 305. For partial lists of litigation related to forced laborers, POWs, and "comfort women," see "POWs/Forced Labor: Japan."

165. Kitano 2002.

166. Koga 2013, 494. See also Levin 2008, 154.

167. Kattoulas 2001.

168. *Japan Times Online* 2001.

169. Yamaguchi 2001. See also Yoshida 2014, 107. Note that the name of the Ministry of Education was changed in 2001; for simplicity's sake, I refer throughout to the Ministry of Education.

170. Kakuchi 2001; *Kyodo News* 2001.

171. Quoted in Millett 2001.

172. S. Park 2011, 230.

173. The three major newspapers in Japan were against his visits, as were former PMs Kaifu, Miyazawa, Murayama, Hashimoto, and Mori (*Japan Echo* 2005a; *Yomiuri Shimbun* 2005). For Diet members' views, see Ryu 2007, 717. For domestic criticisms, see Ibison 2004; *Japan Echo* 2005b; Yomiuri Shimbun and Asahi Shimbun 2005. On domestic contestation, see Masshardt 2007.

174. On the strengthening of the power of the PM's office under Koizumi, see Shinoda 2007. On the electoral-political considerations behind Koizumi's shrine visits, see Cheung 2010.

175. Quoted in Dickie and Pilling 2005. See also Deans 2007; Ryu 2007; Lai 2014, 122–50. Several interviewees made the points in this paragraph (interview with political analyst [J-1], Tokyo, July 2008; interview with *New York Times* journalist [J-2], Tokyo, July 2008; interview with former senior Japanese Foreign Ministry official [J-3], Tokyo, July 2008; interview with foreign diplomat [J-4], Tokyo, July 2008).

176. Quoted in Rose 2005, 108.

177. Ministry of Foreign Affairs of Japan 2001.

178. Quoted in Schauble 2001.

179. Shinoda 2006; interview with *New York Times* journalist [J-2], Tokyo, July 2008.

180. Dickie and Pilling 2005.

181. Roy 2004, 96; McDonald and Cameron 2005.

182. Ministry of Foreign Affairs of Japan 2006; interview with government adviser [J-18], Tokyo, July 2008; S. Park 2011.

183. Chea 2005; interview with government adviser [J-18], Tokyo, July 2008.

184. Edwards 2005; Onishi 2005; Weiss 2014, 127–59.

185. *OsterDowJones Commodity Wire* 2005.

186. Quoted in Ang 2005.

187. Quoted in Pearson 2005.

188. Yao 2005.

189. Onishi and French 2005.

190. Cheung 2010, 540–42.

191. Interview with former senior Japanese Foreign Ministry official [J-3], Tokyo, July 2008. Moreover, it suggests that Koizumi's insistence on visiting the shrine to "normalize" relations with Japan's Asian neighbors might have had its intended effect.

192. Interview with foreign diplomat [J-4], Tokyo, July 2008.

193. One interviewee noted that the Chinese government was worried that pressing Japan on history issues might further aggravate bilateral relations (anonymous interview [J-8], Tokyo, July 2008). See also Weiss 2014.

194. Interview with *New York Times* journalist [J-2], Tokyo, July 2008.

195. On the "nationalist resurgence" in Japan, see Kingston 2015. See also Takenaka 2014.

196. Evans 2013.

CONCLUSION

1. Zinn 2005.

2. Krebs (2015) emphasizes the structural importance of settled versus unsettled moments in relation to narratives' dominance. Aktürk (2011) similarly emphasizes the conjuncture of ideas, electoral politics, and agency in explaining changes in citizenship policies.

3. See *Bakalian v. Republic of Turkey* 2010. See also Yeghiayan and Associates 2010.

4. The islands in dispute with Russia are inhabited.

5. Arai, Goto, and Wang 2012.

6. Yang 2001, 77.

7. G. Jenkins 2001, 16.

8. On domestic debates and attitudes, see Saaler 2005; Seraphim 2006; Seaton 2007; Yoshida 2014; Hashimoto 2015. On textbooks, see Rose 1998; Barnard 2003; Nozaki 2008. On the Yasukuni Shrine, see Breen 2008. On apologies, see Yamazaki 2006; Dudden 2008; Lind 2008; Jeffery 2011.

9. For example, Lind 2008; He 2009; Berger 2012.

10. Brooks 1999; Gibney et al. 2008; Sikkink 2011.

11. For example, Finnemore and Sikkink 1998; Keck and Sikkink 1998; Price 1998; Risse, Ropp, and Sikkink 1999, 2013; Simmons 2009.

12. On naming and shaming, see, e.g., Hafner-Burton 2008; Meernik et al. 2012; Hendrix and Wong 2013.

13. Hovannisian 1986, 128.

14. Keck and Sikkink 1998. For the report, see ECOSOC 1985.

15. Günaysu 2008a.

16. For example, Zarakolu 2008b; Günaysu 2009a. See also Berktay's comment mentioned in chapter 4, note 73.

17. On learning, see Nye 1987; Finnemore 1993; Dobbin, Simmons, and Garrett 2007, 460–62.

18. S. Park 2011. See also Arrington 2016.

19. See Bazyler 2011.

20. Interview with political analyst [J-1], Tokyo, July 2008; interview with leftist activist [J-14], Tokyo, July 2008.

21. Ben-Josef Hirsch and Dixon 2017. For references to the costs and benefits of norm compliance and violation, see Legro 1997, 53; Finnemore and Sikkink 1998, 895; Ayoub 2015, 312. See also Kelley 2008; Hyde 2011.

22. Quoting from Ben-Josef Hirsch 2007a, 191.

23. Dixon 2017.

24. On stigma and Turkey's position, see Zarakol 2010. Ulgen (2010a, 12) notes that "denial existed in highly sophisticated modalities before the term 'genocide' came to bear prominence in the post-WW2 world order."

25. On memory and generational change, see Schuman and Scott 1989; Schuman and Rodgers 2004; Lebow, Kansteiner, and Fogu 2006. On memory activists, see Gutman 2017. On carriers of memory, see Schudson 1992.

26. On the Turkish case, for example, Bloxham (2005) primarily looks at great power politics, whereas Göçek (2015) focuses on domestic structures and ideologies in seeking to explain Turkey's long denial of the Armenian Genocide.

27. Leebaw (2011) makes this point.

28. Here I am using "denial" in a broader sense than it is defined in chapter 1.

APPENDIX 1. RESEARCH CONDUCTED

1. I also conducted a handful of interviews in the United States.

2. Interviews were conducted in English or Turkish, depending on the interviewee's fluency in English and preference.

3. The High School History III course was used (until the late 1990s) in the tenth grade, and covered Ottoman and European political and social history from the fifteenth to the twentieth centuries, generally stopping at WWII. The History of the Revolution of the Turkish Republic and Atatürkism textbook addresses more contemporary political history and is used in eleventh grade. It covers the first part of the twentieth century, focusing particularly on the creation of the Republic of Turkey and Atatürk's role in this process.

4. For published bibliographies, see R. G. Hovannisian 1978; Vassilian 1992; İlter 1997.

5. I conducted some of the interviews in English, while others were conducted in Japanese with my research assistant translating.

References

100 Soruda Ermeni Sorunu (Ankara: Genelkurmay Basım Evi, 2001).

Dilaver Arıkan Açar and İnan Rüma, "External Pressure and Turkish Discourse on 'Recognition of the Armenian Genocide,'" *Southeast European and Black Sea Studies*, vol. 7, no. 3 (2007), pp. 449–65.

Amitav Acharya, "How Ideas Spread: Whose Norms Matter? Norm Localization and Institutional Change in Asian Regionalism," *International Organization*, vol. 58, no. 2 (2004), pp. 239–75.

Hülya Adak, "Identifying the 'Internal Tumors' of World War I: *Talat Paşa'nın Hatıraları* [Talat Paşa's memoirs], or the Travels of a Unionist Apologia into 'History,'" in Andreas Baehr, Peter Burschel, and Gabriele Jancke, eds., *Raueme des Selbst* (Köln: Böhlau Verlag, 2007), pp. 151–69.

James Ring Adams, "Facing Up to an Armenian Genocide," *Wall Street Journal* (12 August 1983), p. 20.

Theodor W. Adorno, "What Does Coming to Terms with the Past Mean?" in Geoffrey H. Hartman, ed., *Bitburg in Moral and Political Perspective* (Bloomington: Indiana University Press, 1986 [1959]), pp. 114–29.

Agence France-Presse, "Another Cabinet Minister Denies Japan's War of Aggression" (12 August 1994).

——, "Turkey Condemns French Recognition of Armenian 'Genocide'" (29 May 1998).

——, "Japan Tries to Soothe Chinese Concerns over Rightists" (6 March 2000).

"Agreement between Japan and the Republic of Korea concerning the Settlement of Problems in Regard to Property and Claims and Economic Co-operation," *International Legal Materials*, vol. 5, no. 1 (1966), pp. 111–17.

Paloma Aguilar, "Transitional or Post-Transitional Justice? Recent Developments in the Spanish Case," *South European Society and Politics*, vol. 13, no. 4 (2008), pp. 417–33.

Taner Akçam, *Türk Ulusal Kimliği ve Ermeni Sorunu* (İstanbul: İletişim Yayınları, 1992).

——, *From Empire to Republic: Turkish Nationalism and the Armenian Genocide* (London: Zed Books, 2004).

——, *A Shameful Act: The Armenian Genocide and the Question of Turkish Responsibility* (New York: Metropolitan Books, 2006a).

——, "The Ottoman Documents and the Genocidal Policies of the Committee for Union and Progress (İttihat ve Terakki) toward the Armenians in 1915," *Genocide Studies and Prevention*, vol. 1, no. 2 (2006b), pp. 127–48.

——, "A Shameful Campaign," *Armenian Reporter* (24 March 2007).

——, *'Ermeni Meselesi Hallolunmuştur': Osmanlı Belgelerine göre Savaş Yıllarında Ermenilere Yönelik Politikalar* (İstanbul: İletişim Yayınları, 2008).

——, *The Young Turks' Crime against Humanity: The Armenian Genocide and Ethnic Cleaning in the Ottoman Empire* (Princeton, NJ: Princeton University Press, 2012).

——, "Sorry, but We're No Longer Impressed: We've Changed," *Armenian Weekly* (7 May 2014).

Taner Akçam and Ümit Kurt, *The Spirit of the Laws: The Plunder of Wealth in the Armenian Genocide* (New York: Berghahn Books, 2015).

İdris Akdin, Muhittin Çakmak, and Mustafa Genç, *Türkiye Cumhuriyeti İnkılâp Tarihi ve Atatürkçülük Lise 3* (İstanbul: Ilıcak Matbaacılık A.Ş., 2005).

Akşam, "523 Bin Türk Katledildi" (18 April 2005).

Gündüz Aktan, "Pedagogy of Genocide," *Turkish Daily News* (9 August 2001).

——, "A Turkish View on the Applicability of the Genocide Convention to the Armenian Incidents and the ICTJ's Report," *Turkish Daily News* (19 February 2003).

Ayhan Aktar, *Varlık Vergisi ve "Türkleştirme" Politikaları* (İstanbul: İletişim Yayınları, 2000).

——, "Debating the Armenian Massacres in the Last Ottoman Parliament, November–December 1918," *History Workshop Journal*, no. 64 (2007), pp. 241–70.

——, ed., *Yüzbaşı Sarkis Torosyan: Çanakkale'den Filistin Cephesi'ne* (İstanbul: İletişim Yayınları, 2012).

Şener Aktürk, "Regimes of Ethnicity: Comparative Analysis of Germany, the Soviet Union/ Post-Soviet Russia, and Turkey," *World Politics*, vol. 63, no. 1 (2011), pp. 115–64.

——, "Politics of History in Turkey: Revisionist Historiography's Challenge to the Official Version of the Turkish War of Independence," in Alexei Miller and Maria Lipman, eds., *The Convolutions of Historical Politics* (Budapest: Central European University Press, 2012), pp. 279–307.

Hasan B. Ali, President, American Turkish Association, letter to the editor, "Assassinations, Atrocities and the Armenians," *Washington Post* (9 February 1982), p. A18.

Ali Hikmet Alp, "Today's Armenia and Motives behind the Genocide Accusations," *Ermeni Araştırmaları*, vol. 2 (2001), available at: http://www.eraren.org/index.php ?Lisan=en&Page=DergiIcerik&IcerikNo=225.

Ayşe Gül Altınay, "In Search of Silenced Grandparents: Ottoman Armenian Survivors and Their (Muslim) Grandchildren," in Hans-Lukas Kieser and Elmar Plozza, eds., *Der Völkermord an den Armeniern, die Türkei und Europa* (Zürich: Chronos, 2006), pp. 117–32.

Ayşe Gül Altınay and Yektan Türkyılmaz, "Unraveling Layers of Gendered Silencing: Converted Armenian Survivors of the 1915 Catastrophe," in Amy Singer, Christoph K. Neumann, and Selçuk Akşin Somel, eds., *Untold Histories of the Middle East: Recovering Voices from the 19th and 20th Centuries* (London: Routledge, 2011), pp. 25–53.

Eriko Amaha, "Abridging the Great Divide," *Far Eastern Economic Review*, vol. 161, no. 2 (8 January 1998), p. 63.

Benedict Anderson, *Imagined Communities: Reflections on the Origin and Spread of Nationalism* (London: Verso, 1983).

Margaret Lavinia Anderson, "Who Still Talked about the Extermination of the Armenians? German Talk and German Silence," in Ronald Grigor Suny, Fatma Müge Göçek, and Norman M. Naimark, eds., *A Question of Genocide: Armenians and Turks at the End of the Ottoman Empire* (New York: Oxford University Press, 2011), pp. 199–217.

——, "Shooting an Elephant," *Journal of Genocide Research*, vol. 15, no. 4 (2013), pp. 464–72.

Audra Ang, "Japan Confirms Meeting with Chinese President," *Associated Press Newswires* (23 April 2005).

Ankara Anatolia, "Foreign Ministry on California Governor's Donation," in FBIS, Daily Report: Western Europe, FBIS-WEU-85-153 (8 August 1985), p. T1.

——, "Evren Unviels [*sic*] Monument for Victims of Massacre," in FBIS, Daily Report: Western Europe, FBIS-WEU-86-132 (10 July 1986), p. T1.

——, "Ambassador to Moscow Denies Armenian Allegations," in FBIS, Daily Report: West Europe, FBIS-WEU-91-092 (13 May 1991), p. 39.

Ankara Domestic Service, "Evren Stresses Resistance to Outside Pressures," in FBIS, Daily Report: Western Europe, FBIS-WEU-81-115 (16 June 1981), p. T1.

——, "Ulusu News Conference on Economy, Foreign Policy," in FBIS, Daily Report: Western Europe, FBIS-WEU-82-201 (18 October 1982), p. T1.

——, "Ozal: U.S. Missile Deployment 'Out of Question,'" in FBIS, Daily Report: Western Europe, FBIS-WEU-84-011 (17 January 1984), p. T2.

——, "President Evren on Armenian Massacre Claims," in FBIS, Daily Report: Western Europe, FBIS-WEU-86-133 (11 July 1986), p. T1.

——, "Evren, Halefoglu on European Resolution on Armenians: President Evren Comments," in FBIS, Daily Report: West Europe, FBIS-WEU-87-118 (19 June 1987a), p. Q1.

——, "Ministry Welcomes U.S. Rejection of Armenian Bill," in FBIS, Daily Report: West Europe, FBIS-WEU-87-153 (10 August 1987b), p. Q1.

——, "Evren, Ozal Send Letters to Bush," in FBIS, Daily Report: West Europe, FBIS-WEU-89-197 (13 October 1989), p. 29.

Tatsushi Arai, Shihoko Goto, and Zheng Wang, eds., *Clash of National Identities: China, Japan, and the East China Sea Territorial Dispute* (Washington, DC: Wilson Center, 2012).

Maki Arakawa, "A New Forum for Comfort Women: Fighting Japan in United States Federal Court," *Berkeley Women's Law Journal*, vol. 16 (2001), pp. 174–200.

Fahri Aral, ed., *İmparatorluğun Çöküş Döneminde Osmanlı Ermenileri: Bilimsel Sorumluluk ve Demokrasi Sorunları* (İstanbul: İstanbul Bilgi Üniversitesi Yayınları, 2011).

Armenian Genocide Reparations Study Group, *Resolution with Justice: Reparations for the Armenian Genocide* (March 2015), available at: www.armeniangenocidereparations.info/?p=245#more-245.

Armenian National Committee, Ad 434, "Mr. Ecevit, We Demand Reparations and Return of Our Territories!" *New York Times* (28 May 1978), p. E5.

Armenian Weekly, "Commission on Human Rights Votes to Recommend Special Rapporteur Reinstate Paragraph 30," vol. 56, no. 4 (24 March 1979).

Celeste Arrington, "Japan-South Korea Relations and Litigation," in *Challenges Facing Japan: Perspectives from the U.S.-Japan Network for the Future* (Washington, DC: The Maureen and Mike Mansfield Foundation, 2014), pp. 11–19.

——, *Accidental Activists: Victim Movements and Government Accountability in Japan and South Korea* (Ithaca, NY: Cornell University Press, 2016).

Arşiv Belgeleriyle Ermeni Faaliyetleri 1914–1918 (Ankara: Genelkurmay Basım Evi, 2005).

David Art, *The Politics of the Nazi Past in Germany and Austria* (Cambridge: Cambridge University Press, 2006).

Asahi Evening News, "Asahi on Asian Criticism of History Textbook," in FBIS, Daily Report: ASIA & PACIFIC, ANNEX, FBIS-APA-86-118-A (17 June 1986).

Asian Political News Kyodo News International, "Japan's New Political Scene Offers Hope for War Victims" (2 August 1993).

——, "Japan Allows War-Redress Descriptions in Textbooks" (4 July 1994).

Asian Women's Fund, "The Legal Position of the Japanese Government Regarding Implications of Acceptance of Support from Asian Women's Fund Projects" (October 1996), available at: www.awf.or.jp/e6/statement-16.html.

——, "The Statement by President of the Asian Women's Fund Murayama at the Final Press Conference" (6 March 2007), available at: www.awf.or.jp/pdf/0209.pdf.

David Askew, "The Nanking Incident: Recent Research and Trends," *Electronic Journal of Contemporary Japanese Studies* (2002).

——, "Part of the Numbers Issue: Demography and Civilian Victims," in Bob Tadashi Wakabayashi, ed., *The Nanking Atrocity 1937–38: Complicating the Picture* (New York: Berghahn Books, 2007).

Robert W. Aspinall, "The Rise and Fall of Nikkyōso: Classroom Idealism, Union Power and the Three Phases of Japanese Politics since 1955," in Rikki Kersten and David Williams, eds., *The Left in the Shaping of Japanese Democracy: Essays in Honour of J.A.A. Stockwin* (London: Routledge, 2006), pp. 65–81.

Aspirations et Agissements Révolutionnaires des Comités Arméniens Avant et Après la Proclamation de la Constitution Ottomane (Istanbul, 1917).

Aspirations et Mouvements Révolutionnaires Arméniens (Constantinople: Ahmed Ingan, 1915).

Associated Press Newswires, "Turkey's $1 Million Gift to UCLA Highlights Growing Dilemma" (24 November 1997).

Stephan H. Astourian, "The Nagorno-Karabakh Conflict: Dimensions, Lessons, and Prospects," *Mediterranean Quarterly*, vol. 5, no. 4 (1994), pp. 85–109.

——, "From Ter-Petrosian to Kocharian: Leadership Change in Armenia," Working Paper Series, Paper 2000_04'asto, Berkeley Program in Soviet and Post-Soviet Studies (2000).

——, "State, Homeland, and Diaspora: The Armenian and Azerbaijani Cases," in Touraj Atabaki and Sanjyot Mehendale, eds., *Central Asia and the Caucasus: Transnationalism and Diaspora* (London: Routledge, 2005), pp. 80–112.

——, "Armenian Foreign Policy: An Assessment of Some Key Issues," Occasional Paper of the Armenian Studies Program at UC Berkeley, no. 2 (2016).

Ferudun Ata, *İşgal İstanbul'unda Tehcir Yargılamaları* (Ankara: TTK Yayınları, 2005).

ATAA, *Armenian Allegations: Myth and Reality: A Handbook of Facts and Documents* (Washington, DC: ATAA, 1986).

ATA-USA, "Happy 60th Anniversary Turkish Republic," *Bulletin of the Assembly of Turkish American Associations*, vol. 4, no. 4 (October 1983), copy on file with author.

Türkkaya Ataöv, *Talât Paşa'ya Atfedilen Andonian "Belgeler"i Sahtedir* (Ankara: Barok Ofset, 1984a).

——, *A Brief Glance at the "Armenian Question"* (Ankara: Sistem Ofset, 1984b).

——, *Hitler and the "Armenian Question"* (Ankara: Sistem Ofset, 1985a).

——, *Deaths Caused by Disease, in Relation to the Armenian Question* (Ankara: Sistem Ofset, 1985b).

——, *The Ottoman Archives and the Armenian Question* (Ankara: Sistem Ofset, 1986).

Atılım, "Mecliste Ermeni Soykırımı Gerginliği" (22 December 2008).

Varoujan Attarian, *Le Génocide des Arméniens devant l'ONU* (Bruxelles: Éditions Complexe, 1997).

Boaz Atzili, *Good Fences, Bad Neighbors: Border Fixity and International Conflict* (Chicago: University of Chicago Press, 2012).

Yair Auron, *The Banality of Denial: Israel and the Armenian Genocide* (New Brunswick, NJ: Transaction Publishers, 2003).

Australian Government, "Prime Minister Kevin Rudd, MP—Apology to Australia's Indigenous Peoples" (13 February 2008), available at: http://www.australia.gov.au/about-australia/our-country/our-people/apology-to-australias-indigenous-peoples.

Séverine Autesserre, "Dangerous Tales: Dominant Narratives on the Congo and Their Unintended Consequences," *African Affairs*, vol. 111, no. 443 (2012), pp. 202–22.

Vahagn Avedian, "State Identity, Continuity, and Responsibility: The Ottoman Empire, the Republic of Turkey and the Armenian Genocide," *European Journal of International Law*, vol. 23, no. 3 (2012), pp. 797–820.

Awaya Kentarō, "Emperor Shōwa's Accountability for War," *Japan Quarterly*, vol. 38, no. 4 (1991), pp. 386–98.

——, "The Tokyo Tribunal, War Responsibility and the Japanese People" (5 February 2006), available at: www.zcommunications.org/the-tokyo-tribunal-war-responsibility-and -the-japanese-people-by-kentaro-awaya.

Bilgin Ayata, "Searching for Alternative Approaches to Reconciliation: A Plea for Armenian-Kurdish Dialogue," *Armenian Weekly* (26 April 2008), pp. 38–42.

——, "Critical Interventions: Kurdish Intellectuals Confronting the Armenian Genocide," *Armenian Weekly* (29 April 2009).

——, "The Kurds in the Turkish-Armenian Reconciliation Process: Double-Bind or Double-Blind?," *International Journal of Middle East Studies*, vol. 47, no. 4 (2015), pp. 807–12.

Phillip M. Ayoub, "Contested Norms in New-Adopter States: International Determinants of LGBT Rights Legislation," *European Journal of International Relations*, vol. 21, no. 2 (2015), pp. 293–322.

Tuncay Babalı, "Turkey at the Energy Crossroads: Turkey, Present and Past," *Middle East Quarterly*, vol. 16, no. 2 (2009), pp. 25–33.

Cristina G. Badescu and Thomas G. Weiss, "Misrepresenting R2P and Advancing Norms: An Alternative Spiral?," *International Studies Perspectives*, vol. 11, no. 4 (2010), pp. 354–74.

Anny P. Bakalian, *Armenian-Americans: From Being to Feeling American* (New Brunswick, NJ: Transaction Publishers, 1993).

Bakalian v. Republic of Turkey, No. 2:10-cv-09596-DMG-SS (C.D. Cal. Dec. 15, 2010).

Onur Bakiner, "Is Turkey Coming to Terms with Its Past? Politics of Memory and Majoritarian Conservatism," *Nationalities Papers*, vol. 41, no. 5 (2013), pp. 691–708.

——, *Truth Commissions: Memory, Power, and Legitimacy* (Philadelphia: University of Pennsylvania Press, 2015a).

——, "One Truth among Others?: Truth Commissions' Struggle for Truth and Memory," *Memory Studies*, vol. 8, no. 3 (2015b), pp. 345–60.

Peter Balakian, *The Burning Tigris: The Armenian Genocide and America's Response* (New York: HarperCollins Publishers, 2003).

Frank Baldwin, "Translator's Note," in Saburō Ienaga, *The Pacific War: World War II and the Japanese, 1931–1945* (New York: Random House, 1978), pp. vii–x.

Rıfat N. Bali, *Model Citizens of the State: The Jews of Turkey during the Multi-Party Period* (Lanham, MD: Fairleigh Dickinson University Press, 2012).

Murat Bardakçı, *Talât Paşa'nın Evrak-ı Metrûkesi: Sadrazam Tâlat Paşa'nın Özel Arşivinde Bulunan Ermeni Tehciri Konusundaki Belgeler ve Hususî Yazışmalar* (İstanbul: Everest Yayınları, 2008).

Elazar Barkan, *The Guilt of Nations: Restitution and Negotiating Historical Injustices* (New York: W. W. Norton, 2000).

Elazar Barkan and Alexander Karn, eds., *Taking Wrongs Seriously: Apologies and Reconciliation* (Stanford, CA: Stanford University Press, 2006).

Christopher Barnard, *Language, Ideology and Japanese History Textbooks* (London: RoutledgeCurzon, 2003).

Cameron W. Barr, "Japan Teeters between Apology and Denial," *Christian Science Monitor* (15 August 1995a).

——, "Japan Sidesteps Claims," *Christian Science Monitor* (15 August 1995b), p. 12.

Nanore Barsoumian, "WikiLeaks: Stepping Out of Ottoman Archives, Diplomat Says 'We Really Slaughtered Them!'" *Armenian Weekly* (10 September 2011a).

——, "Scholar Becomes Target of Turkish Groups," *Armenian Weekly* (15 December 2011b).

Bulent Basol, on behalf of the Board of Directors of the American-Turkish Association of Southern California, letter to the editor, "'Anguish and Policy' over Martyrs Day Resolution," *Los Angeles Times* (8 May 1986), p. D6.

Gary Jonathan Bass, *Stay the Hand of Vengeance: The Politics of War Crimes Tribunals* (Princeton, NJ: Princeton University Press, 2000).

Seyhan Bayraktar, "Nothing but Ambiguous: The Killing of Hrant Dink in Turkish Discourse," *Armenian Weekly* (26 April 2008), pp. 6–10.

——, *Politik und Erinnerung: Der Diskurs über den Armeniermord in der Türkei zwischen Nationalismus und Europäisierung* (Bielefeld: transcript Verlag, 2010).

Michael J. Bazyler, "From 'Lamentation and Liturgy to Litigation': The Holocaust-Era Restitution Movement as a Model for Bringing Armenian Genocide-Era Restitution Suits in American Courts," *Marquette Law Review*, vol. 95, no. 1 (2011), pp. 245–303.

BBC Monitoring Asia Pacific—Political, "Foreign Ministry Rejects Chinese Complaint on Court Ruling" (25 December 1998a).

——, "China's 'Righteous Indignation' over Japanese Court Verdict on Nanjing Massacre" (28 December 1998b).

BBC Monitoring Service: Asia-Pacific, "Commentary Says Japanese Leader's Visit to War Shrine Shows 'Hawk' Nature" (2 August 1996).

——, "Foreign Ministry Reiterates No Change in China Policy" (17 May 1999).

BBC Monitoring Service: Central Europe and Balkans, "President Asks French Counterpart to 'Use Influence' over Genocide Bill" (6 June 1998).

——, "Turkish Foreign Minister Ismail Cem Has Warned US Secretary . . ." (8 May 2000), originally published in *Hürriyet*, 3 May 2000.

Edward R. Beauchamp and James M. Vardaman, Jr., eds., *Japanese Education since 1945: A Documentary Study* (Armonk, NY: M.E. Sharpe, 1994).

Lawrence W. Beer, *Freedom of Expression in Japan: A Study in Comparative Law, Politics, and Society* (Tokyo: Kodansha International, 1984).

Steven T. Benfell, "Why Can't Japan Apologize? Institutions and War Memory since 1945," *Harvard Asia Quarterly*, vol. 6, no. 2 (2002), pp. 4–11.

Osman Bengür, "Turkey's Image and the Armenian Question," *Turkish Policy Quarterly*, vol. 8, no. 1 (2009), pp. 43–48.

Michal Ben-Josef Hirsch, "Agents of Truth and Justice: Truth Commissions and the Transitional Justice Epistemic Community," in David Chandler and Volker Heins, eds., *Rethinking Ethical Foreign Policy: Pitfalls, Possibilities and Paradoxes* (Oxford: Routledge, 2007a), pp. 184–205.

——, "From Taboo to the Negotiable: The Israeli New Historians and the Changing Representation of the Palestinian Refugee Problem," *Perspectives on Politics*, vol. 5, no. 2 (2007b), pp. 241–58.

——, "Ideational Change and the Emergence of the International Norm of Truth and Reconciliation Commissions," *European Journal of International Relations*, vol. 20, no. 3 (2014), pp. 810–33.

——, "Historical Acknowledgment as a Negotiation Strategy: Insights from Israel/Palestine," paper presented at the Historical Dialogues, Justice and Memory Network Annual Conference, Columbia University, New York (8 December 2017).

Michal Ben-Josef Hirsch and Jennifer M. Dixon, "A Tale of Two Norms: Assessing the Strength of Transitional Justice Norms," paper presented at the Seventh Annual Conference of the Historical Justice and Memory Network, Columbia University, New York (8 December 2017).

Michal Ben-Josef Hirsch, Megan MacKenzie, and Mohamed Sesay, "Measuring the Impacts of Truth and Reconciliation Commissions: Placing the Global 'Success' of TRCs in Local Perspective," *Cooperation and Conflict*, vol. 47, no. 3 (2012), pp. 386–403.

Thomas U. Berger, *Cultures of Antimilitarism: National Security in Germany and Japan* (Baltimore: Johns Hopkins University Press, 1998).

——, "The Construction of Antagonism: The History Problem in Japan's Foreign Relations," in G. John Ikenberry and Takashi Inoguchi, eds., *Reinventing the Alliance: U.S.–Japan Security Partnership in an Era of Change* (New York: Palgrave Macmillan, 2003), pp. 63–88.

——, "Different Beds, Same Nightmare: The Politics of History in Germany and Japan," *AICGS Policy Report*, no. 39 (2009).

——, *War, Guilt, and World Politics after World War II* (New York: Cambridge University Press, 2012).

Michael Bernhard and Jan Kubik, eds., *Twenty Years after Communism: The Politics of Memory and Commemoration* (New York: Oxford University Press, 2014a).

——, "The Politics and Culture of Memory Regimes: A Comparative Analysis," in Michael Bernhard and Jan Kubik, eds., *Twenty Years after Communism: The Politics of Memory and Commemoration* (New York: Oxford University Press, 2014b), pp. 261–96.

Matthias Bjørnlund, "The 1914 Cleansing of Aegean Greeks as a Case of Violent Turkification," *Journal of Genocide Research*, vol. 10, no. 1 (2008), pp. 41–57.

——, "'A Fate Worse Than Dying': Sexual Violence during the Armenian Genocide," in Dagmar Herzog, ed., *Brutality and Desire: War and Sexuality in Europe's Twentieth Century* (London: Palgrave Macmillan, 2009), pp. 16–58.

David W. Blight, *Race and Reunion: The Civil War in American Memory* (Cambridge, MA: Harvard University Press, 2001).

Wolf Blitzer, "Turkey Seeks Help of Israel and U.S. Jews to Fight U.S. Senate Resolution Marking Armenian Genocide," *Jerusalem Post* (24 October 1989).

Alan Bloomfield, "Norm Antipreneurs and Theorizing Resistance to Normative Change," *Review of International Studies*, vol. 42, no. 2 (2016), pp. 310–33.

Donald Bloxham, "Determinants of the Armenian Genocide," in Richard G. Hovannisian, ed., *Looking Backward, Moving Forward: Confronting the Armenian Genocide* (New Brunswick, NJ: Transaction Publishers, 2003a), pp. 23–50.

——, "The Armenian Genocide of 1915–1916: Cumulative Radicalization and the Development of a Destruction Policy," *Past and Present*, no. 181 (2003b), pp. 141–91.

——, *The Great Game of Genocide: Imperialism, Nationalism, and the Destruction of the Ottoman Armenians* (Oxford: Oxford University Press, 2005).

Michael Bobelian, *Children of Armenia: A Forgotten Genocide and the Century-Long Struggle for Justice* (New York: Simon and Schuster, 2009).

Gözde Boğa, "An Analysis of the Role of Media in Conflict Escalation: The Case of the 'Armenian Conference' in Turkey," MA thesis, Sabancı University (2006).

Neil Boister and Robert Cryer, eds., *Documents on the Tokyo International Military Tribunal: Charter, Indictment and Judgments* (Oxford: Oxford University Press, 2008a).

Neil Boister and Robert Cryer, "Introduction," in Neil Boister and Robert Cryer, eds., *Documents on the Tokyo International Military Tribunal: Charter, Indictment and Judgments* (Oxford: Oxford University Press, 2008b), pp. xxxiii–lxxxiv.

John H. Boyle, "Review of *The Nanjing Massacre: A Japanese Journalist Confronts Japan's National Shame* by Honda Katsuichi; Frank Gibney; Karen Sandness," *American Historical Review*, vol. 106, no. 1 (2001), pp. 148–49.

Laurie A. Brand, *Official Stories: Politics and National Narratives in Egypt and Algeria* (Stanford, CA: Stanford University Press, 2014).

John Breen, "Introduction: A Yasukuni Genealogy," in John Breen, ed., *Yasukuni, the War Dead and the Struggle for Japan's Past* (New York: Columbia University Press, 2008), pp. 1–21.

Timothy Brook, ed., *Documents on the Rape of Nanking* (Ann Arbor: University of Michigan Press, 1999).

——, "The Tokyo Judgment and the Rape of Nanking," *Journal of Asian Studies*, vol. 60, no. 3 (2001), pp. 673–700.

Roy L. Brooks, ed., *When Sorry Isn't Enough: The Controversy over Apologies and Reparations for Historical Injustice* (New York: New York University Press, 1999).

Susanne Buckley-Zistel, "Narrative Truths: On the Construction of the Past in Truth Commissions," in Susanne Buckley-Zistel, Teresa Koloma Beck, Christian Braun, and Friederike Mieth, eds., *Transitional Justice Theories* (London: Routledge, 2014), pp. 144–62.

Susanne Buckley-Zistel, Teresa Koloma Beck, Christian Braun, and Friederike Mieth, eds., *Transitional Justice Theories* (London: Routledge, 2014).

Tom Burgis, "Man in the News: Paul Kagame," *Financial Times* (13 August 2010).

Charles Burress, "Most Japanese Support Apology / Nation No Longer Has 'Historic Amnesia' about World War II," *San Francisco Chronicle* (18 August 1995), p. B2.

Richard C. Bush III, "Thoughts on the Nanjing Massacre," *Brookings Northeast Asia Commentary* (December 2007).

Zoltán I. Búzás, "Evading International Law: How Agents Comply with the Letter of the Law but Violate Its Purpose," *European Journal of International Relations*, vol. 23, no. 4 (2017), pp. 857–83.

——, "Is the Good News about Law Compliance Good News about Norm Compliance?: The Case of Racial Equality," *International Organization*, vol. 72, no. 2 (2018), pp. 351–85.

Necip Çakır, "Asılsız Soykırım İddiaları Konferansta Ele Alındı," *Zaman* (17 May 2003).

Cansu Çamlıbel, "Turkey Needs Post-2015 Strategy on Armenian Genocide Claims, Says Turkish Diplomat," *Hürriyet Daily News* (10 November 2014).

Brendon J. Cannon, "Politicizing History and Legislating Reality: History, Memory, and Identity as Explanations for Armenian Claims of Genocide," PhD diss., University of Utah (2009).

David Capie, "Localization as Resistance: The Contested Diffusion of Small Arms Norms in Southeast Asia," *Security Dialogue*, vol. 39, no. 6 (2008), pp. 637–58.

——, "The Responsibility to Protect Norm in Southeast Asia: Framing, Resistance, and the Localization Myth," *Pacific Review*, vol. 25, no. 1 (2012), pp. 75–93.

Sonia Cardenas, "Norm Collision: Explaining the Effects of International Human Rights Pressure on State Behavior," *International Studies Review*, vol. 6, no. 2 (2004), pp. 213–31.

——, *Conflict and Compliance: State Responses to International Human Rights Pressure* (Philadelphia: University of Pennsylvania Press, 2007).

R. Charli Carpenter, "Studying Issue (Non-)Adoption in Transnational Advocacy Networks," *International Organization*, vol. 61, no. 3 (2007), pp. 643–67.

——, "Vetting the Advocacy Agenda: Network Centrality and the Paradox of Weapons Norms," *International Organization*, vol. 65, no. 1 (2011), pp. 69–102.

Mitat Çelikpala, "360 Degrees Diplomacy," *On Turkey* series of the German Marshall Fund of the United States (19 July 2009).

Center for Eurasian Studies, *2015 Annual Report* (Ankara: AVİM, 2016).

Centre for Economics and Foreign Policy Studies, "Turks Regretful over the Armenian Tragedy of 1915 but Refuse to Qualify It as a Genocide," Public Opinion Surveys of Turkish Foreign Policy 2015/1 (2015), available at: http://edam.org.tr/en/turks

-regretful-over-the-armenian-tragedy-of-1915-but-refuse-to-qualify-it-as-a
-genocide/.

Frank Chalk and Kurt Jonassohn, *The History and Sociology of Genocide: Analyses and Case Studies* (New Haven, CT: Yale University Press, 1990).

Iris Chang, *The Rape of Nanking: The Forgotten Holocaust of World War II* (New York: Penguin Books, 1997).

——, "Japan Must Pay for Its War Crimes," *Newsday* (19 February 1998), p. A37.

Yvonne Chang, "Japan Scholar Wins Rare Victory in Textbook Case," *Reuters News* (31 August 1997a).

——, "Japan Textbook Crusader Worried about Backlash," *Reuters News* (2 September 1997b).

——, "Japan City Allows Meeting Denying Nanjing Massacre," *Reuters News* (19 January 2000).

Israel W. Charny, "The Conference Crisis: The Turks, Armenians and the Jews," in Israel W. Charny and Shamai Davidson, eds., *The Book of the International Conference on the Holocaust and Genocide: Book One* (Tel Aviv: Institute of the International Conference on the Holocaust and Genocide, 1983), pp. 269–315.

——, "The Psychology of Denial of Known Genocides," in Israel W. Charny, ed., *Genocide: A Critical Bibliographic Review*, Vol. 2 (Jerusalem: Institute on the Holocaust and Genocide, 1991), pp. 3–37.

——, "Toward a Generic Definition of Genocide," in George J. Andreopoulos, ed., *Genocide: Conceptual and Historical Dimensions* (Philadelphia: University of Pennsylvania Press, 1994), pp. 64–94.

——, "A Classification of Denials of the Holocaust and Other Genocides," *Journal of Genocide Research*, vol. 5, no. 1 (2003), pp. 11–34.

Israel W. Charny and Shamai Davidson, eds., *The Book of the International Conference on the Holocaust and Genocide: Book One, The Conference Program and Crisis* (Tel Aviv: Institute of the International Conference on the Holocaust and Genocide, 1983).

Israel W. Charny and Daphna Fromer, "Denying the Armenian Genocide: Patterns of Thinking as Defence-Mechanisms," *Patterns of Prejudice*, vol. 32, no. 1 (1998), pp. 39–49.

Terrence Chea, "Chinese Americans Seek to Hold Japan Accountable for WWII Atrocities," *Associated Press* (11 June 2005).

Jeffrey T. Checkel, "Why Comply? Social Learning and European Identity Change," *International Organization*, vol. 55, no. 3 (2001), pp. 553–88.

——, "International Institutions and Socialization in Europe: Introduction," *International Organization*, vol. 59, no. 4 (2005), pp. 801–26.

Vicken Cheterian, *War and Peace in the Caucasus: Ethnic Conflict and the New Geopolitics* (New York: Columbia University Press, 2008).

——, *Open Wounds: Armenians, Turks and a Century of Genocide* (New York: Oxford University Press, 2015).

Mong Cheung, "Political Survival and the Yasukuni Controversy in Sino-Japanese Relations," *Pacific Review*, vol. 23, no. 4 (2010), pp. 527–48.

Chicago Sun-Times Wires, "Japan Official Ousted over War Remarks // No Retraction, Says Okuno" (14 May 1988), p. 5.

Children and Textbooks Japan Network 21, "The Falsification of History under the Guise of 'Self-Censorship' Has Been Forced onto Textbook Publishers: We Will Not Tolerate the Actions of the Government and the Ministry of Education," statement issued on 21 September 2000, copy on file with author.

Susan Chira, "Tokyo Funeral Forces Choice by Old Foes," *New York Times* (13 January 1989).

Ray Christensen, *Ending the LDP Hegemony: Party Cooperation in Japan* (Honolulu: University of Hawai'i Press, 2000).

Leonidas T. Chrysanthopoulos, *Caucasus Chronicles: Nation-Building and Diplomacy in Armenia, 1993–1994* (Princeton, NJ: Gomidas Institute Books, 2002).

Chuo Koron, "* Challenge for Diplomacy of Future Viewed," in FBIS, Daily Report: East Asia, Annex, FBIS-EAS-92-060-A (1 February 1992), pp. 80–91.

Kemal Çiçek, *Ermenilerin Zorunlu Göçü 1915–1917* (Ankara: TTK Yayınları, 2005).

Karisa Cloward, "False Commitments: Local Misrepresentation and the International Norms against Female Genital Mutilation and Early Marriage," *International Organization*, vol. 68, no. 3 (2014), pp. 495–526.

"Comfort Women: Asia," Memory & Reconciliation in the Asia-Pacific (Washington, DC: The George Washington University, n.d.), available at: https://www.gwu.edu /%7Ememory/data/judicial/comfortwomen_japan/comfort_women_japan.html.

Stanley Cohen, *States of Denial: Knowing about Atrocities and Suffering* (Cambridge, UK: Polity Press, 2001).

Lee Condon, "Sins of the Past; Armenians Demand Recognition of Genocide," *Los Angeles Daily News* (24 April 1999), p. N3.

Congressional Record, "Proceedings and Debates of the 90th Congress, Second Session: House of Representatives" (6 March 1968), pp. 5395–459.

——, "Extensions of Remarks" (7 June 1974), pp. 18353–54.

Paul Connerton, "Seven Types of Forgetting," *Memory Studies*, vol. 1, no. 1 (2008), pp. 59–71.

The Constitution of Japan (3 May 1947), available at: japan.kantei.go.jp/constitution_and _government_of_japan/constitution_e.html.

Alvin D. Coox, "Waking Old Wounds," in *An Overview of the Nanjing Debate: Reprints of Articles from* Japan Echo, *1998–2007 with New Commentaries* (Tokyo: Japan Echo, 2008), pp. 88–99.

Andrew P. Cortell and James W. Davis, Jr., "Understanding the Domestic Impact of International Norms: A Research Agenda," *International Studies Review*, vol. 2, no. 1 (2000), pp. 65–87.

Herve Couturier, "Japan, Neighbors Irked over Attempt to Rewrite History," *Globe and Mail* (27 July 1982), p. P11.

Roger Crabb, "Most Japanese See Need for Apology to China," *Reuters News* (14 October 1992).

——, "Japan Crusader Wins Rare Victory on War History," *Reuters News* (20 October 1993).

Kate Cronin-Furman, "Just Enough: The Politics of Accountability for Mass Atrocities," PhD diss., Columbia University (2015).

Consuelo Cruz, "Identity and Persuasion: How Nations Remember Their Pasts and Make Their Futures," *World Politics*, vol. 52, no. 3 (2000), pp. 275–312.

Vahakn N. Dadrian, "The Events of April 24 in Moscow—How They Happened and under What Circumstances," *Armenian Review*, vol. 20, no. 2 (1967), pp. 9–26.

——, "The Role of the Turkish Military in the Destruction of Ottoman Armenians: A Study in Historical Continuities," *Journal of Political and Military Sociology*, vol. 20, no. 2 (1992), pp. 257–88.

——, "The Secret Young-Turk Ittihadist Conference and the Decision for the World War I Genocide of the Armenians," *Holocaust and Genocide Studies*, vol. 7, no. 2 (1993), pp. 173–201.

——, *The History of the Armenian Genocide: Ethnic Conflict from the Balkans to Anatolia to the Caucasus* (New York: Berghahn Books, 1995a).

——, *Ulusal ve Uluslararası Hukuk Sorunu Olarak Jenosid: 1915 Ermeni Olayı ve Hukuki Sonuçları* (İstanbul: Belge Yayınları, 1995b).

——, "The Turkish Military Tribunal's Prosecution of the Authors of the Armenian Genocide: Four Major Court-Martial Series," *Holocaust and Genocide Studies*, vol. 11, no. 1 (1997), pp. 28–59.

Vahakn N. Dadrian and Taner Akçam, eds., *Judgment at Istanbul: The Armenian Genocide Trials* (New York: Berghahn Books, 2011).

Ihsan D. Dagi, "Turkey in the 1990s: Foreign Policy, Human Rights, and the Search for a New Identity," *Mediterranean Quarterly*, vol. 4, no. 4 (1993), pp. 60–77.

Xinyuan Dai, *International Institutions and National Policies* (New York: Cambridge University Press, 2007).

Daily Yomiuri/Yomiuri Shimbun, "Court Acknowledges Nanjing Massacre as Historical Fact, but Rules Out Damages" (24 September 1999).

James Dao, "Parents' Nightmare, Children's Quest," *New York Times* (16 May 1998), p. 9.

Geoff Davidian and Pamela Ferchl, "Armenians Want 'Justice' for Their Dead," *Globe and Mail* (28 August 1982), p. 11.

Leslie A. Davis, *The Slaughterhouse Province: An American Diplomat's Report on the Armenian Genocide, 1915–1917* (New Rochelle, NY: Aristide D. Caratzas, 1989).

Davoyan v. Republic of Turkey, No. 2:10-cv-05636-DMG-SS (C.D. Cal. July 29, 2010).

William Dawkins and Gordon Cramb, "Quest for Clear View of the Past," *Financial Times* (12 August 1995), p. 8.

Phil Deans, "Diminishing Returns? Prime Minister Koizumi's Visits to the Yasukuni Shrine in the Context of East Asian Nationalisms," *East Asia*, vol. 24, no. 3 (2007), pp. 269–94.

Nicole Deitelhoff and Lisbeth Zimmermann, "Things We Lost in the Fire: How Different Types of Contestation Affect the Validity of International Norms," PRIF Working Paper, no. 18 (2013), pp. 1–17.

Uğurhan Demirbaş, ed., *Osmanlı Belgelerinde Ermeni-Fransız İlişkileri (1918–1919)*, vol. 2 (Ankara: Başbakanlık Osmanlı Devlet Arşivleri Genel Müdürlüğü, 2002).

Bedross Der Matossian, "The Taboo within the Taboo: The Fate of Armenian Capital at the End of the Ottoman Empire," *European Journal of Turkish Studies* (2011a), available at: http://journals.openedition.org/ejts/4411.

——, "The Genocide Archives of the Armenian Patriarchate of Jerusalem," *Armenian Review*, vol. 52, nos. 3–4 (2011b), pp. 17–39.

Katharine Derderian, "Common Fate, Different Experience: Gender-Specific Aspects of the Armenian Genocide, 1915–1917," *Holocaust and Genocide Studies*, vol. 19, no. 1 (2005), pp. 1–25.

Edward W. Desmond, "Finally, a Real Apology," *TIME*, vol. 146, no. 9 (28 August 1995), p. 47.

Thomas de Waal, *Great Catastrophe: Armenians and Turks in the Shadow of Genocide* (New York: Oxford University Press, 2015).

Matteo Dian, "Interpreting Japan's Contested Memory: Conservative and Progressive Traditions," *International Relations*, vol. 29, no. 3 (2015), pp. 363–77.

Mure Dickie and David Pilling, "Unbowed: Koizumi's Assertive Japan Is Standing Up Increasingly to China," *Financial Times* (14 February 2005), p. 17.

Julian Dierkes, *Postwar History Education in Japan and the Germanys: Guilty Lessons* (London: Routledge, 2010).

Hasan Dilan, *Fransız Diplomatik Belgelerinde Ermeni Olayları 1914–1918 Cilt I–VI / Les Evenements Armeniens dans les Documents Diplomatiques Français 1914–1918* (Ankara: TTK Yayınları, 2005–6).

Jennifer M. Dixon, "Education and National Narratives: Changing Representations of the Armenian Genocide in History Textbooks in Turkey," *International Journal for Education Law and Policy* (2010a), pp. 103–26.

——, "Defending the Nation?: Maintaining Turkey's Narrative of the Armenian Genocide," *South European Society and Politics*, vol. 15, no. 3 (2010b), pp. 467–85.

——, "Rhetorical Adaptation and Resistance to International Norms," *Perspectives on Politics*, vol. 15, no. 1 (2017), pp. 83–99.

Jennifer M. Dixon and Jennifer L. Erickson, "The Instrumental Uses of Norms in World Politics," paper presented at ISA annual meeting, Baltimore (24 February 2017).

Frank Dobbin, Beth Simmons, and Geoffrey Garrett, "The Global Diffusion of Public Policies: Social Construction, Coercion, Competition, or Learning?," *Annual Review of Sociology*, vol. 33 (2007), pp. 449–72.

Michael Dobbs, "Lawyers Target Japanese Abuses; WWII Compensation Effort Shifts from Europe to Asia," *Washington Post* (5 March 2000), p. A1.

K. Donabedian, Armenian National Committee (Boston), letter to the editor, "Of Turkey and an Armenian Anniversary," *New York Times* (30 May 1977), p. 14.

Pierre-Antoine Donnet, "Ghosts from the Past Again Haunt Japan," *Agence France-Presse* (31 January 1997).

R. P. Dore, "Textbook Censorship in Japan: The Ienaga Case," *Pacific Affairs*, vol. 43, no. 4 (1970–71), pp. 548–56.

John W. Dower, *Embracing Defeat: Japan in the Aftermath of World War II* (London: Penguin Books, 1999).

——, *Ways of Forgetting, Ways of Remembering: Japan in the Modern World* (New York: New Press, 2012).

Alexis Dudden, *Troubled Apologies among Japan, Korea, and the United States* (New York: Columbia University Press, 2008).

Laura Dugan, Julie Y. Huang, Gary LaFree, and Clark McCauley, "Sudden Desistance from Terrorism: The Armenian Secret Army for the Liberation of Armenia and the Justice Commandos of the Armenian Genocide," *Dynamics of Asymmetric Conflict*, vol. 1, no. 3 (2008), pp. 231–49.

Fuat Dündar, *Modern Türkiye'nin Şifresi: İttihat ve Terakki'nin Etnisite Mühendisliği (1913–1918)* (İstanbul: İletişim Yayınları, 2008).

——, *Crime of Numbers: The Role of Statistics in the Armenian Question (1878–1918)* (New Brunswick, NJ: Transaction Publishers, 2010).

Paul Eckert, "Japan's Murayama Remembers War at China Memorial," *Reuters News* (3 May 1995).

ECOSOC (United Nations Economic and Social Council), Commission on Human Rights, Sub-Commission on Prevention of Discrimination and Protection of Minorities, "Progress Report by Mr. Nicodème Ruhashyankiko, Study of the Question of the Prevention and Punishment of the Crime of Genocide," Document E/CN.4/Sub.2/L.583 (25 June 1973).

——, Commission on Human Rights, Sub-Commission on Prevention of Discrimination and Protection of Minorities, "Study Prepared by Mr. Nicodème Ruhashyankiko, Special Rapporteur, Study of the Question of the Prevention and Punishment of the Crime of Genocide," Document E/CN.4/Sub.2/416 (4 July 1978).

——, Commission on Human Rights, Sub-Commission on Prevention of Discrimination and Protection of Minorities, "Report of the Sub-Commission on Prevention of Discrimination and Protection of Minorities on Its Thirty-Seventh Session," Document E/CN.4/Sub.2/1984/43 (19 October 1984).

——, Commission on Human Rights, Sub-Commission on Prevention of Discrimination and Protection of Minorities, "Revised and Updated Report on the Question of the

Prevention and Punishment of the Crime of Genocide Prepared by Mr. B. Whitaker," Document E/CN.4/Sub.2/1985/6 (2 July 1985).

——, Commission on Human Rights, "Report on the Mission to the Democratic People's Republic of Korea, the Republic of Korea and Japan on the Issue of Military Sexual Slavery in Wartime," Document E/CN.4/1996/53/Add.1 (4 January 1996).

Sibel Edmonds and Philip Giraldi, "Who's Afraid of Sibel Edmonds?," *American Conservative* (November 2009).

Steven Edwards, "60 Years, and Still No Shame: Failure to Atone for Wartime Atrocities Diminishes Japan," *National Post* (13 April 2005), p. A16.

Lerna Ekmekçioğlu, "A Climate for Abduction, a Climate for Redemption: The Politics of Inclusion during and after the Armenian Genocide," *Comparative Studies in Society and History*, vol. 55, no. 3 (2013), pp. 522–53.

——, "Republic of Paradox: The League of Nations Minority Protection Regime and the New Turkey's Step-Citizens," *International Journal of Middle East Studies*, vol. 46, no. 4 (2014), pp. 657–79.

——, "Scholarship on the Armenian Genocide as a Gendered Event and Process," *New Perspectives on Turkey*, vol. 53 (2015), pp. 185–90.

——, *Recovering Armenia: The Limits of Belonging in Post-Genocide Turkey* (Stanford, CA: Stanford University Press, 2016).

Anne Elizabeth Elbrecht, *Telling the Story: The Armenian Genocide in* The New York Times *and* Missionary Herald, *1914–1918* (London: Gomidas Institute, 2012).

Şükrü Elekdağ, Ambassador of Turkey, Washington, "Letters: Turkey's Jews Are Under No Threat," *New York Times* (10 June 1982), p. A30.

——, Ambassador of the Turkish Republic, Washington, "Letters to the Editor: The Turkish Ambassador Replies," *Washington Post* (26 April 1983a), p. A18.

——, Ambassador of the Turkish Embassy, Washington, "Letters: Turkish-Armenian Issue: The Complex Tragedy of 1915," *New York Times* (11 May 1983b), p. A22.

——, Ambassador of Turkey, Washington, "Letters to the Editor: Armenians vs. Turks: The View from Istanbul," *Wall Street Journal* (21 September 1983c), p. 33.

——, "Letters: The Descendants of Turks and Armenians Alike Deserve Better," *New York Times* (23 May 1985), p. A26.

——, "In Turkey, Democracy Is a Fact," *New York Times* (1 October 1988).

——, "The Target Is Our Main Artery," *Milliyet* (1 July 2001), published as "Armenia Said Aiming at Breaking Turkish-U.S. Ties" (6 July 2001), World News Connection.

Esra Elmas, "Towards 2015: Media in Turkey on the Armenian Genocide," in Alexis Demirdjian, ed., *The Armenian Genocide Legacy* (London: Palgrave Macmillan, 2016), pp. 183–96.

Jon Elster, *Closing the Books: Transitional Justice in Historical Perspective* (Cambridge: Cambridge University Press, 2004).

Omar G. Encarnación, *Democracy without Justice in Spain: The Politics of Forgetting* (Philadelphia: University of Pennsylvania Press, 2014).

Hülya Eraslan, "*AGOS* (1996–2005): Türkiye'de Yayınlanan Türkçe-Ermenice Gazete Üzerine İnceleme," MA thesis, Ankara University (2007).

Ayda Erbal, "Mea Culpas, Negotiations, Apologias: Revisiting the 'Apology' of Turkish Intellectuals," in Birgit Schwelling, ed., *Reconciliation, Civil Society, and the Politics of Memory: Transnational Initiatives in the 20th and 21st Century* (Bielefeld: transcript Verlag, 2012), pp. 51–94.

Recep Tayyip Erdoğan, "Letter to Robert Kocaryan" (10 April 2005), available at: www.turkishembassy.com/ii/O/ErdogantoKocaryan.htm.

——, "Congress and Armenia," *Wall Street Journal* (19 October 2007).

Jennifer L. Erickson, "Leveling the Playing Field: Cost Diffusion and the Promotion of 'Responsible' Arms Export Norms," *International Studies Perspectives*, vol. 18, no. 3 (2017), pp. 323–42.

Nihat Erman, Consul General, Republic of Turkey, Los Angeles, "Turkey and Armenians," *Los Angeles Times* (27 October 1986), p. B4.

Ermeniler Tarafından Yapılan Katliam Belgeleri (1914–1919), Yayın Nu: 49 (Ankara: T.C. Başbakanlık Devlet Arşivleri Genel Müdürlüğü Osmanlı Arşivi Daire Başkanlığı, 2001).

European Parliament, "Resolution on a Political Solution to the Armenian Question," Doc. A2-33/87 (18 June 1987).

——, "European Parliament Resolution on the 1999 Regular Report from the Commission on Turkey's Progress towards Accession (COM(1999) 513 C5-0036/2000—2000/2014(COS))," A5-0297/2000 (15 November 2000).

——, "European Parliament Resolution on the 2003 Regular Report of the Commission on Turkey's Progress towards Accession (COM(2003) 676—SEC(2003)1212—C5-0535/2003–2003/2204(INI))," P5_TA(2004)0274 (1 April 2004).

——, "European Parliament Resolution on the Opening of Negotiations with Turkey," P6_TA(2005)0350 (28 September 2005).

——, "European Parliament Resolution of 24 October 2007 on EU-Turkey Relations," P6_TA-PROV(2007)0472 (24 October 2007).

European Stability Initiative, "Noah's Dove Returns. Armenia, Turkey and the Debate on Genocide," Berlin / Istanbul / Yerevan (21 April 2009), available at: www.esiweb.org /index.php?lang=en&id=156&document_ID=108.

Gareth Evans, "Japan and the Politics of Guilt," *East Asia Forum* (6 February 2013), available at: http://www.eastasiaforum.org/2013/02/06/japan-and-the-politics-of-guilt/.

Mark Eykholt, "Aggression, Victimization, and Chinese Historiography of the Nanjing Massacre," in Joshua A. Fogel, ed., *The Nanjing Massacre in History and Historiography* (Berkeley: University of California Press, 2000), pp. 11–69.

Bedil Faik, "We Are Still Waiting," *Hürriyet*, 18 October 1981, p. 6, in FBIS, Daily Report: Western Europe, FBIS-WEU-81-202, "Hurriyet Calls for Armenian Patriotic Loyalty" (20 October 1981), p. T3.

Randall Fegley, *A History of Rwandan Identity and Trauma: The Mythmakers' Victims* (London: Lexington Books, 2016).

Judy Feigin, "The Office of Special Investigations: Striving for Accountability in the Aftermath of the Holocaust," Department of Justice (December 2006), available at: nsarchive.gwu.edu/NSAEBB/NSAEBB331/OSI_report_complete.pdf.

Helen Fein, "A Formula for Genocide: Comparison of the Turkish Genocide (1915) and the German Holocaust (1939–1945)," in Richard F. Tomasson, ed., *Comparative Studies in Sociology* (Greenwich: Jai Press, 1978), pp. 271–94.

——, "Genocide: A Sociological Perspective," *Current Sociology*, vol. 38, no. 1 (1990), pp. 1–7.

Norma Field, *In the Realm of a Dying Emperor: Japan at Century's End* (New York: Vintage Books, 1993 [1991]).

——, "The Stakes of Apology," *Japan Quarterly*, vol. 42, no. 4 (1995), pp. 405–18.

Martha Finnemore, "International Organizations as Teachers of Norms: The United Nations Educational, Scientific, and Cultural Organization and Science Policy," *International Organization*, vol. 47, no. 4 (1993), pp. 565–97.

Martha Finnemore and Kathryn Sikkink, "International Norm Dynamics and Political Change," *International Organization*, vol. 52, no. 4 (1998), pp. 887–917.

Patrick Finney, "The Ubiquitous Presence of the Past? Collective Memory and International History," *International History Review*, vol. 36, no. 3 (2014), pp. 443–72.

Orfeo Fioretos, "Historical Institutionalism in International Relations," *International Organization*, vol. 65, no. 2 (2011), pp. 367–99.

Laurel E. Fletcher, Harvey M. Weinstein, and Jamie Rowen, "Context, Timing and the Dynamics of Transitional Justice: A Historical Perspective," *Human Rights Quarterly*, vol. 31, no. 1 (2009), pp. 163–220.

Joshua A. Fogel, "Review of Iris Chang, *The Rape of Nanking: The Forgotten Holocaust of World War II*; and George Hicks, *Japan's War Memories: Amnesia or Concealment*," *Journal of Asian Studies*, vol. 57, no. 3 (1998), pp. 818–20.

——, "Introduction: The Nanjing Massacre in History," in Joshua A. Fogel, ed., *The Nanjing Massacre in History and Historiography* (Berkeley: University of California Press, 2000a), pp. 1–9.

——, ed., *The Nanjing Massacre in History and Historiography* (Berkeley: University of California Press, 2000b).

Foreign Policy Institute, *The Armenian Issue in Nine Questions and Answers* (Ankara: Foreign Policy Institute, 1982 [1985; 1992]).

Clive Foss, "Armenian History as Seen by Twentieth-Century Turkish Historians," *Armenian Review*, vol. 45, nos. 1–2 (1992), pp. 1–52.

Howard W. French, "Internet Raiders in Japan Denounce Rape of Nanjing," *New York Times* (31 January 2000), p. 9.

Donna-Lee Frieze, ed., *Totally Unofficial: The Autobiography of Raphael Lemkin* (New Haven, CT: Yale University Press, 2013).

Leora Eren Frucht and Ariel Jerozolimski, "A Tragedy Offstage No More," *Jerusalem Post* (12 May 2000).

T. Fujitani, Geoffrey M. White, and Lisa Yoneyama, eds., *Perilous Memories: The Asia-Pacific War(s)* (Durham, NC: Duke University Press, 2001).

Fujiwara Akira, "The Nanking Atrocity: An Interpretive Overview," *Japan Focus* (23 October 2007).

Fujiwara Kiichi, "Japan: Remembering the War—Japanese Style," *Far Eastern Economic Review*, vol. 168, no. 11 (16 December 2005), pp. 51–55.

Fukatsu Masumi, "A State Visit to Yasukuni Shrine," *Japan Quarterly*, vol. 33, no. 1 (1986), pp. 19–24.

Lily Gardner Feldman, *Germany's Foreign Policy of Reconciliation: From Enmity to Amity* (Lanham, MD: Rowman and Littlefield, 2012).

David Gaunt, *Massacres, Resistance, Protectors: Muslim-Christian Relations in Eastern Anatolia during World War I* (Piscataway: Gorgias Press, 2006).

Ernest Gellner, *Nations and Nationalism* (Ithaca, NY: Cornell University Press, 1983).

Frank Gibney, "Editor's Introduction," in Honda Katsuichi (with Frank Gibney, ed.), *The Nanjing Massacre: A Japanese Journalist Confronts Japan's National Shame* (Armonk, NY: M.E. Sharpe, 1999), pp. vii–xxi.

Mark Gibney, Rhoda E. Howard-Hassmann, Jean-Marc Coicaud, and Niklaus Steiner, eds., *The Age of Apology: Facing Up to the Past* (Philadelphia: University of Pennsylvania Press, 2008).

John R. Gillis, ed., *Commemorations: The Politics of National Identity* (Princeton, NJ: Princeton University Press, 1994).

Ryan Gingeras, *Sorrowful Shores: Violence, Ethnicity, and the End of the Ottoman Empire, 1912–1923* (New York: Oxford University Press, 2009).

——, "Last Rites for a 'Pure Bandit': Clandestine Service, Historiography and the Origins of the Turkish 'Deep State,'" *Past & Present*, vol. 206, no. 1 (2010), pp. 151–74.

Richard Giragosian, "Turkish-U.S. Relations: The Role of the Armenian Issue," *Turkish Policy Quarterly*, vol. 4, no. 1 (2005), pp. 1–12.

Carol Gluck, "*Sekinin*/Responsibility in Modern Japan," in Carol Gluck and Anna Lowenhaupt Tsing, eds., *Words in Motion: Toward a Global Lexicon* (Durham: Duke University Press, 2009), pp. 83–108.

Fatma Müge Göçek, "Reading Genocide: Turkish Historiography on the Armenian Deportations and Massacres of 1915," in Israel Gershoni, Amy Singer, and Y. Hakan Erdem, eds., *Middle East Historiographies: Narrating the Twentieth Century* (London: I.B. Tauris, 2006), pp. 101–27.

——, "Furor against the West: Nationalism as the Dangerous Underbelly of Modern Turkey," in Ireneusz Paweł Karolewski and Andrzej Marcin Suszycki, eds., *Nationalism and European Integration: The Need for New Theoretical and Empirical Insights* (London: Continuum, 2007), pp. 168–80.

——, "Dünyanın Bildiği, Türkiye'nin Bilmediği: Ermeni Meselesindeki Bilgi Birikimine Sosyolojik Bir Yaklaşım," in Ragıp Zarakolu, ed., *Sivil Toplumda Türk-Ermeni Diyaloğu* (İstanbul: Pencere Yayınları, 2008), pp. 220–36.

——, *The Transformation of Turkey: Redefining State and Society from the Ottoman Empire to the Modern Era* (London: I.B. Tauris, 2011).

——, *Denial of Violence: Ottoman Past, Turkish Present, and Collective Violence against the Armenians, 1789–2009* (New York: Oxford University Press, 2015).

Nigar Göksel, "A Brave New World for Turkey and Armenia?," *On Turkey Analysis*, German Marshall Fund of the United States (1 October 2009), pp. 1–3.

Richard Gordon, Bonnie Oh, Iris Chang, and Toshiaki Miura, with host Ted Koppel, "Profile: Remembrance: When History Hurts; Japanese Prime Minister's Visit to Shrine of War Dead Infuriates China, Korea, and Some in the United States," *ABC News: Nightline* (15 August 2001).

Aybars Görgülü, *Turkey-Armenia Relations: A Vicious Circle* (Istanbul: TESEV Publications, Foreign Policy Analysis Series-8, 2008).

——, "Towards a Turkish-Armenian Rapprochement?," *Insight Turkey*, vol. 11, no. 2 (2009), pp. 19–29.

Aybars Görgülü, Sabiha Senyücel Gündoğar, Alexander Iskandaryan, and Sergey Minasyan, *Turkey-Armenia Dialogue Series: Breaking the Vicious Circle*, TESEV-Caucasus Institute Joint Report (Istanbul: TESEV Publications, 2009).

Aybars Görgülü, Alexander Iskandaryan, and Sergey Minasyan, *Turkey-Armenia Dialogue Series: Assessing the Rapprochement Process* (Istanbul: TESEV Publications, 2010).

Government of the Republic of Armenia, "Armenian Declaration of Independence" (23 August 1990), available at: www.gov.am/en/independence/.

Kelly M. Greenhill, *Weapons of Mass Migration: Forced Displacement, Coercion, and Foreign Policy* (Ithaca, NY: Cornell University Press, 2010).

Kelly M. Greenhill and Ben Oppenheim, "Rumor Has It: The Adoption of Unverified Information in Conflict Zones," *International Studies Quarterly*, vol. 61, no. 3 (2017), pp. 660–76.

Peter Hays Gries, *China's New Nationalism: Pride, Politics, and Diplomacy* (Berkeley: University of California Press, 2004).

——, "Anti-Japanese Feeling among Chinese Has Historic Roots," *Denver Post* (22 May 2005), p. E1.

Abdullah Gül, "Politicizing the Armenian Tragedy," *Washington Times* (28 March 2007), op-ed page.

Mehmet Gültekin, "Our Grief Is Buried," *Cumhuriyet*, 10 February 1989, p. 14, in FBIS, Daily Report: West Europe, FBIS-WEU-89-060, "Museum Opens Section on Massacre by Armenians" (30 March 1989), p. 30.

Ayşe Günaysu, "The Schism in the Turkish Left," *Armenian Weekly* (20 September 2008a).

——, "Ya Kendi Düşüncemize Vurduğumuz Zincirler? (II)," *Savaş Karşıtları* (26 September 2008b).

——, "Learnings from the Sari Gelin Case," *Armenian Weekly* (4 March 2009a).

——, "Armenians and Kurds," *Armenian Weekly* (5 August 2009b).

——, "Kurdish MP Challenges Turkish Parliament on Armenian Genocide," *Armenian Weekly* (8 November 2009c).

——, "Are We 'Righteous Turks'?," *Keghart.com* (16 June 2013).

Güneş, "Gunes Cites Ozal Remarks on 'Armenian Issue,'" 13 February 1985, p. 1, 11, in FBIS, Daily Report: Western Europe, FBIS-WEU-85-035 (21 February 1985), p. T6.

Michael M. Gunter, *Armenian History and the Question of Genocide* (New York: Palgrave Macmillan, 2011).

Rasit Gurdilek, "Turkey Opens Archives to Counter Armenian Claims," *The Times* (4 January 1989).

Vigen Guroian, "Collective Responsibility and Official Excuse Making: The Case of the Turkish Genocide of the Armenians," in Richard G. Hovannisian, ed., *The Armenian Genocide in Perspective* (New Brunswick, NJ: Transaction Publishers, 1986), pp. 135–52.

Yaprak Gürsoy, "The Changing Role of the Military in Turkish Politics: Democratization through Coup Plots?," *Democratization*, vol. 19, no. 4 (2012), pp. 735–60.

Erol Gurun, President, Federation of Turkish American Societies Inc., letter to the editor, "Other Side of the Story," *New York Times* (8 June 1985), p. 22.

Kâmuran Gürün, *Ermeni Dosyası* (Ankara: TTK Yayınları, 1983 [1985]).

——, *Le Dossier Arménien* (Paris: Triangle, 1984).

——, *The Armenian File: The Myth of Innocence Exposed* (London: K. Rustem and Brother, 1985).

——, *Fırtınalı Yıllar: Dışişleri Müsteşarlığı Anıları* (İstanbul: Milliyet Yayınları, 1995).

Wolfgang Gust, ed., *The Armenian Genocide: Evidence from the German Foreign Office Archives, 1915–1916* (New York: Berghahn Books, 2014).

Yifat Gutman, *Memory Activism: Reimagining the Past for the Future in Israel-Palestine* (Nashville, TN: Vanderbilt University Press, 2017).

Clyde Haberman, "Japanese Official Fires New Furor on the War," *New York Times* (11 May 1988).

Emilie M. Hafner-Burton, "Sticks and Stones: Naming and Shaming the Human Rights Enforcement Problem," *International Organization*, vol. 62, no. 4 (2008), pp. 689–716.

Yusuf Halaçoğlu, *Ermeni Tehciri ve Gerçekler (1914–1918)* (Ankara: TKK Yayınları, 2001).

——, *Facts on the Relocation of Armenians 1914–1918* (Ankara: Turkish Historical Society, 2002).

Maurice Halbwachs, *The Collective Memory*, trans. Francis J. Ditter Jr. and Vida Yazdi Ditter (New York: Harper and Row, 1980 [1950]).

Akiko Hashimoto, *The Long Defeat: Cultural Trauma, Memory, and Identity in Japan* (New York: Oxford University Press, 2015).

Ryutaro Hashimoto, "Letter from Prime Minister to the Former Comfort Women," Documents of the Japanese Government and the Asian Women's Fund (Digital Museum: The Comfort Women Issue and the Asian Women's Fund, 1996), available at: http://www.awf.or.jp/e6/statement-12.html.

Ron E. Hassner, "The Path to Intractability: Time and the Entrenchment of Territorial Disputes," *International Security*, vol. 31, no. 3 (2006/7), pp. 107–38.

Hata Ikuhiko, "The Nanking Atrocities: Fact and Fable," *Japan Echo*, vol. 25, no. 4 (1998), pp. 47–57.

Hatano Sumio, "History and the State in Postwar Japan," in Sven Saaler and Christopher W. A. Szpilman, eds., *Routledge Handbook of Modern Japanese History* (Oxon: Routledge, 2018), pp. 421–39.

Hirofumi Hayashi, "Disputes in Japan over the Japanese Military 'Comfort Women' System and Its Perception in History," *ANNALS of the American Academy of Political and Social Science*, vol. 617 (2008), pp. 123–32.

Priscilla B. Hayner, *Unspeakable Truths: Confronting State Terror and Atrocity* (New York: Routledge, 2001).

Yinan He, "History, Chinese Nationalism and the Emerging Sino-Japanese Conflict," *Journal of Contemporary China*, vol. 16, no. 50 (2007a), pp. 1–24.

——, "Remembering and Forgetting the War: Elite Mythmaking, Mass Reaction, and Sino-Japanese Relations, 1950–2006," *History and Memory*, vol. 19, no. 2 (2007b), pp. 43–74.

——, *The Search for Reconciliation: Sino-Japanese and German-Polish Relations since World War II* (New York: Cambridge University Press, 2009).

Martin O. Heisler, "Challenged Histories and Collective Self-Concepts: Politics in History, Memory, and Time," *ANNALS of the American Academy of Political and Social Science*, no. 617 (2008), pp. 199–211.

Cullen S. Hendrix and Wendy H. Wong, "When Is the Pen Truly Mighty? Regime Type and the Efficacy of Naming and Shaming in Curbing Human Rights Abuses," *British Journal of Political Science*, vol. 43, no. 3 (2013), pp. 651–72.

Jeffrey Herf, *Divided Memory: The Nazi Past in the Two Germanys* (Cambridge, MA: Harvard University Press, 1997).

Holger H. Herwig, "Clio Deceived: Patriotic Self-Censorship in Germany after the Great War," *International Security*, vol. 12, no. 2 (1987), pp. 5–44.

Edmund Herzig, *The New Caucasus: Armenia, Azerbaijan and Georgia* (London: Royal Institute of International Affairs, 1999).

George Hicks, *The Comfort Women: Japan's Brutal Regime of Enforced Prostitution in the Second World War* (New York: W. W. Norton, 1995).

——, *Japan's War Memories: Amnesia or Concealment?* (Aldershot: Ashgate, 1997).

Higashinakano Shudo, *The Nanking Massacre: Fact versus Fiction, a Historian's Quest for the Truth* (Tokyo: Sekai Shuppan, 2005).

Ben Hills, "Minister Sacked for War Comments," *Sydney Morning Herald* (15 August 1994), p. 13.

Mutsumi Hirano, *History Education and International Relations: A Case Study of Diplomatic Disputes over Japanese Textbooks* (Folkestone: Global Oriental, 2009).

Andy Ho, "Read It and Weep," *Straits Times* (13 May 2005a).

——, "Much More to Yasukuni Shrine Than War Criminals," *Straits Times* (28 May 2005b).

Eric Hobsbawm and Terence O. Ranger, eds., *The Invention of Tradition* (Cambridge: Cambridge University Press, 1983).

Tessa Hofmann, *Armenians in Turkey Today: A Critical Assessment of the Situation of the Armenian Minority in the Turkish Republic* (Brussels: EU Office for the Armenian Associations of Europe, October 2002), pp. 1–46.

Lorien Holland, "Storm over War Apology at Japan-China Summit," *Agence France-Presse* (26 November 1998).

Peter I. Holquist, "'Crimes against Humanity': Genealogy of a Concept, 1815–1945," unpublished manuscript (n.d.).

David Holthouse, "State of Denial: Turkey Spends Millions to Cover Up Armenian Genocide," Intelligence Report, Southern Poverty Law Center (Summer 2008).

William H. Honan, "Princeton Is Accused of Fronting for the Turkish Government," *New York Times* (22 May 1996), p. 1.

Honda Katsuichi, *The Nanjing Massacre: A Japanese Journalist Confronts Japan's National Shame* (Armonk, NY: M.E. Sharpe, 1999).

Hora Tomio, *Kindai Senshi no Nazo* (Tōkyō: Jinbutsu Ōraisha, 1967).

Raffi K. Hovannisian, "Addressing Turkey and Its Blockade of Armenia: The Double-Edged Sword of the Treaties of Kars and Moscow," The National Citizens' Initiative (1994).

Richard G. Hovannisian, *Armenia on the Road to Independence, 1918* (Berkeley: University of California Press, 1967).

——, *The Armenian Holocaust: A Bibliography Relating to the Deportations, Massacres, and Dispersion of the Armenian People, 1915–1923* (Cambridge, MA: NAASR, Armenian Heritage Press, 1978).

——, "Genocide and Denial: The Armenian Case," in Israel W. Charny, ed., *Toward the Understanding and Prevention of Genocide: Proceedings of the International Conference on the Holocaust and Genocide* (Boulder, CO: Westview Press, 1984), pp. 84–99.

——, "The Armenian Genocide and Patterns of Denial," in Richard G. Hovannisian, ed., *The Armenian Genocide in Perspective* (New Brunswick, NJ: Transaction Publishers, 1986), pp. 111–33.

——, ed., *The Armenian Genocide: History, Politics, Ethics* (London: St. Martin's Press, 1992).

——, "The Armenian Question in the Ottoman Empire 1876 to 1914," in Richard G. Hovannisian, ed., *The Armenian People from Ancient to Modern Times, Volume II, Foreign Dominion to Statehood: The Fifteenth Century to the Twentieth Century* (New York: St. Martin's Press, 1997), pp. 203–38.

——, "Denial of the Armenian Genocide in Comparison with Holocaust Denial," in Richard G. Hovannisian, ed., *Remembrance and Denial: The Case of the Armenian Genocide* (Detroit: Wayne State University Press, 1999a), pp. 201–36.

——, ed., *Remembrance and Denial: The Case of the Armenian Genocide* (Detroit: Wayne State University Press, 1999b).

——, ed., *Looking Backward, Moving Forward: Confronting the Armenian Genocide* (New Brunswick, NJ: Transaction Publishers, 2003).

——, "The Armenian Genocide: Wartime Radicalization or Premeditated Continuum?," in Richard G. Hovannisian, ed., *The Armenian Genocide: Cultural and Ethical Legacies* (New Brunswick, NJ: Transaction Publishers, 2007), pp. 3–17.

——, "Denial of the Armenian Genocide 100 Years Later: The New Practitioners and Their Trade," *Genocide Studies International*, vol. 9, no. 2 (2015), pp. 228–47.

Jane Howard, "Archives May Help Resolve Armenian Question," *Sydney Morning Herald* (5 January 1989), p. 5.

Marvine Howe, "Turkey Denies It Threatened Jews over Tel Aviv Parley on Genocide," *New York Times* (5 June 1982), p. 3.

William Lee Howell, "The Inheritance of War: Japan's Domestic Politics and International Ambitions," in Gerrit W. Gong, ed., *Remembering and Forgetting: The Legacy of War and Peace in East Asia* (Boulder, CO: Westview Press, 1997), pp. 82–102.

Shi Hua, "Fight for Justice," *Shanghai Star* (29 February 2000).

Ian Hurd, "Legitimacy and Authority in International Politics," *International Organization*, vol. 53, no. 2 (1999), pp. 379–408.

Hürriyet, "Genelkurmay: Gökçen Ata'nın Armağanıdır" (22 February 2004).

——, "Tapu Arşivlerini 'Sınırlı' Kullanın" (19 September 2006).

Susan D. Hyde, "Catch Us If You Can: Election Monitoring and International Norm Diffusion," *American Journal of Political Science*, vol. 55, no. 2 (2011), pp. 356–69.

David Ibison, "Koizumi Visits to War Shrine Attacked," *Financial Times* (26 November 2004), p. 9.

Ahmet İçduygu, Şule Toktaş, and B. Ali Soner, "The Politics of Population in a Nation-Building Process: Emigration of Non-Muslims from Turkey," *Ethnic and Racial Studies*, vol. 31, no. 2 (2008), pp. 358–89.

ICTJ (International Center for Transitional Justice), "The Applicability of the United Nations Convention on the Prevention and Punishment of the Crime of Genocide to Events Which Occurred during the Early Twentieth Century" (10 February 2003), available at: ictj.org/publication/applicability-un-convention-prevention-and-punishment-crime-genocide-events-which.

ICTR (International Criminal Tribunal for Rwanda), *Prosecutor v. Jean-Paul Akayesu*, Case No. ICTR-96-4-T (2 September 1998).

———, *Prosecutor v. Clément Kayishema and Obed Ruzindana*, Case No. ICTR-95-1-T (21 May 1999).

ICTY (International Criminal Tribunal for the Former Yugoslavia), *Prosecutor v. Goran Jelisić*, Case No. IT-95-10-T (14 December 1999).

Saburo Ienaga, "The Glorification of War in Japanese Education," *International Security*, vol. 18, no. 3 (1993–94), pp. 113–33.

Erdal İlter, *Türk-Ermeni İlişkileri Bibliyografyası* (Ankara: Ankara Üniversitesi Osmanlı Tarihi Araştırma ve Uygulama Merkezi Yayınları, 1997).

Efraim Inbar, "Israel's Strategic Relations with Turkey and India," in Robert O. Freedman, ed., *Contemporary Israel: Domestic Politics, Foreign Policy, and Security Challenges* (Boulder, CO: Westview Press, 2009), pp. 227–51.

Irie Yoshimasa, "The History of the Textbook Controversy," *Japan Echo*, vol. 24, no. 3 (1997), pp. 34–38.

Emre İşeri and Nihat Çelik, "Turkish Nation-State Identity and Foreign Policy on Armenia: The Roles of Sèvresphobia and 'Brotherly' Azerbaijan," *Turkish Review*, vol. 3, no. 3 (2013), pp. 274–79.

Kazuo Ishii, "War Lawsuits against Japan on Rise in U.S.," *Daily Yomiuri/Yomiuri Shimbun* (18 September 1999).

Chiaki Ishimura, "Condemnation in Japan and South Korea over Shimamura Comments," *Agence France-Presse* (10 August 1995).

Shingo Ito, "Zhu Urges 'New Pages' in Sino-Japanese Bitterness," *Agence France-Presse* (13 October 2000).

Japan Echo, "Chronology: May–June," vol. 32, no. 4 (2005a).

———, "Chronology: September–October 2005," vol. 32, no. 6 (2005b).

Japan Economic Newswire, "Japan Must Apologize for Nanjing Massacre: U.S. Writer" (2 December 1998).

———, "Court Rejects Damage Claims, Admits Japan's Wartime Role" (22 September 1999).

———, "New Japanese Textbook Drafts Say Less about Sex Slaves" (30 June 2000).

"Japan-Korea Treaty on Basic Relations," *International Legal Materials*, vol. 4, no. 5 (1965), pp. 924–27.

Japan Quarterly, "Basic Trends: Political" and "Chronology: September to November, 1955," vol. 3, no. 1 (1956), pp. 1–8, 125–30.

———, "Political: Japan's Peripatetic Premier," vol. 5, no. 2 (1958), pp. 131–34.

———, "Chronology: December 1967–February 1968," vol. 15, no. 2 (1968), pp. 270–78.

———, "Chronology: December 1969–February 1970," vol. 17, no. 2 (1970), pp. 221–36.

———, "Chronology: September–November 1970," vol. 18, no. 1 (1971), pp. 115–28.

———, "Chronology: September–November 1971," vol. 19, no. 1 (1972a), pp. 111–20.

———, "Chronology: December 1971–February 1972," vol. 19, no. 2 (1972b), pp. 242–48.

———, "Chronology: March–May 1979," vol. 26, no. 3 (1979), pp. 427–36.

———, "Chronology: December 1982–February 1983," vol. 30, no. 2 (1983), pp. 221–28.

———, "Chronology: September–November 1983," vol. 31, no. 1 (1984a), pp. 115–22.

——, "Chronology: December 1983–February 1984," vol. 31, no. 2 (1984b), pp. 229–37.

——, "Chronology: December 1984–February 1985," vol. 32, no. 2 (1985a), pp. 221–28.

——, "Chronology: June–August 1985," vol. 32, no. 4 (1985b), pp. 450–56.

Japan Times Online, "Mori Slips Up with 'Shina' Comment" (11 January 2001).

——, "Bones of Presumed Military Experiment Victims Laid to Rest" (28 March 2002).

Japan Today, "On Yasukuni: Full Interview Transcript with Yomiuri and Asahi Editors" (17 October 2003).

Scott Jaschik, "Suit over 'Unreliable Websites,'" *Inside Higher Ed* (1 December 2010a).

——, "Unlikely Foes," *Inside Higher Ed* (20 December 2010b).

——, "Refusing to Back Down," *Inside Higher Ed* (6 December 2011).

Roger B. Jeans, "Victims or Victimizers? Museums, Textbooks, and the War Debate in Contemporary Japan," *Journal of Military History*, vol. 69, no. 1 (2005), pp. 149–95.

Renee Jeffery, "When Is an Apology Not an Apology?: Contrition Chic and Japan's (Un) apologetic Politics," *Australian Journal of International Affairs*, vol. 65, no. 5 (2011), pp. 607–17.

David Jenkins, "Japanese 'Sorrow' Is No Apology," *Sydney Morning Herald* (25 February 1992a), p. 9.

——, "Akihito—and an Apology—Welcome," *Sydney Morning Herald* (29 September 1992b).

Gareth Jenkins, "The Military and Turkish Society," *Adelphi Series*, vol. 41, no. 337 (2001), pp. 9–20.

JOAK Television, "Text of Fukuda Speech," in FBIS, Daily Report: Asia and Pacific, FBIS-APA-78-206 (24 October 1978), p. C2.

Clayton Jones, "Japanese Shrine Stirs Controversy," *Christian Science Monitor* (15 August 1993).

Torben Jørgensen, "Turkey, the US and the Armenian Genocide," in Steven L. B. Jensen, ed., *Genocide: Cases, Comparisons and Contemporary Debates* (Copenhagen: Danish Center for Holocaust and Genocide Studies, 2003), pp. 193–223.

Joe Joseph and Catherine Sampson, "Takeshita Comments Land Japan in Diplomatic Row," *The Times* (22 February 1989).

Journal: Armenian Assembly of America, "U.S. Academicians and Lobbying: Turkey Uses Advertisement as Political Tool," vol. 14, no. 1 (1987), pp. 1, 6–8, 12.

Hiroshi Kaihara, "The Advent of a New Japanese Politics: Effects of the 1994 Revision of the Electoral Law," *Asian Survey*, vol. 47, no. 5 (2007), pp. 749–65.

Hilmar Kaiser, "From Empire to Republic: The Continuities of Turkish Denial," *Armenian Review*, vol. 48, nos. 3–4 (2003), pp. 1–24.

Suvendrini Kakuchi, "Japan-China: Once-Testy Ties Take Somewhat Warmer Tone," *Inter Press Service* (17 October 2000).

——, "Japan: New History Texts Called Propaganda by Asian Neighbors," *Inter Press Service* (13 April 2001).

Kenan Kalecikli, *Türkiye Cumhuriyeti İnkılâp Tarihi ve Atatürkçülük 1* (İstanbul: Gendaş A.Ş., 1994).

Dikran M. Kaligian, "The Use and Abuse of Armeno-Turkish Dialogue," *Armenian Review*, vol. 50, nos. 1–4 (2008), pp. 75–97.

——, *Armenian Organization and Ideology under Ottoman Rule, 1908–1914* (New Brunswick, NJ: Transaction Publishers, 2009).

——, "Anatomy of Denial: Manipulating Sources and Manufacturing a Rebellion," *Genocide Studies International*, vol. 8, no. 2 (2014), pp. 208–23.

M. Kalman, *Batı-Ermenistan (Kürt İlişkileri) ve Jenosid* (İstanbul: Peri Yayınları, 1994).

Nüzhet Kandemir, letter to the editor, *Washington Post* (4 May 1990).

Kankai, "* Senior Officers Discuss SDF Future," in FBIS, Daily Report: East Asia, Annex, FBIS-EAS-91-151-A (1 June 1991), pp. 60–75.

Wulf Kansteiner, "From Exception to Exemplum: The New Approach to Nazism and the 'Final Solution,'" *History and Theory,* vol. 33, no. 2 (1994), pp. 145–71.

——, "Finding Meaning in Memory: A Methodological Critique of Collective Memory Studies," *History and Theory,* vol. 41, no. 2 (2002), pp. 179–97.

Şenol Kantarcı, Kamer Kasım, İbrahim Kaya, and Sedat Laçiner, eds., *Ermeni Sorunu El Kitabı* (Ankara: ASAM, 2002).

Sam Kaplan, *The Pedagogical State: Education and the Politics of National Culture in Post-1980 Turkey* (Stanford, CA: Stanford University Press, 2006).

Kemal Kara, *Lise Türkiye Cumhuriyeti İnkılap Tarihi ve Atatürkçülük* (İstanbul: Önde Yayıncılık, 2007).

Hülya Karabağlı, "Biri Azınlıkları 40 Yıldır Gözetliyor," *Sabah* (8 November 2003).

Taha Niyazi Karaca, *Ermeni Sorununun Gelişim Sürecinde Yozgat'ta Türk Ermeni İlişkileri* (Ankara: TTK Yayınları, 2005).

Recep Karacakaya, *Kaynakçalı Ermeni Meselesi Kronolojisi (1878–1923),* Yayın Nu: 52 (İstanbul: Başbakanlık Devlet Arşivleri Genel Müdürlüğü, 2001).

Kasahara Tokushi, *Nankin Jiken* (Tōkyō: Iwanami Shoten, 1997).

——, "Higashinakano Osamichi: The Last Word in Denial," in Bob Tadashi Wakabayashi, ed., *The Nanking Atrocity, 1937–38: Complicating the Picture* (New York: Berghahn Books, 2007), pp. 304–29.

Kamer Kasım and Sedat Laçiner, eds., *The Armenian Diaspora in France, the United Kingdom, Germany and Australia* (Ankara: Türk-Ermeni İlişkileri Milli Komitesi Yayınları, 2003).

Velisarios Kattoulas, "Japan—Sorry Is the Hardest Word," *Far Eastern Economic Review,* vol. 164, no. 9 (8 March 2001), p. 56.

Peter J. Katzenstein, "Introduction: Alternative Perspectives on National Security," in Peter J. Katzenstein, ed., *The Culture of National Security: Norms and Identity in World Politics* (New York: Columbia University Press, 1996), pp. 1–32.

Stuart J. Kaufman, "Symbolic Politics or Rational Choice?: Testing Theories of Extreme Ethnic Violence," *International Security,* vol. 30, no. 4 (2006), pp. 45–86.

Chaim Kaufmann, "Threat Inflation and the Failure of the Marketplace of Ideas: The Selling of the Iraq War," *International Security,* vol. 29, no. 1 (2004), pp. 5–48.

Ilhan Kaya, "Turkish-American Immigration History and Identity Formations," *Journal of Muslim Minority Affairs,* vol. 24, no. 2 (2004), pp. 295–308.

——, "Identity across Generations: A Turkish American Case Study," *Middle East Journal,* vol. 63, no. 4 (2009), pp. 617–32.

Nurcan Kaya, *Forgotten or Assimilated? Minorities in the Education System of Turkey* (London: Minority Rights Group International, 2009).

Margaret E. Keck and Kathryn Sikkink, *Activists beyond Borders: Advocacy Networks in International Politics* (Ithaca, NY: Cornell University Press, 1998).

Judith Kelley, "International Actors on the Domestic Scene: Membership Conditionality and Socialization by International Institutions," *International Organization,* vol. 58, no. 3 (2004), pp. 425–57.

——, "Assessing the Complex Evolution of Norms: The Rise of International Election Monitoring," *International Organization,* vol. 62, no. 2 (2008), pp. 221–55.

Ferhat Kentel and Gevorg Poghosyan, "Armenian and Turkish Citizens' Mutual Perceptions and Dialogue Project" (Yerevan-Istanbul: TESEV and Sociological and Marketing Research Center, 2005).

Rikki Kersten, "Defeat and the Intellectual Culture of Postwar Japan," *European Review,* vol. 12, no. 4 (2004), pp. 497–512.

Eren Keskin, "Armenian Genocide 'Yesterday and Today,'" *University of Saint Thomas Journal of Law & Public Policy*, vol. 4, no. 2 (2009–10), pp. 31–35.

——, "1915 Soykırımdır!," *Özgür Gündem* (26 April 2011).

Raymond Kévorkian, *The Armenian Genocide: A Complete History* (London: I.B. Tauris, 2011).

Altemur Kılıç, Press Attaché, Turkish Embassy, Washington, "Letters to the Times: Visit of Turkish President," *New York Times* (1 February 1957), p. 24.

——, Information Counselor, Turkish Embassy, Washington, "Letters to the Editor of The Times: Turkish Citizens All," *New York Times* (4 May 1965), p. 42.

Hun Joon Kim, "Local, National, and International Determinants of Truth Commission: The South Korean Experience," *Human Rights Quarterly*, vol. 34, no. 3 (2012), pp. 726–50.

——, *The Massacres at Mt. Halla: Sixty Years of Truth Seeking in South Korea* (Ithaca, NY: Cornell University Press, 2014).

Kimura Takuji, "Nanking: Denial and Atonement in Contemporary Japan," in Bob Tadashi Wakabayashi, ed., *The Nanking Atrocity, 1937–38: Complicating the Picture* (New York: Berghahn Books, 2007), pp. 330–54.

David King and Miles Pomper, "The U.S. Congress and the Contingent Influence of Diaspora Lobbies: Lessons from U.S. Policy toward Armenia and Azerbaijan," *Journal of Armenian Studies*, vol. 8, no. 1 (2004), pp. 72–98.

Elisabeth King, "Memory Controversies in Post-Genocide Rwanda: Implications for Peacebuilding," *Genocide Studies and Prevention*, vol. 5, no. 3 (2010), pp. 293–309.

——, *From Classrooms to Conflict in Rwanda* (New York: Cambridge University Press, 2014).

Jeff Kingston, "Coded Rebuke as Japan's Crown Prince Says: Remember War 'Correctly,'" *CNN* (26 February 2015), available at: http://www.cnn.com/2015/02/26/opinion/japan-crown-prince-ww2-comments/index.html.

Masayuki Kitano, "Japan Court Rules for Chinese Victim of Nanjing," *Reuters News* (10 May 2002).

Richard D. Kloian, ed., *The Armenian Genocide: News Accounts from the American Press, 1915–1922* (Berkeley, CA: Anto Printing, 1985).

Yukiko Koga, "Accounting for Silence: Inheritance, Debt, and the Moral Economy of Legal Redress in China and Japan," *American Ethnologist*, vol. 40, no. 3 (2013), pp. 494–507.

——, "Between the Law: The Unmaking of Empire and Law's Imperial Amnesia," *Law & Social Inquiry*, vol. 41, no. 2 (2016), pp. 402–34.

Osman Köker, "Diyarbakırlı Bir Ermeni'nin Öyküsü," *Yazin Dergisi* (1 September 1995), available at: www.arasyayincilik.com/index.php?dispatch=pages.view&page_id=499.

——, ed., *100 Yıl Önce Türkiye'de Ermeniler: Orlando Carlo Calumeno Koleksiyonu'ndan Kartpostallarla* (İstanbul: Birzamanlar Yayıncılık, 2005).

Koshida Takashi, "Zenshin o Togetekita Kingendaishi Kijutsu," in Ishiwata Nobuo and Koshida Takashi, eds., *Sekai no Rekishi Kyōkasho* (Tōkyō: Akashi Shoten, 2002), pp. 265–72.

Dickran Kouymjian, "The Destruction of Armenian Historical Monuments as a Continuation of the Turkish Policy of Genocide," in Permanent Peoples' Tribunal, *A Crime of Silence: The Armenian Genocide* (London: Zed Books, 1985), pp. 173–85.

Alan Kramer, "The First Wave of International War Crimes Trials: Istanbul and Leipzig," *European Review*, vol. 14, no. 4 (2006), pp. 441–55.

Ronald R. Krebs, *Narrative and the Making of US National Security* (Cambridge: Cambridge University Press, 2015).

Ronald R. Krebs and Jennifer K. Lobasz, "Fixing the Meaning of 9/11: Hegemony, Coercion, and the Road to War in Iraq," *Security Studies*, vol. 16, no. 3 (2007), pp. 409–51.

Neil J. Kritz, ed., *How Emerging Democracies Reckon with Former Regimes, Volume I: General Considerations* (Washington, DC: USIP Press Books, 1995).

Jan Kubik and Michael Bernhard, "A Theory of the Politics of Memory," in Michael Bernhard and Jan Kubik, eds., *Twenty Years after Communism: The Politics of Memory and Commemoration* (New York: Oxford University Press, 2014), pp. 7–34.

Leo Kuper, *Genocide: Its Political Use in the Twentieth Century* (New Haven, CT: Yale University Press, 1981).

Dilek Kurban, "Unravelling a Trade-Off: Reconciling Minority Rights and Full Citizenship in Turkey," *European Yearbook of Minority Issues*, vol. 4 (2004/5), pp. 341–72.

——, "The Draft Law on Foundations Does Not Solve the Problems of Non-Muslim Foundations" (Istanbul: TESEV Democratization Program, 2007).

Dilek Kurban and Kezban Hatemi, *Bir 'Yabancı'laştırma Hikâyesi: Türkiye'de Gayrimüslim Cemaatlerin Vakıf ve Taşınmaz Mülkiyeti Sorunu* (İstanbul: TESEV Yayınları, 2009).

Ümit Kurt, "Legal and Official Plunder of Armenian and Jewish Properties in Comparative Perspective: The Armenian Genocide and the Holocaust," *Journal of Genocide Research*, vol. 17, no. 3 (2015), pp. 305–26.

Ümit Kurt and Bezen Balamir Coşkun, "History vs. Geopolitics: An Overview of Turkish-Armenian Relations in the 2000s," *Turkish Review*, vol. 3, no. 3 (2013), pp. 244–50.

Tuncer M. Kuzay, United Turkish Americans, letter to the editor, "Armenians' Fate: A Turkish View," *Wall Street Journal* (19 May 1983), p. 35.

Kwan Weng Kin, "The 'Sorry' That Sticks in Japan's Throat," *Straits Times* (14 May 1995).

——, "Tokyo Soothes Beijing over Governor-Elect's Remarks," *Straits Times* (20 April 1999).

Kyodo, "Ministry Explains Revisions," in FBIS, Daily Report: Asia and Pacific, FBIS-APA-82-154 (10 August 1982), p. C1.

——, "Spokesman Cited on 'Subdued' Response," in FBIS, Daily Report: East Asia, FBIS-EAS-89-111 (9 June 1989).

——, "Kaifu's Foreign Policy Speech," in FBIS, Daily Report: East Asia, FBIS-EAS-91-086 (3 May 1991).

——, "Dailies Welcome Emperor's Oct Visit to China," in FBIS, Daily Report: East Asia, FBIS-EAS-92-166 (26 August 1992a).

——, "'Full Text' of Miyazawa 30 Oct Policy Speech," in FBIS, Daily Report: East Asia, FBIS-EAS-92-211 (30 October 1992b).

——, "Political Scene 'May Be Good' for War Victims," in FBIS, Daily Report: East Asia, FBIS-EAS-93-144 (29 July 1993).

——, "SDPJ Urges Hata to Sack Nagano," in FBIS, Daily Report: East Asia, FBIS-EAS-94-088 (6 May 1994).

Kyodo News, "3RD LD: Japan Approves Nationalist-Authored History Text" (3 April 2001).

Lai Yew Meng, *Nationalism and Power Politics in Japan's Relations with China: A Neoclassical Realist Interpretation* (London: Routledge, 2014).

Lam Peng Er, ed., *Japan's Relations with Southeast Asia: The Fukuda Doctrine and Beyond* (Oxon: Routledge, 2012).

Eric Langenbacher, "Collective Memory as a Factor in Political Culture and International Relations," in Eric Langenbacher and Yossi Shain, eds., *Power and the Past: Collective Memory and International Relations* (Washington, DC: Georgetown University Press, 2010), pp. 13–49.

Eric Langenbacher and Yossi Shain, eds., *Power and the Past: Collective Memory and International Relations* (Washington, DC: Georgetown University Press, 2010).

Richard Ned Lebow, Wulf Kansteiner, and Claudio Fogu, eds., *The Politics of Memory in Postwar Europe* (Durham, NC: Duke University Press, 2006).

Bronwyn Anne Leebaw, "The Irreconcilable Goals of Transitional Justice," *Human Rights Quarterly*, vol. 30, no. 1 (2008), pp. 95–118.

——, *Judging State-Sponsored Violence, Imagining Political Change* (New York: Cambridge University Press, 2011).

Joanne Lee-Young, "Security Talks Hold Key to Ties, Says Japanese Envoy," *South China Morning Post* (10 December 1997).

Jeffrey W. Legro, "Which Norms Matter? Revisiting the 'Failure' of Internationalism," *International Organization*, vol. 51, no. 1 (1997), pp. 31–63.

Raphael Lemkin, *Axis Rule in Occupied Europe: Laws of Occupation—Analysis of Government—Proposals for Redress* (Washington, DC: Carnegie Endowment for International Peace, 1944).

——, "Genocide," *American Scholar*, vol. 15, no. 2 (1946), pp. 227–30.

Mark Levene, "Creating a Modern 'Zone of Genocide': The Impact of Nation- and State-Formation on Eastern Anatolia, 1878–1923," *Holocaust and Genocide Studies*, vol. 12, no. 3 (1998), pp. 393–433.

——, *Genocide in the Age of the Nation State The Meaning of Genocide.* Vol. 1. (London: I.B. Tauris, 2005).

Mark A. Levin, "Nishimatsu Construction Co. v. Song Jixiao et al.; Kō Hanako et al. v. Japan," *American Journal of International Law*, vol. 102, no. 1 (2008), pp. 148–54.

Jack S. Levy, "Case Studies: Types, Designs, and Logics of Inference," *Conflict Management and Peace Science*, vol. 25, no. 1 (2008), pp. 1–18.

Library of Congress, *House Joint Resolution 148*, 94th Congress (1975–1976), passed House on 8 April 1975.

——, *House Joint Congressional Resolution 126*, 105th Congress (1997–1998), 1st Session, introduced on 25 July 1997.

Dennis Lim, "Armenians Protest over Proposed Turkish Studies Chair," *Daily Bruin* (23 November 1997).

Jennifer Lind, *Sorry States: Apologies in International Politics* (Ithaca, NY: Cornell University Press, 2008).

Deborah E. Lipstadt, *Denying the Holocaust: The Growing Assault on Truth and Memory* (New York: Free Press, 1993).

O. Faruk Logoglu, "To Reconcile Turks and Armenians," *Washington Times* (2 May 2005).

Heath W. Lowry, "Leave Armenia's History to Historians," *Wall Street Journal* (15 November 1989).

——, "The State of the Field: A Retrospective Overview and Assessment of Ottoman Studies in the United States of America and Canada," *Turkish Studies Association Bulletin*, vol. 24, no. 1 (2000), pp. 65–119.

Cyanne E. Loyle and Christian Davenport, "Transitional Injustice: Subverting Justice in Transition and Postconflict Societies," *Journal of Human Rights*, vol. 15, no. 1 (2016), pp. 126–49.

Nava Löwenheim, "A Haunted Past: Requesting Forgiveness for Wrongdoing in International Relations," *Review of International Studies*, vol. 35, no. 3 (2009), pp. 531–55.

John Lubbock, "In Eastern Turkey, Walking in the Shadow of Genocide," *Global Voices* (30 April 2015), available at: https://globalvoices.org/2015/04/30/in-eastern-turkey-walking-in-the-shadow-of-genocide/.

Nicholas S. Ludington, "Soviet Hand Is Evident in Armenian Issue," *Los Angeles Times* (15 March 1983), p. C5.

Ömer Engin Lütem, ed., *Ermeni Sorunu: Temel Bilgi ve Belgeler* (Ankara: ASAM Yayınları, 2007).

——, *Armenian Terror* (Ankara: ERAREN, 2008).

Benjamin Madley, *An American Genocide: The United States and the California Indian Catastrophe, 1846–1873* (New Haven, CT: Yale University Press, 2016).

Charles S. Maier, *The Unmasterable Past: History, Holocaust, and German National Identity* (Cambridge, MA: Harvard University Press, 1988).

——, "Doing History, Doing Justice: The Narrative of the Historian and of the Truth Commission," in Robert I. Rotberg and Dennis Thompson, eds., *Truth v. Justice: The Morality of Truth Commissions* (Princeton, NJ: Princeton University Press, 2000), pp. 261–78.

Mainichi Daily News, "Undercurrents of National Security (1)—Nanking Issue Clouding US-Japan Ties" (2 June 1998).

Marc A. Mamigonian, "From Idea to Reality: The Development of Armenian Studies in the U.S. from the 1890s to 1969," *Journal of Armenian Studies*, vol. 10, nos. 1 and 2 (2012–13), pp. 153–84.

——, "Academic Denial of the Armenian Genocide in American Scholarship: Denialism as Manufactured Controversy," *Genocide Studies International*, vol. 9, no. 1 (2015), pp. 61–82.

Michael Mann, *The Dark Side of Democracy: Explaining Ethnic Cleansing* (New York: Cambridge University Press, 2005), pp. 111–79.

Levon Marashlian, "The Armenian Question from Sèvres to Lausanne: Economics and Morality in American and British Policies, 1920–1923," PhD diss., University of California, Los Angeles (1992).

Recep Maraşlı, *Ermeni Ulusal Demokratik Hareketi ve 1915 Soykırımı* (İstanbul: Peri Yayınları, 2008).

Michael R. Marrus, "Official Apologies and the Quest for Historical Justice," *Journal of Human Rights*, vol. 6, no. 1 (2007), pp. 75–105.

Trevor Marshallsea, "China Reminds Hashimoto to Remember History," *Asia Pulse* (5 September 1997).

Harutyun Marutyan, "Iconography of Historical Memory and Armenian National Identity at the End of the 1980s," in Tsypylma Darieva and Wolfgang Kaschuba, eds., *Representations on the Margins of Europe: Politics and Identities in the Baltic and South Caucasian States* (Frankfurt: Campus Verlag, 2007), pp. 89–113.

——, *Iconography of Armenian Identity, Vol. 1: The Memory of Genocide and the Karabagh Movement* (Yerevan: Gitutyun Publishing House, 2009).

Brian Masshardt, "Mobilizing from the Margins: Domestic Citizen Politics and Yasukuni Shrine," *East Asia*, vol. 24, no. 3 (2007), pp. 319–35.

Fukatsu Masumi, "The Eclipse of Shōwa Taboos and the Apology Resolution," *Japan Quarterly*, vol. 42, no. 4 (1995), pp. 419–25.

Lou Ann Matossian, "Institute of Turkish Studies Chair Was Ousted for Acknowledging Genocide," *Armenian Reporter*, no. 66 (31 May 2008a), pp. 1, 3.

——, "Turkish Officials Controlled Institute for Turkish Studies Pursestrings, Limiting Academic Freedom," *Armenian Reporter*, no. 73 (19 July 2008b), pp. 1, 3.

Justin McCarthy and Carolyn McCarthy, *Turks and Armenians: A Manual on the Armenian Question* (Washington, DC: Assembly of Turkish American Associations, 1989).

Terry McCarthy, "Country Wary of Emperor's Trip to China," *The Independent—London* (29 July 1992), p. 9.

Gavan McCormack, "The Japanese Movement to 'Correct' History," in Laura Hein and Mark Selden, eds., *Censoring History: Citizenship and Memory in Japan, Germany, and the United States* (Armonk, NY: M.E. Sharpe, 2000), pp. 53–73.

——, "New Tunes for an Old Song: Nationalism and Identity in Post-Cold War Japan," in Roy Starrs, ed., *Nations under Siege: Globalization and Nationalism in Asia* (New York: Palgrave, 2002), pp. 137–68.

Hamish McDonald and Deborah Cameron, "Rivalry Erupts into Rancour," *The Age* (16 April 2005), p. 4.

Peter McGill and Roy K. Akagawa, "Life—Crime and Confession on the Net (3757)," *Asahi Shimbun/Asahi Evening News* (22 August 1998).

Keith McLaughlin, "Chinese-Americans Seek to Make World Aware of 'Forgotten Holocaust,'" *Buffalo News* (15 August 1993), p. H10.

David McNeill and Mark Selden, "Japan's Past a Threat to Its Future," *Straits Times* (13 April 2005).

James Meernik, Rosa Aloisi, Marsha Sowell, and Angela Nichols, "The Impact of Human Rights Organizations on Naming and Shaming Campaigns," *Journal of Conflict Resolution*, vol. 56, no. 2 (2012), pp. 233–56.

Robert Melson, *Revolution and Genocide: On the Origins of the Armenian Genocide and the Holocaust* (Chicago: Chicago University Press, 1992).

David A. Mendeloff, "Truth-Telling and Mythmaking in Post-Soviet Russia: Pernicious Historical Ideas, Mass Education, and Interstate Conflict," PhD diss., Massachusetts Institute of Technology (2001).

——, "Truth-Seeking, Truth-Telling, and Postconflict Peacebuilding: Curb the Enthusiasm?," *International Studies Review*, vol. 6, no. 3 (2004), pp. 355–80.

——, "'Pernicious History' as a Cause of National Misperceptions: Russia and the 1999 Kosovo War," *Cooperation and Conflict*, vol. 43, no. 31 (2008), pp. 31–56.

——, "Trauma and Vengeance: Assessing the Psychological and Emotional Effects of Post-Conflict Justice," *Human Rights Quarterly*, vol. 31, no. 3 (2009), pp. 592–623.

MFA (Ministry of Foreign Affairs, Republic of Turkey), "Presentation by Ambassador Gündüz Aktan at the House Committee on International Relations on September 14, 2000" (2000), available at: www.mfa.gov.tr/presentation-by-ambassador-gunduz-aktan-at-the-house-committee-on-international-relations-on-september-14_-2000_.en.mfa.

——, "The Prime Minister of the Republic of Turkey, Recep Tayyip Erdoğan, on the Events of 1915, 24 April 2014" (23 April 2014), available at: www.mfa.gov.tr/basbakan-sayin-recep-tayyip-erdogan_in-1915-olaylarina-iliskin-mesaji_-23-nisan-2014.tr.mfa.

——, "Press Release regarding the Resolution by the European Parliament on the 1915 Events," No. 117 (15 April 2015), available at www.mfa.gov.tr/no_-117_-15-april-2015_-press-release-regarding-the-press-release-regarding-the-resolution-by-the-european-parliament-on-the-1915-events.en.mfa.

Middle East Studies Association, "Letter to Prime Minister Recep Tayyip Erdoğan," signed by Mervat Hatem, MESA President (27 May 2008), available at: mesa.wns.ccit.arizona.edu/caf/letters_turkey.html#May27Turkey.

Manus I. Midlarsky, *The Killing Trap: Genocide in the Twentieth Century* (Cambridge: Cambridge University Press, 2005).

Carol Migdalovitz, "92109: Armenia-Azerbaijan Conflict," *CRS Issue Brief* (3 December 1996).

Donald E. Miller and Lorna Touryan Miller, *Survivors: An Oral History of the Armenian Genocide* (Berkeley: University of California Press, 1993).

Manjari Chatterjee Miller, *Wronged by Empire: Post-Imperial Ideology and Foreign Policy in India and China* (Stanford, CA: Stanford University Press, 2013).

Michael Millett, "Japan's Take on History Upsets Neighbors," *Sydney Morning Herald* (3 March 2001), p. 20.

Milliyet, "Korutürk: Herkes Gözünü Biraz da Dış Âleme Çevirmeli" (2 April 1975).

Edward Minasian, "The Forty Years of Musa Dagh: The Film That Was Denied," *Journal of Armenian Studies*, vol. 3, nos. 1–2 (1986–87), pp. 121–32.

Richard H. Minear, *Victor's Justice: The Tokyo War Crimes Trial* (Princeton, NJ: Princeton University Press, 1971).

Ministry of Foreign Affairs of Japan, "Joint Communique of the Government of Japan and the Government of the People's Republic of China" (29 September 1972), available at: www.mofa.go.jp/region/asia-paci/china/joint72.html.

——, "Statement by Chief Cabinet Secretary Kiichi Miyazawa on History Textbooks" (26 August 1982), available at: www.mofa.go.jp/policy/postwar/state8208.html.

——, "Statement by Chief Cabinet Secretary Koichi Kato on the Issue of the So-Called 'Wartime Comfort Women' from the Korean Peninsula" (6 July 1992), available at: www.mofa.go.jp/policy/postwar/state9207.html.

——, "Statement by the Chief Cabinet Secretary Yohei Kono on the Result of the Study on the Issue of 'Comfort Women'" (4 August 1993), available at: www.mofa.go.jp/policy/women/fund/state9308.html.

——, "Statement by Prime Minister Tomiichi Murayama on the 'Peace, Friendship, and Exchange Initiative'" (31 August 1994), available at: www.mofa.go.jp/announce/press/pm/murayama/state9408.html.

——, "Statement by Prime Minister Tomiichi Murayama on the Occasion of the Establishment of the 'Asian Women's Fund'" (July 1995a), available at: www.mofa.go.jp/policy/women/fund/state9507.html.

——, "Statement by Prime Minister Tomiichi Murayama 'On the Occasion of the 50th Anniversary of the War's End'" (15 August 1995b), available at: www.mofa.go.jp/announce/press/pm/murayama/9508.html.

——, "Visit to the People's Republic of China by Prime Minister Junichiro Koizumi: Meeting with President Jiang Zemin (Overview and Evaluation)" (8 October 2001), available at: www.mofa.go.jp/region/asia-paci/china/pmv0110/meet-2.html.

——, "The First Meeting of the Japan-China Joint History Research Committee (Summary)" (December 2006), available at: www.mofa.go.jp/region/asia-paci/china/meet0612.html.

Ministry of National Education, "'Ermeni, Yunan-Pontus ve Süryaniler' ile İlgili Konuların Orta Öğretim Tarih 1, Tarih 2 ve T.C. İnkılâp Tarihi ve Atatürkçülük Dersi Öğretim Programlarında Yer Alması," *Tebliğler Dergisi*, vol. 65, no. 2538 (2002a), pp. 530–55.

——, "Ermeni Sorunu ile İlgili Programlara Girecek Konuların Açıklaması," *Tebliğler Dergisi*, vol. 65, no. 2539 (2002b), pp. 702–3.

Martha L. Minow, *Between Vengeance and Forgiveness: Facing History after Genocide and Mass Violence* (Boston: Beacon Press, 1998).

Alla Mirzoyan, *Armenia, the Regional Powers, and the West: Between History and Geopolitics* (New York: Palgrave Macmillan, 2010).

Rana Mitter, "Remembering the Forgotten War," *History Today*, vol. 55, no. 8 (2005), pp. 17–19.

Jennifer Mitzen, "Ontological Security in World Politics: State Identity and the Security Dilemma," *European Journal of International Relations*, vol. 12, no. 3 (2006), pp. 341–70.

Eugene Moosa, "Japanese Cabinet Minister Fired in Korean History Controversy," *Associated Press* (8 September 1986).

Henry Morgenthau, *Ambassador Morgenthau's Story* (Ann Arbor, MI: Gomidas Institute, 2000 [1918]).

Leonardo Morlino, "Authoritarian Legacies, Politics of the Past and the Quality of Democracy in Southern Europe: Open Conclusions," *South European Society and Politics*, vol. 15, no. 3 (2010), pp. 507–29.

James Morrison, "'Genocide' Denied," *Washington Times* (12 May 1994), p. A13.

———, "Remembering Armenia," *Washington Times* (3 May 1995), p. A12.

———, "Armenia's Proposals . . . ," *Washington Times* (8 October 1998), p. A15.

Tessa Morris-Suzuki, "Introduction: Confronting the Ghosts of War in East Asia," in Tessa Morris-Suzuki, Morris Low, Leonid Petrov, and Timothy Y. Tsu, eds., *East Asia beyond the History Wars: Confronting the Ghosts of Violence* (London: Routledge, 2013), pp. 1–26.

Khatchig Mouradian, "From Yeghern to Genocide: Armenian Newspapers, Raphael Lemkin, and the Road to the UN Genocide Convention," *Haigazian Armenological Review*, vol. 29 (2009), pp. 127–37.

———, "The Meskeneh Concentration Camp, 1915–1917: A Case Study of Power, Collaboration, and Humanitarian Resistance during the Armenian Genocide," *Journal of the Society of Armenian Studies*, vol. 24, no. 3 (2015), pp. 44–55.

———, "Genocide and Humanitarian Resistance in Ottoman Syria, 1915–1916," *Études Arméniennes Contemporaines*, vol. 7 (2016), pp. 87–103.

Steven Mufson, "Japanese Leader Makes Near Apology for World War II Aggression in China," *Washington Post* (5 May 1995), p. A30.

Pat Murdo, "Textbook Controversies in Japan: How Dead Are They?," *JEI Report*, vol. 1996, no. 5 (9 February 1996).

Mutsuko Murakami, "Writing New History," *South China Morning Post* (22 March 2003), p. 16.

Jan-Werner Müller, *Memory and Power in Post-War Europe: Studies in the Presence of the Past* (Cambridge: Cambridge University Press, 2002).

Norman M. Naimark, *Fires of Hatred: Ethnic Cleansing in Twentieth-Century Europe* (Cambridge, MA: Harvard University Press, 2001), pp. 17–56.

Yasuhiro Nakasone, *Japan—A State Strategy for the Twenty-First Century*, trans. Lesley Connors and Christopher P. Hood (London: RoutledgeCurzon, 2002).

Louise Nalbandian, *The Armenian Revolutionary Movement: The Development of Armenian Political Parties through the Nineteenth Century* (Los Angeles: University of California Press, 1963).

Monika Nalepa, *Skeletons in the Closet: Transitional Justice in Post-Communist Europe* (New York: Cambridge University Press, 2010).

Bogos Natanyan, *Sivas 1877*, ed. Arsen Yarman (İstanbul: Birzamanlar Yayıncılık, 2008).

National Archives and Records Administration, Document RG 59, 867.4016/67 (28 May 1915), Microfilm Publication M353: *Records of the Department of State Relating to the Internal Affairs of Turkey, 1910–1929*, Roll 43; General Records of the Department of State, Record Group 59.

National Diet of Japan, House of Representatives, "Resolution to Renew the Determination for Peace on the Basis of Lessons Learned from History" (9 June 1995), available at: www.mofa.go.jp/announce/press/pm/murayama/address9506.html.

Tigran Nazaryan, "Papazyan: It Is Difficult for Us to Be Friends with Turkey," *Hürriyet* (29 August 1993), p. 16, in FBIS, "Foreign Minister Discusses Relations with Turkey," Daily Report: Central Eurasia, FBIS-SOV-93-169 (2 September 1993), p. 56.

Mehmet Necef, "The Turkish Media Debate on the Armenian Massacre," in Steven L. B. Jensen, ed., *Genocide: Cases, Comparisons and Contemporary Debates* (Copenhagen: Danish Center for Holocaust and Genocide Studies, 2003), pp. 225–62.

Jeff Nesmith and Andrew Alexander, "U.S. Resolution on Armenian Deaths Is Threatening to Alienate Turkey," *Atlanta Journal-Constitution* (26 March 1987), p. A34.

Rafi Nets-Zehngut, "Origins of the Palestinian Refugee Problem: Changes in Historical Memory of Israelis/Jews 1949–2004," *Journal of Peace Research*, vol. 48, no. 2 (2011), pp. 235–48.

Rafi Nets-Zehngut and Daniel Bar-Tal, "Transformation of the Official Memory of Conflict: A Tentative Model and the Israeli Memory of the 1948 Palestinian Exodus," *International Journal of Politics, Culture, and Society*, vol. 27, no. 1 (2014), pp. 67–91.

New York Times, "Turkey Denies It Threatened Jews over Tel Aviv Parley on Genocide" (5 June 1982a).

——, "Newspeak in Japan" (25 August 1982b), editorial page.

——, "Turkey Warns of Retaliation" (16 July 1983), p. 10.

——, "U.S. House Resolution Angers Turkish Premier" (15 September 1984), p. 4.

——, "A Japanese View of World War II Is Attacked" (27 April 1988, late city final edition).

——, "U.S. Thinks Twice about Armenian Measure" (5 November 1989).

——, Editorial Board, "Turkey's Willful Amnesia" (17 April 2015).

Leyla Neyzi and Hranush Kharatyan-Araqelyan, *Speaking to One Another: Personal Memories of the Past in Armenia and Turkey* (Bonn: dvv international, 2010).

NHK General Television, "Text of Miyazawa Policy Speech," in FBIS, Daily Report: East Asia, FBIS-EAS-93-013 (22 January 1993).

NHK General Television Network, "Kaifu Delivers Policy Speech to Diet," in FBIS, Daily Report: East Asia, FBIS-EAS-91-150 (5 August 1991).

——, "Prime Minister Miyazawa Gives Diet Policy Speech," in FBIS, Daily Report: East Asia, FBIS-EAS-92-016 (24 January 1992a).

——, "Foreign Minister Watanabe's Diet Policy Speech," in FBIS, Daily Report: East Asia, FBIS-EAS-92-017 (24 January 1992b).

NHK Television Network, "Okita Delivers Foreign Policy Speech at Diet Reopening," in FBIS, Daily Report: Asia and Pacific, FBIS-APA-80-020 (29 January 1980), p. C1.

——, "Suzuki Gives Press Conference 23 August," in FBIS, Daily Report: Asia and Pacific, FBIS-APA-82-166 (26 August 1982), p. C1.

——, "Nakasone Delivers Policy Speech at Diet Session," in FBIS, Daily Report: Asia and Pacific, FBIS-APA-83-017 (25 January 1983), p. C4.

Colin Nickerson, "Neighbors Fear a Japan Militarily Resurgent: Troop-Movement Decision Raises Old Alarms," *Boston Globe* (28 June 1992), p. 68.

Sevan Nişanyan, *Hayali Coğrafyalar: Cumhuriyet Döneminde Türkiye'de Değiştirilen Yeradları* (İstanbul: TESEV Yayınları, 2011).

Melissa Nobles, *The Politics of Official Apologies* (New York: Cambridge University Press, 2008).

Pierre Nora, "Between Memory and History: Les Lieux de Memoire," *Representations*, no. 26 (Spring 1989), pp. 7–24.

Yoshiko Nozaki, "Japanese Politics and the History Textbook Controversy, 1982–2001," *International Journal of Education Research*, vol. 37, nos. 6 and 7 (2002), pp. 603–22.

——, *War Memory, Nationalism and Education in Postwar Japan, 1945–2007: The Japanese History Textbook Controversy and Ienaga Saburo's Court Challenges* (London: Routledge, 2008).

Nozaki Yoshiko and Inokuchi Hiromitsu, "Japanese Education, Nationalism, and Ienaga Saburō's Textbook Lawsuits," in Laura Hein and Mark Selden, eds., *Censoring History: Citizenship and Memory in Japan, Germany, and the United States* (Armonk, NY: M.E. Sharpe, 2000), pp. 96–126.

Joseph S. Nye, Jr., "Nuclear Learning and U.S.-Soviet Security Regimes," *International Organization*, vol. 41, no. 3 (1987), pp. 371–402.

Obata Misao, "In the Magazines," *Japan Quarterly*, vol. 17, no. 1 (1970), pp. 92–98.

David Oberman, "A Guilty Emperor?," *Jerusalem Post* (9 January 1989).

Official Journal of the European Communities, "Resolution on a Political Solution to the Armenian Question," Doc. A2-33/87, No. C 190/119-120 (18 June 1987).

Shuko Ogawa, "The Difficulty of Apology: Japan's Struggle with Memory and Guilt," *Harvard International Review*, vol. 22, no. 3 (2000), pp. 42–46.

Takushi Ohno, "United States Policy on Japanese War Reparations, 1945–1951," *Asian Studies*, vol. 13, no. 3 (1975), pp. 23–45.

Hisahiko Okazaki, "Insights into the World: Let Historians Handle Japanese History," *Daily Yomiuri/Yomiuri Shimbun* (17 April 2000).

Ertuğrul Zekâi Ökte, ed., *Ottoman Archives: Yıldız Collection: The Armenian Question*, 3 vols. (İstanbul: Tarihi Araştırmalar ve Dokümantasyon Merkezleri Kurma ve Geliştirme Vakfı Yayınları, 1989).

Emre Öktem, "Turkey: Successor or Continuing State of the Ottoman Empire?" *Leiden Journal of International Law*, vol. 24, no. 3 (2011), pp. 561–83.

Kerem Öktem, "The Nation's Imprint: Demographic Engineering and the Change of Toponymes in Republican Turkey," *European Journal of Turkish Studies*, vol. 7 (2008), available at: http://journals.openedition.org/ejts/2243.

——, *Angry Nation: Turkey Since 1989* (London: Zed Books, 2011).

Jeffrey K. Olick, "What Does It Mean to Normalize the Past? Official Memory in German Politics Since 1989," *Social Science History*, vol. 22, no. 4 (1998), pp. 547–71.

——, "Genre Memories and Memory Genres: A Dialogical Analysis of May 8, 1945 Commemorations in the Federal Republic of Germany," *American Sociological Review*, vol. 64, no. 3 (1999), pp. 381–402.

——, *The Politics of Regret: On Collective Memory and Historical Responsibility* (New York: Routledge, 2007).

Jeffrey K. Olick and Daniel Levy, "Collective Memory and Cultural Constraint: Holocaust Myth and Rationality in German Politics," *American Sociological Review*, vol. 62, no. 6 (1997), pp. 921–36.

Jeffrey K. Olick and Joyce Robbins, "Social Memory Studies: From 'Collective Memory' to the Historical Sociology of Mnemonic Practices," *Annual Review of Sociology*, vol. 24 (1998), pp. 105–40.

Jeffrey K. Olick, Vered Vinitzky-Seroussi, and Daniel Levy, "Introduction," in Jeffrey K. Olick, Vered Vinitzky-Seroussi, and Daniel Levy, eds., *The Collective Memory Reader* (New York: Oxford University Press, 2011), pp. 3–62.

Robert W. Olson, "The Remains of Talat: A Dialectic between Republic and Empire," *Die Welt des Islams*, vol. 26, no. 1 (1986), pp. 46–56.

Barry O'Neill, *Honor, Symbols, and War* (Ann Arbor: University of Michigan Press, 1999).

Mark O'Neill, "China Victims to Take First War Claim to Tokyo," *Reuters News* (5 July 1995).

Norimitsu Onishi, "Japan Lodges Protest in Response to Demonstrations in China," *New York Times* (10 April 2005).

Norimitsu Onishi and Howard W. French, "Ill Will Rising between China and Japan as Old Grievances Fuel New Era of Rivalry," *New York Times* (3 August 2005), p. 7.

Baskın Oran, *Türkiye'de Azınlıklar: Kavramlar, Lozan, İç Mevzuat, İçtihat, Uygulama* (İstanbul: TESEV Yayınları, 2004).

Şinasi Orel and Süreyya Yuca, *Ermenilerce Talât Paşa'ya Atfedilen Telgrafların Gerçek Yüzü* (Ankara: TTK Yayınları, 1983).

——, *The Talât Pasha "Telegrams": Historical Fact or Armenian Fiction?* (London: K. Rustem & Brother, 1986).

James J. Orr, *The Victim as Hero: Ideologies of Peace and National Identity in Japan* (Honolulu: University of Hawai'i Press, 2001).

OsterDowJones Commodity Wire, "Japan War Record Comment Not Seen as Breaking New Ground" (22 April 2005).

John Owen-Davies, "Turkey Says Armenians Join Forces with Kurds," *Reuters News* (7 December 1989).

Ichirō Ozawa, *Blueprint for a New Japan: The Rethinking of a Nation*, trans. Louisa Rubinfien (Tokyo: Kodansha International, 1994).

Sadullah Özcan, "Ermeni Üst Kurulu Oluşturuldu, Başkanı Devlet Bahçeli," *Zaman* (18 May 2002).

Hikmet Özdemir, *Salgın Hastalıklardan Ölümler 1914–1918* (Ankara: TTK Yayınları, 2005).

——, *Ermeni İddiaları Karşısında Türkiye'nin Birikimi* (Ankara: TBMM Basımevi, 2008).

Hikmet Özdemir, Kemal Çiçek, Ömer Turan, Ramazan Çalık, and Yusuf Halaçoğlu, *Ermeniler: Sürgün ve Göç* (Ankara: TTK Yayınları, 2004).

Oktay Ozel, "My Hrant, or Historian's Guilt," *Armenian Weekly* (12 February 2009).

Ayhan Ozer, Public Relations Director, Federation of Turkish American Societies, letter to the editor, "Armenian Insurgencies," *New York Times* (10 May 1986), p. 26.

Özgür Politika, "Soykırım Olsa Ermeni Kalır mıydı?" (24 May 2003).

Esra Özyürek, "Introduction: The Politics of Public Memory in Turkey," in Esra Özyürek, ed., *The Politics of Public Memory in Turkey* (Syracuse, NY: Syracuse University Press, 2007), pp. 1–15.

Ahmet Bekir Palazoğlu and Osman Bircan, *Türkiye Cumhuriyeti İnkılâp Tarihi ve Atatürkçülük 1* (İstanbul: Koza Eğitim ve Yayıncılık Ltd. Şti., 1995).

Razmik Panossian, "Between Ambivalence and Intrusion: Politics and Identity in Armenia-Diaspora Relations," *Diaspora: A Journal of Transnational Studies*, vol. 7, no. 2 (1998), pp. 149–96.

Cheol Hee Park, "Conservative Conceptions of Japan as a 'Normal Country': Comparing Ozawa, Nakasone, and Ishihara," in Yoshihide Soeya, Masayuki Tadokoro, and David A. Welch, eds., *Japan as a 'Normal Country'?: A Nation in Search of Its Place in the World* (Toronto: University of Toronto Press, 2011), pp. 98–120.

Soon-Won Park, "A History That Opens the Future: The First Common China-Japan-Korea History Teaching Guide," in Gi-Wook Shin and Daniel C. Sneider, eds., *History Textbooks and the Wars in Asia: Divided Memories* (Oxon: Routledge, 2011), pp. 230–45.

İsmet Parmaksızoğlu, *Ortaokul Türkiye Cumhuriyeti İnkılâp Tarihi ve Atatürkçülük* (İstanbul: Milsan Basın Sanayi A.Ş., 1988).

Rachel Anderson Paul, "Grassroots Mobilization and Diaspora Politics: Armenian Interest Groups and the Role of Collective Memory," *Nationalism and Ethnic Politics*, vol. 6, no. 1 (2000), pp. 24–47.

Edwin W. Pauley, "Report on Japanese Reparations to the President of the United States, November 1945 to April 1946," Department of State Publication 3174, Far Eastern Series 25 (Washington, DC: Division of Publications, Office of Public Affairs, 1946).

Natalie Obiko Pearson, "Japanese Education Minister Says More Patriotism Necessary in Schools," *Associated Press Newswires* (11 June 2005).

T. J. Pempel, *Regime Shift: Comparative Dynamics of the Japanese Political Economy* (Ithaca, NY: Cornell University Press, 1998).

Christine Philliou, "The Armenian Genocide and the Politics of Knowledge," *Public Books* (1 May 2015), available at: www.publicbooks.org/nonfiction/the-armenian-genocide-and-the-politics-of-knowledge.

David L. Phillips, *Unsilencing the Past: Track Two Diplomacy and Turkish-Armenian Reconciliation* (New York: Berghahn Books, 2005).

——, "Diplomatic History: The Turkey-Armenia Protocols," Report, Institute for the Study of Human Rights, Columbia University (2012).

Paul Pierson, "Increasing Returns, Path Dependence, and the Study of Politics," *American Political Science Review*, vol. 94, no. 2 (2000), pp. 251–67.

——, *Politics in Time: History, Institutions, and Social Analysis* (Princeton, NJ: Princeton University Press, 2004).

Nicola Piper, "Transnational Women's Activism in Japan and Korea: The Unresolved Issue of Military Sexual Slavery," *Global Networks*, vol. 1, no. 2 (2001), pp. 155–70.

Mehmet Polatel, Nora Mıldanoğlu, Özgür Leman Eren, and Mehmet Atılgan, *2012 Declaration: The Seized Properties of Armenian Foundations in Istanbul* (İstanbul: Hrant Dink Foundation Publications, 2012).

"POWs/Forced Labor: Japan," Memory & Reconciliation in the Asia-Pacific (Washington, DC: The George Washington University, n.d.), available at: https://www.gwu.edu /%7Ememory/data/judicial/POWs_and_Forced_Labor_Japan/pows_forcedlabor _japan.html.

John Prendergast and David Smock, *Post-Genocidal Reconstruction: Building Peace in Rwanda and Burundi*, United States Institute of Peace, Special Report no. 53 (1999).

Richard Price, "Reversing the Gunsights: Transnational Civil Society Targets Landmines," *International Organization*, vol. 52, no. 3 (1998), pp. 613–44.

Prime Minister of the Republic of Turkey, "Statement by His Excellency Mr. Ahmet Davutoğlu, Prime Minister of the Republic of Turkey on the Ottoman Armenians Who Lost Their Lives during the Last Years of the Ottoman Empire" (April 2015), available at: www.basbakanlik.gov.tr/Forms/_Article/pg_Article.aspx?Id=7dfcf217 -12f7-4354-b37b-6e78664fbe8f.

Kenneth B. Pyle, *Japan Rising: The Resurgence of Japanese Power and Purpose* (New York: PublicAffairs, 2007).

Donald Quataert, "The Massacres of Ottoman Armenians and the Writing of Ottoman History," *Journal of Interdisciplinary History*, vol. 37, no. 2 (2006), pp. 249–59.

John Rabe, *The Good Man of Nanking: The Diaries of John Rabe* (New York: Alfred A. Knopf, 1998).

Kevin Rafferty, "Emperor Akihito Will Not Apologise for Past during Visit to China," *The Guardian* (25 August 1992).

——, "Hosokawa Rules Out Cash Settlement for War Victims," *The Guardian* (26 August 1993), p. 7.

Elizabeth Redden, "Turkey's Take Back," *Inside Higher Ed* (22 December 2015).

James Reston Jr., "How Japan Teaches Its Own History: The Nation Is Debating Revisions in Its Textbooks," *New York Times* (27 October 1985), p. SM52.

Reuters News, "Turkish President Urges Bush to Stop Pro-Armenian Resolution" (13 October 1989a).

——, "Turkey Links Armenians with Kurdish Rebels" (6 December 1989b).

Michael Reynolds, "Missing Context," *Journal of Genocide Research*, vol. 15, no. 4 (2013), pp. 472–78.

Thomas Risse, "International Norms and Domestic Change: Arguing and Communicative Behavior in the Human Rights Area," *Politics and Society*, vol. 27, no. 4 (1999), pp. 529–59.

Thomas Risse, Stephen C. Ropp, and Kathryn Sikkink, eds., *The Power of Human Rights: International Norms and Domestic Change* (Cambridge: Cambridge University Press, 1999).

——, eds., *The Persistent Power of Human Rights: From Commitment to Compliance* (Cambridge: Cambridge University Press, 2013).

Thomas Risse-Kappen, "Public Opinion, Domestic Structure, and Foreign Policy in Liberal Democracies," *World Politics*, vol. 43, no. 4 (1991), pp. 479–512.

——, "Ideas Do Not Float Freely: Transnational Coalitions, Domestic Structures, and the End of the Cold War," *International Organization*, vol. 48, no. 2 (1994), pp. 185–214.

Natasha Robinson, "Armenian Genocide the Final Frontier—ANZAC DAY 2010," *Weekend Australian* (24 April 2010), p. 9.

Naomi Roht-Arriaza and Javier Mariezcurrena, eds., *Transitional Justice in the Twenty-First Century: Beyond Truth versus Justice* (Cambridge: Cambridge University Press, 2006).

Caroline Rose, *Interpreting History in Sino-Japanese Relations* (London: Routledge, 1998).

——, *Sino-Japanese Relations: Facing the Past, Looking to the Future?* (London: Routledge, 2005).

Denny Roy, "Stirring Samurai, Disapproving Dragon: Japan's Growing Security Activity and Sino-Japan Relations," *Asian Affairs*, vol. 31, no. 2 (2004), pp. 86–101.

Amy Magaro Rubin, "Critics Accuse Turkish Government of Manipulating Scholarship," *Chronicle of Higher Education* (27 October 1995).

R. J. Rummel, *Death by Government* (New Brunswick, NJ: Transaction Publishers, 1994).

Yongwook Ryu, "The Yasukuni Controversy: Divergent Perspectives from the Japanese Political Elite," *Asian Survey*, vol. 47, no. 5 (2007), pp. 705–26.

Sven Saaler, *Politics, Memory and Public Opinion: The History Textbook Controversy and Japanese Society* (Tokyo: Deutsches Institut für Japanstudien, 2005).

——, "Book Review: *War Memory and Social Politics in Japan, 1945–2005*," *Social Science Journal Japan* (25 February 2008), available at: http://ssjj.oxfordjournals.org/cgi/content/full/jyn004v1?ck=nck.

——, "Nationalism and History in Contemporary Japan," *Japan Focus*, vol. 14, no. 20 (2016), pp. 1–17.

Richard J. Samuels, "Japan in 1989: Changing Times," *Asian Survey*, vol. 30, no. 1 (1990), pp. 42–51.

——, "Kishi and Corruption: An Anatomy of the 1955 System," JPRI Working Paper, No. 83 (December 2001).

——, *Securing Japan: Tokyo's Grand Strategy and the Future of East Asia* (Ithaca, NY: Cornell University Press, 2007).

San Francisco Chronicle, "Turkey Criticizes Report on Armenian Genocide" (20 August 1985), p. 14.

Rebecca Sanders, "Legal Frontiers: Targeted Killing at the Borders of War," *Journal of Human Rights*, vol. 13, no. 4 (2014), pp. 512–36.

——, "Norm Proxy War and Resistance through Outsourcing: The Dynamics of Transnational Human Rights Contestation," *Human Rights Review*, vol. 17, no. 2 (2016), pp. 165–91.

Ara Sarafian, ed., *United States Official Documents on the Armenian Genocide* (Watertown, MA: Armenian Review Press, 1993a).

——, "The Issue of Access to the Ottoman Archives," *Zeitschrift für Türkeistudien*, vol. 6, no. 1 (1993b), pp. 93–99.

——, "The New Thinking Revisited: Gerard Libaridian Speaks at Princeton University," *Armenian Forum*, vol. 1, no. 2 (1998), p. 139.

——, "The Ottoman Archives Debate and the Armenian Genocide," *Armenian Forum*, vol. 2, no. 1 (1999), pp. 35–44.

——, "The Absorption of Armenian Women and Children into Muslim Households as a Structural Component of the Armenian Genocide," in Omer Bartov and Phyllis Mack, eds., *In God's Name: Genocide and Religion in the Twentieth Century* (New York: Berghahn Books, 2001), pp. 209–17.

Lale Sarıibrahimoğlu, "Ankara to Renew Diplomatic Action on Armenia," *Today's Zaman* (14 April 2007).

Joachim J. Savelsberg, "Tribunals, Collective Memory, and Prospects of Human Rights," in Werner Gephart, Jürgen Brokoff, Andrea Schütte, and Jan Christoph Suntrup, eds., *Tribunale: Literarische Darstellung und juridische Aufarbeitung von Kriegsverbrechen im globalen Kontext* (Frankfurt am Main: Klostermann, 2013), pp. 117–34.

Dominik J. Schaller and Jürgen Zimmerer, eds., *Late Ottoman Genocides: The Dissolution of the Ottoman Empire and Young Turkish Population and Extermination Policies* (London: Routledge, 2009).

John Schauble, "A Bridge Long in the Crossing," *The Age* (13 October 2001), p. 4.

Eric Schickler, *Disjointed Pluralism: Institutional Innovation and the Development of the U.S. Congress* (Princeton, NJ: Princeton University Press, 2001).

Frank Schimmelfennig, "Strategic Calculation and International Socialization: Membership Incentives, Party Constellations, and Sustained Compliance in Central and Eastern Europe," *International Organization*, vol. 59, no. 4 (2005), pp. 827–60.

——, "EU Political Accession Conditionality after the 2004 Enlargement: Consistency and Effectiveness," *Journal of European Public Policy*, vol. 15, no. 6 (2008), pp. 918–37.

Leonard J. Schoppa, "Two-Level Games and Bargaining Outcomes: Why *Gaiatsu* Succeeds in Japan in Some Cases but Not Others," *International Organization*, vol. 47, no. 3 (1993), pp. 353–86.

Mark Lawrence Schrad, *The Political Power of Bad Ideas: Networks, Institutions, and the Global Prohibition Wave* (New York: Oxford University Press, 2010).

Michael Schudson, *Watergate in American Memory: How We Remember, Forget, and Reconstruct the Past* (New York: BasicBooks, 1992).

Howard Schuman and Willard L. Rodgers, "Cohorts, Chronology, and Collective Memories," *Public Opinion Quarterly*, vol. 68, no. 2 (2004), pp. 217–54.

Howard Schuman and Jacqueline Scott, "Generations and Collective Memories," *American Sociological Review*, vol. 54, no. 3 (1989), pp. 359–81.

Barry Schwartz, "Rethinking Conflict and Collective Memory: The Case of Nanking," in Jeffrey C. Alexander, Ronald N. Jacobs, and Philip Smith, eds., *The Oxford Handbook of Cultural Sociology* (Oxford: Oxford University Press, 2012), pp. 529–63.

Philip A. Seaton, *Japan's Contested War Memories: The 'Memory Rifts' in Historical Consciousness of World War II* (London: Routledge, 2007).

Sekai, "Owada, Asahi Editor Discuss Tokyo's Diplomacy," in FBIS, Daily Report: East Asia, Annex, FBIS-EAS-92-025-A (1 December 1991), pp. 34–47.

Jacques Sémelin, *Purify and Destroy: The Political Uses of Massacre and Genocide* (New York: Columbia University Press, 2007).

Banu Şenay, "Trans-Kemalism: The Politics of the Turkish State in the Diaspora," *Ethnic and Racial Studies*, vol. 35, no. 9 (2011), pp. 1615–33.

——, *Beyond Turkey's Borders: Long-Distance Kemalism, State Politics and the Turkish Diaspora* (London: I.B. Tauris, 2013).

Nabi Şensoy, Ambassador of Turkey, Washington, "Turks and Armenians," *New York Times* (24 May 2006), p. A26.

——, "Turkey's Response to ADL Controversy," *The Advocate* (5 September 2007).

Güler Şenünver, H. Samim Kesim, Rıfat Turgut, and Aliye Akay, *Orta Okullar İçin Türkiye Cumhuriyeti İnkılâp Tarihi ve Atatürkçülük III* (Ankara: Türk Tarih Kurumu Basımevi, 1989).

Franziska Seraphim, *War Memory and Social Politics in Japan, 1945–2005* (Cambridge, MA: Harvard University Asia Center, 2006).

Setting the Record Straight on Armenian Propaganda against Turkey (Ankara: Dış Politika Enstitüsü, 1982).

Ali Ferda Sevin, President, Assembly of Turkish American Associations, letter to the editor, "Turkish Ordeal," *Washington Post* (8 June 1991), p. A20.

Menachem Shalev, "Embassy Went Too Far in Armenian Affair," *Jerusalem Post* (24 October 1989).

Shaul R. Shenhav, *Analyzing Social Narratives* (New York: Routledge, 2015).

Daiki Shibuichi, "Japan's History Textbook Controversy: Social Movements and Governments in East Asia, 1982–2006," *Electronic Journal of Contemporary Japanese Studies*, Discussion Paper 4 (March 2008).

——, "The Japan Conference (Nippon Kaigi): An Elusive Conglomerate," *East Asia*, vol. 34, no. 3 (2017), pp. 179–96.

Shuji Shimokoji, "'Historical Issues' in Japanese Diplomacy toward Neighboring Countries," Fellows Program of the Weatherhead Center for International Affairs, Harvard University (2003).

Gi-Wook Shin, "History Textbooks, Divided Memories, and Reconciliation," in Gi-Wook Shin and Daniel C. Sneider, eds., *History Textbooks and the Wars in Asia: Divided Memories* (Oxon: Routledge, 2011), pp. 3–19.

Tomohito Shinoda, "Japan's Top-Down Policy Process to Dispatch the SDF to Iraq," *Japanese Journal of Political Science*, vol. 7, no. 1 (2006), pp. 71–91.

——, *Koizumi Diplomacy: Japan's Kantei Approach to Foreign and Defense Affairs* (Seattle: University of Washington Press, 2007).

Shukan Jiji, "Sakurai on Fate of 'Illegitimate Coalition,'" in FBIS, Daily Report: East Asia, FBIS-EAS-94-186 (3 September 1994), pp. 27–29.

Aline Sierp and Jenny Wüstenberg, "Linking the Local and the Transnational: Rethinking Memory Politics in Europe," *Journal of Contemporary European Studies*, vol. 23, no. 3 (2015), pp. 321–29.

Kathryn Sikkink, *The Justice Cascade: How Human Rights Prosecutions Are Changing World Politics* (New York: W. W. Norton, 2011).

Beth A. Simmons, *Mobilizing for Human Rights: International Law in Domestic Politics* (New York: Cambridge University Press, 2009).

Bilâl N. Şimşir, *The Genesis of the Armenian Question* (Ankara: Turkish Historical Society, 1982a [1984; 2003]).

——, ed., *British Documents on Ottoman Armenians, Volume I (1856–1880)* (Ankara: TTK Printing Office, 1982b).

——, ed., *British Documents on Ottoman Armenians, Volume II (1880–1890)* (Ankara: TTK Printing Office, 1983).

——, ed., *British Documents on Ottoman Armenians, Volume III: 1891–1895* (Ankara: TTK Basımevi, 1989).

——, ed., *British Documents on Ottoman Armenians, Volume IV: 1895* (Ankara: TTK Basımevi, 1990).

——, *Şehit Diplomatlarımız*, 2 vols. (Ankara: Bilgi Yayınevi, 2000).

Charles Smith, "Foot in the Mouth: Minister's Comments Upset Asian Neighbors," *Far Eastern Economic Review*, vol. 157, no. 20 (19 May 1994a), p. 30.

——, "War and Remembrance," *Far Eastern Economic Review*, vol. 157, no. 34 (25 August 1994b), pp. 22–24.

——, "The Textbook Truth: Children Finally Exposed to Wartime Facts," *Far Eastern Economic Review*, vol. 157, no. 34 (25 August 1994c), pp. 26–27.

Roger W. Smith, "Genocide and Denial: The Armenian Case and Its Implications," *Armenian Review*, vol. 42, no. 1 (1989), pp. 1–38.

Sheila A. Smith, *Intimate Rivals: Japanese Domestic Politics and a Rising China* (New York: Columbia University Press, 2015).

Janet Snyder, "China to Get Same War Apology from Japan as SKorea," *Reuters News* (9 October 1998).

Yoshihide Soeya, "A 'Normal' Middle Power: Interpreting Changes in Japanese Security Policy in the 1990s and After," in Yoshihide Soeya, Masayuki Tadokoro, and David A. Welch, eds., *Japan as a 'Normal Country'?: A Nation in Search of Its Place in the World* (Toronto: University of Toronto Press, 2011), pp. 72–97.

Yoshihide Soeya, Masayuki Tadokoro, and David A. Welch, "Introduction: What Is a 'Normal Country'?," in Yoshihide Soeya, Masayuki Tadokoro, and David A. Welch, eds., *Japan as a 'Normal Country'?: A Nation in Search of Its Place in the World* (Toronto: University of Toronto Press, 2011a), pp. 3–15.

——, eds., *Japan as a 'Normal Country'?: A Nation in Search of Its Place in the World* (Toronto: University of Toronto Press, 2011b).

C. Sarah Soh, "Japan's Responsibility toward Comfort Women Survivors," JPRI Working Paper No. 77, Japan Policy Research Institute (May 2001), available at: http://www .jpri.org/publications/workingpapers/wp77.html.

——, *The Comfort Women: Sexual Violence and Postcolonial Memory in Korea and Japan* (Chicago: University of Chicago Press, 2008).

Felix Soh, "Japanese Nationalism 'Could Re-emerge,'" *Straits Times* (31 August 1996).

Salâhi R. Sonyel, "Armenian Deportations: A Re-appraisal in the Light of New Documents," *Belleten*, vol. 36, no. 141 (1972), pp. 51–69.

——, "Turco-Armenian Relations in the Context of the Jewish Holocaust," *Belleten*, vol. 54, no. 210 (1990), pp. 757–72.

——, *Turkey's Struggle for Liberation and the Armenians* (Ankara: Ministry of Foreign Affairs, SAM, 2001).

South China Morning Post, "Japan Announces Goodwill Visit by Emperor Akihito" (26 August 1992a.)

——, "Akihito Must Follow the Japanese Script during His Visit to China" (18 October 1992b).

"Speech by Takeo Fukuda," *Contemporary Southeast Asia*, vol. 2, no. 1 (1980), pp. 69–73.

Lavinia Stan, *Transitional Justice in Post-Communist Romania: The Politics of Memory* (New York: Cambridge University Press, 2012).

Ervin Staub, *The Roots of Evil: The Origins of Genocide and Other Group Violence* (Cambridge: Cambridge University Press, 1989).

Patricia G. Steinhoff, "Doing the Defendant's Laundry: Support Groups as Social Movement Organizations in Contemporary Japan," *Japanstudien*, vol. 11, no. 1 (1999), pp. 55–78.

Straits Times, "Miyazawa 'Won't Let Akihito Say Sorry during China Visit'" (6 August 1992).

——, "War of Words over Japan's Militarist Past" (26 January 1997).

Scott Straus, *The Order of Genocide: Race, Power, and War in Rwanda* (Ithaca, NY: Cornell University Press, 2006).

——, "Second-Generation Comparative Research on Genocide," *World Politics*, vol. 59, no. 3 (2007), pp. 476–501.

——, "Retreating from the Brink: Theorizing Mass Violence and the Dynamics of Restraint," *Perspectives on Politics*, vol. 10, no. 2 (2012), pp. 343–62.

——, *Making and Unmaking Nations: War, Leadership, and Genocide in Modern Africa* (Ithaca, NY: Cornell University Press, 2015).

Wolfgang Streeck and Kathleen Thelen, eds., *Beyond Continuity: Institutional Change in Advanced Political Economies* (Oxford: Oxford University Press, 2005).

Mükerrem K. Su and Ahmet Mumcu, *Lise Türkiye Cumhuriyeti İnkılâp Tarihi ve Atatürkçülük* (İstanbul: Milli Eğitim Basımevi, 1983).

Jelena Subotić, *Hijacked Justice: Dealing with the Past in the Balkans* (Ithaca, NY: Cornell University Press, 2009).

——, "Expanding the Scope of Post-Conflict Justice: Individual, State and Societal Responsibility for Mass Atrocity," *Journal of Peace Research*, vol. 48, no. 2 (2011), pp. 157–69.

——, "Stories States Tell: Identity, Narrative, and Human Rights in the Balkans," *Slavic Review*, vol. 72, no. 2 (2013), pp. 306–26.

——, "Bargaining Justice: A Theory of Transitional Justice Compliance," in Susanne Buckley-Zistel, Teresa Koloma Beck, Christian Braun, and Friederike Mieth, eds., *Transitional Justice Theories* (London: Routledge, 2014), pp. 127–43.

Talin Suciyan, *The Armenians in Modern Turkey: Post-Genocide Society, Politics and History* (London: I. B. Tauris, 2016).

Lena H. Sun, "Emperor Regrets War Acts in China; Japan's Akihito Stops Short of an Apology," *Washington Post* (24 October 1992).

Ronald Grigor Suny, *Looking toward Ararat: Armenia in Modern History* (Bloomington, IN: Indiana University Press, 1993).

——, "*AHR Forum*: Truth in Telling: Reconciling Realities in the Genocide of the Ottoman Armenians," *American Historical Review* (October 2009), pp. 930–46.

——, "*They Can Live in the Desert but Nowhere Else*": *A History of the Armenian Genocide* (Princeton, NJ: Princeton University Press, 2015).

Ronald Grigor Suny and Fatma Müge Göçek, "Introduction: Leaving It to the Historians," in Ronald Grigor Suny, Fatma Müge Göçek, and Norman M. Naimark, eds., *A Question of Genocide: Armenians and Turks at the End of the Ottoman Empire* (New York: Oxford University Press, 2011), pp. 3–11.

Ronald Grigor Suny, Fatma Müge Göçek, and Norman M. Naimark, eds., *A Question of Genocide: Armenians and Turks at the End of the Ottoman Empire* (New York: Oxford University Press, 2011).

Supreme Commander for the Allied Powers, "Special Proclamation: Establishment of an International Military Tribunal for the Far East" (19 January 1946), available at: http://www.un.org/en/genocideprevention/documents/atrocity-crimes/Doc.3_1946%20Tokyo%20Charter.pdf.

Pulat Tacar, "Soykırım İddiaları Nedeniyle Oluşan Uyuşmazlığın Çözüm Yolları Konusunda Düşünceler," *Gazi Akademik Bakış*, vol. 1, no. 1 (2007), pp. 127–53.

——, "Ermenilerin Soykırımı Savını Yadsıyanların Cezalandırılması veya Türkiye'den Tazminat Almak Amacı İle Yaptıkları Yargı Mücadeleleri," *Ermeni Araştırmaları*, no. 46 (2013), pp. 55–128.

Pulat Tacar and Maxime Gauin, "State Identity, Continuity, and Responsibility: The Ottoman Empire, the Republic of Turkey and the Armenian Genocide: A Reply to Vahagn Avedian," *European Journal of International Law*, vol. 23, no. 3 (2012), pp. 823–26.

Vahé Tachjian, "Expulsion of the Armenian Survivors of Urfa and Diarbekir, 1923–1930," in Richard G. Hovannisian, ed., *Armenian Tigranakert/Diarbekir and Edessa/Urfa* (Costa Mesa, CA: Mazda Publishers, 2006), pp. 519–35.

Takahashi Tetsuro, Kaneko Kotaro, and Inokuma Tokuro, "Fighting for Peace after War: Japanese War Veterans Recall the War and Their Peace Activism after Repatriation," *Japan Focus*, vol. 6, no. 11 (1 November 2008), pp. 1–13.

Takemoto Tadao and Ohara Yasuo, *The Alleged 'Nanking Massacre': Japan's Rebuttal to China's Forged Claims* (Tokyo: Meisei-sha, 2000).

Akiko Takenaka, "Reactionary Nationalism and Museum Controversies: The Case of 'Peace Osaka,'" *Public Historian*, vol. 36, no. 2 (2014), pp. 75–98.

Namık Tan, "Turkey and Human Rights," *New York Times* (27 July 2012).

Tan Tarn How, "China to Mark Victory in Sino-Japanese War in Big Way," *Straits Times* (2 July 1995).

Hiroshi Tanaka, "Why Is Asia Demanding Postwar Compensation Now?" *Hitotsubashi Journal of Social Studies*, vol. 28, no. 1 (1996), pp. 1–14.

Tanaka Masaaki, *"Nankin Gyakusatsu" no Kyokō* (Tōkyō: Nihon kyōbunsha, 1984).

Yuki Tanaka, *Hidden Horrors: Japanese War Crimes in World War II* (Boulder, CO: Westview Press, 1996).

——, *Japan's Comfort Women: Sexual Slavery and Prostitution during World War II and the US Occupation* (Oxon: Routledge, 2002).

——, "Crime and Responsibility: War, the State, and Japanese Society," *Japan Focus* (20 August 2006).

Shiping Tang, "Reconciliation and the Remaking of Anarchy," *World Politics*, vol. 63, no. 4 (2011), pp. 711–49.

Taraf, "Ders Kitaplarında Sözde ve Asılsız İddiaları, 1915 Olaylarına Dönüyor" (22 January 2009).

Nicholas Tavuchis, *Mea Culpa: A Sociology of Apology and Reconciliation* (Stanford, CA: Stanford University Press, 1991).

T. B. M. M. Gizli Celse Zabıtları, vol. 1 (Ankara: Türkiye İş Bankası Kültür Yayınları, 1985).

T. C. Başbakanlık Basın-Yayın ve Enformasyon Genel Müdürlüğü, *Ayın Tarihi* (17 May 2002).

Ruti G. Teitel, *Transitional Justice* (Oxford: Oxford University Press, 2000).

——, *Globalizing Transitional Justice: Contemporary Essays* (New York: Oxford University Press, 2014).

Yves Ternon, *Ermeni Tabusu* (İstanbul: Belge Yayınları, 1993).

Kathleen Thelen, "Historical Institutionalism in Comparative Politics," *Annual Review of Political Science*, vol. 2 (1999), pp. 369–404.

Marilyn W. Thompson, "An Ex-Leader in Congress Is Now Turkey's Man in the Lobbies of Capitol Hill," *New York Times* (17 October 2007).

The Times, "Interview with Recep Tayyip Erdogan in Full" (21 October 2007).

Times of India, "China Raps Japan for Textbooks Airbrushing War History" (13 September 2000).

Kazuhiko Togo, ed., *Japan and Reconciliation in Post-War Asia: The Murayama Statement and Its Implications* (New York: PalgravePivot, 2013).

Haruo Tohmatsu, "Japanese History Textbooks in Comparative Perspective," in Gi-Wook Shin and Daniel C. Sneider, eds., *History Textbooks and the Wars in Asia: Divided Memories* (Oxon: Routledge, 2011), pp. 115–39.

Khachig Tololyan, "Cultural Narrative and the Motivation of the Terrorist," *Journal of Strategic Studies*, vol. 10, no. 4 (1987), pp. 217–33.

John Torpey, "'Making Whole What Has Been Smashed': Reflections on Reparations," *Journal of Modern History*, vol. 73, no. 2 (2001), pp. 333–58.

——, "Dynamics of Denial: Responses to Past Atrocities in Germany, Turkey, and Japan," in Gi-Wook Shin, Soon-Won Park, and Daqing Yang, eds., *Rethinking Historical Injustice and Reconciliation in Northeast Asia: The Korean Experience* (New York: Routledge, 2007), pp. 173–91.

John Torpey and Maxine Burkett, "The Debate over African American Reparations," *Annual Review of Law and Social Science*, vol. 6 (2010), pp. 449–67.

Meline Toumani, "The Burden of Memory," *The Nation*, vol. 279, no. 8 (20 September 2004), pp. 39–42.

——, "Minority Rules," *New York Times Magazine* (17 February 2008).

Treaty of Sèvres, or The Treaty of Peace between the Allied and Associated Powers and Turkey (10 August 1920), available at: wwi.lib.byu.edu/index.php/Section_I,_Articles _1_-_260.

TRT Television Network, "Akbulut, Party Leaders Address National Assembly: Akbulut Speaks on U.S. Ties," in FBIS, Daily Report: West Europe, FBIS-WEU-90-037 (23 February 1990a), p. 21.

——, "Inonu Discusses Armenian Bill," in FBIS, Daily Report: West Europe, FBIS-WEU-90-037 (23 February 1990b), p. 25.

Takashi Tsuchiya, "The Imperial Japanese Experiments in China," in Ezekiel J. Emanuel, Christine Grady, Robert A. Crouch, Reidar K. Lie, Franklin G. Miller, and David Wendler, eds., *The Oxford Textbook of Clinical Research Ethics* (Oxford: Oxford University Press, 2008), pp. 31–45.

Mete Tunçay, "Son Beş Yılda Ermeni Sorunu Nasıl Tartışıldı?," in Ragıp Zarakolu, ed., *Sivil Toplumda Türk-Ermeni Diyaloğu* (İstanbul: Pencere Yayınları, 2008), pp. 237–44.

Ali Naci Tuncer, "Önsöz," in *Arşiv Belgelerine Göre Kafûkaslar'da ve Anadolu'da Ermeni Mezâlimi, I (1906–1918)*, Yayın Nu: 23 (Ankara: Başbakanlık Devlet Arşivleri Genel Müdürlüğü Osmanlı Arşivi Daire Başkanlığı, 1995), pp. V–VIII.

Berna Türkdoğan, "Türk-Ermeni İlişkileri Uluslararası Sempozyumu," *Atatürk Araştırma Merkezi Dergisi*, vol. 15, no. 45 (1999).

Turkish Daily News, "FM Cem - Genocide Bill Will Harm Turco-French Relations" (29 May 1998a).

——, "French Bill Continues to Spark Harsh Reaction" (3 June 1998b).

——, "Ankara Blasts 'Genocide' Memorial in France" (9 June 1999).

——, "Turkey Protests EP Resolution on 'Armenian Genocide'" (2 March 2002a).

——, "So-Called Armenian Genocide Claims Will Be Taught at Schools" (20 August 2002b).

——, "Celik Sheds Light on Armenian 'Genocide' in Journal" (10 May 2003).

Turkish Weekly, "Turkish PM: We'll Retaliate against States That Recognize So-Called 'Genocide'" (19 May 2005).

Türkiye Büyük Millet Meclisi, *Tutanak Dergisi*, 23rd term, 3rd legislative year, vol. 35, 33rd session (21 December 2008).

——, *Tutanak Dergisi*, 23rd term, 4th legislative year, vol. 51, 9th session (21 October 2009).

Michelle Tusan, "'Crimes against Humanity': Human Rights, the British Empire, and the Origins of the Response to the Armenian Genocide," *American Historical Review*, vol. 119, no. 1 (2014), pp. 47–77.

Tuzla Ermeni Çocuk Kampı: Bir El Koyma Öyküsü (Ankara: İnsan Hakları Derneği, 2000).

Nurer Uğurlu and Esergül Balcı, *Tarih Lise 3* (İstanbul: Serhat Yayınları A.Ş./Örgün Yayınları Ltd., 1989).

Fatma Ulgen, "'Sabiha Gökçen's 80-Year-Old Secret': Kemalist Nation Formation and the Ottoman Armenians," PhD diss., University of California, San Diego (2010a).

——, "Reading Mustafa Kemal Atatürk on the Armenian Genocide of 1915," *Patterns of Prejudice*, vol. 44, no. 4 (2010b), pp. 369–91.

Sayuri Umeda, "Japan: WWII POW and Forced Labor Compensation Cases," Law Library of Congress (September 2008), available at: https://www.loc.gov/law/help/pow-compensation/japan.php.

UN (United Nations), "Convention on the Prevention and Punishment of the Crime of Genocide," General Assembly Resolution 260 (III) (9 December 1948).

——, General Assembly, "Thirty-Seventh Session, 15th Plenary Meeting, Agenda Item 9, Document A/37/PV.15," *Official Records* (4 October 1982), pp. 255–72.

William Underwood, "Chinese Forced Labor, the Japanese Government and the Prospects for Redress," *Japan Focus* (8 July 2005).

——, "The Japanese Court, Mitsubishi and Corporate Resistance to Chinese Forced Labor Redress," *Japan Focus* (29 March 2006a).

——, "NHK's Finest Hour: Japan's Official Record of Chinese Forced Labor," *Japan Focus* (8 August 2006b).

——, "Redress Crossroads in Japan: Decisive Phase in Campaigns to Compensate Korean and Chinese Wartime Forced Laborers," *Japan Focus*, article no. 3387 (26 July 2010).

Uğur Ümit Üngör, "Seeing Like a Nation-State: Young Turk Social Engineering in Eastern Turkey, 1913–50," *Journal of Genocide Research*, vol. 10, no. 1 (2008a), pp. 15–39.

——, "Geographies of Nationalism and Violence: Rethinking Young Turk 'Social Engineering,'" *European Journal of Turkish Studies*, vol. 7, no. 7 (2008b), available at: http://ejts.revues.org/2583.

——, "'Turkey for the Turks': Demographic Engineering in Eastern Anatolia, 1914–1945," in Ronald Grigor Suny, Fatma Müge Göçek and Norman M. Naimark, eds., *A Question of Genocide: Armenians and Turks at the End of the Ottoman Empire* (New York: Oxford University Press, 2011a), pp. 287–305.

——, *The Making of Modern Turkey: Nation and State in Eastern Anatolia, 1913–1950* (Oxford: Oxford University Press, 2011b).

——, "The Armenian Genocide: New Sources and Research Directions," *Haigazian Armenological Review*, vol. 31 (2011c), pp. 9–31.

——, "Rethinking the Violence of Pacification: State Formation and Bandits in Turkey, 1914–1937," *Comparative Studies in Society and History*, vol. 54, no. 4 (2012), pp. 746–69.

Uğur Ümit Üngör and Mehmet Polatel, *Confiscation and Destruction: The Young Turk Seizure of Armenian Property* (London: Continuum, 2011).

United Nations Treaty Series, "No. 1021. Convention on the Prevention and Punishment of the Crime of Genocide. Adopted by the General Assembly of the United Nations on 9 December 1948" (1951), pp. 278–86.

——, "Treaty of Peace with Japan. Signed at San Francisco, on 8 September 1951," vol. 136, no. 1832 (1952a), pp. 44–164.

——, "Protocol to the Treaty of Peace between the Republic of China and Japan," vol. 138, no. 1858 (1952b), pp. 44–48.

——, "Treaty of Peace and Friendship between Japan and the People's Republic of China," vol. 1225, no. 19784 (1978), pp. 268–70.

United Turkish Americans, "H. Res. 142 and H.J. Res. 192: Why We Object!" (October 1985), copy on file with author.

Ferhat Ünlü, "Non-Governmental Organisations," in Ümit Cizre, ed., *Almanac Turkey 2005: Security Sector and Democratic Oversight* (Istanbul: TESEV Publications, 2006), pp. 190–203.

Esat Uras, *Tarihte Ermeniler ve Ermeni Meselesi* (Ankara: Yeni Matbaa, 1950).

——, *The Armenians in History and the Armenian Question* (Istanbul: Documentary Publications, 1988).

Ali Eşref Uzundere, *İnsanlık Suçu; Iğdır ve Çevresinde Ermeniler'in Türk Kırımı* (Ankara: T.C. Kültür Bakanlığı, 2002).

Benjamin A. Valentino, *Final Solutions: Mass Killing and Genocide in the Twentieth Century* (Ithaca, NY: Cornell University Press, 2004).

Théo Van Boven, "Paragraph 30: Note on the Deleted Reference to the Massacre of the Armenians in the Study on the Question of the Prevention and the Punishment of the Crime of Genocide," in Permanent Peoples' Tribunal, *A Crime of Silence: The Armenian Genocide: The Permanent Peoples' Tribunal* (London: Zed Books, 1985), pp. 168–72.

Stephen Van Evera, "Hypotheses on Nationalism and War," *International Security*, vol. 18, no. 4 (1994), pp. 5–39.

Hamo B. Vassilian, ed., *The Armenian Genocide: A Comprehensive Bibliography and Library Resource Guide* (Glendale, CA: Armenian Reference Books, 1992).

Ernesto Verdeja, *Unchopping a Tree: Reconciliation in the Aftermath of Political Violence* (Philadelphia: Temple University Press, 2009).

Speros Vryonis, Jr., *The Turkish State and History: Clio Meets the Grey Wolf* (New Rochelle, NY: Aristide D. Caratzas, 1991).

——, *The Mechanism of Catastrophe: The Turkish Pogrom of September 6–7, 1955, and the Destruction of the Greek Community of Istanbul* (New York: Greekworks.com, 2005).

Bob Tadashi Wakabayashi, "The Nanking 100-Man Killing Contest Debate, 1971–75," in Wakabayashi, ed., *The Nanking Atrocity, 1937–38: Complicating the Picture* (New York: Berghahn Books, 2007a), pp. 115–48.

——, ed., *The Nanking Atrocity 1937–38: Complicating the Picture* (New York: Berghahn Books, 2007b).

Wakamiya Yoshibumi, *The Postwar Conservative View of Asia: How the Political Right Has Delayed Japan's Coming to Terms with Its History of Aggression in Asia* (Tokyo: LTCB International Library Foundation, 1998).

Wakamiya Yoshibumi and Watanabe Tsuneo, "Yomiuri and Asahi Editors Call for a National Memorial to Replace Yasukuni," *Japan Focus*, vol. 4, no. 2 (16 February 2006).

Ming Wan, *Sino-Japanese Relations: Interaction, Logic, and Transformation* (Stanford, CA: Stanford University Press, 2006).

Zheng Wang, *Never Forget National Humiliation: Historical Memory in Chinese Politics and Foreign Relations* (New York: Columbia University Press, 2012).

Washington Post, Ad 90, placed by the Action Committee for Armenian Rights, "We Charge Genocide! We Demand Justice for the Armenian People!" (23 April 1971), p. C2.

——, "Attention Members of the U.S. House of Representatives," advertisement paid for by the Assembly of Turkish American Associations (19 May 1985), p. A4.

Keith David Watenpaugh, "'Are There Any Children for Sale?': Genocide and the Transfer of Armenian Children (1915–1922)," *Journal of Human Rights*, vol. 12, no. 3 (2013), pp. 283–95.

Brian A. Weiner, *Sins of the Parents: The Politics of National Apologies in the United States* (Philadelphia: Temple University Press, 2005).

Jessica Chen Weiss, *Powerful Patriots: Nationalist Protest in China's Foreign Relations* (New York: Oxford University Press, 2014).

Kenneth R. Weiss, "UCLA Rejects $1-Million Turkish Gift," *Los Angeles Times* (6 December 1997).

Alexander Wendt, "On Constitution and Causation in International Relations," *Review of International Studies*, vol. 24, no. 5 (1998), pp. 101–17.

——, *Social Theory of International Politics* (Cambridge: Cambridge University Press, 1999).

Allen S. Whiting, "Assertive Nationalism in Chinese Foreign Policy," *Asian Survey*, vol. 23, no. 8 (1983), pp. 913–33.

——, *China Eyes Japan* (Berkeley: University of California Press, 1989).

Richard Ashby Wilson, "Humanity's Histories: Evaluating the Historical Accounts of International Tribunals and Truth Commissions," *politix*, vol. 20, no. 80 (2007), pp. 31–59.

Wilson Quarterly, "Japan's Unfinished War," vol. 29, no. 3 (1 July 2005), p. 106.

Jay Winter, *Sites of Memory, Sites of Mourning: The Great War in European Cultural History* (Cambridge: Cambridge University Press, 1995).

——, "Under Cover of War: The Armenian Genocide in the Context of Total War," in Robert Gellately and Ben Kiernan, eds., *The Specter of Genocide: Mass Murder in Historical Perspective* (New York: Cambridge University Press, 2004), pp. 189–214.

——, "Historical Remembrance in the Twenty-First Century," *ANNALS of the American Academy of Political and Social Science*, vol. 617 (2008), pp. 6–13.

——, "Thinking about Silence," in Efrat Ben-Ze'ev, Ruth Ginio, and Jay Winter, eds., *Shadows of War: A Social History of Silence in the Twentieth Century* (Cambridge: Cambridge University Press, 2010), pp. 3–31.

Jenny Wüstenberg, *Civil Society and Remembrance in Postwar Germany* (New York: Cambridge University Press, 2017).

Mari Yamaguchi, "Japan's Rightists, Lawmakers Launch New Nationalist Campaign," *Associated Press Newswires* (30 May 1997).

——, "Japan Approves History Textbook," *AP Online* (3 April 2001).

Masahiro Yamamoto, *Nanking: Anatomy of an Atrocity* (Westport, CT: Praeger, 2000).

Jane W. Yamazaki, *Japanese Apologies for World War II: A Rhetorical Study* (London: Routledge, 2006).

Yanada Hiroyoshi, "From the Newspapers and Magazines," *Japan Quarterly*, vol. 26, no. 3 (1979), pp. 414–19.

Daqing Yang, "A Sino-Japanese Controversy: The Nanjing Atrocity as History," *Sino-Japanese Studies*, vol. 3, no. 1 (1990), pp. 14–35.

——, "Convergence or Divergence? Recent Historical Writings on the Rape of Nanjing," *American Historical Review*, vol. 104, no. 3 (1999), pp. 842–65.

——, "The Challenges of the Nanjing Massacre: Reflections on Historical Inquiry," in Joshua A. Fogel, ed., *The Nanjing Massacre in History and Historiography* (Berkeley: University of California Press, 2000), pp. 133–79.

——, "The Malleable and the Contested: The Nanjing Massacre in Postwar China and Japan," in T. Fujitani, Geoffrey M. White, and Lisa Yoneyama, eds., *Perilous Memories: The Asia-Pacific War(s)* (Durham, NC: Duke University Press, 2001), pp. 50–86.

——, "Revisionism and the Nanjing Atrocity," *Critical Asian Studies*, vol. 43, no. 4 (2011), pp. 625–48.

Yao Ying, "Japan's Youth Deserves the Truth," *China Daily* (14 June 2005).

Jim Yardley and Sebnem Arsu, "Pope Calls Killing of Armenians Genocide, Provoking Turkish Anger," *New York Times* (13 April 2015), p. A7.

Yeghiayan and Associates, "Land under U.S. Airbase Stolen by Turkey during Armenian Genocide, According to Lawsuit Filed by Yeghiayan & Associates," press release, *Cision PR Newswire* (15 December 2010), available at: https://www.prnewswire.com/news-releases/land-under-us-airbase-stolen-by-turkey-during-armenian-genocide-according-to-lawsuit-filed-by-yeghiayan-associates-111950024.html.

Yelda, *İstanbul'da, Diyarbakır'da Azalırken* (İstanbul: Belge Yayınları, 2000 [1996]).

Yomiuri Shimbun, "'Private Citizen' Koizumi's Visits to Yasukuni Shrine and Japanese Diplomacy: A Call for a New Nonreligious War Memorial" (4 June 2005), reprinted in "Yasukuni Shrine, Nationalism and Japan's International Relations," *Japan Focus* (6 June 2005).

Yomiuri Shimbun and Asahi Shimbun, "Yasukuni Shrine, Nationalism and Japan's International Relations," *Japan Focus* (6 June 2005).

Takashi Yoshida, "A Battle over History: The Nanjing Massacre in Japan," in Joshua A. Fogel, ed., *The Nanjing Massacre in History and Historiography* (Berkeley: University of California Press, 2000), pp. 70–132.

——, "A War over Words: Changing Descriptions of Nanjing in Japanese History Textbooks," *Asian Cultural Studies*, no. 14 (March 2005), pp. 59–71.

——, "The Nanjing Massacre: Changing Contours of History and Memory in Japan, China, and the U.S.," *Japan Focus* (19 December 2006a).

——, *The Making of the "Rape of Nanking": History and Memory in Japan, China, and the United States* (New York: Oxford University Press, 2006b).

——, "Advancing or Obstructing Reconciliation? Changes in History Education and Disputes over History Textbooks in Japan," in Elizabeth A. Cole, ed., *Teaching the Violent Past: History Education and Reconciliation* (Lanham, MD: Rowman and Littlefield, 2007), pp. 51–79.

——, *From Cultures of War to Cultures of Peace: War and Peace Museums in Japan, China, and South Korea* (Portland, ME: MerwinAsia, 2014).

Yoshimi Yoshiaki, *Comfort Women: Sexual Slavery in the Japanese Military during World War II* (New York: Columbia University Press, 2000).

M. Can Yüce, "The Essence of the Current Enmity toward Armenians," *Özgür Gündem*, 20 December 1993, p. 2, in FBIS, Daily Report: West Europe, FBIS-WEU-93-246, "Government Claim of PKK-Armenian Links Viewed" (27 December 1993), p. 39.

Amberin Zaman, "Armenian Church Caught Up in Ethnic Enmity," *Los Angeles Times* (25 December 2002), p. 12.

——, "Turkish Civil Society Paves Way for Erdoğan's Armenian Opening," *Al-Monitor* (25 April 2014).

Ayşe Zarakol, "Ontological (In)security and State Denial of Historical Crimes: Turkey and Japan," *International Relations*, vol. 24, no. 3 (2010), pp. 3–23.

——, *After Defeat: How the East Learned to Live with the West* (Cambridge: Cambridge University Press, 2011).

Ragıp Zarakolu, ed., *Sivil Toplumda Türk-Ermeni Diyaloğu* (İstanbul: Pencere Yayınları, 2008a).

——, "Giriş: Monologdan Diyaloğa Doğru," in Ragıp Zarakolu, ed., *Sivil Toplumda Türk-Ermeni Diyaloğu* (İstanbul: Pencere Yayınları, 2008b), pp. 11–31.

——, "Ermeni Soykırımını Tartışmanın Bedeli," in Ragıp Zarakolu, ed., *Sivil Toplumda Türk-Ermeni Diyaloğu* (İstanbul: Pencere Yayınları, 2008c), pp. 245–58.

Mehmet Zarif, "Kompozisyon Genelgesinin Sır Yönetmeliği," *BİA Haber Merkezi* (10 December 2003).

Fang Zhou, "China-Japan Ties Need Improvement," *China Daily* (19 March 2005).

Lisbeth Zimmermann, "Same Same or Different? Norm Diffusion between Resistance, Compliance, and Localization in Post-Conflict States," *International Studies Perspectives*, vol. 17, no. 1 (2016), pp. 98–115.

——, *Global Norms with a Local Face: Rule-of-Law Promotion and Norm Translation* (Cambridge: Cambridge University Press, 2017).

Howard Zinn, "Against Discouragement," commencement speech delivered at Spelman College, Atlanta, Georgia (15 May 2005), available at: www.tomdispatch.com/dialogs/print/?id=2728.

Erik Jan Zürcher, *The Unionist Factor: The Role of the Committee of Union and Progress in the Turkish National Movement, 1905–1926* (Leiden: E. J. Brill, 1984).

——, *Turkey: A Modern History* (London: I.B. Tauris, 1998 [1993]).

Michael Zürn and Jeffrey T. Checkel, "Getting Socialized to Build Bridges: Constructivism and Rationalism, Europe and the Nation-State," *International Organization*, vol. 59, no. 4 (2005), pp. 1045–79.

Index

Page numbers in italics refer to figures.